W9-CWN-953

SAP PRESS e-books

Print or e-book, Kindle or iPad, workplace or airplane: Choose where and how to read your SAP PRESS books! You can now get all our titles as e-books, too:

- ▶ By download and online access
- ▶ For all popular devices
- ▶ And, of course, DRM-free

Convinced? Then go to **www.sap-press.com** and get your e-book today.

Implementing SAP® Business Suite on SAP HANA®

 **PRESS**

SAP PRESS is a joint initiative of SAP and Rheinwerk Publishing. The know-how offered by SAP specialists combined with the expertise of Rheinwerk Publishing offers the reader expert books in the field. SAP PRESS features first-hand information and expert advice, and provides useful skills for professional decision-making.

SAP PRESS offers a variety of books on technical and business-related topics for the SAP user. For further information, please visit our website: *www.sap-press.com*.

Merz, Hügens, Blum
Implementing SAP BW on SAP HANA
2015, 467 pages, hardcover
ISBN 978-1-4932-1003-9

Jens Krüger
SAP Simple Finance: An Introduction
2015, 407 pages, hardcover
ISBN 978-1-4932-1215-6

Schneider, Westenberger, Gahm
ABAP Development for SAP HANA
2014, 609 pages, hardcover
ISBN 978-1-59229-859-4

Haun, Hickman, Loden, Wells
Implementing SAP HANA, 2nd edition
2015, 860 pages, hardcover
ISBN 978-1-4932-1176-0

Michael Pytel

Implementing SAP® Business Suite on SAP HANA®

Rheinwerk®
Publishing

Bonn • Boston

Editor Meagan White
Acquisitions Editor Kelly Grace Weaver
Copyeditor Julie McNamee
Cover Design Graham Geary
Photo Credit iStockphoto.com/10806973/© RapidEye
Layout Design Vera Brauner
Production Nicole Carpenter
Typesetting III-satz, Husby (Germany)
Printed and bound in the United States of America, on paper from sustainable sources

ISBN 978-1-4932-1257-6

© 2016 by Rheinwerk Publishing, Inc., Boston (MA)
1st edition 2016

Library of Congress Cataloging-in-Publication Data
Pytel, Michael, author.
Implementing SAP business suite on SAP HANA / Michael Pytel. -- 1st edition.
pages cm
Includes index.
ISBN 978-1-4932-1257-6 (print : alk. paper) -- ISBN 1-4932-1257-5 (print : alk. paper) -- ISBN 978-1-4932-1258-3 (ebook) --
ISBN (invalid) 978-1-4932-1259-0 (print and ebook : alk. paper) 1. SAP ERP. 2. Systems migration. 3. Management infor-
mation systems. I. Title.
QA76.9.S9P97 2015
658.4'038011--dc23
2015030308

All rights reserved. Neither this publication nor any part of
it may be copied or reproduced in any form or by any
means or translated into another language, without the
prior consent of Rheinwerk Publishing, 2 Heritage Drive,
Suite 305, Quincy, MA 02171.

Rheinwerk Publishing makes no warranties or representa-
tions with respect to the content hereof and specifically dis-
claims any implied warranties of merchantability or fitness
for any particular purpose. Rheinwerk Publishing assumes
no responsibility for any errors that may appear in this publication.

"Rheinwerk Publishing" and the Rheinwerk Publishing logo
are registered trademarks of Rheinwerk Verlag GmbH,
Bonn, Germany. SAP PRESS is an imprint of Rheinwerk Verlag GmbH and Rheinwerk Publishing, Inc.

All of the screenshots and graphics reproduced in this book
are subject to copyright © SAP SE, Dietmar-Hopp-Allee 16,
69190 Walldorf, Germany.

SAP, the SAP logo, ABAP, BAPI, Duet, mySAP.com, mySAP,
SAP ArchiveLink, SAP EarlyWatch, SAP NetWeaver, SAP
Business ByDesign, SAP BusinessObjects, SAP Business-
Objects Rapid Mart, SAP BusinessObjects Desktop Intelli-
gence, SAP BusinessObjects Explorer, SAP Rapid Marts,
SAP BusinessObjects Watchlist Security, SAP Business-
Objects Web Intelligence, SAP Crystal Reports, SAP
GoingLive, SAP HANA, SAP MaxAttention, SAP MaxDB,
SAP PartnerEdge, SAP R/2, SAP R/3, SAP R/3 Enterprise,
SAP Strategic Enterprise Management (SAP SEM), SAP
StreamWork, SAP Sybase Adaptive Server Enterprise (SAP
Sybase ASE), SAP Sybase IQ, SAP xApps, SAPPHIRE NOW,
and Xcelsius are registered or unregistered trademarks of
SAP SE, Walldorf, Germany.

All other products mentioned in this book are registered or
unregistered trademarks of their respective companies.

Contents at a Glance

Dear Reader,

SAP HANA has been called many things—"revolutionary," "game-changing," "transformative," and "you want *me* to implement *what*?" (I admit the last one may not be a direct quote.) However, it's true that migrating to SAP Business Suite on SAP HANA is a big undertaking, and one that can be more than a little bit intimidating. That's where this book comes in.

Between these pages, author Michael Pytel has given you everything you need to confidently execute your migration to SAP HANA. He covers preparation, making sure you know where to find all the information you need, how to use it, and how to keep your new system secure. He covers go-live, showing you how to test, monitor, and ensure a smooth transition. He covers optimization, demonstrating settings and solutions you can implement to customize your system. All of this is in addition to his step-by-step instructions, screenshots, and tips for your actual migration—the heart of the book. In short, he's given you everything you need bring your business to the next level.

As always, your comments and suggestions are the most useful tools to help us make our books the best they can be. Let us know what you thought about *Implementing SAP Business Suite on SAP HANA*! Please feel free to contact me and share any praise or criticism you may have.

Thank you for purchasing a book from SAP PRESS!

Meagan White
Editor, SAP PRESS

Rheinwerk Publishing
Boston, MA

meaganw@rheinwerk-publishing.com
www.sap-press.com

Contents

PART I Preparation

PART II Migration

PART IV Optimizations

Introduction

What does it mean to run a real-time business? Although more information and more data don't make a business run better, they *do* make people run better. Organizations today are the sum of the individuals that operate the processes within their specific line of business. From the top of an organization to the bottom, people are making decisions every day that either add or subtract from the bottom line. Many of the decisions people make are driven by data with an unknown level of accuracy or age. SAP Business Suite powered by SAP HANA will never replace a person's experience in making decisions that help run a business, but when that person needs to rely on data to make a decision, SAP Business Suite on SAP HANA can help. The access to more information more quickly that SAP Business Suite on SAP HANA can provide won't replace gut instinct but instead enhance and validate it.

SAP Business Suite on SAP HANA isn't just about speed. It's a platform on which you can grow and expand, as well as deploy new user interfaces (UIs) for SAP Business Suite. It's a new analytics platform for SAP Business Suite and a platform on which you can integrate the Internet of Things with SAP ERP. Organizations are made up of people, and people need an interface that enables them to interact with a system that is fluid, intuitive, able to predict what they want next, and able to provide easy access to information that can power decisions. SAP has more than 200 different software products with numerous UIs. SAP Business Suite on SAP HANA coupled with SAP's new UI strategy will deliver new functionality to your users and enable them to access more SAP systems from any device, anywhere. The migration to SAP Business Suite on SAP HANA is the first step to enabling access to this new world of functionality and technology. The goals are to remove the constraints of the desktop with multiple UIs and graphical UIs (GUIs) and enable a unified view of both the transactional and analytical data within your SAP landscape to simplify the user experience. SAP Business Suite on SAP HANA is the platform to deliver these goals.

Note	[«]
Please note that the SAP Business Suite on SAP HANA includes SAP ERP, SAP CRM, and SAP SCM. The screenshots in this book were largely taken within SAP ERP, but the process is applicable for all three solutions.	

Audience

We expect three main types of readers to pick up this book: those who understand the value proposition of SAP Business Suite on SAP HANA and need to understand the effort required to migrate to build a business case; those who have been told they are migrating, but still don't quite understand the value proposition; and those who understand the value proposition and are well on their way to a migration to SAP Business Suite on SAP HANA. This book exists for those people who need a resource to guide themselves and their team members on how to migrate to SAP Business Suite on SAP HANA—and not just from a technical perspective. How we do plan for the migration? How can we measure the impact of change? What resources, both human capital and technology, will be required? When we're ready for the production migration to SAP Business Suite on SAP HANA, what can we expect? This book will answer these questions and more. The goal in writing this book was to provide a single resource that can arm people with the information they need on all resources available to them to complete a migration to SAP Business Suite on SAP HANA.

Structure of the Book

We organized the book into four parts. Preparation, the first part, will help guide you on setting project scope, defining the resources required for the project, and the technical infrastructure decisions you'll need to make. In this part, we'll discuss the use of SAP Solution Manager to document your current production system and then analyze the impact of an enhancement package with the SAP Scope and Effort Analyzer (SEA). When you run an SAP Business Suite on SAP HANA migration, you don't need to guess what business processes will be impacted. Within this part, we'll show you how to reverse-document the transactions and programs your users execute today within your production environment, and we'll capture interface-related programs as well. After SAP Solution Manager contains this repository of technical objects, we'll perform a detailed impact analysis at the object level. From here we can estimate effort for ABAP remediation and end-user testing. This part will also cover details on identifying dependencies between SAP components, add-on compatibility, and how to define your target SAP ERP version for the migration. Do we migrate as-is, or do we upgrade and migrate? You'll know your options by the end of this part. We'll cover some important security topics in this part as well. What do I need to be aware of when including SAP Business Suite on SAP HANA in my security plan? What type of access is common for a developer, administrator, or operator? We'll provide advice on what to look for, as well as highlight some security aspects you may be missing.

The second part, Migration, will focus on the migration to SAP Business Suite on SAP HANA. As an SAP customer you have access to two different tools for the migration. The one you should choose and which one applies to your scenario will depend on the target version you selected in Part 1 and your source version of SAP ERP. We'll talk about the migration process and include those activities you'll need to execute if you aren't already running Unicode. In this part, we'll also talk about the new features of the software logistics toolset (SL Toolset) delivered by SAP. We provide detailed step-by-step instructions on how to benchmark a migration to get some measure of estimated time based on the hardware in your landscape. We'll also walk through the standalone table comparison tools made available to customers to validate a SAP Business Suite on SAP HANA migration. To close out this part of the book, we perform a migration to SAP Business Suite on SAP HANA using both tools with detailed screenshots. Each customer scenario will vary slightly, but this chapter will give the reader a solid understanding of the migration tools, options, execution, and troubleshooting for any issues that may occur.

The third part, Go-Live, focuses on the planning of preparation activities you'll need to perform before the migration project completes. We talk about testing and change management strategies during an SAP Business Suite on SAP HANA migration. We focus on tools included with your SAP Enterprise and SAP Standard Maintenance Agreements, which can be leveraged during your project. Did you know SAP Solution Manager contains a test planning, execution, and management tool? Or that SAP Solution Manager can control and manage transports between SAP ERP releases? We provide answers to these questions and show how you can activate proactive, real-time monitoring of your new SAP Business Suite on SAP HANA landscape using both the SAP Fiori administrative applications and the traditional SAP Database Administration Cockpit (DBA Cockpit) within SAP GUI. You'll finish this part knowing how you to manage the logistics of change during your SAP Business Suite on SAP HANA project and how to plan for the cutover activities as you work your way through the project to the production system.

The fourth and final part of the book, Optimizations, focuses on enhancements and optimizations you can make postmigration. After you migrate to SAP Business

Suite on SAP HANA (and for many customers that will include SAP ERP EHP 7), you'll have numerous opportunities to enhance your SAP ERP system. Within EHP 7 alone, there are more than 1,000 enhancements delivered by SAP. We'll focus on those delivered with EHP 7 that highlight SAP HANA capabilities. You may not realize the full value of your software maintenance if you run SAP ERP 6.0 EHP 7 and don't activate these enhancements! The enhancements within SAP ERP Financials (FI), Production Planning (PP, including materials requirements planning [MRP]), and Procurement will change how people work within SAP ERP and SAP GUI. The enhancements we cover don't even scratch the surface of the available enhancements. SAP ERP EHP 7 provides numerous business process, reporting, and UI enhancements (think SAP Screen Personas and SAP Fiori). In Part 4, we'll also provide an overview of how to find ABAP code to optimize, and then we'll provide detailed step-by-step instructions on installing SAP HANA Live and enabling end user access to SAP HANA Live content through securely developed SAP HANA roles. Lastly, we'll cover the detailed step-by-step instructions to install SAP S/4HANA Finance from target component identification to installation. We provide the first step in your journey to SAP S/4HANA Finance after you complete your SAP Business Suite on SAP HANA migration. SAP S/4HANA Finance will be required to run SAP S/4HANA and its complementary components.

Purpose and Objective

The goal of this book is to serve as a practical guide to the planning, execution, and optimization of SAP Business Suite on SAP HANA. You'll find detailed screenshots for each step in the process, and you'll have the opportunity to maximize your investment in SAP enterprise maintenance by fully using SAP Solution Manager throughout the process. SAP Solution Manager is your gateway to SAP Support, but it's also a key component to the delivery of SAP enhancements. With SAP Solution Manager, you can remove the guesswork in defining test scope or trying to understand how your end users leverage SAP Business Suite. Using the tools provided by SAP, you can get a detailed understanding of the utilization of your SAP Business Suite system, which enables your project team to know where you're going.

Acknowledgments

This book is the culmination of my experience as a SAP customer, consultant, blogger, speaker, and writer—without being an SAP employee. I sought to write a book that could be used as a field guide for those upgrading and migrating to SAP HANA. I wanted to ensure the important ancillary systems such as SAP Solution Manager were described in detail so someone could use this book to plan, execute, and support the upgrade and migration. I began my career in SAP as a Basis Administrator, then moved into SAP Solution Manager, and most recently applied focus to all things SAP Business Suite on SAP HANA.

My career in SAP and IT started with a gift from two mentors that I can't thank enough. They set me down a path for a career in which I'm able to provide for my family and enjoy the work I do. I'm passionate about technology and thankful that Kirk Schamel and Floyd Alexander saw this in me while working in a warehouse of a small wheelchair manufacturing company. Kirk is an exceptional leader who has given opportunities to unlikely characters like myself only to see them blossom into thought leaders and IT professionals. Floyd Alexander is an exceptional program manager who taught me to think like a developer when working as a system administrator. From these two gentlemen, I learned that IT needs the business users more than the users need IT. The role of IT is that of a customer service organization, and we should conduct ourselves in a manner than supports the business users first. Without these two individuals, I wouldn't have gained the solid foundation in IT processes and procedures that enabled me to grow into the IT professional I am today.

Chapter 4 on security is a special chapter for me because it was co-written by a close friend and colleague Gary Prewett. There are lots of people to thank at NIMBL for supporting me in writing this book—Gabe Mensching, Rob Kelly, Vanita Mody, and more. I had help installing new RHEL kernels, setting up storage, networking, troubleshooting errors during backups, finding bad ABAP code, and so on. Gary contributed in a way that exceeded my expectations. I wanted a chapter in the book with a sole focus on security. There are more threats to SAP customers than ever before, and I hope Chapter 4 provides the opportunity to start a new conversation on how IT approaches security and SAP. Gary is a seasoned security professional who provided valuable input that I think every reader will derive value from.

I co-founded NIMBL with Yosh Eisbart more than six years ago with the hopes of creating a company that could provide opportunities for people to grow both their professional and personal lives. Yosh, a fellow SAP Press author and SAP thought leader, has been extremely supportive of me while writing this book. He's the best business partner and friend I could have asked for on this journey.

Lastly, I need to thank the person who provided more mental support than anyone else. My wife, Leah, is an extraordinary person who keeps me grounded and motivated to complete challenges I never thought I would accomplish. From running a marathon to completing this book—none of those goals would have been achieved without my true best friend and partner for life.

PART I
Preparation

What is SAP Business Suite on SAP HANA? And what is SAP S/4HANA? How are they different? In this chapter, we're going to tackle these questions and describe what your new SAP Business Suite on SAP HANA landscape might look like.

1 SAP HANA, SAP ERP, and SAP S/4HANA

It's a good time to be an SAP customer not only because of the innovation offered by SAP but also because of the choices available as SAP customers today. You can choose when to apply innovation within your SAP Business Suite systems using the enhancement package strategy supplied by SAP. You're no longer forced to adopt innovation when changing releases, and you can selectively activate the functionality that is most valuable to your business when you're ready. With the release of SAP Business Suite on SAP HANA (often referred to as Suite on HANA or SoH), you have the option to change the underlying database for SAP Business Suite without impacting application logic or business processes within your environment. Granted, there are technical release levels you must move to in order to run SAP Business Suite on SAP HANA. However, for most customers, the business processes that are supported by both standard and custom transactions will process as-is when migrating to SAP Business Suite on SAP HANA, which is fantastic!

In this chapter, we're going to provide some high-level information on the landscape and the definition of the components in your new SAP Business Suite on SAP HANA landscape. For some, this will be review (especially if you're already SAP HANA certified), but for others, this chapter will help highlight what makes SAP Business Suite on SAP HANA different and how to migrate to SAP S/4HANA after the SAP Business Suite on SAP HANA migration. SAP describes the ability to run SAP Business Suite on SAP HANA as "transformative innovation without disruption," which is definitely a mouthful. Let's break it down.

How is SAP Business Suite on SAP HANA transformative? It changes the way people work, and that doesn't mean it creates more work for IT. Let's take an example of a planner within a manufacturing company. Prior to SAP Business Suite on SAP HANA, this planner would run your traditional material requirements planning (MRP) programs in the background—submit and forget, and then come back in a few hours to review the results. If the job ran too long, he would break it up into multiple jobs to run separately and then review the results. But due to the dynamic changes in business, how can we respond when only one or two iterations of a plan can be created each day? Buy too many or too few materials, and the business suffers. With SAP Business Suite on SAP HANA and the introduction of MRP Live, you can change the way the planner works. SAP HANA provides the ability to run jobs interactively that you once were forced to run in the background. Now, that planner can run MRP with multiple iterations before committing a plan. The planner is engaged, actively working with the data, and able to make better decisions because he has better access to information.

We can make better decisions when we can get more information more quickly. This is a key benefit of running SAP Business Suite on SAP HANA. When running SAP Business Suite on any other database, we treat that database as a black box. By "black box," we mean that we treat the database as a repository only—we don't leverage any vendor-specific features or capabilities. SAP HANA, on the other hand, is both an application platform and database. With SAP HANA, that black box is now a transparent box. We need to understand the capabilities of the database (and the platform) to further optimize SAP Business Suite. With SAP Business Suite on SAP HANA, SAP has delivered real innovation by combining online transaction processing (OLTP) and online analytical processing (OLAP) within one system. More specifically, SAP HANA Live is both software and content delivered by SAP that enables an organization to perform analytical activities against its transactional database without fear of impacting business processes. Let's use the example of a company that manufactures and sells low-margin products. It's a volume-based business, where decisions need to be made quickly. Within the traditional data warehouse model, that organization would need development staff to write and execute extracts, store the data, maintain the hardware, write the reports, and perform time-based delta extracts throughout the day. With SAP HANA Live, this process changes. There is no need for extracts, duplicate data storage, or additional hardware. Users connect to analytical views over SAP Business Suite transactional data with SAP Lumira, SAP Business-Objects, or even the SAP HANA client-enabled Microsoft Excel. This fantastic innovation enables true self-service analytics.

In the twenty-first century, the term "disruptive" doesn't always have a negative connotation. We hear about disruptive technologies and businesses in the media every week. In the case of your primary business system—SAP Business Suite— disruption is bad, however. Ideally, you want to offer your business users innovation without disruption. The primary focus of this book is on how to migrate to SAP Business Suite on SAP HANA with minimal disruption to the business. How do we ensure business processes run as-is and the migration will require as little downtime as possible? The software logistics toolset (SL Toolset) developed by SAP to assist in the migration to SAP HANA is so advanced that it's self-learning. The Software Update Manager (SUM) learns from each SAP Business Suite on SAP HANA migration you execute so that when it comes time for the production migration, you've optimized the migration process and reduced business time to as little as possible. If downtime is still a problem, SAP offers Near Zero Downtime (nZDM) capabilities with SAP Landscape Transformation (SLT). When paired with SUM and the appropriate hardware resources, you can achieve even less downtime. It's a good time to be an SAP customer. It's good to have choices.

1.1   What Is SAP ERP on SAP HANA?

SAP ERP is software that was written to run on any database and was also originally written for disk-based databases. Table structures, program logic, and the overall data model were all constructed with the limitations of disk-based systems in mind. Developers built a system that could scale for customers large and small and on any database platform. With the release of SAP HANA, SAP first needed to ensure that the existing SAP ERP code base could run on this new in-memory platform. SAP uses a proprietary SQLDBC library (or database shared library [DBSL]) for connectivity to the database. After this was written, Support Package Stacks (SP Stacks) were released for Enhancement Package 6 (EHP 6) and Enhancement Package 7 (EHP 7), which allowed SAP ERP to run directly on SAP HANA in the scale-up scenario (more on that in Section 1.5). SAP uses Open SQL to abstract the database from the developers and the users, which is probably why the ability to run SAP Business Suite on SAP HANA was released by SAP so quickly after SAP HANA's release.

After the code base was solidified on SAP HANA, SAP then focused on delivering enhancements. With the release of SP Stacks for EHP 6, SAP ERP Financials (FI) was the first to receive updates with new transactions ending in "H" (Transaction FBL1H, Transaction FBL3H, Transaction FAGLL03H, etc.). With EHP 7, lots of new enhancements were made for SAP ERP in general but a handful became SAP HANA only. We'll talk more about some impactful enhancements in Chapter 12. SAP has said additional enhancement packages will be delivered for SAP ERP, and they will include enhancements that are applicable to any database. As we said before—it's good to have choices. What we know today from both conferences and published roadmaps is that SAP will support two code bases for SAP ERP: one for any database and one optimized for SAP HANA. How sustainable that future will be depends on the adoption. Adoption depends on the ease at which people can use the innovation being offered. After reading this book, we think you'll realize the migration to SAP HANA will be the easy part of the project. Choosing which innovation to implement first will be more difficult.

[»] **Note**

Need to know more about SAP-published roadmaps for both SAP ERP and SAP HANA? Check out *http://service.sap.com/roadmaps*, and choose PRODUCT & SOLUTION ROADMAPS • CROSS TOPICS.

1.1.1 Software

What software will make up your new landscape? You already know the makeup of the SAP ERP system as an ABAP application server. We'll review some of the key components and the differences between an ABAP system on SAP HANA versus any other database. When running SAP ERP on any other database, you typically only have to maintain patches to the database. With SAP HANA, you'll have a few more components to maintain. Think back to our statement on SAP HANA becoming a transparent box instead of black box. Many of the enhancements offered by SAP Business Suite on SAP HANA exist on the periphery. Don't misunderstand—there are lots of enhancements for SAP Business Suite on SAP HANA that reside in ABAP. But some of the true innovation when running SAP Business Suite on SAP HANA will come from components that exist on the outside. The following list is only a sample of the many components delivered with SAP HANA:

▸ **SAP HANA Live**
SAP-delivered and predefined OLAP content installed outside of SAP Business Suite but inside SAP HANA. It creates a virtual data model.

- **SAP Fiori Smart Business Apps**
  SAPUI5 applications access both transactional tables in SAP Business Suite and analytical content in SAP HANA Live.

- **Real-time replication**
  When using Central Finance or other solutions, you have to maintain the components supporting real-time data replication.

- **Free text search**
  SAP HANA provides a text search capability that can be extended to search help and more in SAP Business Suite.

When writing this book, we leveraged the latest SAP HANA release available. SAP HANA 1.0 SP 10 includes numerous enhancements that are part of the platform. However, your SAP Business Suite on SAP HANA runtime license will prevent you from accessing all of the features without an additional license. In terms of which software license is required to run SAP Business Suite on SAP HANA, you'll need the runtime license (as of August 2015). There are essentially three editions of SAP HANA separate from the runtime licenses: SAP HANA Enterprise, SAP HANA Platform, and SAP HANA Base. Each version provides a different level of functionality, with SAP HANA Enterprise being the all-inclusive version. If your organization hasn't licensed the SAP Business Suite runtime SAP HANA license, none of the SAP HANA media (and, more specifically, the SAP NetWeaver kernel for SAP HANA) will be available for you to download.

1.1.2   Hardware

In this book, we'll cover sizing SAP Business Suite on SAP HANA. We'll provide you with enough details to execute a sizing for an existing SAP Business Suite system, which can then be shared with your infrastructure team members or a hardware partner. SAP HANA hardware can be implemented using two methods:

- **SAP certified HANA appliance partners**
  There are more than 17 certified hardware partners with 900+ server configurations. This method includes both hardware and operating system (OS) support with SAP HANA preinstalled and preconfigured.

- **Tailored data center integration (TDI)**
  Customer-provided hardware with SAP HANA installation is performed by a certified SAP HANA administrator. This method enables you to leverage existing IT investment if hardware meets the SAP HANA requirements.

▷ In August 2015, SAP announced support for SAP HANA on IBM Power Systems in addition to the Intel Haswell-based systems being offered. From an OS perspective, SUSE Linux was certified first for use with SAP HANA, with Red Hat Enterprise Linux (RHEL) certified shortly after. We recommend Enterprise Support Agreements when using either OS. During the writing of this book, we implemented SAP HANA 1.0 SP 10 on RHEL, which required one major OS kernel update to provide system stability. Customers are still able to leverage Microsoft Windows Server as an ABAP application server with SAP HANA as the database platform. In fact, you can continue to use any SAP-supported OS platform as your application server platform. The migration demonstrated within Chapter 6 using SUM provides examples migrating from a Windows Server and SQL environment to a Windows Server and SAP HANA database landscape.

▷ As you read about the different hardware configurations, keep in mind that as of Q3 2015, SAP Business Suite on SAP HANA was only supported in the scale-up scenario (more on that in Section 1.5). Appliances certified for SAP Business Warehouse (SAP BW) on SAP HANA scale up aren't the same as those certified for SAP Business Suite on SAP HANA. SAP Business Suite on SAP HANA has a different memory-to-CPU ratio, which aligns to the heavier OLTP environment. Don't think your environment can fit on one system? SAP believes 99% of its customers can run SAP Business Suite on one SAP HANA node because current hardware can scale to 12TB of memory with 188 CPU Core on one appliance. This means you could theoretically migrate a 40TB row-store database to a column-store database in SAP HANA. (Who remembers working on 5.25" floppies?)

[»] **Note**

For a list of SAP Certified HANA Appliance partners head over to the SAP Community Network (SCN) page at *http://scn.sap.com/docs/DOC-52522*. If you want to know more about TDI, then check out the FAQ on SCN at *https://scn.sap.com/docs/DOC-62942*.

1.2   What Is SAP S/4HANA?

SAP S/4HANA is the next generation of SAP ERP optimized for SAP HANA. SAP ERP 6 EHP 7 has a common code base that supports any database, including SAP HANA. With SAP S/4HANA, SAP has taken the first step to simplify the SAP ERP data model and optimize the code base for SAP HANA as an in-memory database.

SAP has worked to remove the constraints of the traditional row-store disk-based database and to consolidate tables, reducing the amount of stored derived data. SAP HANA is able to process calculations at runtime so quickly that you no longer need specific tables in SAP ERP to store calculated values. The first simplification of the data model was delivered with SAP S/4HANA Finance. We also anticipate that SAP S/4HANA Logistics will include optimizations for Sales, Materials Management (MM), Production Planning (PP), Procurement, Asset Management, and more. SAP S/4HANA Finance has been released for use with core SAP ERP in addition to 25 industry solutions. All future solutions built in SAP S/4HANA will require SAP S/4HANA Finance first. This means that you can't migrate to SAP S/4HANA Logistics without first completing the migration to SAP S/4HANA Finance.

SAP S/4HANA is more than an installation; it's a group of migration activities for those customers currently running SAP Business Suite. For new customers, SAP S/4HANA is the initial install, so there is no data migration within SAP Business Suite. For those of you who already run SAP Business Suite, you'll need to prepare your system for the SAP S/4HANA migration, which starts with the activation of SAP S/4HANA Finance. As you read through this book, we'll talk about planning your upgrade and migration to SAP Business Suite on SAP HANA without including the SAP S/4HANA (SAP S/4HANA Finance) components. This is deliberate. SAP S/4HANA Finance is a data migration post-installation of specific ABAP components. You can include SAP S/4HANA Finance as part of the SAP Business Suite on SAP HANA migration project—it's technically feasible—and it would enable your organization to use the latest innovations and business process optimizations. However, by introducing these changes, you're also extending your project time line. With an as-is migration to SAP Business Suite on SAP HANA, you apply support packages and change the underlying database, but your business processes/transactions will remain as-is. During the planning section of this book, we walk through a migration approach that can be completed in 12 weeks from project kickoff to go-live in production with SAP Business Suite on SAP HANA. If you choose to include SAP S/4HANA Finance, then you have to coordinate with a financial calendar because the migration has significant impact on the functionality within SAP ERP Financials (FI).

In Figure 1.1, we've outlined in red some of the key components that will be part of the SAP S/4HANA Finance On-Premise installation. This book not only shows you how to migrate to SAP Business Suite on SAP HANA but also similarly shows you how to perform the technical installation of SAP S/4HANA Finance (a key component of SAP S/4HANA) postmigration to SAP Business Suite on SAP HANA.

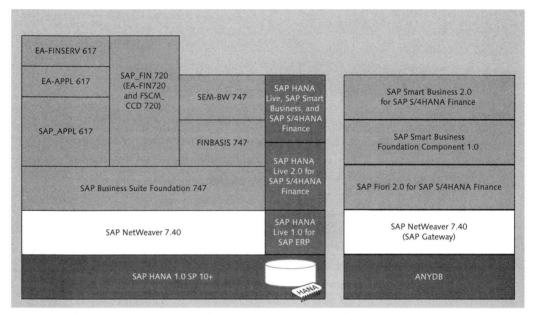

Figure 1.1 Key Components of SAP S/4HANA Finance Installation

We'll cover more on the installation of SAP S/4HANA Finance in Chapter 13. We'll also cover the installation of SAP HANA Live in Chapter 14, which is required to run SAP S/4HANA Finance. When you move to SAP S/4HANA, you'll not only have new ABAP components and a series of functional SAP Business Suite configuration tasks to complete, but you'll also need to rethink your security model. In the past, you operated SAP Business Suite on any database and typically never provided an end user or interface direct access to the database. With the installation of SAP HANA Live, your users will be able to connect directly to the database. You'll have another component of your landscape exposed to the user community and therefore will need some hardening. In Chapter 4, we provide some examples of what to plan for and how to scope the effort for security during your SAP Business Suite on SAP HANA migration.

1.3   SAP HANA and the Relational Database Management System

SAP HANA is a relational database, but it has been described as the reinvention of the database. It's true that SAP HANA as a database is both SQL-92 and ACID (atomicity, consistency, isolation, and durability) compliant. This means that you can run the most common and latest SQL commands within SQLScript. ACID compliant means that SAP HANA performs like any modern database system because it processes transactions that follow a set of rules, maintain consistencies of the transactions, isolate transactions from each other, and ensure any committed transaction won't be lost; these are the four guiding principles of database theory. Where SAP HANA breaks from the Relational Database Management System (RDBMS) mold is that it stores all transactions in memory first, in columnar format, and compressed. Many in-memory databases available on the market today require you to store data within a disk-based database first and then replicate to a memory cache. With SAP HANA, end-user transactions are read and written from memory first and then synchronized to disk and committed to logs.

SAP HANA is open and supports Open Database Connectivity (ODBC), Java Database Connectivity (JDBC), multidimensional expressions (MDX), OLE DB for OLAP (ODBO), ADO.NET, ABAP, and Extensible Markup Language (XML; REST [Representational State Transfer] and JSON [JavaScript Object Notation]), providing external access to both the database and its application platform. SAP HANA is an enterprise platform because it offers a database and an application platform that provides advanced text analysis, a spatial reference (geospatial), virtual OLAP, a web application server, and an advanced data replication engine. It's an entire application stack in one system. You could deploy a web application running SAP Fiori on the SAP HANA platform leveraging all of the components listed previously and only need to maintain one system. With other software vendors, this might require two to four different systems. SAP HANA also offers the disaster recovery and system replication features you would expect from an enterprise platform. You can replicate within the data center or across multiple geographically dispersed data centers—it's all supported and configured with a GUI in SAP HANA Studio.

Additionally, SAP HANA is available as both a cloud and on-premise platform. Again, it's a good time to be an SAP customer because you have choices. You can choose to run SAP HANA in a hybrid scenario or use services from SAP and its partners, which offer SAP HANA as a platform as a service (PaaS) in addition to the traditional infrastructure as a service (IaaS). In this book, we cover the migration to SAP Business Suite on SAP HANA. The planning tasks, migration procedures, screenshots, and post-install activities covered here apply to any scenario you choose. If you choose to leverage SAP HANA Enterprise Cloud, the tools we cover could be used to both convert your database and move your organization to the cloud. As a database platform, your IT staff will find the database familiar to work with if they have used Oracle, DB2, or MS SQL in the past. What might surprise them most is the seamless integration from database to applications included in the platform. They'll be able to leverage spatial and text search functionality within the same program without having to call another system or service. For administrators, they will learn to administer the database just like any other database.

1.4   In-Memory Database versus Caching

An in-memory database is different from a database in memory. Even with IBM's first database in 1968, we had the ability as customers to run a database that could pin tables to memory. A `commit` operation would exist at the disk level, and a process would copy the data to main memory. This is often referred to as a disk-block cache. The industry term in-memory database management systems (IMDBMS) was coined to describe databases that store the entire database structure in-memory with all operations (such as `select`, `insert`, `update`) occurring in memory without the need for an input/output (I/O) instruction to disk. SAP BW Accelerator (BWA) is a great example of a database in memory. We could load specific data from SAP BW into the main memory of another server, which would be used for OLAP operations (read only). It could be an index of a table or a group of indexes, but the main point here is that databases which cached data in memory were not used for the OLTP workload.

SAP HANA is an IMDMS that uses a column store and multiple compression algorithms to store the entire database in memory. It works closely with the Linux OS (Red Hat or SUSE Linux) to manage memory and correctly allocate memory tools for the most efficient storage of data. People always ask how much compression they will get by moving to SAP HANA, and the answer depends on the nature of the data, the number of repeated values, and the indexes. One great feature is that SAP HANA manages the tables for you, and it determines the compression algorithms (dictionary, run-length encoding (RLE), sparse, and others) to be used by column. Multiple columns within a table in memory could be using different compression types. And not all columns are loaded into memory. Sometimes referred to as "lazy loading," SAP HANA loads column into memory on first use. Columns that aren't used aren't loaded, thereby avoiding memory waste.

Figure 1.2 illustrates a breakdown of the virtual memory with SAP HANA running on Linux. SAP HANA is a collection of processes to the operating system, which requests memory from the OS based on demand. When the virtual memory needs to be used, it is mapped to physical memory or resident memory. The OS uses an algorithm to swap the old process out of resident memory. However, in a correctly sized SAP HANA system, this swapping should never occur.

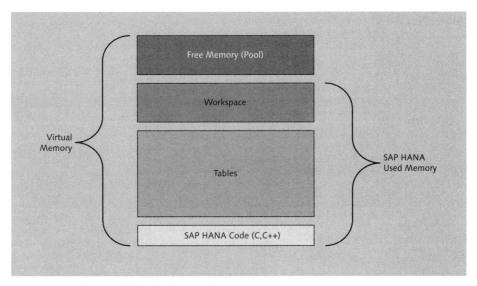

Figure 1.2 Explanation of SAP HANA Virtual Memory

Later in Chapter 3, we'll talk about SAP HANA sizing for SAP Business Suite on SAP HANA. As more memory is required, the SAP HANA memory manager will request and reserve more memory from the OS. By default, SAP HANA allocates 90% of the first 64GB and then 97% of the remaining memory. This allocation limit can be changed in scenarios where you have multiple SAP HANA instances on the same appliance.

As SAP HANA has matured, SAP has provided its customers with the tools needed to manage memory in SAP HANA. You have commands to load all tables into memory to get the "worst case" measurement. And you can view snapshots of memory usage over a period of time. SAP HANA is a true IMDBMS that can be managed much like a traditional RDBMS. Instead of monitoring disk space for tables, your database administrators will be monitoring memory and table growth to ensure your database systems can operate without error. (You still have to monitor the disk space in SAP HANA, and all transactions are written to the data and log files too.)

In the next section, we'll talk about architecture options with SAP Business Suite on SAP HANA now that you've got a foundation on how memory is managed with SAP HANA.

1.5   SAP HANA Architecture Options

There are entire books and white papers written on the topic of SAP HANA architecture. What you need to know going into the migration to SAP Business Suite on SAP HANA is that SAP HANA supports all major functionalities you would expect from an enterprise class database. SAP HANA supports a point-in-time recovery with the ability to configure High Availability (HA) and Disaster Recovery (DR) to meet any customer's requirements. From local disaster recovery to site-to-site replication, SAP has delivered out-of-the-box functionality to support most scenarios. There is no additional license to buy to leverage these advanced features. There are well-documented procedures and step-by-step guides, tutorials, and education for each scenario supported by SAP. In this section, we'll give you primer on what is available and some potential architecture options.

SAP HANA as a database has two options for scale, as it relates to database growth. SAP HANA can be deployed in the scale up or the scale out scenario. With scale up, we deploy as many resources as possible to a single host to support the current database and future database growth. With the scale out scenario, we add additional SAP HANA hosts alongside the primary host to add additional capacity for the database to grow. In the scale out scenario, data is distributed amongst the hosts supporting the database; thus we have to plan for and managed this data distribution. In the scale up scenario all data resides within one host which is easier to manage. As of August 2015, SAP Business Suite on SAP HANA is only supported on the scale up scenario.

Currently, you might have a single stack with an ABAP application server sharing the same host as the database. Or you might have a separate, clustered, primary application server (PAS) with standalone dialog servers and a clustered database. With SAP, many scenarios are supported. In our examples, we'll first look at the most basic scenario and then a complex one. Just know that there are too many options to list, so your organization might fall somewhere in between.

Let's start with the most basic configuration where the ABAP application server and the SAP HANA database share the same host. In this scenario, if one host fails, you have to recover both the database and the application server. Disaster Recovery and High Availability (HA/DR) are managed independently of the component. When you configure HA/DR for SAP HANA, it doesn't account for the ABAP application server and vice versa.

> **Note** [«]
>
> If you're only interested in running SAP Business Suite on SAP HANA in the cloud, you won't need to design your architecture because that will be the responsibility of the cloud provider. It's still good to review the items in this section to better under the service options available to you as a customer.

In Figure 1.3, we've configured one of the most basic DR scenarios. This DR environment could be within the same data center or at another site. We've configured SAP HANA System Replication, which requires no additional licenses and ensures that we have a copy of our production database ready to start. SAP HANA does support vendor-supplied storage replication technologies as an option.

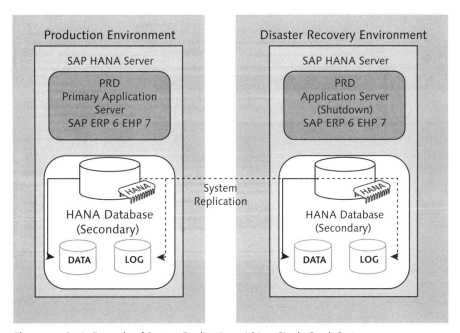

Figure 1.3 Basic Example of System Replication within a Single Stack System

Note that small- to medium-enterprise customers can run SAP Business Suite on SAP HANA in a cost-effective manner and still provide great recovery point objectives (RPO) and recovery time objectives (RTO). The RPO can be up to the minute, which is fantastic. SAP HANA can handle the automatic host failover at the database layer. The ABAP application server failover is manual and requires DNS changes, but it can be executed in under an hour or even under 30 minutes if well scripted. This assumes you're using SAP Solution Manager to monitor system availability so manual processes can be started in the event of a failure.

In terms of the system replication types, which can be used in a multitier strategy, you should be aware of the following modes:

▶ **Asynchronous**
The primary system commits the transaction after sending the log without waiting for a response from the secondary system. This mode is most useful when the secondary site is more than 100KM away from the primary site or when reducing latency is critical.

▶ **Synchronous In-Memory**
The primary system commits the transaction after it receives a reply that the log was received by the secondary system, but before it was persisted. The delay in the primary system is shorter because it only includes the network transmission time.

▶ **Synchronous**
The primary system waits to commit the transaction until it receives a reply that the log is persisted in the secondary system. This mode guarantees immediate consistency between both systems at a cost of delaying the transaction by the time for data transmission and persisting in the secondary system.

▶ **Synchronous Full Sync**
Another option determines what to do if the replication fails due to a network or system issue. The options are to fail the transaction or commit the transaction.

In Figure 1.3, we set the SAP HANA system replication configuration to synchronous. What if you want replication within the data center and a remote site? In the examples shown Figure 1.4 and Figure 1.5, we configure synchronous replication to another appliance within the same data center. We then configure asynchronous system replication to an appliance in another data center. Meanwhile, you could be using either SAP HANA appliance for QA, development, or as a sandbox as long as it doesn't interfere with the system replication. You've got options.

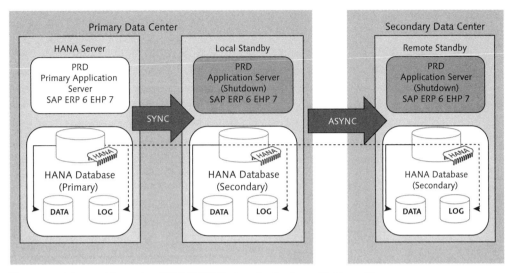

Figure 1.4 Advanced Example of SAP HANA System Replication with Theee Tiers

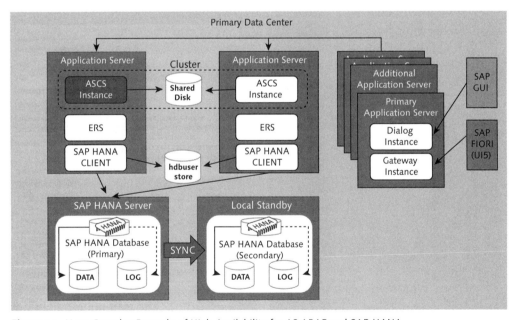

Figure 1.5 More Complex Example of High Availability for AS ABAP and SAP HANA

Now that you understand the options at the database layer, let's talk about the application layer. High Availability (HA) for Application Server (AS) ABAP has been available for more than 10 years. It's well documented and easy to set up. A variety of options are available to you as the customer. The really neat (neat as in fully automated) failover between data centers is typically delivered with some functionality provided at the virtualization layer. Automated failover within a data center is supported out of the box with SAP NetWeaver. If you want to failover to another data center automatically, you need to look at virtualization capabilities within VMware, Windows Hyper-V, HP UX vPars or nPars, AIX logical partitions (LPARs), or others. Let's use the example of HA for AS ABAP and SAP HANA in the same data center.

In Figure 1.5, we've covered most of the single point of failures (SPOFs) at the application and OS layer. From here, your team will then drill into the underlying infrastructure to ensure the storage and network layer have the appropriate redundancy. ABAP SAP Central Services (ASCS) is the cluster-aware service that is managed at the OS level. This functionality comes out of the box with Microsoft Windows Server. For a list of other OSs and the required components to support a similar scenario for UNIX, see Table 1.1. Enqueue Replication Service (ERS) is the function that manages locks within SAP. When using a replicated enqueue, you get better throughput. In this example, the ERS shares the host with the ASCS. For maximum throughput, you can put the ERS on two additional hosts. This obviously increases the number of systems to manage but is an SAP recommendation. We talk about the standalone enqueue server later in Chapter 3, Section 3.1.

Partner	Solution
HP	Serviceguard A.11.20
NEC	ExpressCluster 3.1 on Linux x86_64
Oracle	Clusterware 11g (Rel. 2)
Red Hat	Enterprise Linux 6
SUSE	Linux Enterprise High Availability 11 on Linux x86_64
Symantec	Veritas InfoScale

Table 1.1 SAP High Availability Certified Partners and Solutions for UNIX

[»] **Note**

To learn more about HA configuration, check out the SCN page at *http://scn.sap.com/docs/DOC-8541*. For more information on SAP HANA HA and DR options, see the white paper "Introduction – SAP HANA in Data Centers" at *http://scn.sap.com/docs/DOC-60341*.

1.6 Summary

It's a great time to be an SAP customer. SAP Business Suite on SAP HANA brings true innovation that will excite and motivate your business and IT teams. In this chapter, we highlighted some of the differences between SAP Business Suite on SAP HANA and SAP S/4HANA. SAP S/4HANA is a collection of ABAP components and configuration that will facilitate the migration from your current core SAP ERP Financials (FI). When migrating to SAP Business Suite on SAP HANA, you can choose whether to include those ABAP components for SAP S/4HANA. You can migrate to SAP Business Suite on SAP HANA with EHP 7 to begin using operational and analytical improvements, including SAP HANA Live and SAP Smart Business Applications. Then, as your IT teams prepare the organization for the process changes with SAP S/4HANA Finance, you can activate functionality and deploy as a pure functional upgrade to the business community. Migrating to SAP Business Suite on SAP HANA without SAP S/4HANA Finance will mean most of your transactions and processes will run as-is, requiring little remediation. When activating SAP S/4HANA Finance, you'll have both process change and user interface changes.

With this background information, you're now ready to begin the planning, estimating, executing, and management of your SAP Business Suite on SAP HANA migration project. Remember, you don't need to be a SAP HANA database or architecture expert to run an SAP Business Suite on SAP HANA migration project. You do, however, need those SAP HANA experts for installation and administration at various points in the project. We won't cover the SAP HANA DB installation in this book, as that's been well covered in other sources and can be completed quickly for simple installation scenarios. Instead, we'll cover in depth the tools and migration process for SAP Business Suite on SAP HANA.

Next, let's get started with defining your project scope.

The SAP Business Suite on SAP HANA project will have many moving parts, and you need to look at all of them to determine your project scope. Use this chapter as your guide in defining what will be changing during the SAP Business Suite on SAP HANA migration.

2   Establishing Project Scope

Both a clearly defined project scope and project charter are key to any project in IT. Let's cover how to define the project scope for your SAP Business Suite on SAP HANA migration. The project scope will dictate resources, time lines, effort, and, consequently, cost. As you plan and execute a migration to SAP Business Suite on SAP HANA, you should ask the following questions: Do we upgrade first and then migrate? Do we migrate as-is if we already have the minimum supported software components? How will this impact our third-party software components and interfaces with SAP Business Suite?

As a customer, you have several available options when migrating to SAP Business Suite on SAP HANA. You can choose to include a Support Package Stack (SP Stack) in the migration, or you can include an entire enhancement package when migrating to SAP HANA. We'll discuss how and what level of change you should include with your migration to maximize all resources.

Landscape planning is also a key component to a successful migration project. You'll need to know what your client strategy will be, as well as how many systems will be required to support both production support changes and any development required during the project. We'll discuss several approaches to the landscape along with the pros and cons of each approach. At the end of this chapter, you'll have a better understanding of the questions to ask and how to mitigate risk.

Running SAP Business Suite systems in a silo isn't a real-world scenario. We know that your organization's SAP Business Suite system will have multiple interfacing scenarios, third-party add-ons installed, potentially industry solutions activated, and numerous customizations. We'll cover the tools made available from SAP to understand dependencies between SAP components, industry solutions, and certified SAP third-party add-ons, as well as the risk during the migration for those noncertified applications connecting to SAP ERP. We'll also cover how the migration will affect the application layer within SAP ERP so you'll have a better understanding if homegrown applications will still interface after the migration.

SAP Solution Manager and its Build SAP Like a Factory toolsets will play a key component role in the migration. Initially, you'll use SAP Solution Manager to reverse-document your production SAP ERP system, and later in Chapter 8, we'll talk about how SAP Solution Manager supports testing and impact analysis. In this chapter, we cover Solution Documentation tool, which you use to document the transactions and programs in use within your production systems.

We'll conclude this chapter with a discussion of resource planning and the use of SAP Best Practices for the SAP Business Suite on SAP HANA migration. During the various phases of the project, we'll cover the types of resources required and how to calculate the number of each resource required. Armed with example project team roles and training plans, this chapter will provide the foundation for your successful SAP Business Suite on SAP HANA migration.

2.1 Upgrade and Migration Dependencies

There are six specific areas to review to determine your project scope: enhancement packages, support packages, add-ons, Unicode, dual stacks, and custom code. We'll cover the dual stack in Chapter 3 and custom code in Chapter 11. Reviewing add-ons will be the only topic area that might prevent a company from a migration to SAP HANA today due to support provided by SAP (not all add-ons and industry solutions are support by SAP HANA today—more on that topic in Section 2.1.3). All other areas are items you need to plan for but none should prevent you from migrating SAP ERP to SAP HANA.

In addition to helping you find information on what versions and components are required to migrate to SAP HANA, we'll attempt answer the following: How much change is too much change? How can you best leverage the testing dollars you plan on spending during this project? What can you do if you're an SAP R/3 customer today?

2.1.1 Enhancement Packages

Enhancement packages split the installation of new functionality with the implementation of enhancements. You can now install enhancements without impacting existing business processes and then selectively activate enhancements when they are ready. When coupled with the correct usage of the Business Process Change Analyzer (BPCA) in SAP Solution Manager (see Chapter 8), a customer can also measure the impact of enabling specific enhancements. Enhancement packages can be included with normal support package installations performed by a customer (ideally on an annual basis) and not directly impact the level of testing required. Enhancements are delivered as part of maintenance agreements with SAP, and it's up to the customer to install and then activate.

> **Note** [«]
>
> Want to know more about potential enhancements your organization could be using? Check out the SAP Innovation & Discovery page (*https://apps.support.sap.com/innovation-discovery/index.html*). This page links information from your company's SAP ERP usage (based on SAP EarlyWatch Alerts) to enhancements delivered by SAP. A Service Marketplace user ID is required to access this page.

Finding Your Target SAP ERP Version

When planning your SAP Business Suite on SAP HANA migration, there are specific SAP ERP release levels that are supported for the migration (see Table 2.1). The source release for a migration to SAP Business Suite on SAP HANA can be any version of SAP ECC 5.0 or SAP ERP 6.0. The target release depends on the release strategy within your organization. If we follow SAP's recommendation for the migration, the target release will be EHP 7 for SAP ERP 6.0 SPS 05 at a minimum. If you're already running SAP ERP 6.0 EHP 6, then you can migrate as-is to SAP Business Suite on SAP HANA using the Software Provisioning Manager (SWPM).

> **Note** [«]
>
> Per SAP Note 1768031, it's not recommended to start new implementation projects using the initial version of SAP Business Suite powered by SAP HANA. The latest enhancement package versions as outlined previously should be used. Please refer to SAP Note 1903842, which explains as well the nonavailability of the former version for new installation downloads on the Service Marketplace.

The Software Tool column in Table 2.1 represents the two applications provided by SAP that you can us to migrate to SAP Business Suite on SAP HANA. The Software Update Manager (SUM) and Software Provisioning Manager (SWPM) are delivered as part of the software logistics toolset (SL Toolset) from SAP. We'll cover these tools in detail in Chapter 5. There are two key points to take away from the this table. First, if you're currently running SAP R/3, then you need to upgrade to SAP ERP 6.0 EHP 7 and then use the SWPM tool to migrate. Getting all of these activities to complete within a weekend is challenging, but we'll explain how to speed up the process in Chapter 6 and Chapter 7 when we perform the actual migration.

Source Release	Intermediary Release	Software Tool	Target Release
=< SAP R/3 4.7c	SAP ERP 6.0 EHP 7	SUM and SWPM	SAP ERP 6.0 EHP 7 on SAP HANA
ECC 5.0 Any SP Level	N/A	SUM	SAP ERP 6.0 EHP 7 on SAP HANA
ERP 6.0 Any SP or EHP Level	N/A	SUM	SAP ERP 6.0 EHP 7 on SAP HANA
SAP ERP 6.0 EHP 6+	N/A	SWPM	SAP ERP 6.0 EHP 6+ on SAP HANA*

Table 2.1 SAP Recommended Targets

The second key point from the table comes from SAP Note 1768031. If your organization's release strategy is N-1, this might dictate that you must apply EHP 6 instead of EHP 7 (N-1 refers to the IT strategy of installing software one revision lower than the current release with the idea the newest release is not the most stable). Essentially, this isn't permitted because SAP won't even allow the Maintenance Optimizer to download the media needed for this migration type. The N-1 philosophy is better applied to SP Stacks, not enhancement packages. Keep in mind that enhancement packages are installed dormant. They won't impact your system unless activated via the Switch Framework (Transaction SFW5). SP Stacks are collections of fixes provided by SAP that will directly impact your transactions and programs in use within your environment. Adopting an N-1 strategy for SP Stacks is allowed during the migration to SAP Business Suite on SAP HANA. This is an option when you execute the Maintenance Optimizer to download the required upgrade software components. Based on the current SAP recommendations and published roadmaps at the time of this writing, we recommend setting your target release to SAP ERP 6.0 EHP 7 if you're not already on that release. If you're currently running EHP 7, then see the next section.

Follow these instructions to find your current SAP ERP version:

1. Log on to your SAP ERP system with a valid user ID and password.

2. Select SYSTEM • STATUS from the SAP GUI toolbar as shown in Figure 2.1.

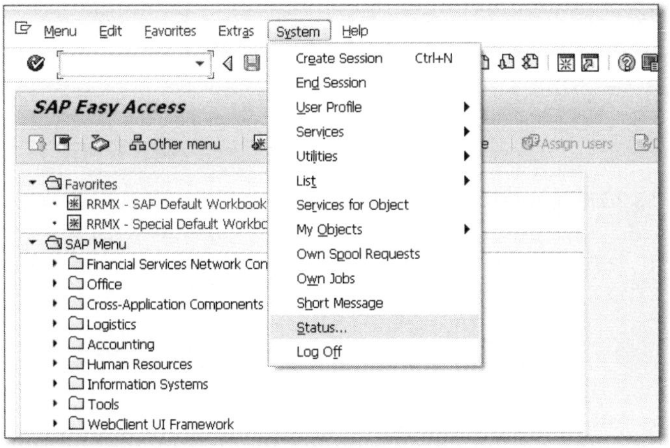

Figure 2.1 Status Menu Selection

3. Check the COMPONENT VERSION field, which should display your current release information, as shown in Figure 2.2. If it reads, SEE COMPONENT INFORMATION, click the COMPONENT INFORMATION button under the COMPONENT VERSION field.

Figure 2.2 Component Version Information Displayed

4. After clicking the Component Information button, you'll see a list of software components that make up SAP ERP. Click the Installed Product Versions tab.

5. Note the current enhancement package version. SAP ERP 6.0 EHP 7 is the version installed in Figure 2.3.

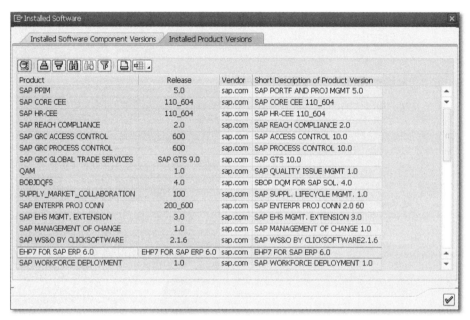

Figure 2.3 Installed Product Versions

[+]   Tip

To find the latest available enhancement package for SAP ERP, access the following SAP Support Portal page *http://service.sap.com/erp-EHP*. Under the Spotlight section, SAP displays the latest enhancement package version.

2.1.2   Support Packages

In addition to planning the target enhancement package level you'll apply when migrating to SAP HANA, you also need to determine the SP Stack level. A SP Stack is a collection of support packages that SAP has tested as a release to the customer base. A support package is a collection of fixes or SAP Notes for a specific version of an SAP product. In practice, it's best that you always run a consistent SP Stack delivered by SAP. You do have the option of upgrading specific individual components, but this isn't recommended.

To determine which SP Stack you should implement during your SAP Business Suite on SAP HANA migration project, you need to take into account SAP's maintenance strategy. SAP regularly updates its SP Stack schedule within the Service Marketplace. For example, if you know you're going to start a migration project in Q4 2015, then the SP Stack schedule helps you understand the current SP Stack level available and the planned release date for the next available SP Stack. In general, SAP recommends installing the latest available SP Stack.

Support Package Stack Schedule

Let's go over the steps you need to follow to view the SP Stack schedule:

1. Go to the SAP Support Portal with a valid user ID and password as shown in Figure 2.4 via the URL *https://support.sap.com/release-upgrade-maintenance/ package-stack-schedules.html.*

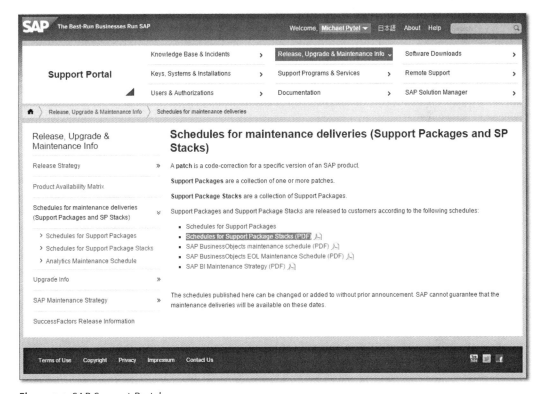

Figure 2.4 SAP Support Portal

2. Click the link for SCHEDULES FOR SUPPORT PACKAGE STACKS (PDF) to open a PDF schedule of support packages for multiple SAP software products. SAP updates this schedule frequently.
3. Navigate in the document to EHP 7 FOR SAP ERP 6.0. In the example in Figure 2.5, you can see the SP Stack level 9 was planned for release in July 2015.

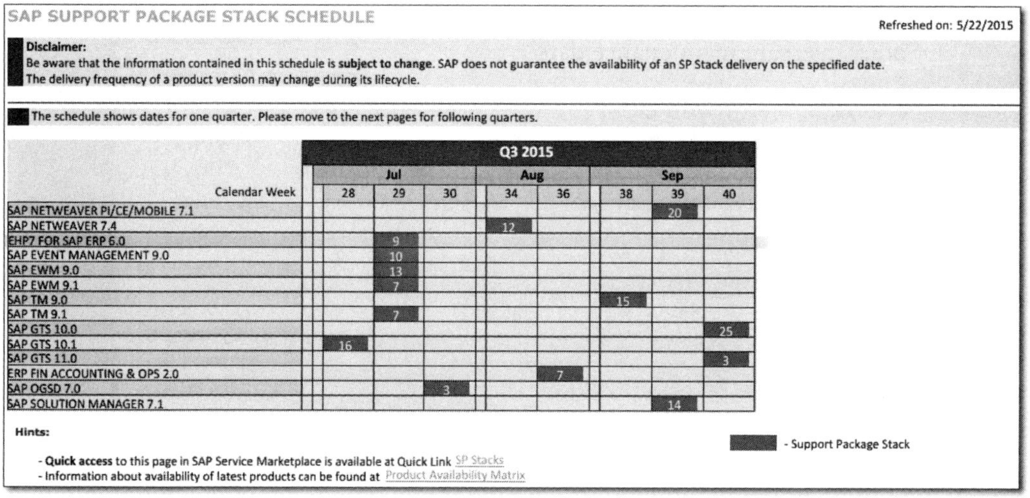

SAP SUPPORT PACKAGE STACK SCHEDULE

Refreshed on: 5/22/2015

Disclaimer:
Be aware that the information contained in this schedule is **subject to change**. SAP does not guarantee the availability of an SP Stack delivery on the specified date.
The delivery frequency of a product version may change during its lifecycle.

The schedule shows dates for one quarter. Please move to the next pages for following quarters.

	Q3 2015							
	Jul			Aug		Sep		
Calendar Week	28	29	30	34	36	38	39	40
SAP NETWEAVER PI/CE/MOBILE 7.1							20	
SAP NETWEAVER 7.4				12				
EHP7 FOR SAP ERP 6.0		9						
SAP EVENT MANAGEMENT 9.0		10						
SAP EWM 9.0		13						
SAP EWM 9.1		7						
SAP TM 9.0						15		
SAP TM 9.1		7						
SAP GTS 10.0								25
SAP GTS 10.1	16							
SAP GTS 11.0								3
ERP FIN ACCOUNTING & OPS 2.0					7			
SAP OGSD 7.0			3					
SAP SOLUTION MANAGER 7.1							14	

Hints:

- **Quick access** to this page in SAP Service Marketplace is available at Quick Link SP Stacks
- Information about availability of latest products can be found at Product Availability Matrix

- Support Package Stack

Figure 2.5 Excerpt from SAP Support Package Stack Schedule

Product Availability Matrix

When planning your target release for the SAP Business Suite on SAP HANA migration, it's also useful to understand the maintenance schedule and supported versions for the software components included in your project scope. The product availability matrix (PAM) provides detailed information regarding specific components that will support your SAP Business Suite on SAP HANA system. You can find details there on the supported OS versions, SAP HANA support package levels, supported browsers, supported Java versions, and more. To start, navigate the PAM to determine your supported OS, DB version, and ABAP add-ons by following these steps:

1. Log on to the SAP Support Portal at *http://support.sap.com/pam.* Enter your SAP Support Portal user ID and password when prompted.
2. Click the ENTER THE PRODUCT AVAILABILITY MATRIX button.

3. In the search box (upper right), type "ERP" and press ⌈Enter⌉.

4. Navigate to the enhancement package version you determined in Section 2.1.1, and select it. In this example, we selected EHP 7 FOR SAP ERP 6.0. From here, you can find the following information (see Figure 2.6):

   ▷ Current status

   ▷ Release to customer date

   ▷ End of mainstream maintenance date

   ▷ Related installation documentation

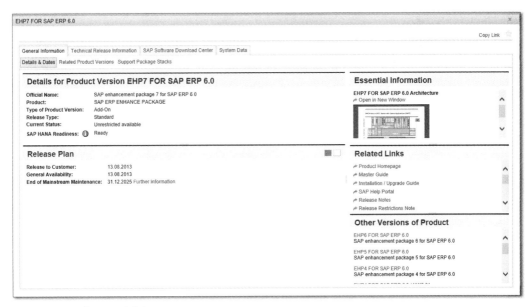

Figure 2.6 Product Availability Matrix

5. Click on the RELATED PRODUCT VERSIONS button (see Figure 2.7).

   Within this screen, you can view the ABAP ADD-ON PRODUCT VERSIONS that have been released for this specific enhancement package. (For more on add-on compatibility, see Section 2.1.3.)

   You can also view the successor product versions within the UPGRADE TO section if this version isn't the latest enhancement package release.

6. Click on the TECHNICAL RELEASE INFORMATION tab, and then click on the DATA-BASE PLATFORMS button. Under the DATABASE selection criteria, choose SAP HANA DATABASE. This will display the combinations of Application Server operating system (OS) and SAP Kernel versions that are supported with the SAP HANA database.

Figure 2.7 Related Product Versions from the Product Availability Matrix

7. You can further define your filter criteria by selecting your organization's preferred OS. In the example in Figure 2.8, we've selected LINUX ON X86_64 and the latest SAP KERNEL 7.42 64-BIT UNICODE.

Using the PAM, you can determine the target version for each component of your landscape. You must also find the right balance of in-house expertise and long-term supportability. In Figure 2.8, you'll notice the SUPPORT UNTIL dates are drastically different between SUSE Enterprise and Red Hat Enterprise. In this example, if we leverage Red Hat Enterprise Linux instead of SUSE Enterprise, we could potentially extend our vendor maintenance period by five years. That's significant if we decide we want to avoid OS upgrades long term. How much different is SUSE versus Red Hat for your administrators? This is one question your organization will need to answer. The same argument applies to Microsoft, HP-UX, IBM AIX, IBM OS/400, IBM Z/OS, and Solaris. Be sure to note the SUPPORT UNTIL dates when planning your target OS version for the Application Servers.

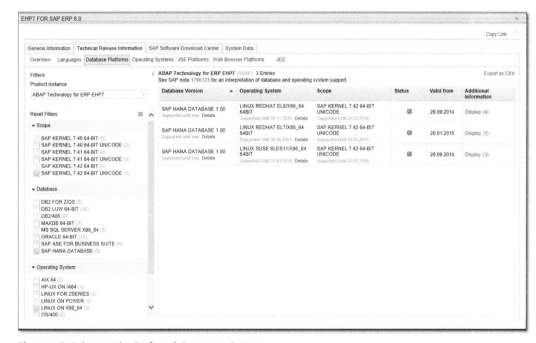

Figure 2.8 Selecting the Preferred Operating System

> **Note** [«]
>
> At the time of this book's publication, the only OS's supported as the SAP HANA database server were Red Hat Enterprise and SUSE Enterprise. To find the latest information on supported OS versions for the SAP HANA database server, search for "SAP HANA Platform Edition" within the PAM.

2.1.3 Add-On Compatibility

ABAP add-ons installed in your SAP Business Suite systems are either provided by SAP or by third parties. SAP-delivered ABAP add-ons are defined as supported or unsupported in SAP Notes and the PAM previously described. These ABAP add-ons are the easiest to determine whether support will be provided by SAP during your migration to SAP Business Suite on SAP HANA. Using the process described earlier in Figure 2.2, you can determine the ABAP add-ons installed in your system. After you've determined the ABAP add-ons, review Table 2.2 to determine whether or not the add-on is supported when migrating to SAP Business Suite on SAP HANA. You must review add-ons for both SAP NetWeaver AS ABAP 7.4 on SAP HANA and SAP ERP 6.0 EHP 7 version for SAP HANA 1.0.

Add-On Name	Supported	Successor
SAP DECISION SERVICE MGMT. 1.0	Yes	
MOB PATIENT MGMNT INT 1.0.0	Yes	
MULTICHANNEL FOR UTILITIES 1.0	Yes	
SAP ACCESS CONTROL 5.3 (only component VIRSANH 530_731)	Yes	
SAP ACCESS CONTROL 10.0 (only component SAP GRC 10.0 PLUGIN NW 7.31)	Yes	
SAP ACCESS CONTROL 10.1 (only component SAP GRC 10.0 PLUGIN NW 7.31)	Yes	
SAP AII 7.1	Yes	
SAP CPM 1.0	Yes	
SAP CPROJECT SUITE 4.50	Yes	
SAP EHP 1 FOR SAP NW MOBILE 7.3	Yes	
SAP EVENT MANAGEMENT 9.0	Yes	
SAP FIN. CLOSING COCKPIT 1.0	Yes	
SAP FIN. CLOSING COCKPIT 2.0	Yes	
SAP FINANCIAL CLOSING COCKPIT 1.0	Yes	
SAP LANDSCAPE TRANSFORMATION 1	Yes	
SAP LANDSCAPE TRANSFORMATION 2	Yes	
SAP LT REPLICATION SERVER 1.0	Yes	
SAP LT REPLICATION SERVER 2.0	Yes	
SAP GATEWAY 2.0	Yes	
SAP NFE 10.0	Yes	
SAP PROCESS CONTROL 10.0 (only component SAP GRC 10.0 PLUGIN NW 7.31)	Yes	
SAP PROCESS CONTROL 10.1 (only component SAP GRC 10.0 PLUGIN NW 7.31)	Yes	
SAP SUPPL. LIFECYCLE MGMT. 1.0	Yes	

Table 2.2 Add-On Support

Add-On Name	Supported	Successor
SAP TDMS 3.0	Yes	
SAP TDMS 4.0	Yes	
SAP TDMS EXT BPL 3.0	Yes	
SAP WORKFORCE DEPLOYMENT 1.0	Yes	
SBOP PC 10.0 FOR SAP NW	Yes	
SL TOOLSET 1.0	Yes	
UI5 APPROVE ALL UIO 1.0.0	Yes	
UI5 CARTAPPROVAL UIO 1.0.0	Yes	
UI5 LEAVEAPPROVAL UIO 1.0.0	Yes	
UI5 LEAVEREQUEST UIO 1.0.0	Yes	
SAP CPROJECT SUITE 4.00	Yes	
SAP GTS 10.1	Yes	
SAP QUALITY ISSUE MGMT 1.0	Yes	
SAP AII 4.0	No	Upgrade to AII 7.1
SAP Notes Management 10.0	Yes	
SAP RISK MANAGEMENT 10.1	No	Released for EHP 7, not on SAP HANA
SAP WORKFORCE MANAGEMENT 3.1	No	Check Support Portal

Table 2.2 Add-On Support (Cont.)

> **Note** [«]
>
> If you don't find the add-on you're looking for either in Table 2.2 or in the related notes, contact SAP Support (under component XX-SER-REL) or contact the specific partner (non-SAP products).
>
> See SAP Notes 1760306 and 1812713 for updated information on the SAP-supported ABAP add-ons when migrating to SAP Business Suite on SAP HANA.

Third-party ABAP add-ons are more difficult to verify because they require the developer of the add-on to recertify the solution with SAP Business Suite on SAP HANA. SAP Note 1855666 is continually updated with information regarding third-party add-ons that have been qualified. The most common ABAP add-ons from Vistex, OpenText, and Nakisa have all been certified for use with SAP Business Suite on SAP HANA (as long as you're running the latest version of their software). Create a message for SAP support using component XXX-SER-REL if you're unable to find specific SAP Notes that validate your third-party solution.

2.1.4 Non-Unicode versus Unicode

SAP HANA only supports Unicode, so any SAP Business Suite system currently running in non-Unicode must be converted. The Database Migration Option (DMO) in SUM supports a Unicode conversion during the SAP HANA migration and upgrade but only if your non-Unicode system is currently configured with a single code page. If your system is Multidisplay/Multiprocessing (MDMP), then your Unicode conversion must take place before the migration to SAP Business Suite on SAP HANA. The SUM tool doesn't support a Unicode conversion and migration to SAP HANA in one step for MDMP systems.

SAP has provided several utilities for customers to use to prepare their systems for a Unicode migration, as we'll discuss in the following subsections. These preparation tasks can be completed weeks or months in advance of the SAP HANA migration. We'll discuss those tools at a high level and explain how to determine what type of non-Unicode version exists in your system. For the most up to date guide and information, refer to SAP Note 1968508.

Determining Unicode Status

To ascertain the Unicode status, follow these steps:

1. Log on to your SAP ERP system with the SAP GUI using a valid user ID and password.
2. On the toolbar, click SYSTEM • STATUS.
3. Under the SAP SYSTEM DATA subsection, you'll see the UNICODE SYSTEM field. If YES appears in the field, then the system is already running Unicode. If NO, see the next section to determine whether the system is single code page or MDMP.

Determining the Non-Unicode Type

To determine the non-Unicode type, follow these steps:

1. Log on to your SAP ERP system with the SAP GUI using a valid user ID and password.

2. Run Transaction SE16. In the TABLE NAME field, enter "TCPDB", as shown in Figure 2.9. Press Enter.

Figure 2.9 Entering the Table Name

3. Leave the selection criteria empty, as shown in Figure 2.10. Click the EXECUTE button.

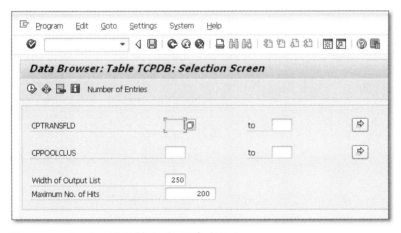

Figure 2.10 Leaving All Fields in the Default State

> ▷ If one record is displayed, then your system is a single code page and can be migrated to SAP Business Suite on SAP HANA using the SUM tool with DMO.

> ▷ If more than one record is displayed, then your system is MDMP and must be first converted to Unicode and then migrated to SAP Business Suite on SAP HANA using the heterogeneous system copy process within the SWPM (covered in Chapter 5).

> ▷ If no records are displayed, your system is already Unicode.

Unicode Preparation

All details and exceptions to the Unicode conversion process are covered in the document "Release Change & Single Code Page Conversion to Unicode with DMO" attached to SAP Note 1968508. The document covers specific issues with specific single code page conversions in detail, and it should be reviewed prior to executing the migration to SAP Business Suite on SAP HANA with the SUM tool for any non-Unicode system. We'll cover the two primary tools used when preparing your non-Unicode system.

The first tool we'll cover enables customers to check the Unicode compliance of any customer-created ABAP program on the non-Unicode system. This utility transaction can be run weeks or months before the actual migration project starts. It's not advisable to run the program for SAP and customer-created programs because you only need to execute for the objects your organization has created. It's best to run the program on any system that will be upgraded and migrated to SAP Business Suite on SAP HANA. For example, if you only run on the development system, you might miss an object in QA or production (despite your best efforts to keep all environments consistent). Some may argue that you only execute the report in production, remediate in development, and then transport through the landscape. If a program is missed in development, the only potential risk is that the program isn't executable postmigration to SAP Business Suite on SAP HANA. In essence, run the program in production, and its output will be the work instructions for the ABAP development team within the development environment.

To use this utility, follow these steps:

1. Log on to your non-Unicode SAP ERP system with a valid user ID and password.
2. Execute Transaction UCCHECK.
3. Leave all fields as default (see Figure 2.11), and the utility will check for Unicode compliance against all customer-created objects, ignoring any object created within a temporary development package.
4. You can update the Maximum Number of Programs field to a larger value, but this might cause timeout issues (long program runtimes).

    This utility is meant to drive work instructions and can be used iteratively. Programs identified can be remediated and then the transaction executed again.

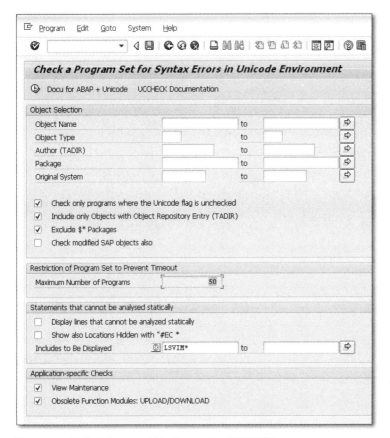

Figure 2.11 Default Screen within Transaction UCCHECK

5. If you change the MAXIMUM NUMBER OF PROGRAMS to a larger value, then you need to execute it as a background job. From the toolbar, click PROGRAM • EXECUTE IN BACKGROUND.

6. Click the EXECUTE button if you leave all fields as default.

7. After the transaction completes, a list of objects to be remediated is displayed. This task is typically handled by an ABAP developer who will ensure each object is set to be ABAP 6.10 compliant.

The next tool will be executed closer to the migration to SAP Business Suite on SAP HANA. Transaction SPUMG is meant to prepare the database tables for the conversion to Unicode. This assumes your migration strategy is an upgrade, Unicode conversion, and migration in one step using SUM with DMO. The results of

Transaction SPUMG are stored in the Export Control Table and provide inputs for the DMO. Before running Transaction SPUMG, you must first update the data it uses as an exception list. The exception list in this case includes tables that only exist in one language. The exception list is updated by SAP and attached to SAP Note 996990. Let's walk through updating the exception list and executing the preparation tasks:

1. Log on to your non-Unicode SAP system with a valid user ID and password.

2. Execute Transaction SPUMG

3. Click the DOWNLOAD EXCEPTION LIST FROM NOTE 996990 button, as shown in Figure 2.12.

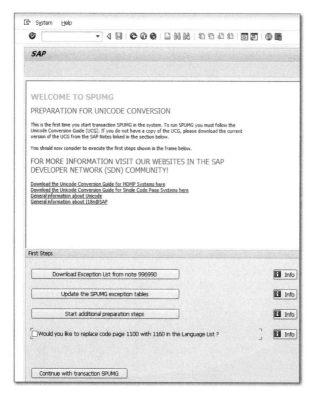

Figure 2.12 Transaction SPUMG

4. This will open a web browser. Read the note carefully to determine the most recent version of the XML file to download. At the time of this writing, the latest version was 028.

5. Scroll down to the ATTACHMENTS section of the SAP Note, as shown in Figure
   2.13 Right-click on the latest version of the exception list zip file, and click SAVE
   TARGET AS.

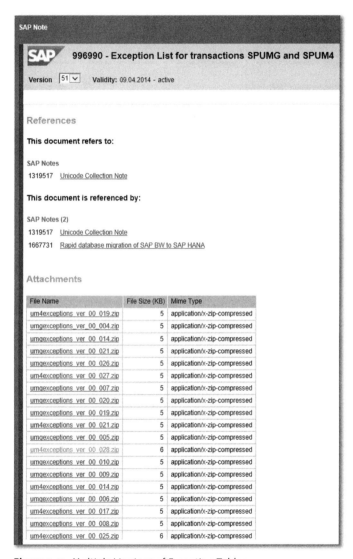

SAP Note

SAP   **996990 - Exception List for transactions SPUMG and SPUM4**

Version   51   Validity: 09.04.2014 - active

References

This document refers to:

SAP Notes
1319517   Unicode Collection Note

This document is referenced by:

SAP Notes (2)
1319517   Unicode Collection Note
1667731   Rapid database migration of SAP BW to SAP HANA

Attachments

File Name	File Size (KB)	Mime Type
um4exceptions_ver_00_019.zip	5	application/x-zip-compressed
umgexceptions_ver_00_004.zip	5	application/x-zip-compressed
umgexceptions_ver_00_014.zip	5	application/x-zip-compressed
umgexceptions_ver_00_021.zip	5	application/x-zip-compressed
umgexceptions_ver_00_026.zip	5	application/x-zip-compressed
um4exceptions_ver_00_027.zip	5	application/x-zip-compressed
umgexceptions_ver_00_007.zip	5	application/x-zip-compressed
umgexceptions_ver_00_020.zip	5	application/x-zip-compressed
umgexceptions_ver_00_019.zip	5	application/x-zip-compressed
um4exceptions_ver_00_021.zip	5	application/x-zip-compressed
umgexceptions_ver_00_005.zip	5	application/x-zip-compressed
um4exceptions_ver_00_028.zip	6	application/x-zip-compressed
umgexceptions_ver_00_010.zip	5	application/x-zip-compressed
umgexceptions_ver_00_009.zip	5	application/x-zip-compressed
um4exceptions_ver_00_014.zip	5	application/x-zip-compressed
umgexceptions_ver_00_006.zip	5	application/x-zip-compressed
um4exceptions_ver_00_017.zip	5	application/x-zip-compressed
umgexceptions_ver_00_008.zip	5	application/x-zip-compressed
um4exceptions_ver_00_025.zip	6	application/x-zip-compressed

Figure 2.13 Multiple Versions of Exception Tables

6. Store the zip file on your local computer. Return to the folder with the zip file,
   and extract its contents.

7. Return to the SAP GUI and Transaction SPUMG. Click the UPDATE THE SPUMG EXCEPTION TABLES button.

8. When prompted, navigate to the XML file you extracted in the previous steps.

9. Select the XML file, and click OPEN. Confirm the system message UPLOAD OF EXCEPTIONS SUCCESSFULLY FINISHED.

10. Click the START ALL PREPARATION STEPS button.

11. You'll be presented with a list of jobs, as shown in Figure 2.14, to be executed to prepare the system for a Unicode conversion. Click the EXECUTE ALL IN BACKGROUND button.

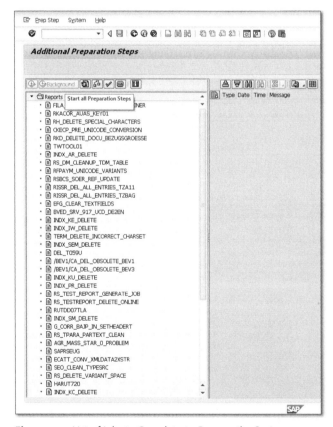

Figure 2.14 List of Jobs to Complete to Prepare the System

12. Click the REFRESH button to confirm the background job completion. You can also view the job status in Transaction SM37.

After you've completed these transactions and all tasks defined within the attachment to SAP Note 1968508, the system is ready for migration to SAP Business Suite on SAP HANA using SUM DMO.

Another utility to ensure your system is ready for the Unicode migration is to define the ABAP system profile parameter `abap/unicode_check` to `on`. This parameter, when set on a non-Unicode system, will ensure only Unicode-enabled objects can be executed. It's another option available to SAP customers which helps verify that your non-Unicode systems are ready to be migrated before you begin the process with SUM DMO.

2.1.5   Upgrade Dependency Analyzer

The SAP application portfolio includes numerous components, and landscapes typically consist of more SAP software than just SAP ERP. How do we understand application interdependencies if we're upgrading SAP ERP to EHP 7 during the migration to SAP HANA? For example, if we're running SAP ERP, SAP Process Integration (SAP PI), and SAP Customer Relationship Management (SAP CRM), how do we upgrade and migrate SAP ERP independently from SAP CRM and SAP PI?

During the planning phases for your project, SAP has a utility to help you calculate these interdependencies. There is obviously no replacement for regression testing regardless of the reports and utilities you use during the planning stages. However, the Upgrade Dependency Analyzer is a useful tool when defining your project scope. It will help you define the applications or components to be upgraded at a high level.

In this section, we'll cover how to access and use the tool, which is available online and within SAP Solution Manager. We'll focus on the online tool, which is immediately available to any SAP customer with a valid SAP Support Portal user ID and password.

1. Log on to *http://support.sap.com/upgrade,* and navigate to UPGRADE TOOLS • UPGRADE DEPENDENCY ANALYZER • TOOL ACCESS.

2. Click START APPLICATION (this will open a new window).

3. Under TARGET COMPONENT, input the target version of SAP ERP you want to simulate. In Figure 2.15, we selected the following:

   ▸ PRODUCT: SAP ERP ENHANCE PACKAGE

▶ PRODUCT VERSION: EHP 7 FOR SAP ERP 6.0

▶ PRODUCT INSTANCE: ERP CENTRAL COMPONENT (ECC)

Figure 2.15 Simulating the Impact of an Upgrade with Upgrade Dependency Analyzer

4. Under EXISTING COMPONENT in Figure 2.15, input the component you want to know if there is a known dependency for in the SAP ERP upgrade. For this example, we made the following entries:

▶ PRODUCT: SAP SCM

▶ PRODUCT VERSION: SAP SCM 7.0

▶ PRODUCT INSTANCE: SCM SERVER

5. In Figure 2.15, you can see the text NO KNOWN UPGRADE DEPENDENCIES, INDEPENDENT UPGRADE POSSIBLE, which means, for this example, we can upgrade SAP ERP without having to upgrade SAP Supply Chain Management (SAP SCM).

6. The Upgrade Dependency Analyzer is the first tool you use to understand the potential impact of SAP ERP to the rest of your SAP landscape. It requires no setup and very little input to get an answer. If there is an impact, then the tool will highlight where you can get additional information.

2.2   Landscape Planning

As you continue to define your project scope, you must define the project landscape to be used during your SAP Business Suite on SAP HANA migrations. The project landscape plan will include a list of systems, system clients if applicable, and software components to be used during your project. If we stick with the example used in Section 2.1.5, the landscape might consist of SAP ERP, SAP CRM, and SAP PI. When you embark on your SAP Business Suite on SAP HANA migration, you're going to need an isolated landscape (albeit temporarily) where you can test your migration procedures, perform application regression tests, and potentially perform cutover testing. Because your SAP landscapes are so interconnected within each SAP system, you need to define a plan for the number of systems, where they will reside, how long they will exist, and how you'll manage changes during your project (more on change management tools in Chapter 8). Referring to our example, if we create a test system for the SAP Business Suite on SAP HANA migration project, do we need a corresponding SAP CRM and SAP PI test system? The answer isn't always cut and dried, so we'll explain some guiding principles you can follow to determine what other systems will be part of your SAP Business Suite on SAP HANA migration project.

2.2.1 Connected Systems Questions

If you answer yes to any of the following questions, it's safe to say you'll need a corresponding test system for any connected system as part of the SAP Business Suite on SAP HANA migration project:

▸ Does the connected system *not* support connections to more than one SAP ERP system at the same time?

▸ Do you have a 1:1 relationship between the connected system and the systems in your SAP ERP landscape (e.g., DEV SAP ERP connected to DEV SAP CRM)?

▸ Are you unable to implement a manual interfacing method if the connected system is unavailable or a defect arises at go-live?

These additional systems will only be required for the test cycles you execute during your project. For an upgrade and migration project, ideally you should limit your total testing time to two to four weeks (there are exceptions for regulated industries where test cycles might be longer). Keep in mind that you're changing the underlying database but not activating new functionality during the migration. Depending on your approach, you might also be applying SP Stacks, which, as we mentioned previously, are collections of notes. So your test cycles will typically be focused on regression testing—not user acceptance or unit testing. In this section, we'll focus on planning the number of systems and the length of time they will be required.

2.2.2 System Strategy

When referring to the system strategy as part of the overall landscape strategy, we're referring to the representation of two components:

- How many SAP ERP systems will you need during your project to support existing SAP ERP operations and the project?

- How many SAP ERP connected systems (e.g., SAP CRM and SAP PI) will you need during your project?

The latter will be driven by the definition of systems for the former. There are two main system strategies we see in the SAP community when customers execute an SAP Business Suite on SAP HANA migration. The first strategy is probably the most common, and it's referred to as the *five-system landscape*. In this scenario, you have your normal development, quality, and production systems along with two project-related systems supporting development and testing.

The second strategy (and coincidentally the least expensive to implement) involves the usage of only one additional system in the landscape. It's been called the five-in-one landscape, but for simplicity, let's refer to it as the *four-system landscape*. Let's explore each scenario to determine which landscape might best fit your organization in the following subsections.

Five-System Landscape

The five-system landscape enables a project team to work as fast or as slow as they want without impacting the production support landscape. This scenario is by far the most common one that we encounter when working with customers on any enhancement project. As you see in Figure 2.16, one major downside of the five-system landscape is the cost of infrastructure and change management to keep a large landscape in sync for the duration of the project. When thinking about this strategy, you need to keep in mind the number of connected systems you'll also need to replicate to support this landscape.

In Figure 2.16, you'll see the addition of two systems to your traditional landscape; development SAP Business Suite on SAP HANA and QA SAP Business Suite on SAP HANA. These systems are ideally a copy of the production environment before the upgrade and migration to SAP Business Suite on SAP HANA. Why a copy of production? When running your project, you need to remember that the end goal of the project is to upgrade and migrate production to SAP Business Suite on SAP HANA. All development and testing you complete for the project should be done on the systems that most closely resemble the end target, that is, production. The eventual migration of production support systems (development and QA) will happen after the production go-live. You typically don't upgrade and migrate development and QA systems during the project because those systems are often not a good representation of production. They might contain table definitions, Data Dictionary (DDIC) objects, and/or programs that were created once and never transported to production. The upgrade and migration process will only be complicated by migrating these systems, and the lessons learned from them won't always apply to production. By copying production down to the project landscape for both development and QA, you ensure all activities and lessons learned can be applied to the eventual production upgrade and migration to SAP Business Suite on SAP HANA.

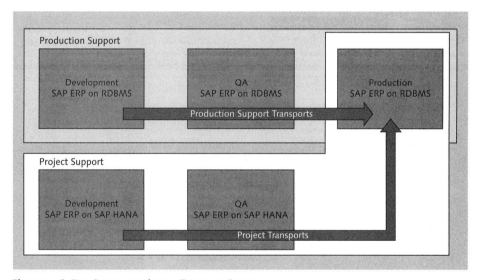

Figure 2.16 Five-System Landscape Transport Routes

Some people might argue that the project development system should be a copy of the production support development system so that we have a copy of the repository. In most cases, the repository history can be accessed via the standard code compare tools within the Development Workbench in SAP. And the number of new objects created will be minimized because this is an upgrade and migration without the activation of enhancements within the enhancement package.

In Figure 2.17, you'll notice transports that originate in project development will make their way through project QA and eventually into production. How do you get these transports from the project landscape to the production support landscape after production go-live? After go-live, you'll embark on an upgrade and migration of the production support development system. You don't want to refresh production support development from production because this could overwrite your repository and any developments you've started there that aren't ready for movement to QA. You could upgrade the production support QA system and migrate it to SAP HANA, or rebuild it using a system copy from production. However, this assumes you've got a good handle on change control and understand what transports you potentially need to account for. (More information on change management can be found in Chapter 8.) The system copy process when running SAP Business Suite on SAP HANA is vastly simplified over previous system copy procedures for non-SAP databases.

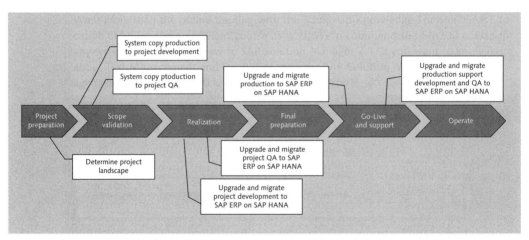

Figure 2.17 Example Number of System Copies, Upgrades, and Migrations

The five-system landscape is very common and flexible enough to reduce code freeze periods. You can work on project environments while enabling production support to exist with minimal disruption. You will, however, have greater infrastructure and change management costs. It's also worth noting that the longer you run your project, the more expensive the five-system landscape is to maintain. Whether using tools or manual process, change management for five systems can be burdensome. Ideally, these additional project systems exist for three to six months (or the duration of your project), but keep in mind the number of connected systems that must also be accounted for. For each project support landscape system, you might have a copy of a connected system (e.g., SAP CRM or SAP PI). These additional systems will add to your operational cost.

Four-System Landscape

The four-system landscape is a variation that is becoming more prevalent. It significantly reduces the number of systems you need to maintain but also requires detailed planning, as a single system will assume multiple roles during the project. We often use this approach when we want to run a lean project to get a customer's entire SAP ERP environment on SAP HANA within 10–12 weeks. This approach also reduces the number of connected systems you need to configure and maintain. Because you're only adding one additional system to the landscape, you should be able to survive with only one additional copy of connected systems such as SAP CRM, SAP PI, and so on. Let's explore this option using an example project time line running 12 weeks. Your project time line may vary; however, the roles each system plays within the four-system landscape scenario will be the same.

In Figure 2.18, you'll notice that we system copy production down to a system we'll call support. We'll avoid the word sandbox, as this implies the system is a playground instead of the controlled system we need. This support system will be the first system you upgrade and migrate to SAP Business Suite on SAP HANA. It's an exact copy of production from an application version standpoint. (You don't need an exact replica of hardware at this point.)

Next, your ABAP team will sign into the support system to perform their Transaction SPAU and Transaction SPDD activities. At this point, we've given the Basis team two weeks to complete their first upgrade and migration, and we've given the development team one week to complete their DDIC and base SAP modification remediation, as shown in Figure 2.19. These remediation activities are saved into a transport, which the Basis team will save off to another location.

During week 3, the Basis team will essentially uninstall SAP Business Suite on SAP HANA, refresh the support system from production again, and repeat the upgrade and migration procedure. The only new step in the process will be the inclusion of the Transaction SPAU and Transaction SPDD transport during the initial upgrade and migration.

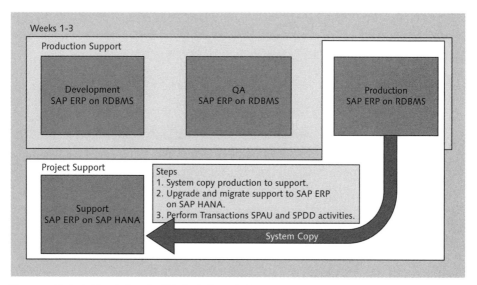

Figure 2.18 Activities during the Weeks 1 through 3

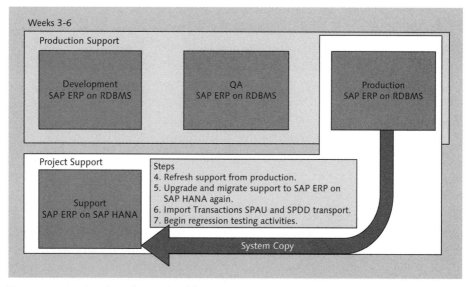

Figure 2.19 Week 3 through 6 Explained

After this second upgrade and migration to SAP Business Suite on SAP HANA is complete, the functional team will start regression testing for two weeks (for more information on test scope identification see Chapter 8). The approach is structured this way because we need to regression test the Transaction SPAU and Transaction SPDD modification transport in addition to the upgrade. This is how we'll upgrade the production system, so this is how we must test the support system.

During week 7, the role of the support system will shift. Ideally, at this point, you've completed your regression testing and documented and resolved any defects, or you're able to move forward with some open defects knowing you'll resolve them within the development or QA upgrades. The upgrade and migration on development is started, and the support system is rebuilt once again as a copy of production. The support system now becomes the emergency break/fix path to production because your development system is now a different release of SAP ERP. Officially, SAP doesn't support moving transports from a higher release level to a lower release level. Refreshing support as a copy of production enables your team to support the production landscape and run the upgrade in development. During this time, you also enter a quasi-code freeze. Any developments within the development system that need to be in production before the SAP Business Suite on SAP HANA go-live can move to the QA system for further testing.

In Figure 2.20, you can see the support system is now on the same release as the production system, which provides the emergency break/fix capabilities you need to support your landscape. At this point, any enhancement work that needs to be imported into production before the go-live of SAP Business Suite on SAP HANA will need to occur in QA or within the support system. If you're wondering how you keep new objects created in the support system in sync with the production support landscape if they aren't transported to those systems, you essentially have two options. First, you can initiate a phase of manual dual maintenance where any work completed in the support system is then manually repeated in the development system. Given the short duration of your project, this might be acceptable for some organizations but will require detailed tracking to ensure all objects are consistent. Keep in mind that after the production go-live, the QA system should be refreshed with a copy of production to ensure a consistent test environment. The second option is to use the software tools within SAP Solution Manager to track the transports created in the support system and then retrofit them into the development system automatically via Change Request Management (ChaRM) or Quality Gate Management (QGM). You can find more information on the Retrofit tool in Chapter 8.

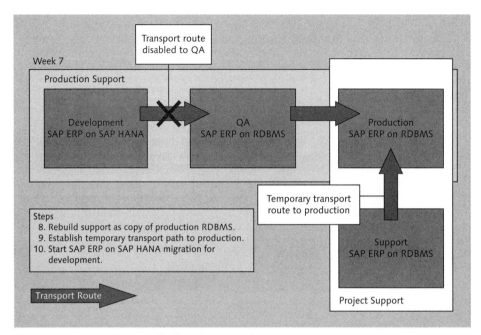

Figure 2.20 Support System Refreshed during Week 7

As you can see in Figure 2.21, in week 8, the QA system is upgraded and migrated to SAP Business Suite on SAP HANA, and the support system continues to play its role as a production support system. At this point in the project, enhancement work can begin again in development but can't move to QA until the additional regression test cycle is completed. Keep in mind that you already completed the primary regression tests during weeks 3 and 4.

Ideally, this additional regression test cycle is focused on two primary areas: interfaces you weren't able to replicate in the support landscape and business-critical processes that are worthy of another test execution. The Basis team is also preparing for the production upgrade and migration during this time. Next, the project will focus on the production go-live.

In weeks 9 and 10, shown in Figure 2.22, the regression test cycle is completed, defects resolved, and a risk mitigation plan is put into place to account for any defects that might occur during the production upgrade. Over the weekend in week 10, the production system will be migrated to SAP Business Suite on SAP HANA, which will require system downtime. At this point, the support system remains as-is in case of rollback. The remaining weeks in this 12-week example project would cover hyper-care type support where technical project resources remain committed to the project team for quick support.

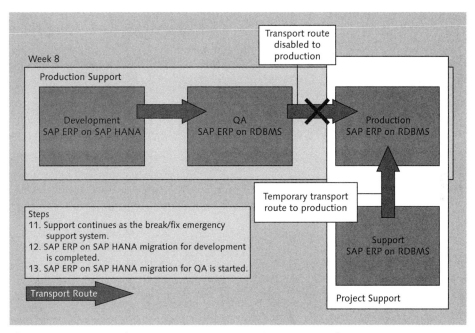

Figure 2.21 QA Migrated to SAP Business Suite on SAP HANA in Week 8

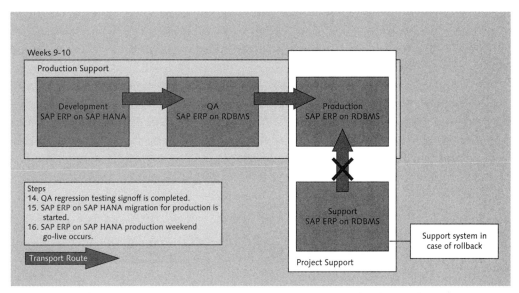

Figure 2.22 Production SAP Business Suite on SAP HANA Migration Completed in Week 10

Summary

Landscape planning and determining your landscape strategy are key components of your SAP Business Suite on SAP HANA migration project scope definition. Determining the number of systems and when they will be leveraged will help drive an effort estimation for both human and hardware resources. The two strategies we covered here are the most common scenarios, and while there are variations and modifications to how each system is used, the underlying requirements remain the same. You should strive to provide a consistent SAP landscape where both project and production support activities can coexist. The environment must be flexible and provide a place for teams to regression test based on a production-like environment. Whether implementing the five-system landscape or four-system landscape, you must focus on change management and governance of the project environment to maintain consistency.

2.3 SAP Solution Manager Tools for Establishing Scope

We'll cover SAP Solution Manager in multiple chapters within this book because its SAP's preferred mechanism for customers to use when deploying, upgrading, or enhancing their SAP solutions. SAP Solution Manager 7.1 includes multiple tools, some of which can be used to help you determine your project scope. In the previous sections, we talked about choosing targeting application versions, verifying add-ons, working with Unicode conversions, and defining a landscape strategy. Next, you need to define what you are upgrading and migrating to SAP Business Suite on SAP HANA. You already know you're impacting the SAP ERP system, but now you need to go deeper. What are the transactions and programs that will potentially be impacted by the migration? What business processes will you need to test, and how can you determine what your users use in production today? How can you estimate the effort for development and testing during your project based on the transactions your users utilize? These are all important questions you must answer to help you determine the scope and ultimately the effort required to complete the SAP Business Suite on SAP HANA migration.

2.3.1 Solution Documentation

Solution Documentation is a toolset to help define what you're implementing or what you've implemented within SAP ERP. Using the Business Process Repository (BPR) within Solution Documentation, you can find example business processes from SAP for new solutions you haven't implemented yet. Or when using the Solution Documentation Assistant (SDA), you can discover the business processes currently active in your production environment based on the data collected by SAP Solution Manager on how your system is utilized. These tools provide important information to your project team so you can determine the true impact of the migration to SAP Business Suite on SAP HANA. Think of SAP Solution Manager as providing a clear understanding of where you are today with your SAP ERP usage in order to better understand where you're going when migrating to SAP HANA.

Solution Documentation Assistant

The Solution Documentation Assistant (SDA) enables you to compare your system utilization data in production with a set of business processes in SAP Solution Manager. For example, SDA allows you to analyze your production SAP ERP system to ensure users are following standard processes for accounts receivable. This assumes that you have your business processes documented in SAP Solution Manager, so the SDA has something to compare SAP ERP usage too. In the event you don't have your business processes documented in SAP Solution Manager, SAP has provided its Enterprise Support customers with example business processes to jump-start their business process documentation. These business process examples are often referred to as content for Reverse Business Process Documentation (RBPD). The content is available to those customers who have agreements with SAP, including SAP Enterprise Support, Product Support for Large Enterprises (PSLE), and SAP MaxAttention. If you're currently an SAP Standard Support customer, please see the utility program we'll cover in the next section.

Now, let's walk through an example of analyzing your SAP ERP system with the SDA. The primary prerequisite for the SDA analysis is that the system to be analyzed must have SAP EarlyWatch Reporting active for that system. If you don't have SAP EarlyWatch Alerts for the production SAP ERP system, first activate them, and then proceed with the SDA.

Note	[«]
Want to know even more about RBPD? See the SAP Service Marketplace landing page for videos, how-to guides, and deep analysis of its features at *http://service.sap.com/rbpd*, or see SAP Note 1591505.	

1. Log on to the SAP Support Portal to download the latest content for the RBPD by navigating to *http://support.sap.com/swdc* and choosing SUPPORT PACKAGES AND PATCHES • A - Z INDEX • "S" • SAP SOLUTION MANAGER • SAP SOLUTION MANAGER 7.1 • ENTRY BY COMPONENT • ADDITIONAL CONTENT • ST-RBPD-ERP 100 • # OS INDEPENDENT.

2. Download the latest version of the content if more than one version is displayed, as shown in Figure 2.23.

Figure 2.23 Downloading the Latest ZIP File Displayed

3. Save the zip file to a folder location local to your PC.

4. Log on to SAP Solution Manager with a valid user ID and password.

5. Execute Transaction SM_WORKCENTER, and wait for your browser to display a list of work centers.

6. Navigate to the SOLUTION DOCUMENTATION ASSISTANT work center, and then select Content Interface.

7. Click on the UPLOAD CONTENT link to the right of the screen (see Figure 2.24).

8. When a new browser window opens, click the Upload button, and navigate to the file you downloaded in step 2.

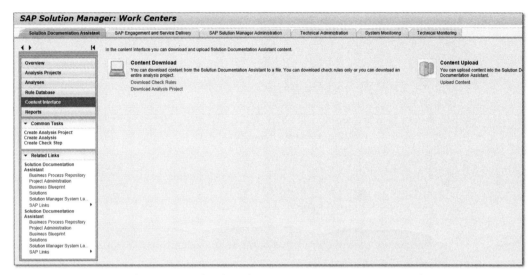

Figure 2.24 Content Interface Menu within the Solution Documentation Assistant Work Center

9. Select the zip file directly. Don't extract the contents of the zip file.

10. Click OK, and then click the Start button (see Figure 2.25).

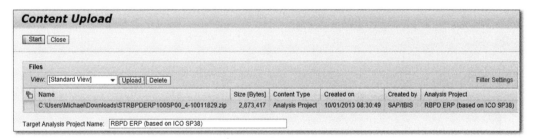

Figure 2.25 Confirmation Screen before Upload to SAP Solution Manager

11. On the next screen (see Figure 2.26), you see a summary of Business Scenarios, Business Processes, and Business Process Steps that will be checked. Leave all fields as default, and click Next.

12. In the Define Profile step, you can input a Logical Component Target specific to your landscape for those products that include SAP ERP transactions.

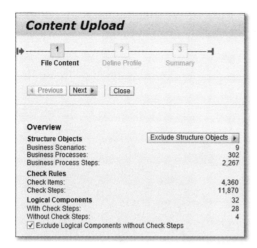

Figure 2.26 Summary of Items to Be Analyzed in RBPD

13. In Figure 2.27, your SAP ERP systems are part of the logical component Z_ERP_60_ECC. This name was generated by your Basis team when setting up SAP EarlyWatch Reporting.

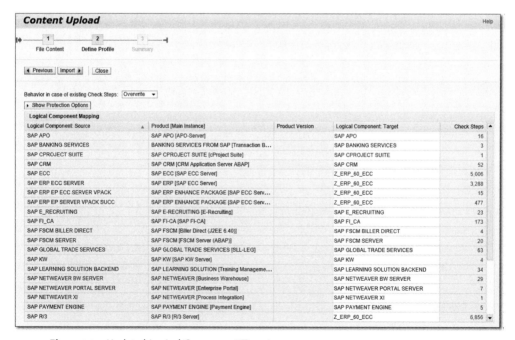

Figure 2.27 Updated Logical Component Target

14. The TARGET LOGICAL COMPONENT is specific to your environment. If you don't know your logical component name, see the SAP Solution Manager or Basis administrator who is responsible for SAP EarlyWatch Reports.

15. Enter your SAP ERP logical component as the LOGICAL COMPONENT TARGET for the following LOGICAL COMPONENT SOURCE systems:

    ▶ SAP ECC

    ▶ SAP ERP ECC SERVER

    ▶ SAP ERP EP ECC SERVER VPACK

    ▶ SAP ERP EP SERVER VPACK SUCC

    ▶ SAP R/3

    ▶ SAP R/3 ENTERPRISE E-SET

16. After the updates are made, click IMPORT.

17. When you see the message CONTENT IMPORTED in the upper-left part of the screen, click CLOSE.

18. Return to the browser window with the SOLUTION DOCUMENTATION ASSISTANT work center displayed.

19. Click on ANALYSIS PROJECTS. Scroll through the grid rows to find the Analysis Project RBPD ERP (BASED ON ICO SP 38) (name is dependent upon the version of content you downloaded).

20. Select the grid row, and then click the CREATE button under ANALYSES BASED ON ANALYSIS PROJECT RBPD ERP (BASED ON ICO SP 38), as shown in Figure 2.28.

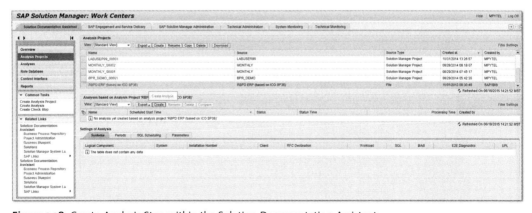

Figure 2.28 Create Analysis Step within the Solution Documentation Assistant

21. In the window that appears, enter a name for the analysis execution. In this example, we used "First Run" to denote this is the first execution. Any name or naming format will suffice.

22. For SCHEDULE MODE, you can select IMMEDIATE or SCHEDULE. Selecting SCHEDULE enables you to execute the analysis at a specific date or time. Because this will execute a read remote function call (RFC) against the production system, you can schedule for off hours. The program doesn't create data in production; it only reads usage information and will consume no more than one dialog process.

23. Click NEXT after you've determined the SCHEDULE MODE.

24. In STEP 2 SPECIFY LOGICAL COMPONENTS, leave the selection defaults, and click NEXT (see Figure 2.29).

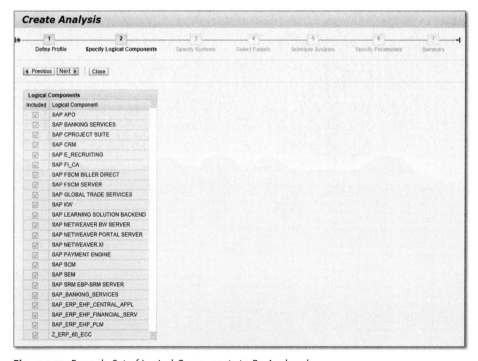

Figure 2.29 Example Set of Logical Components to Be Analyzed

25. In STEP 3 SPECIFY SYSTEMS, you need to select the SYSTEM ROLE to be analyzed. When you enter the step, it will default to DEVELOPMENT SYSTEM (see Figure

2.30). Be sure to change the selection criteria to PRODUCTION (this is where your end users transact, so you need to analyze the production environment).

26. After you select the PRODUCTION SYSTEM next to your SAP ERP system's LOGI-CAL COMPONENT, you should see a green light, which denotes the RFCs are set up for that system, and the analysis can be run.

    If you see a red light, more than likely your RFCs from SAP Solution Manager to the target system aren't correct, or you haven't enabled SAP EarlyWatch Reports for that system. Ensure SAP EarlyWatch Reports are being generated, and then return to this step.

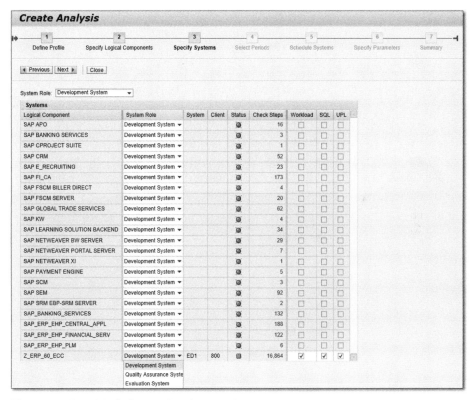

Figure 2.30 Step 3 Defaulting to Development System

27. Click NEXT to select the time period for your analysis.

28. In STEP 4 SELECT PERIODS, by default you can analyze any month where you have SAP EarlyWatch Report data availability. In the example in Figure 2.31,

we have eight months of SAP EarlyWatch Reporting, so we can analyze eight months of end-user activity in the Production SAP ERP system.

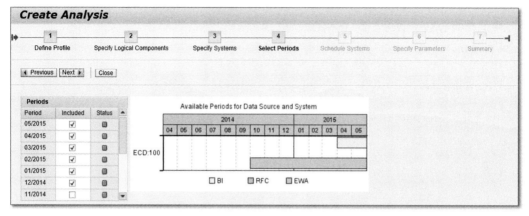

Figure 2.31 Selecting Your Time Period for the Solution Documentation Assistant Analysis

29. After you select the time period to analyze, click NEXT.

30. In STEP 5 SCHEDULE SYSTEMS, you can determine the maximum number of work processes your analysis will utilize on the target system only in the event data must be analyzed in the target system due to missing SAP EarlyWatch Report data.

31. In Figure 2.32, we're limiting the process to three work processes. If the ANALYSIS SYSTEM SCHEDULING table is blank, your SAP Solution Manager has the SAP EarlyWatch Report data it needs to analyze.

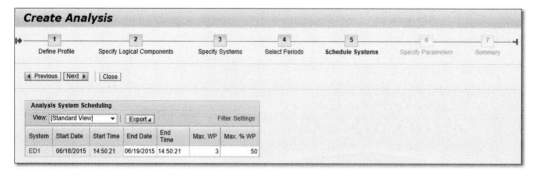

Figure 2.32 Limiting Processing to Three Work Processes for This Example

32. Click NEXT.

33. In STEP 6 SPECIFY PARAMETERS, you need to make several selections (see Figure 2.33):

   ▸ Deselect USE OPTIMIZATION.

   ▸ Under TASK TYPES, click UNMARK ALL, and then select DIALOG.

   ▸ Under NOT USED CUSTOMER OBJECTS, click TRANSACTION and REPORT.

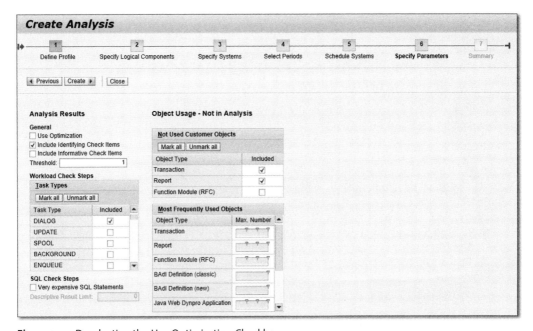

Figure 2.33 Deselecting the Use Optimization Checkbox

34. Click CREATE after all selections have been made.

35. You should avoid selecting USE OPTIMIZATION because it negates some of the check steps. For example, if a business process is supported by three transactions that perform a similar function, it will only analyze the first transaction. You want all transactions analyzed.

36. After clicking CREATE, you get a summary screen (see Figure 2.34). Review, click CLOSE, and return to the SOLUTION DOCUMENTATION ASSISTANT work center.

37. After you return to the SOLUTION DOCUMENTATION ASSISTANT work center, click the REFRESH link under the grid for ANALYSES BASED ON ANALYSIS PROJECT 'RBPD ERP (BASED ON ICO SP 38)'.

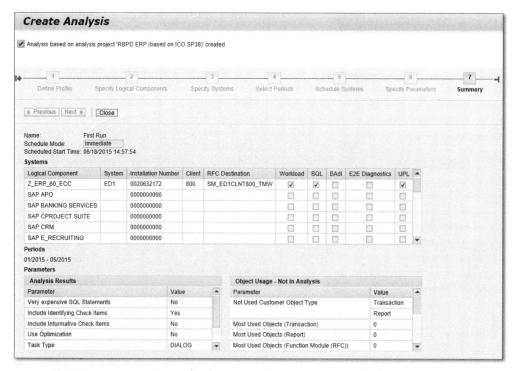

Figure 2.34 Summary Screen for the Solution Documentation Assistant Analysis

38. When the status reads FINISHED, you can analyze the results (see Figure 2.35).

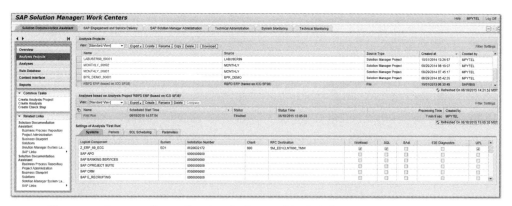

Figure 2.35 Summary Screen Showing the Status of Analysis Projects

39. After the status has updated to FINISHED, click on the name of the analysis you scheduled. In this example, it's called FIRST RUN.

40. A new browser opens displaying the analysis results. The important components of the ANALYSIS RESULTS tab shown in Figure 2.36 are described here:

▷ ANALYSIS STRUCTURE: In this section of the screen, color appears next to each business process the analysis was attempting to find:

– **Gray diamond**: The tool was not able to determine if that process is active.

– **Red light**: The analysis determined this process was not active due to no transaction or program activity and missing table entries.

– **Yellow light**: The analysis determined this process might be active in your system. Transactions or programs weren't executed, but data in specific tables suggests the process is in use.

– **Green light**: The analysis found transactions or programs known to be part of the selected business process as active in your system.

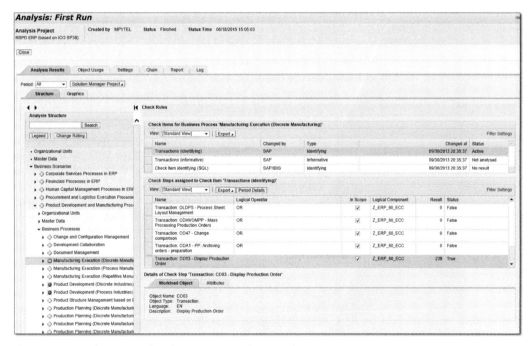

Figure 2.36 Initial Screen within the First Run Analysis Results

▷ CHECK RULES: This section shows a breakdown of what the analysis tool was looking for to determine if that process was active in your SAP ERP system. These are broken down into Check Items:

- TRANSACTIONS (IDENTIFYING): These are the known transactions that your users would execute to signify you're using this scenario in SAP.

- TRANSACTIONS (INFORMATIVE): These are related transactions that are usually part of the process you're analyzing. This check is inactive by default.

- CHECK ITEM IDENTIFYING (SQL): These are SQL table record checks that determine if a business process is active based on the data found within a specific group of tables. A green light here might mean you have a custom transaction updating these tables but aren't using the standard SAP transactions.

41. The OBJECT USAGE tab in Figure 2.37 will provide the same data but in a different view. There are three tabs, two of which contain relevant information:

  ▸ ANALYSIS: These are the transactions and programs the analysis was looking for and the number of times they were executed.

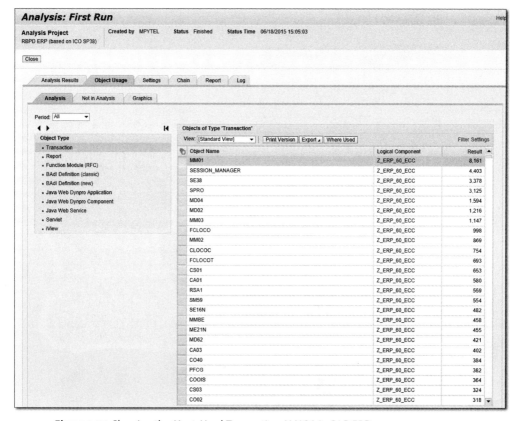

Figure 2.37 Showing the Most-Used Transaction MM01 in SAP ERP

▶ NOT IN ANALYSIS: These are the transactions and programs the analysis found to be running in your system but weren't part of a known SAP business process. In other words, these are the transactions your users use, but the SDA doesn't know which business process they belong to.

42. The data in both tabs, ANALYSIS and NOT IN ANALYSIS, can be exported to Excel. You can then filter transactions and programs that were never executed and combine the lists to get a full list of all transactions your users execute in production SAP ERP.

43. Return to the ANALYSIS RESULTS tab on the top row. Click SOLUTION MANAGER PROJECT • CREATE.

44. Input a name in the PROJECT field, select UPGRADE PROJECT in the TYPE field, enter a TITLE, and set the LANGUAGE field to EN (for English).

45. Leave all other options default, and click OK (see Figure 2.38). A progress bar will display the status. Click CLOSE, and the process will continue in the background, or you can leave the screen open to validate completion.

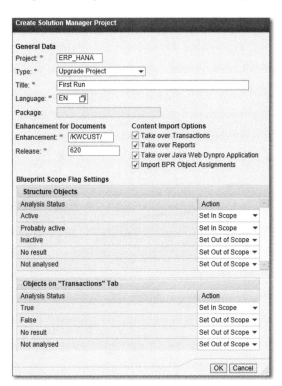

Figure 2.38 Creating a Project from the Solution Documentation Assistant Results

Using the SDA enables you to define how your system is being utilized today so that you can plan for the required testing effort as part of your SAP Business Suite on SAP HANA project. In Chapter 8, we'll cover some of the impact analysis tools that depend on the data collected here. At this point, you now know in detail what transactions and programs your production SAP ERP users execute over a specific time period, effectively establishing a measuring stick that defines how many unit test scripts you should have in your test repository.

Blueprint Generation by Module

In the previous section, we utilized a set of business processes defined by SAP to compare your production SAP ERP system against. While some people like this end-to-end process-based view, it can be difficult to read. In late 2014, as part of an SAP Note, SAP released another reverse documentation utility that can be installed in SAP Solution Manager 7.1 SP 11 and above. This blueprint generation utility program performs a similar function by collecting information about the usage of your SAP ERP system. However, this data is then loaded directly into a SAP Solution Manager project structured by module. This in effect creates a project in SAP Solution Manager from the unit test perspective. Let's explore this utility a little more and demonstrate how it is executed.

Before you can get started, you'll need to install the following SAP Notes in your landscape. Some notes include manual preimplementation and postimplementation instructions that require ABAP developer support. Install the following notes in your production SAP Solution Manager: SAP Note 2061626, 2160438, and 2143379. Now, follow these steps in the Blueprint Generation utility:

1. Log on to your production SAP Solution Manager with a valid user ID and password.
2. Run Transaction SA38. and input the program "RUTILITY_BLUEPRINT_GENERATION", as shown in Figure 2.39. Click the Execute button.
3. Enter the following information on the input screen (see Figure 2.40). Leave all other fields default.
   - ▶ SAP System ID: Enter the production SAP ERP system to be analyzed.
   - ▶ Client: Enter the production SAP ERP client on the system to be analyzed.
   - ▶ Logical Component (optional): Select the logical component for SAP ERP in your landscape.

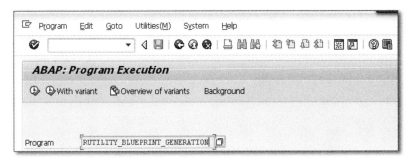

Figure 2.39 First Step in Executing the New Blueprint Generation Utility

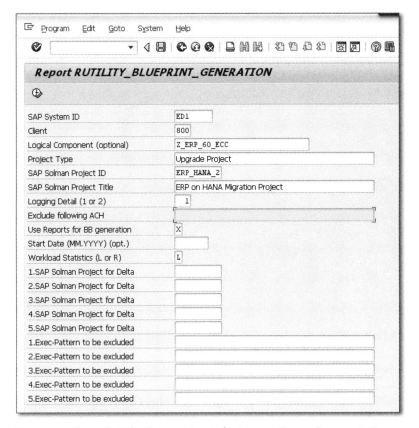

Figure 2.40 Example Utility Program Inputs for Reverse Process Documentation

> ► Project Type: Select any project type. We use an upgrade project in this example.

> ▸ SAP SOLMAN PROJECT ID: Enter a project ID with no spaces.

> ▸ SAP SOLMAN PROJECT TITLE: Enter a text description of the project.

4. After you've entered the relevant data for your landscape, click the EXECUTE button.

5. When you run the program interactively, it will use the SAP Solution Manager READ RFC to connect to the target system to begin collecting the required data. You can also submit the program to the background and check for completion. If you run the program interactively, you should see a result similar to Figure 2.41.

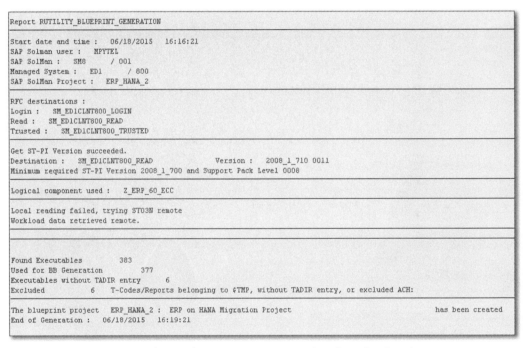

```
Report RUTILITY_BLUEPRINT_GENERATION

Start date and time :   06/18/2015   16:16:21
SAP Solman user :   MPYTEL
SAP SolMan :    SM8      / 001
Managed System :   ED1      / 800
SAP SolMan Project :   ERP_HANA_2

RFC destinations :
Login :    SM_ED1CLNT800_LOGIN
Read :    SM_ED1CLNT800_READ
Trusted :    SM_ED1CLNT800_TRUSTED

Get ST-PI Version succeeded.
Destination :    SM_ED1CLNT800_READ            Version :   2008_1_710 0011
Minimum required ST-PI Version 2008_1_700 and Support Pack Level 0008

Logical component used :    Z_ERP_60_ECC

Local reading failed, trying ST03N remote
Workload data retrieved remote.


Found Executables       383
Used for BB Generation        377
Executables without TADIR entry      6
Excluded       6    T-Codes/Reports belonging to $TMP, without TADIR entry, or excluded ACH:

The blueprint project   ERP_HANA_2 :   ERP on HANA Migration Project                    has been created
End of Generation :   06/18/2015   16:19:21
```

Figure 2.41 Example Completion Summary Screen When the Utility Completes

6. After the program completes, return to the main menu, and run Transaction SOLAR01.

7. When you enter Transaction SOLAR01, select BUSINESS BLUEPRINT • OTHER PROJECT. Choose the project name you input in the earlier step in the utility program. Click the green checkmark.

8. After you've selected the correct project, you're presented with a business blueprint in SAP Solution Manager for your production system organized by

SAP module, then submodule, and finally the transaction or program (see Figure 2.42).

9. Navigate to CUSTOMER • CUSTOMER EXECUTABLES, and locate any custom transactions or programs your production SAP ERP users executed on the system you analyzed.

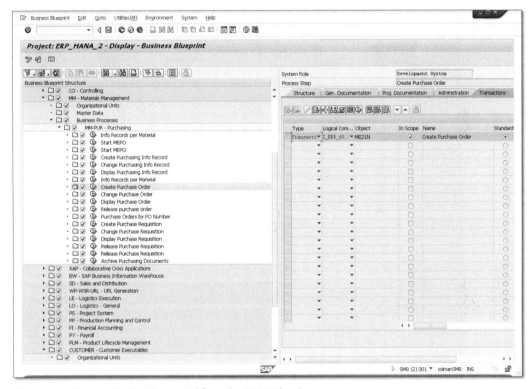

Figure 2.42 Example Project Generated from the SAP Utility Program

10. Custom transactions and program are organized by development package (see Figure 2.43).

At this point, you now have two different perspectives on the usage of your production SAP ERP system. The first view delivered by the SDA attempted to provide an end-to-end process view. The second view provided by the utility program from SAP enabled you to quickly reverse-document your business processes by module. The view by module is very easy to navigate because you typically organize your teams and your work by SAP module. This view will be the easiest to initially deploy and then can be adapted to a process view later. Again, it provides you with a unit test perspective on what transactions and programs are being utilized by your production SAP ERP users. It gives you a sense of the impact as well because now you know every transaction that could be impacted. For a detailed impact analysis, see Chapter 8.

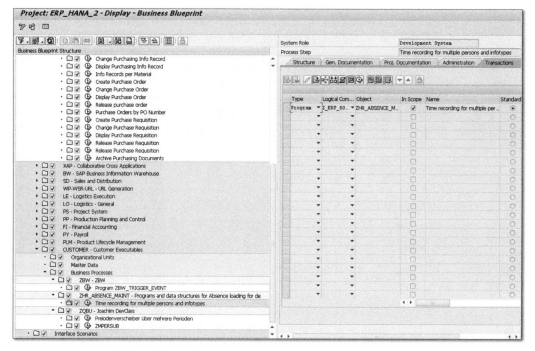

Figure 2.43 Example Custom Transaction Documented by the Utility Program

2.3.2 Scope and Effort Analyzer

In 2014, SAP provide a new utility to help customers understand the scope of effort related to development and testing when installing SAP ERP enhancement packages as part of SAP Solution Manager 7.1 SP 11 and above. The Scope and Effort Analyzer (SEA) built on the capabilities of the BPCA because SEA allows you to run an analysis before even downloading the SAP ERP enhancement package. Remember, if you're including an enhancement package or SP Stack as part of your SAP Business Suite on SAP HANA migration using SUM, you want to know what could potentially be impacted. The SEA helps you define how much

ABAP support will be needed to remediate base SAP modifications. It also helps you define the number of test scripts required to test only those transactions and programs that are impacted by the upgrade. This tool helps support both scope identification and effort estimation, which are key during the planning phases of your SAP Business Suite on SAP HANA migration project. Let's explore how you can execute a scope and effort Analysis for your SAP Business Suite on SAP HANA upgrade and migration. To determine whether SEA is available for your specific SAP components, refer to Table 2.3 as a quick reference.

Scope and Effort Analyzer with Usage and Procedure Logging	Solution Documentation Assistant and Business Process Change Analyzer
► SAP Solution Manager 7.1 SP 11+	► SAP Solution Manager 7.1 SP 1+
► Managed System	► Managed System
► SAP NetWeaver 7.01 SP 10+ or	► SAP NetWeaver 6.40 or higher
► SAP NetWeaver 7.02 SP 09+ or	► Kernel 7.00 patch 264+ or
► SAP NetWeaver 7.31 SP 03+	► Kernel 7.01 patch 116+
► Kernel 7.20 patch 430+ or	► ST-PI 2008_1_XXX SP 06
► Kernel 7.21 patch 120+	
► ST-PI 2008_1_XXX	

Table 2.3 Scope and Effort Analyzer

Note	[«]
If SEA is available in your environment, see SAP Note 2069918 – Prerequisites for Scope and Effort Analyzer (SEA) Tool. This SAP Note provides all details necessary to get started.	

Executing Scope and Effort Analyzer

To execute SEA, follow these steps:

1. Log on to your SAP Solution Manager with a valid user ID and password.

2. Run Transaction SM_WORKCENTER, and navigate to the CHANGE MANAGE-MENT work center.

3. Click on SCOPE AND EFFORT ANALYZER, and then click on the CREATE button (see Figure 2.44).

4. Another browser window opens. You can leave the ANALYSIS NAME field as-is, but you need to enter the PRODUCT SYSTEM (SYSTEM ID) field for the system you plan to update. Typically, you enter your production SAP system ID here. Press Enter, and the PRODUCT VERSION FOR ANALYSIS dropdown becomes available.

5. Select SAP ERP 6.0, and click NEXT.

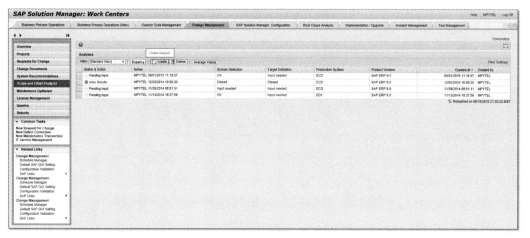

Figure 2.44 Initial Screen for the Scope and Effort Analyzer

6. In STEP 2 SPECIFY ADDITIONAL SYSTEMS, you have the option to enter multiple different systems. Here's an explanation of the system types:

  ▶ SPECIFY SYSTEM TO READ CUSTOM DEVELOPMENTS AND MODIFICATIONS: This is typically the development system in your SAP ERP landscape. SEA will read information about all custom objects created in that system.

  ▶ SPECIFY SYSTEM TO READ USAGE STATISTICS: This is typically the production system where you want to measure how often a custom object is used by the end users.

  ▶ SPECIFY SYSTEM USED FOR TEST SCOPE OPTIMIZATION ACTIVITIES: This is usually the QA system in your landscape. It will be the system from which technical bills of materials (TBOMs) are created and read.

7. In Figure 2.45, you'll notice only one system is defined for this example. In your scenario, please enter the appropriate system ID and client.

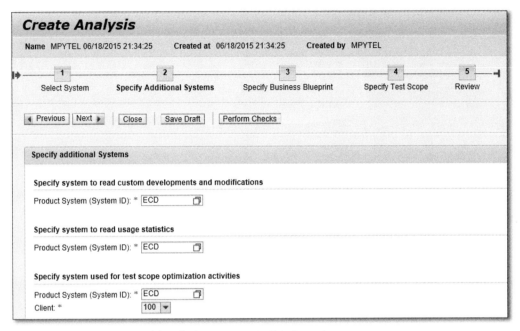

Figure 2.45 System ECD Used for All Three Systems in This Example

8. Click the PERFORM CHECKS button and wait for the results on screen.

9. Confirm the results, and remediate any errors or red lights (see Figure 2.46). The only warning that is acceptable to move forward is related to Usage and Procedure Logging (UPL) data. If your system isn't on the correct kernel version for UPL, this step can be yellow.

10. Click NEXT.

11. Now you can make a decision to use an existing project such as the projects created in an earlier step with the SDA or the utility program. Or you can select CREATE A PROJECT AND BUSINESS BLUEPRINT FOR EXECUTABLES NOT COVERED (see Figure 2.47).

Figure 2.46 Example Results from the Perform Checks Button

12. Select the CREATE option just mentioned to generate another blueprint by module within SAP Solution Manager. This provides you with a third option to generate a business blueprint. This option is technically the same application code as the utility program mentioned earlier.

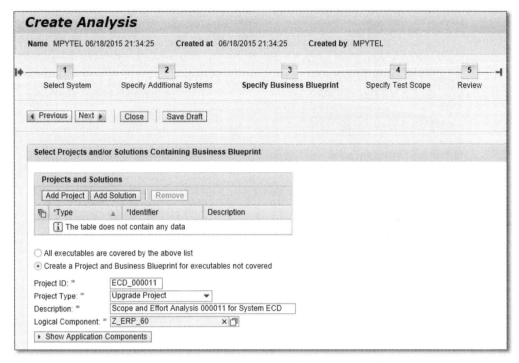

Figure 2.47 Creating a Project in Solution Manager to Store Transactions and Programs

13. Click NEXT.

14. In STEP 4 SPECIFY TEST SCOPE, you have multiple options you can select (see Figure 2.48):

   ▷ TEST MANAGEMENT APPLICATION: In this section of the screen, you can select the Test Management tool to be utilized for testing. You can select the local SAP SOLUTION MANAGER Test Workbench (more about this in Chapter 8) or an SAP PARTNER TEST MANAGEMENT APPLICATION certified partner.

   ▷ OPTIMIZATION APPROACH: If your team has previously configured an optimization approach within SAP Solution Manager, this option can be used. Leave blank if no approach is selectable or suitable for your analysis.

   ▷ TEST COVERAGE (%): This is the test coverage you want to plan for. Assume you'll test all objects impacted.

   ▷ CALCULATE EFFORT FOR CREATION OF AUTOMATED TEST CASES UP TO THE COVERAGE OF: You can define how much test automation you want as part of this project. If you're initially trying to define the manual test effort, deselect this option.

▶ CALCULATE THE EFFORT TO CREATE TEST CASES THAT ARE MISSING WITHIN THE REMAINING TEST COVERAGE BASED ON THE FOLLOWING RULE: You can select the option to calculate effort for creation of manual test cases.

15. Enter your selections, and click NEXT.

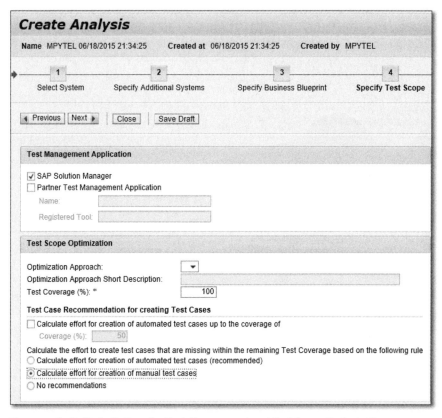

Figure 2.48 Multiple Options for Test Management and Test Scope Optimization

16. In STEP 5 REVIEW, click the CONTINUE WITH TARGET DEFINITION button to open another browser window and execute the Maintenance Optimizer.

17. If you're not familiar with the Maintenance Optimizer, then we recommend utilizing a Basis resource who has used the Maintenance Optimizer before.

18. In the Maintenance Optimizer initial screen, select CALCULATE FILES AUTOMATICALLY – RECOMMENDED. Click CONTINUE (see Figure 2.49).

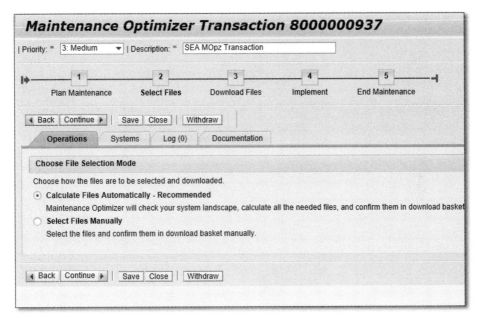

Figure 2.49 Selecting Automatic File Calculation

19. As STEP 2 SELECT FILES continues, the Maintenance Optimizer will connect to the SAP Support Portal to determine the applicable enhancement packages and SP Stacks. The connection and processing of information can take two to three minutes.

20. When the results are retuned, you can select the enhancement package or SP Stack. Because you're already running SAP ERP 6.0 EHP 7, you can select the latest SP Stack for that release.

21. For this example, we leave the SUPPORT PACKAGE STACK radio button selected and click CONTINUE.

22. In STEP 2.1 CHOOSE STACK, you can see the dropdowns for enhancement package and SP Stack versions. You can also see the preselected usage types as defined when you set up SAP EarlyWatch Reports (see Figure 2.50).

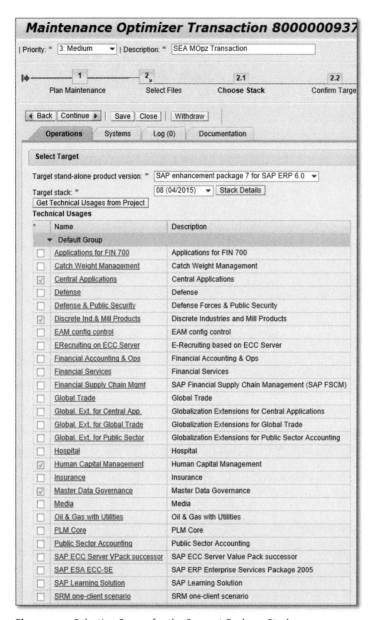

Figure 2.50 Selection Screen for the Support Package Stack

23. You can use this selection screen to choose a prior SP Stack if your organization had an N-1 policy. Otherwise, the latest version is displayed.

24. Click CONTINUE after you've made your selections.

25. On STEP 2.2 CONFIRM TARGET, you can validate the changes you selected. In this example, you can see the version change for both the SAP ERP 6.0 stack level and the SAP NETWEAVER 7.4 stack level (see Figure 2.51).

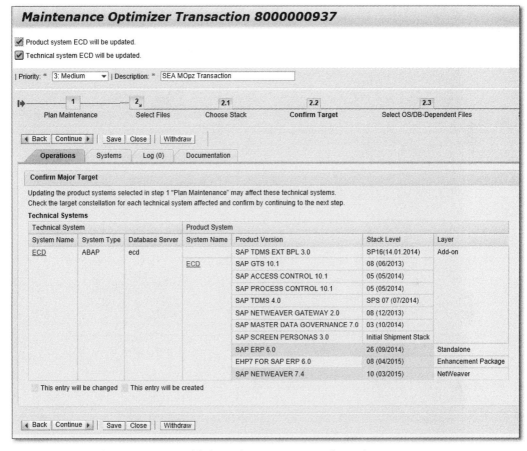

Figure 2.51 SAP Solution Manager Highlighting the Versions to Be Changed

26. Click CONTINUE.

27. On STEP 2.3 CHOOSE ADD-ON PRODUCTS, you can select the add-ons installed in your system that you want to update. In this example, we want to patch the Gateway 2.0 to the latest version but not SAP Governance, Risk, and Compliance (GRC) or SAP Master Data Governance (MDG). These decisions are specific to your environment and covered in Section 2.1.3.

28. Click CONTINUE after your selections are complete.

29. In STEP 2.4 SELECT OS/DB DEPENDENT FILES, you must ensure the correct kernel version is selected for your application and database server version. The versions will automatically be selected if the SAP Host Agent is correctly reporting to the System Landscape Directory (SLD). If not, you must navigate the tree and select the correct version (see Figure 2.52).

30. Always select the SAP IGS and SOFTWARE UPDATE MANAGER upgrades as well.

31. Click CONTINUE.

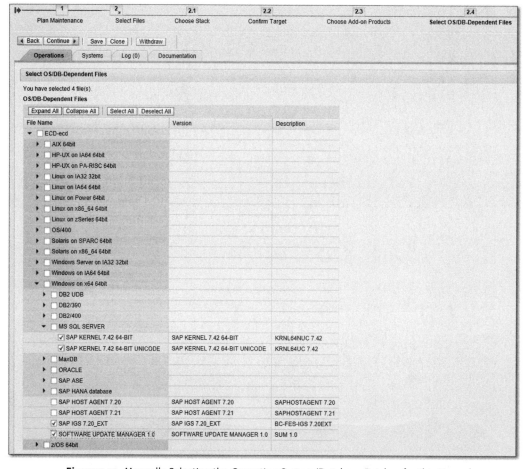

Figure 2.52 Manually Selecting the Operating System/Database Patches for this Example

32. In STEP 2.5, leave the default items selected per SAP recommendations. These are additional add-ons that are recommended for your environment (see Figure 2.53). Click CONTINUE after you've reviewed these.

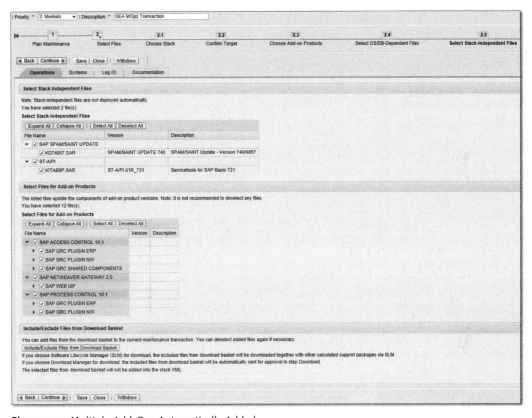

Figure 2.53 Multiple Add-Ons Automatically Added

33. In STEP 2.6, you again are presented with multiple preselected stack dependent files. Leave all items checked as-is, and click CONTINUE (see Figure 2.54).

34. In STEP 2.7 CONFIRM SELECT, leave the default option selected for DOWNLOAD BASKET. Click CONTINUE.

35. In STEP 3 DOWNLOAD FILES, you can forgo downloading any files because the SEA doesn't need the files to actually be downloaded. At this point, click SAVE and then CLOSE.

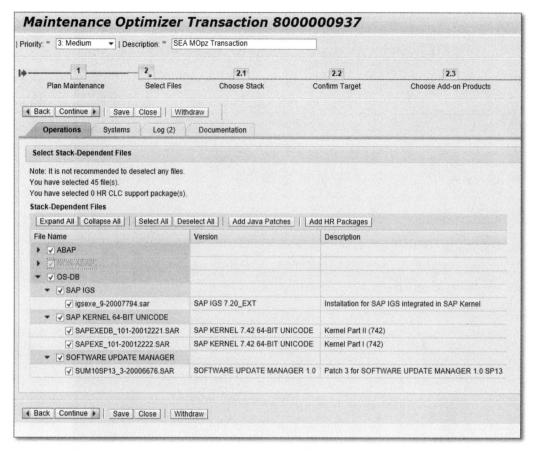

Figure 2.54 Multiple Stack-Dependent Files, Including HR Packages

36. Return to the SAP Solution Manager work center. Go to CHANGE MANAGE-MENT, and then select SCOPE AND EFFORT ANALYZER. Click the REFRESH button on the lower-right position below the grid.

37. You should see a START button next to the analysis you just created, as well as OK displayed under SYSTEM SELECTION and TARGET DEFINITION. This means the SEA knows what enhancement package or SP Stack you're planning to install.

38. Click the START button to begin the analysis (see Figure 2.55).

39. After you click START, you'll see the ANALYSIS STARTED message, and the START button text will change to RUNNING. Continue to click the REFRESH link on the lower-right position of the grid to update the status.

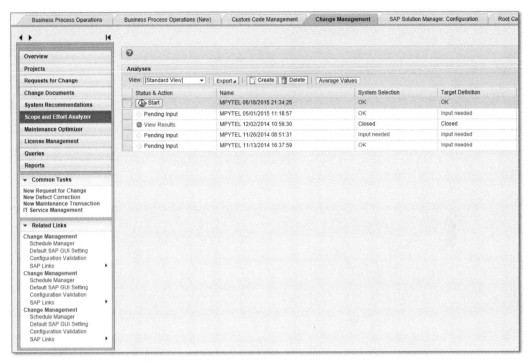

Figure 2.55 Starting the Analysis

40. When the VIEW RESULTS text is displayed in the STATUS & ACTION column, the analysis is complete. It's common for the runtime to be two to three hours.

41. Click the VIEW RESULTS button, and another browser window will open.

42. The initial display is summary information related to the analysis. We'll explain the tabs in order (see Figure 2.56):

  ▷ SUMMARY: This gives you some high-level estimates of the work hours required for custom code and base SAP modification adjustments. It also gives you an estimate on the time required for test script execution.

  ▷ MODIFICATIONS/CUSTOM DEVELOPMENTS: This tab gives more detail on the custom code within the SAP ERP systems. It indicates the number of objects that will require adjustment.

  ▷ TEST MANAGEMENT: This tab shows the estimated test effort in eight-hour days. You can also see the impact of applying test scope optimization, which reduces the number of scenarios you should test based on shared objects.

▶ UPDATED SAP OBJECTS: This graphic gives you an overview of the impacted objects by module and type.

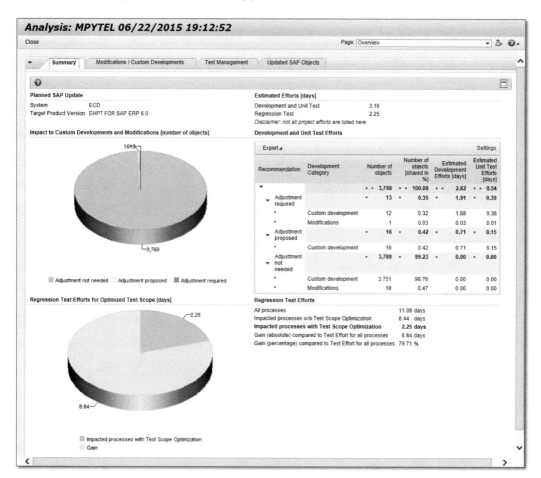

Figure 2.56 Initial Summary Screen for the Scope and Effort Analyzer Analysis

43. You really don't get any real detail at the summary level. Next, click the PAGE dropdown in the upper-right part of the screen. Select DETAILS • MODIFICA-TIONS/CUSTOM DEVELOPMENTS.

44. On the MODIFICATIONS tab, you can see a list of SAP objects that need to be remediated.

45. On the CUSTOM DEVELOPMENTS tab, you can see the list of custom programs and their impact by the upgrade. In Figure 2.57, you can see that the custom program Z_PARTNER_CHECKPASSWORD uses an obsolete SAP function. Therefore, the development team needs to rectify this.

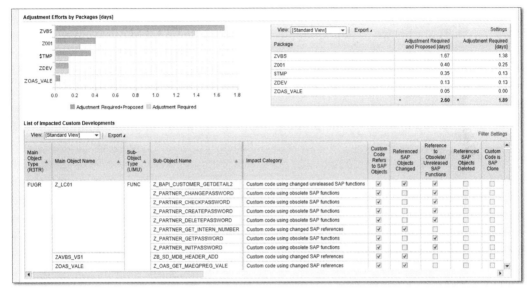

Figure 2.57 Detail from the Scope and Effort Analyzer Identifying Custom Code

46. You now have some valuable content to share with your project team, and you can estimate the development effort required for your project.

47. Return to the PAGE dropdown in the upper-right part of the screen, and select DETAILS • TEST MANAGEMENT. This is where you can get actual transactional details on what needs to be tested.

48. Use the TEST SCOPE OPTIMIZATION RANKING tab to see the impacted process steps at a specific level of test scope coverage. Here you can adjust the test coverage from 100% to 98% and simulate the potential savings in reducing your test effort (see Figure 2.58).

49. Moving to the TEST CASE RECOMMENDATIONS tab, you can estimate the effort to both execute test scripts and build manual test scripts.

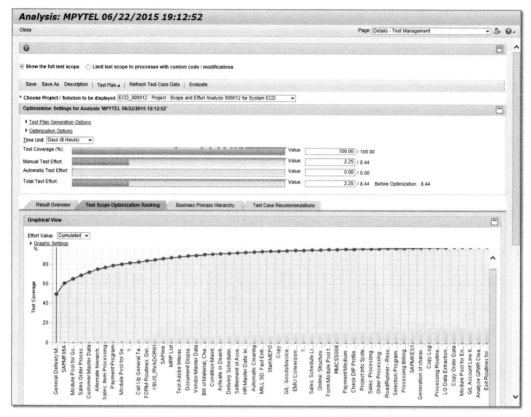

Figure 2.58 Test Scope Optimization from the Scope and Effort Analyzer

50. In Figure 2.59, for our example, we've limited our test scope to 72 programs or transactions. Using the general estimate of 2 hours to create a test script, the tool tells us we'll need 18 days to prepare the test scripts.

51. Scrolling down further in the screen from Figure 2.59, you can get additional details on the transactions and programs impacted by the SP Stack or enhancement package.

What did we accomplish? Before installing the support package or enhancement package in your landscape, you simulated the impact on your SAP ERP system. This enabled you to get a clear picture of the impact on the custom code in your landscape. It also enabled you to understand at a detailed technical level what transactions and programs will be impacted. From here, the impacted transactions/program list can be exported to Excel, can be used to generate a test plan in the SAP Solution Manager Test Workbench, or can be used to create a test plan in HP QC or IBM Rational. This tool is key to supporting your scope and effort identification as you plan for your SAP Business Suite on SAP HANA migration.

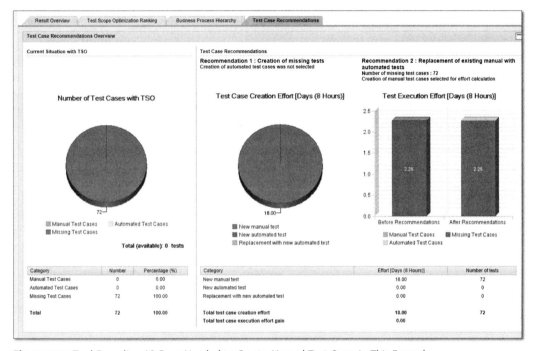

Figure 2.59 Tool Revealing 18 Days Needed to Create Manual Test Cases in This Example

2.4   Resource Planning

As you continue to establish your project scope, you must focus some attention on the human capital that will become part of your project. Remember, the migration (and possibly upgrade) to SAP Business Suite on SAP HANA is a change in the underlying database. There will be no enhancements introduced in the application layer, so you know your testing will be regression focused. You also know that the project will be mostly technical so the project team will be comprised of mostly IT team members. The main value driver behind SAP Business

Suite on SAP HANA is more than just speed—it's analytics, new functionality, and increased capabilities. But for now, let's only focus on the migration to SAP HANA. When talking about resource planning, we'll discuss the roles on a project that you'll need to account for. A role may be supported by one or many people, and a single person can support multiple roles. Each customer environment is different based on size and scope, so let's focus on the project roles you'll need. Your training needs for project team members will also vary based on the size and scope of the project. We'll discuss some of the basic training your team can attend before, during, and after the migration project to best support your new SAP Business Suite on SAP HANA landscape.

2.4.1   Project Team

Your project team is the heart and soul of your SAP Business Suite on SAP HANA project. The success of the project will be the collective sum of individual efforts during the life of the project. It's important everyone understand the roles and responsibilities on the project as well as the communication paths and escalation points. Your project team might consist of internal and external team members. You should consider SAP Active Global Support (AGS) part of your extended team as they will be supporting any technical issues that arise during your project. This section will cover the multiple roles that you'll need to fill on your project to ensure success. Although you may not need all roles in all cases, these project roles will apply to most projects and give you some guidance on staffing your project team.

Project Stakeholders

This role is more likely to be played by a group of people within your organization. A project stakeholder is someone who will be affected by the outcome of the project and has the ability to positively (or negatively) influence the execution of the project. An example title of a project stakeholder might be the CIO, CFO, controller, VP of manufacturing, sales director, or CSO. These are all people who run a business unit or function that will be directly impacted by the system downtime and regressing test effort, and ideally they will be the first to ask for enhancements after the project is complete. The project stakeholders are important to define because they will help define the project schedule, assign power user type resources to support the project, and ultimately sign off on the project before and after go-live.

Project Manager

It goes without saying that the project manager role is essential to a successful project. As you begin searching internally for a project manager, it's more than likely that this person won't have experience managing an SAP ERP migration to SAP HANA. However, it's more important that you find an individual who is good at managing technical projects and even better at communicating with technical people. SAP provides you with Best Practices (covered in Section 2.5), so you'll get content related to phases, deliverables, and common project activities. A good project manager will know how to use this content and when to adapt it to your project environment.

If you engage with a certified SAP Services Partner to deliver some or all of the SAP Business Suite on SAP HANA migration project, you should still have a co-project manager on the project to ensure your organization's best interests are kept in front. Your project manager is ultimately responsible for the project charter, communication plan, and risk plan, and ideally he serves as the conduit between the project team and project stakeholders. The phases of the SAP Business Suite on SAP HANA project will have clear entrance and exit criteria, and the deliverables for each phase will be known. The most successful project managers we've seen on these technical projects are individuals who excel at communication and risk identification. Understanding the risk to your organization's operations and identifying the tasks on the project where you can mitigate risk are key to a successful migration.

Test Manager

Let's keep our focus on project roles before you decide if a single person should play this role on your project. For some organizations that will have hundreds or more test scripts to build and execute as part of a test cycle, they'll need a dedicated resource in this position. The test manager is ultimately responsible for the test cycle planning, execution, defect tracking, test cycle reporting, and exit criteria for the test phase of the project. It's important this person can lead and define the test cycles as part of the project. The test manager defines test script standards for the build of test scripts and their execution by test cycle. The test manager also defines the test plan, which details what resources are required when, and facilitates the logistics of testing. This role provides regular status reports during the build of test scripts as well as the execution of the test script cycles. The test manager is also responsible for defect management during the project. Where will defects be stored? How will resolvers be able to report their resolutions? And how will testers know when to retest? These are all questions the test manager needs to plan for and coordinate.

Test Coordinator

This role is responsible for executing the strategy defined by the test manager. The test coordinator is more tactical in that this person serves as the liaison to business analysts or business users who are responsible for the test script build and execution. During the preparation phase before the test cycle begins, the test coordinator ensures that all scripts conform to a set of standards and even assists with the test script build when required. Ideally, this person is a hands-on administrator of the test planning tool (for more on test tools, see Chapter 8). After the test scripts are loaded into the selected tool, the test coordinator ensures that test scripts are assigned correctly and aids in test script updates and reporting during the execution phase. This role is also responsible for ensuring that all defects are appropriately documented and routed to the correct resolver group. The test coordinator then coordinates retests when possible and provides test cycle reporting to the test manager when required. The primary goal of the test coordinator is to ensure that the testers know how to build test scripts, how to execute them, and where to report defects when they occur.

SAP NetWeaver Administrator (Basis)

This role is the technical focus of the project from beginning to end. This person (or group of persons) is ultimately responsible for the execution of the migration tools for the SAP Business Suite on SAP HANA migration. This role is also responsible for the SAP sizing to be completed as part of the planning phase in addition to providing input on the landscape and client strategy. If you're working with SAP's tailored data center integration (TDI), then this role must be certified by SAP to perform SAP HANA installations (more on training in Section 2.4.2). If you're planning to leverage weekends for both nonproduction and production downtime, then you'll need multiple persons to act in this role. During weekend migrations, it's normal to operate with two to three resources working eight-hour shifts to ensure continual processing and minimization of downtime. Ideal candidates for this role need to be technically sound and provide clear and consistent communication. The process of migrating SAP ERP system to SAP HANA is well documented; however, customer environments always differ even between landscapes. The SAP NetWeaver administrator's primary goal is to clearly communicate the current status of technical activities and provide reasonable estimations for task completion.

SAP (ABAP) Developer

The scope of effort for this role won't be defined until after the execution of the SEA or the BPCA. After either one of these two tools are executed, you should have a good estimate of the effort required to remediate base SAP modifications and how many custom objects will be impacted by the potential installation of an enhancement package or SP Stack. The SAP developer role is responsible for the defect remediation and custom application code adjustment during the project. The developer role's work stream will more than likely be driven by the SAP Solution Manager output and the defects created during testing. The SAP developer is also involved in the test scope identification for interface testing. Ideally, this role should be filled by someone who is familiar with your landscape and its interfaces, and has an overall understanding of why base SAP modifications were made if they exist.

SAP Security Administrator

The SAP security administrator plays a few small roles on the project. During the planning phases, this person needs to understand the systems and clients to be utilized so he can prepare the SAP systems for administrators, developers, and testers. Remember, the migration to SAP Business Suite on SAP HANA isn't activating any new functionality or authorization objects for the functional users. However, you're changing the underlying database and need to determine who will administrate users at the database level. In the past, we've seen the SAP NetWeaver (Basis) administrators be responsible for database security, which typically was created by the SAP installation tools. The SAP migration tools will create the SAP HANA database users needed for the migration. However, they won't create users for the SAP NetWeaver administrators, SAP developers, or any of the analytics team members you might involve postmigration.

SAP Application Tester

This role has two primary responsibilities on the project: build test scripts and test data sets during the preparation for the test cycles, and execute the test scripts and record defects during the test cycle. This role is either filled by IT business analysts or power users within the business. We've seen an even split between the two among the customer projects we've supported in the past. There is tremendous value added in having the business users involved because they live and breathe in the system every day. Their work instructions will be driven by the output of the SEA or the BPCA. These SAP Solution Manager tools define the transactions and programs impacted by the change event, which drive the test scope identification. The SAP application tester role is filled by multiple people who temporarily report to the test manager during the project. If you're planning your migration and test scope correctly, then you should be able to provide detailed schedules to the business users to secure their support.

2.4.2 Training Plan

As part of your SAP Business Suite on SAP HANA migration project, you'll have multiple training opportunities to support your project team and those responsible for maintain your SAP Business Suite on SAP HANA landscape long term. Your training plan should identify the training needs of your project team members for use during the project and the training required to support SAP Business Suite on SAP HANA. The training plan can be as simple as an Excel spreadsheet defining the training events and the planned attendees. Something customers or project managers often forget is that your project team needs training on the tools you use to run your projects. For example, you need to ensure that your project team knows how and where to enter project issues or decisions. Do they use your organization's IT Service Management (ITSM) solution? Or do they need access to a special shared document on a network repository? A dollar spent on training in the beginning of the project will pay dividends later. Let's break down some of the common types of training required for the SAP Business Suite on SAP HANA migration project.

SAP Solution Manager

Your team will need to execute several tools in SAP Solution Manager during the project. In the beginning, you want to ensure that your organization has SAP

EarlyWatch Reports running. As you start the planning phases of the project, the team will then execute Solution Documentation, SEA, and potentially BPCA. Later in the project, your organization will execute a GoingLive Analysis with SAP Support, which is 100% driven through SAP Solution Manager. If you're going to run test cycles with SAP Solution Manager, then your team will need a detailed understanding of the Test Workbench as well. Thankfully, most of the SAP Solution Manager training can be accessed by SAP Enterprise and SAP Standard support customers online for free using the SAP Support Portal:

1. Log on to *https://service.sap.com/rkt-solman* with a valid SAP Support user ID and password.

2. In the center of the screen, select SAP SOLUTION MANAGER 7.1 SP 12 (see Figure 2.60).

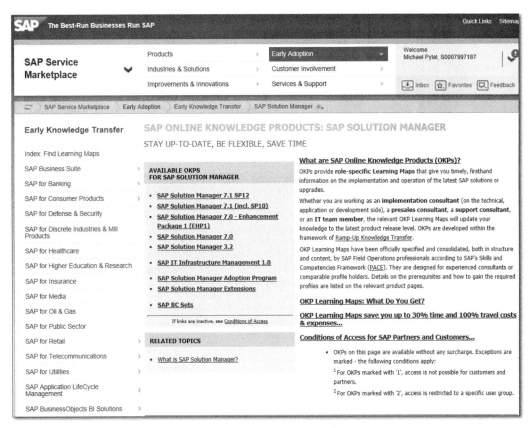

Figure 2.60 SAP's Ramp-Up Knowledge Transfer Content for SAP Solution Manager

3. On the next screen, the content is broken down by area within SAP Solution Manager. If you clicked on SP 12, then the content displayed is only the content specific to that release of SAP Solution Manager.

4. Click BACK, and select the link for SAP SOLUTION MANAGER 7.1 (INCL. SP 10).

5. You can now see more content than the SP 12 link. Select the link for TEST MANAGEMENT under SP 10, and then open BUSINESS PROCESS CHANGE ANALYZER. Two training documents are displayed. The first document covers the benefits of BPCA and the second covers the setup.

The content provided by SAP specific to SAP Solution Manager is included with your organization's SAP support agreement. This training material is best suited for those system administrators who will be responsible for the configuration of SAP Solution Manager during the project.

[»] **Note**

Want more than the online training with the Ramp-Up Knowledge Transfer? SAP Education provides some excellent course as well. We recommend the SM100 course for any system administrator new to SAP Solution Manager 7.1. If you want to know more about Test Management and the BPCA, then the SAP Solution Manager 7.1 Test Management Overview E2E220 is a great classroom option.

Test Tools

Your project team members will need training on whatever testing tools your organization currently uses or plans to implement. The testing cycles of the SAP Business Suite on SAP HANA migration will involve the most people at one time during the project and consequently be the most expensive portion of the project. It's critical that your project team receives training on how to create test scripts, how to execute test scripts, and how to record defects during testing. Whether using a spreadsheet in SharePoint or advanced testing tools such as HP Application Lifecycle Management (ALM) or IBM Test Director, you can't assume that your project team members will know how to use these tools correctly.

SAP HANA

Knowing SAP Business Suite on SAP HANA won't initially impact SAP ERP application functionality, so you can limit the SAP HANA-specific training to your technical team members. SAP HANA is more than a database; it's an application platform that supports more types of integration and application hosting. Initially, SAP HANA will act as the database for your SAP ERP landscape. SAP HANA hardware can be purchased as an appliance with the SAP HANA Platform preinstalled by the hardware manufacturer. You can also install the SAP HANA Platform on your organizations hardware (as long as it meets SAP specifications) but only as long as it's installed by an SAP HANA-certified resource. In addition to SAP NetWeaver administrators, you know operating SAP Business Suite on SAP HANA will impact your developers and security administrators as well. Multiple training options are available for your technical team members. For free online training, we recommend the courses at *http://open.sap.com*. The specific courses we recommend include the following:

▶ **In-Memory Data Management In a Nutshell**
Understand the fundamentals of the in-memory database and columnar store.

▶ **SAP Business Suite powered by SAP HANA**
A good introductory level course on the benefits of running SAP Business Suite on SAP HANA.

▶ **ABAP Development for SAP HANA**
Great discussion of ABAP optimization when running SAP Business Suite on SAP HANA with SAP NetWeaver 7.4.

For classroom (both on-site and virtual live classrooms), we recommend the classes from SAP Education, listed in Table 2.4.

Resource	Class Description	Code
ABAP	ABAP Programming for SAP HANA	HA400
SAP NetWeaver (Basis) administrator	SAP HANA – Operations and Administration	HA200
	Migration to SAP HANA Using DMO	HA250
Security administrator	Authorization, Security, and Scenarios	HA240

Table 2.4 SAP Education Classes

Your training plan will be organization-specific depending on how you staff and organize your project. If you leverage a hosting provider, then your SAP NetWeaver (Basis) administrators likely won't need SAP HANA installation certification. However, your development and security teams will still need training to support future requests, which will begin leveraging the SAP HANA platform.

As for project team members, the most important training you can provide is how to use the document repository for storing project-related documents and how to use your organization's testing tools. Enabling your project team members to accurately report activity tasks and execute defined test scripts is essential for consistent operation of the SAP Business Suite on SAP HANA migration project.

2.5   SAP Best Practices

When working on a variety of projects, customers often ask what the Best Practices are for implementing some solution. It's funny how many times we hear other people talk about Best Practices as something abstract that doesn't tangibly exist. However, SAP Best Practices do exist! SAP has long provided Best Practice guides and toolkits for numerous SAP solutions. SAP has even had a dedicated site to host this content for more than 15 years at *http://help.sap.com/bestpractices*. The Best Practice guides you'll use for the SAP Business Suite on SAP HANA project are stored under a different section of the SAP Support Portal. SAP isn't only a software provider; it also implements its own software as well as supports multiple customers when specific solutions are still new. SAP has been implementing SAP HANA for years now, and all those lessons learned and project documents have been bundled into Rapid Deployment Solutions (RDSs), which SAP customers and partners can utilize on their own SAP Business Suite on SAP HANA migration projects. Let's explore how you access this content and what's included.

1. Log on to *http://service.sap.com/rds* using a valid SAP Support Portal user ID and password.

2. The SAP RAPID DEPLOYMENT SOLUTIONS BUILT ON SAP BEST PRACTICES page is displayed.

3. Click on TECHNOLOGY • IN-MEMORY TECHNOLOGY • SUITE ON SAP HANA • MIGRATION TO SUITE ON SAP HANA.

4. Next to BUILDING BLOCKS, click the DOWNLOAD ALL button.

5. You're taken to the software download center (see Figure 2.61). Click the link for INSTALLATION, and download the zip file displayed. Save the file locally.

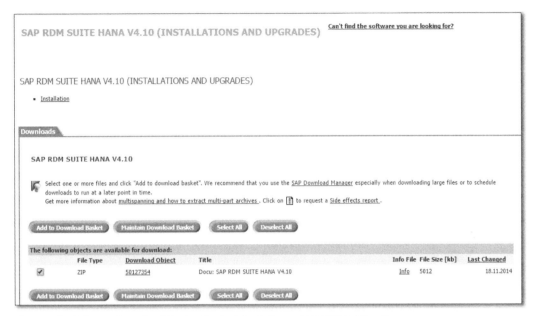

Figure 2.61 Software Download Center Content for Suite on SAP HANA Migration

6. Extract the file contents locally. Right-click on the START.HTM file, and select OPEN WITH • CHROME or FIREFOX (Internet Explorer 10 doesn't display the content correctly).

7. After opening the file, your browser will display the RDS content (see Figure 2.62).

8. Not all content within the RDS package is relevant for your organization's project. The content we recommend includes the following:

   ► SCOPING QUESTIONNAIRE: This document has several tabs that include questions related to the project scope. We've covered most of them in this chapter, but it's worth a review to ensure you haven't missed anything.

   ► SAP SOLUTION MANAGER TEMPLATE DESCRIPTION: This document helps explain the predefined content delivered by SAP for setting up the upgrade project in SAP Solution Manager.

   ► HS1 - DATABASE MIGRATION OF SAP ERP TO SAP HANA: This configuration guide walks you through the high-level steps to perform the SAP Business Suite on SAP HANA migration.

SAP Best Practices Implementation Content

SAP Best Practices quickly turns your SAP software into a live system that handles all your specific business requirements. The preconfigured business processes help you streamline your business without the need for extensive configuration.

SAP Best Practices allows you to evaluate and implement your specific business solution, as well as realize the benefits of your SAP solution faster, with less effort, and less expensively than ever before. The package can be used by companies of all sizes, including global enterprises that need to create a corporate template for their subsidiaries. Different SAP Best Practices packages can also be combined.

SAP Best Practices offers:

- Detailed, step-by-step implementation procedures including automated activities.
- Thorough documentation that can be used for self-study or evaluation, as well as for project team and end-user training.
- Complete preconfiguration settings that allow integrated key processes to be run with reduced implementation effort.

➕ How to use content for evaluation and implementation

Content library for the Rapid database migration of SAP Business Suite to SAP HANA V4

Choose a link to open the document:

Document	Level	Type
[Show all]	▼ [Show all] ▼	[Show all] ▼
Package fact sheet	Solution	Package fact sheet
Software and delivery requirements	Solution	Software and delivery requirements
Scoping questionnaire	Solution	Scoping questionnaire
SAP Note (including Configuration Guide: Getting Started)	Solution	SAP Note
SAP Solution Manager template description	Solution	SAP Solution Manager template description
HS1 - Database Migration of SAP ERP to SAP HANA	Building block	Building block fact sheet
HS1 - Database Migration of SAP ERP to SAP HANA	Building block	Configuration guide
HS2 - Database Migration of SAP CRM to SAP HANA	Building block	Building block fact sheet
HS2 - Database Migration of SAP CRM to SAP HANA	Building block	Configuration guide
HS3 - Database Migration of SAP SCM to SAP HANA	Building block	Building block fact sheet
HS3 - Database Migration of SAP SCM to SAP HANA	Building block	Configuration guide
HS5 - Database Migration of SAP SRM to SAP HANA	Building block	Building block fact sheet

Figure 2.62 SAP Best Practices Content for the SAP Business Suite on SAP HANA Migration

[»] Note

For the latest version of the Rapid Database Migration Guide, see SAP Note 1821999 – Rapid Database Migration of SAP Business Suite to SAP HANA. This SAP Note is updated with the latest information from SAP.

The RDS for the SAP Business Suite on SAP HANA migration is a tangible value that is considered SAP Best Practice for the migration project. It provides you with content to help determine the project scope, activates additional content within SAP Solution Manager, and provides technical configuration guides for the SAP Business Suite on SAP HANA migration. In addition to this book, the RDS content is another source of information to ensure success during your project.

2.6   Summary

Establishing your project scope is a key first step in the SAP Business Suite on SAP HANA migration process. We highlighted the multiple options your organization will have to decide upon with regard to enhancement packages, support packages, and add-on compatibility. Your team will need to decide how much change can be consumed by the organization and how you can effectively use the test cycles you plan to execute during the migration process. For the SAP Business Suite on SAP HANA migration, customers not currently running EHP 6 must upgrade to EHP 7 during the migration. So while your company can't apply an N-1 strategy to enhancement packages, you can apply this principle to the SP Stack, which is also chosen during the planning process.

Your system landscape will have a great impact on cost and the project time line. We covered both the five-system landscape and four-system landscape strategies in this chapter, with the latter considered lean and more cost effective. As you look to optimize the project time line and schedule, we've given you multiple options to consider. Your project scope and time line will also be dictated by the usage of your production SAP ERP system. The more transactions and programs you use, the more testing will be needed. Leveraging SAP Solution Manager and the Solution Documentation tools will give your project team a clear understanding of how your SAP ERP system is used. This information will be critical to understanding the amount of custom code executed in your landscape in addition to the SAP-provided transactions.

Lastly, we talked about the project team roles that are common to an SAP Business Suite on SAP HANA migration project. This section underscored the need for a test manager and test coordinator role as part of the project. Consistency in test scripts creates long-term reusability. Your SAP Business Suite on SAP HANA project can be used as a template for future projects on how test cycles can be planned for and executed. The test coordinator role is often underrated. We'll talk more about the importance of testing in Chapter 8. We ended this section with a discussion of the SAP Rapid Deployment Solutions. Sometimes referred to as SAP Best Practices, this repository of content contains real-world templates and configuration guides on completing an SAP Business Suite on SAP HANA migration project. This content, along with the decisions you've made on SAP ERP versions, system landscapes, project team roles, and the usage of SAP Solution Manager, will guide you on your determination of project scope for the SAP Business Suite on SAP HANA migration.

Running SAP Business Suite on SAP HANA requires infrastructure changes to your SAP landscape because new software components and hardware are installed within your landscape. In addition to ensuring that it's sized appropriately, you need to ensure that it's all backed up and recoverable.

3 Infrastructure Planning

Now that we've defined the project scope, you can focus on the decisions you'll need to make about your infrastructure planning. For those customers whose SAP systems began as SAP NetWeaver 7.31 or above, minimal changes are required. For those customers whose SAP ERP systems were initially installed with SAP R/3 or SAP ERP 6.0 on SAP NetWeaver 7.0 and then upgraded over the years, you'll have some more decisions to make. You'll learn more about why SAP is recommending changes to the primary application server (PAS) and how to comply with those recommendations. What is an enqueue server, and why does SAP want it separate? We'll cover this topic and talk about how it affects sizing. Additionally, if you were a customer who installed a Java stack in addition to the ABAP stack during your initial deployment of SAP ERP 6.0, we'll highlight some of the changes required in your landscape before the migration to SAP Business Suite on SAP HANA. SAP doesn't support the migration of a dual stack system to SAP HANA. We'll cover the how and the why as it relates to your SAP Business Suite on SAP HANA migration.

Sizing your SAP Business Suite on SAP HANA environment will depend on the scope you identified in Chapter 2 and the architecture your team plans to deploy. In Chapter 1, you learned about some of the architecture options when running SAP Business Suite on SAP HANA, which we'll expand upon in this chapter by explaining how each architecture option impacts your sizing requirement. SAP supports running the ABAP PAS on the same hardware as the SAP HANA database, which was previously not an option. We'll break down the additive sizing requirements and discuss the potential benefits of this landscape to those customers with small- to medium-sized environments.

In addition to sizing, we'll also explore some of the backup and recovery options available to SAP customers. There are numerous hardware vendor-provided solutions in addition to the capabilities provided by SAP. We'll show you how to find those certified solutions and provide more details on out-of-the-box solutions. This chapter concludes with information on backup and recovery to support the best decision for your organization's landscape.

3.1 Enqueue Server

The enqueue server is the function within SAP NetWeaver that maintains data about user locks in the lock table in memory; it keeps users operating day to day in SAP ERP without interrupting other users. When a user opens a purchase order, and the message is displayed that another user has the document locked, this is one function the enqueue server supports. Beginning with SAP NetWeaver 7.31 and continuing in SAP NetWeaver 7.4, SAP began splitting the enqueue services from the central instance by default. This means that new installations you delivered had two instances on the PAS host. One instance supports the ABAP dispatcher, work processes, gateway, Internet Communication Manager (ICM), and Internet Graphics Service (IGS), and the other instance supports the message server and enqueue server. If your system was originally an SAP R/3 system, or the initial install was done using a release prior to SAP NetWeaver 7.31, then all these functions were part of a single instance. There are, of course, exceptions. If your SAP ERP landscape was configured for High Availability (HA), it's likely you already have a standalone enqueue server that is replicated to another host for failover purposes. If you're already using the HA scenario with SAP NetWeaver 7.x, then no action is needed with the enqueue server. If you're a customer with the integrated enqueue server on any version of SAP NetWeaver, then SAP recommends that you split the function from the central instance before the migration to SAP HANA. SAP specifically says:

> *SAP strongly recommends using the standalone enqueue server as the better solution. The standalone enqueue server offers better performance and better scalability for large systems (two or more dialog instances). It is already the standard for all new installations and mandatory for high availability setups. In future releases, it will become mandatory for all systems.*

> **Note** [«]
>
> If you want to read SAP's official statement in full, see SAP Note 2019532 – Performance of Integrated Enqueue Server, and SAP Note 2013043 – Performance Problems with Enqueue Work Process.

SAP does provide the tools you need to initially split the enqueue server from the central instance. Using the Software Provisioning Manager 1.0 (SWPM), you can split the instance with minimal application server downtime. Ideally, this is done in the weeks or months before the SAP Business Suite on SAP HANA migration. It's a relatively low-risk activity because you're not moving services to another server. You're keeping the services local but splitting them from the primary instance for performance reasons. In Figure 3.1, you can visualize the changes being made to your system. The update also requires edits to the instance profile for the application servers.

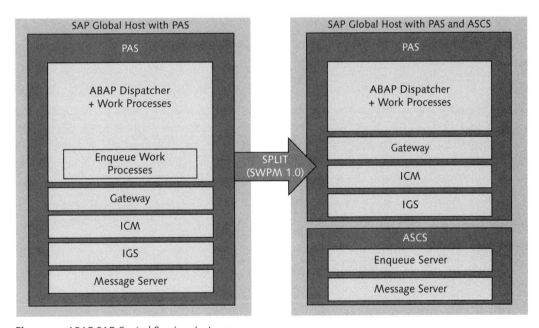

Figure 3.1 ABAP SAP Central Services Instance

Follow these instruction to split the enqueue server from the central instance:

1. Using the SWPM, launch the application on the PAS.

2. In the directory tree, choose <YOUR SAP NETWEAVER RELEASE> • <YOUR DATA-BASE> • ADDITIONAL SAP SYSTEM INSTANCES • SPLIT OFF ASCS INSTANCE FROM EXISTING PRIMARY APPLICATION SERVER INSTANCE (see Figure 3.2).

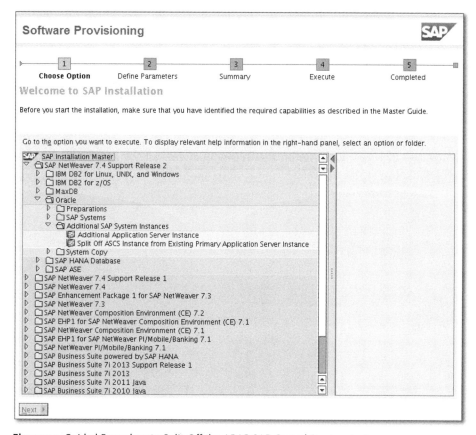

Figure 3.2 Guided Procedure to Split Off the ABAP SAP Central Services Instance

3. Choose TYPICAL as the PARAMETER MODE when prompted.

4. Enter the path to the SAP system profiles in the PROFILE DIRECTORY field shown in Figure 3.3, and click NEXT.

5. Input the DATABASE ID (DBSID) and the DATABASE HOST, and click NEXT.

Figure 3.3 Reading the Profiles to Validate the Process

6. Define the path to the kernel media (which can be downloaded from the SAP Support Portal at *http://support.sap.com/swdc*), as shown in Figure 3.4.

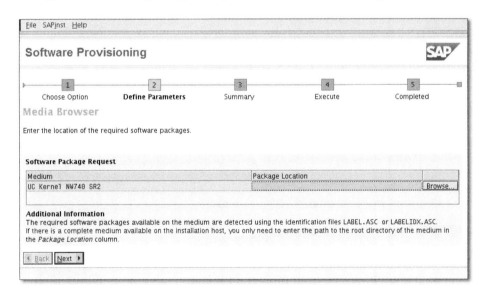

Figure 3.4 Entering the File Path for the Kernel Media

7. The ports for the ABAP message server are read automatically. Validate, and click NEXT.

8. On the SUMMARY step, verify all input. Clicking SHOW DETAIL will give you all parameters used. Then click NEXT, as shown in Figure 3.5.

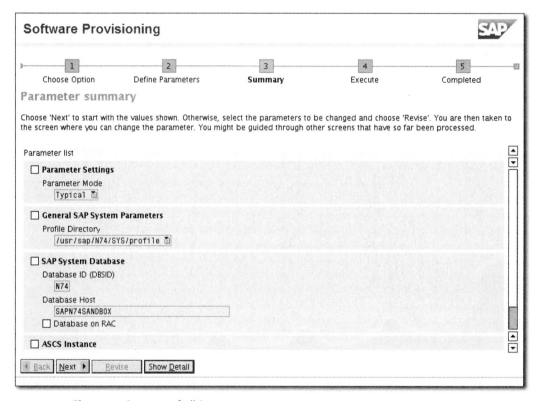

Figure 3.5 Summary of All Parameters

9. The installer processes the information. During this time, the application server instances are restarted with new parameters.

10. When prompted, confirm the completion message.

[»] Note

For information on the process of splitting the ASCS instance and additional settings, see SAP Note 2119669 – How to Split the ASCS from Primary Application Server (PAS).

3.2   Dual Stack Split

SAP no longer supports the update of dual stack systems with the SAP Business Suite. Dual stack systems are defined as a single SAP instance with both an ABAP AS and a Java AS sharing a single system ID and database. This increases maintenance of the system and decreases system performance. Fortunately, SAP provides the SWPM as part of the software logistics toolset (SL Toolset). This program provides a menu-driven wizard tool to export the Java stack, install a new Java stack, and then uninstall the Java stack from the ABAP system. Several options are available to you in terms of where the new Java instance resides. You can install the new Java instance on the same host(s) as the ABAP instance, or use this opportunity to dedicate a host for the Java instance, as shown in Figure 3.6. This answer depends on your current Java instance usage and current hardware sizing. Installing the Java stack on the same host requires additional resources because the new instance will have its own set of binaries, database, and lifecycle.

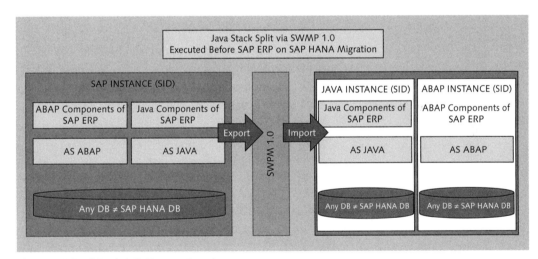

Figure 3.6 Dual Stack Split Process Overview

It's worth noting that the Java stack split creates a completely separate Java instance with its own User Management Engine (UME). This means your SAP ERP (ABAP) users who previously could access the Java stack as part of SAP ERP will no longer have a user ID and password to the Java instance. However, the Java instance UME can be reconfigured to use the ABAP system as the UME, meaning that the Java stack user management database can continue to reside within the ABAP stack.

[»] **Note**

For the latest information on the SL Toolset, which includes SWPM and the Software Update Manager (SUM), check out the SAP Service Marketplace at *http://service.sap.com/sltoolset*. This site is dedicated to release information, installation guides, how to start/stop SAPINST, and direct access to downloads.

Executing Dual Stack Split

To execute the dual stack split, follow these steps:

1. After downloading the latest SWPM from SAP Service Marketplace, log on to the PAS with an administrative account.

2. Start SAPINST, and navigate via the menu to DUAL-STACK SPLIT. The first task you'll execute is EXPORT JAVA STACK, as shown in Figure 3.7.

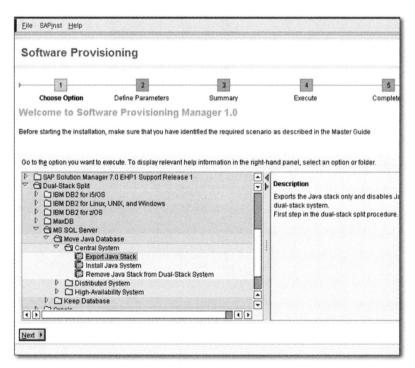

Figure 3.7 Initial Menu in Software Provisioning Manager

3. Select the menu item, and click NEXT.

4. When prompted, enter the path to the SAP PROFILE DIRECTORY, and click NEXT.

5. Enter the PASSWORD OF SAP SYSTEM ADMINISTRATOR when prompted, and click NEXT.

6. Select the correct DATABASE ID (DBSID), and click NEXT.

7. On the next screen, select the EXPORT LOCATION to store the Java export, and leave MANUALLY STOP SYSTEM checked, as shown in Figure 3.8. Typically, 10–20GB will suffice.

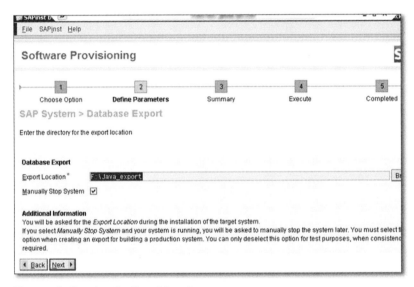

Figure 3.8 Choosing the Export Location

8. Select the option to let the SUM disable the Java stack using the profile parameter `rdisp/j2ee_start=0`. This doesn't stop the system at this point, but it adds the required parameters to disable the Java stack from starting when you restart services. Check the DISABLE APPLICATION SERVER JAVA box, and then click NEXT.

9. On the PARAMETER SUMMARY screen (see Figure 3.9), review all parameters, and click NEXT to begin the export process. You'll need to manually stop SAP services when your team gives you permission.

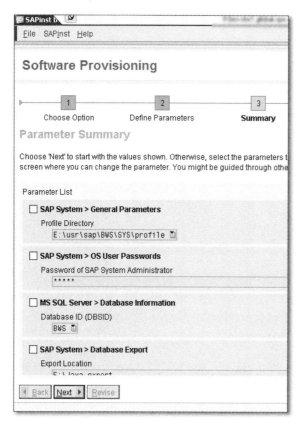

Figure 3.9 Parameter Summary Screen in Software Update Manager

10. At this point, the Java export occurs and should not be restarted until you install the new Java instance.

11. When prompted, stop SAP services, and click OK (see Figure 3.10). Note you only need to stop Java services within the dual stack system using Transaction SMICM.

12. Click OK. The export process continues, and the application server downtime begins for the dual stack split.

13. Verify the results on screen when presented with the completion message (see Figure 3.11).

14. Restart the SAP services using the command Stop SAP, or use the Microsoft Management Console (MMC).

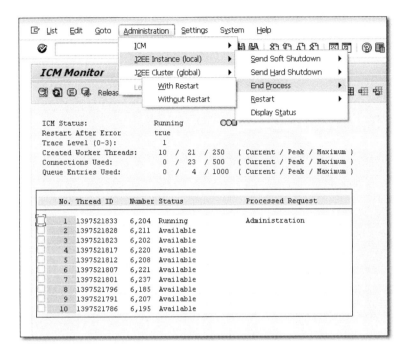

Figure 3.10 Stopping the Java Instance

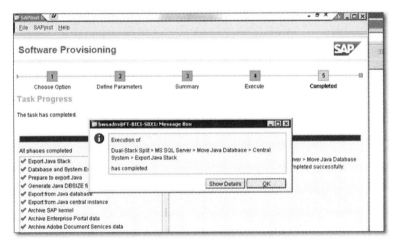

Figure 3.11 Confirmation Message after the Export Completes

15. Return to the SWPM by running SAPINST again. Navigate within the SWPM menu to DUAL-STACK SPLIT • <DATABASE> • MOVE JAVA DATABASE • CENTRAL SYSTEM • INSTALL JAVA SYSTEM (see Figure 3.12).

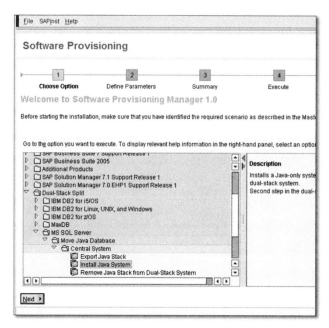

Figure 3.12 Menu Path to Install New Java System

16. When prompted, enter the PACKAGE LOCATION of the Java export created in an earlier step (see Figure 3.13). Click NEXT.

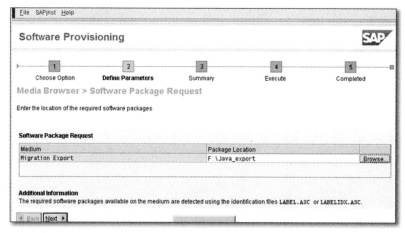

Figure 3.13 Enter the Java Export Directory

17. Select TYPICAL for the PARAMETER MODE, and click NEXT.

18. Enter the new Java System ID (SID) and the location for the new installation directory, which will contain the executables for the Java application server, as shown in Figure 3.14.

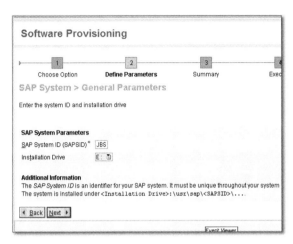

Figure 3.14 SAP Paramters Entry Screen

19. Assign a MASTER PASSWORD, and click NEXT. (Note that the default password for system accounts will be the master password.)

20. Input the SAP SYSTEM ADMINISTRATOR and SAP SYSTEM SERVICE USER passwords, and click NEXT (see Figure 3.15).

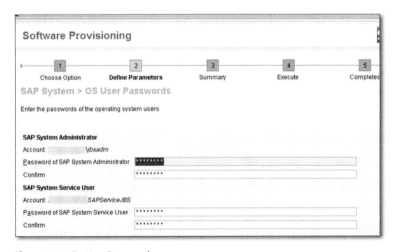

Figure 3.15 Setting Passwords

21. When prompted to select the DATABASE TO USE, click CREATE NEW DATABASE (DBSID = SAPSID), and click NEXT.

22. For the EXPECTED SYSTEM SIZE section, select the system size based on the number of processor cores assigned to this instance (see Figure 3.16). Click NEXT.

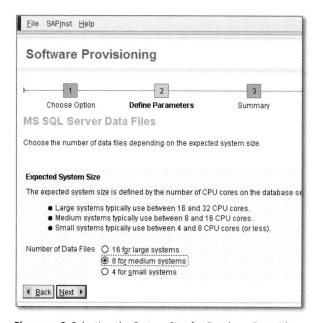

Figure 3.16 Selecting the System Size for Database Data Files

23. In the SOFTWARE PACKAGE REQUEST section, enter the location of the JAVA COMPONENT media in the PACKAGE LOCATION field (see Figure 3.17), which can be downloaded from *https://support.sap.com/swdc*.

24. When prompted, enter the administrator password for the previously exported Java system, and click NEXT.

25. Enter the location of the SAP Cryptographic Library to be used during the installation (see Figure 3.18). This library (or SAR file) can be downloaded per instructions from SAP Note 455033.

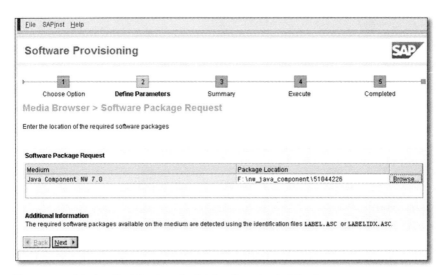

Figure 3.17 Entering the Directory Containing Downloaded Media

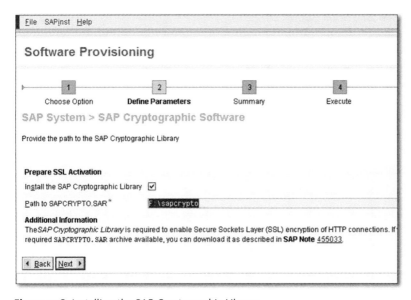

Figure 3.18 Installing the SAP Cryptographic Library

26. On the PARAMETER SUMMARY screen, review the selected criteria and choose NEXT (see Figure 3.19).

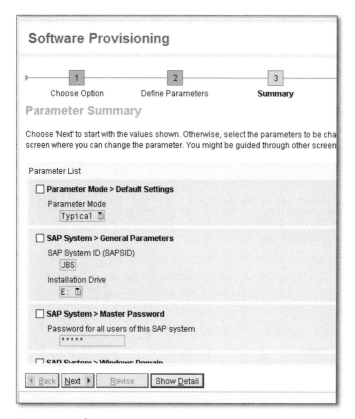

Figure 3.19 Software Povisioning Manager Summary Screen

27. When prompted, verify the ABAP stack is running, and click OK (see Figure 3.20).

28. Verify the results when prompted with a completion message (see Figure 3.21).

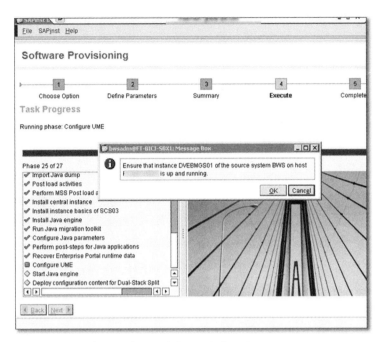

Figure 3.20 Confirming the ABAP System Is Running

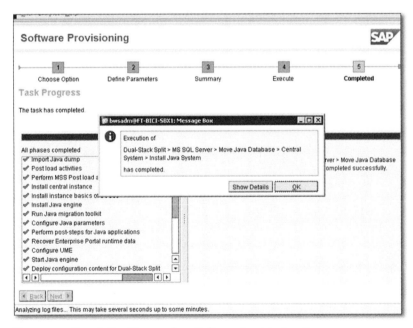

Figure 3.21 Completion Message from Software Provisioning Manager

29. Return to the SWPM, and run SAPINST. Navigate within the SWPM menu to DUAL-STACK SPLIT • <DATABASE> • MOVE JAVA DATABASE • CENTRAL SYSTEM • REMOVE JAVA STACK FROM DUAL-STACK SYSTEM (see Figure 3.22).

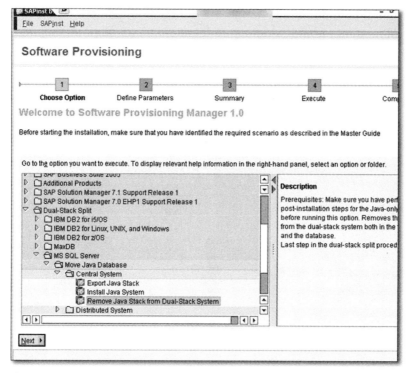

Figure 3.22 Final Step in the Dual Stack Split

30. Enter the path to the ABAP system SAP PROFILE DIRECTORY (see Figure 3.23). Click NEXT.

31. Enter the PASSWORD OF SAP SYSTEM ADMINISTRATOR for the ABAP stack.

32. Next select the DATABASE ID (DBSID) for the ABAP system. Click NEXT.

33. Verify the selection criteria on the PARAMETER SUMMARY screen, and click NEXT to begin the removal process (see Figure 3.24).

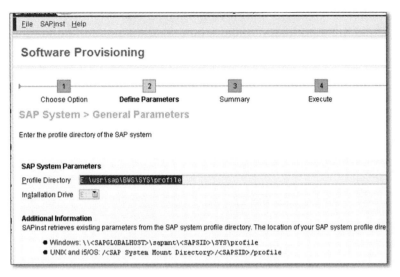

Figure 3.23 Entering the Path to the ABAP System Profiles

Figure 3.24 Parameter Summary Screen

34. On completion of the task, verify the results when prompted (see Figure 3.25). Click OK.

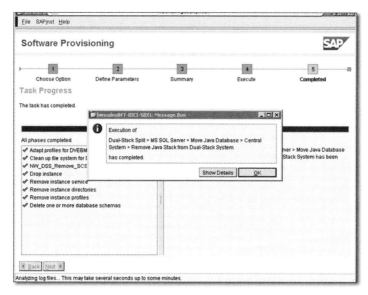

Figure 3.25 Verification of Completion Message from Software Provisioning Manager

35. Confirm the new Java system is running by executing StartSAP as the new Java <SID>ADM user account or by opening MMC to confirm the new instance is running (see Figure 3.26).

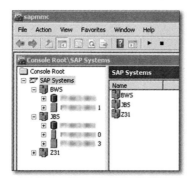

Figure 3.26 New Java System Displayed and Running

Separating the ABAP and Java stack is a requirement that must be completed prior to starting the migration to SAP Business Suite on SAP HANA. These procedures can be executed weeks or months in advance of the migration project. Keep in mind that the screenshots and process in this section assumed no changes in the hardware. The Java instance was separated but remains on the same application servers. This approach limits the amount of change so that testing can be focused at the application layer. If you so choose, you could split the Java stack and move the application server to new hardware or a virtualized OS.

3.3 Sizing

Is SAP sizing more art than science? Some consultants think so. SAP has provided clear guidelines on most if not all components, and while there are spot solutions with fuzzy sizing guidelines, the primary components are well documented. SAP also assumes additive sizing. Do you want to run the ABAP application server on the same host (appliance) as the SAP HANA database? Yes, it's supported. And yes, you add the sizing requirements together (ABAP + SAP HANA) to get the total size required. Keep in mind that sizing isn't done in a silo, and it's not done just once. During your SAP Business Suite on SAP HANA migration project, you're going to learn a lot, and you'll have performance data from all the regression tests. Ideally, you'll mitigate the risk of a bad sizing by running a load test before you go-live.

In the beginning, you'll use the ABAP report provided by SAP to perform a SAP Business Suite on SAP HANA sizing from your production system. This provides an estimate for main memory requirements of the SAP HANA database but won't provide an estimate of SAPS (processing power) required for the application servers. At the start of your project, your sandbox will likely have one PAS connected to a SAP HANA appliance. This might be true for development as well because the load will be small. As your project moves forward, we typically see customers with QA environments that closely match their production environments. This QA landscape that closely resembles production is the ideal environment for a load test. Let's explore some of the sizing methods available to you as a customer. And remember—most hardware partners have an SAP sizing competency center that can help you as well.

What are SAPS?	[«]

SAP Application Performance Standard (SAPS) is a hardware-independent unit of measurement that defines the performance of a system operation in the SAP environment. It was created to independently measure performance across different types or processors.

3.3.1 Ballpark Sizing

There is a formula you can use very easily to calculate the approximate size of the SAP HANA appliance you'll need for your SAP Business Suite on SAP HANA migration. It first requires the size of your existing database, which you can retrieve using Transaction DB02. The recommendation from SAP is that you take half of the size of your disk-based database, include a safety buffer of 20%, and add 50GB for the repository, stack, and other services. Let's look at an example:

1. Log on to your SAP ERP system with a valid user ID and password.

2. Run Transaction DB02, and note the database size displayed (see Figure 3.27).

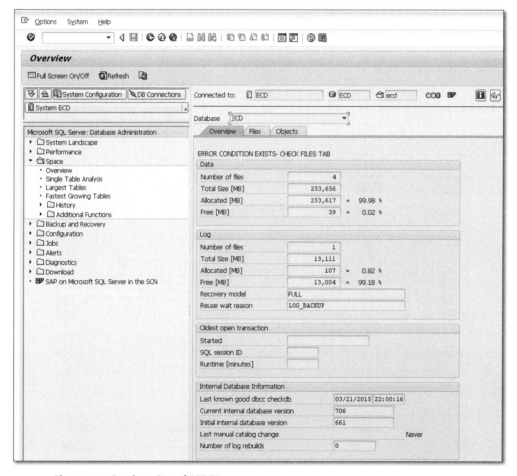

Figure 3.27 Database Size of 253GB

3. Using SAP's formula, you can calculate the approximate size of your SAP HANA database. In this example, this roughly calculates a SAP HANA database of 201GB:

HANA DB Size = (253GB ÷ 2 × 1.2 + 50GB)

3.3.2 SAP Sizing Report for SAP Business Suite on SAP HANA

If your system is already running SAP ERP 6 EHP 7 with the latest versions of the ST-PI ABAP add-on component, then the SAP Business Suite on SAP HANA sizing report already exists in your system. SAP has provided updates to the program, which can be downloaded to your system by implementing SAP Note 2175150 – Suite on SAP HANA Memory Sizing Report. After you've downloaded and implemented the SAP Note, follow these instructions:

1. Log on to your SAP ERP system with a valid user ID and password.

2. Run Transaction SE38, and input the program name "/SDF/HDB_SIZING". Click EXECUTE.

3. By default, you'll leave the LIST OF TABLES fields blank because you want to get the size for the entire system.

4. Uncheck SIZING FOR SAP SIMPLE FINANCE 2.0 (alternate name: SIZING FOR SAP S/4HANA FINANCE) because you're sizing for the migration only. Your team will need to size for SAP S/4HANA Finance later.

> **Note** [«]
>
> If you need to size SAP HANA Enterprise for specific tables in SAP ERP, you can use the same program. If your organization wants to implement the SAP HANA sidecar scenario, you can specify the exact tables to be included and get a good sizing for those specific objects.

5. Under TECHNICAL OPTIONS, enter the NUMBER OF PARALLEL DIALOG PROCESSES you want to use. Leaving this with the default of 1 will result in extremely long runtimes.

6. After you make your selections, select PROGRAM • EXECUTE IN BACKGROUND, as shown in Figure 3.28.

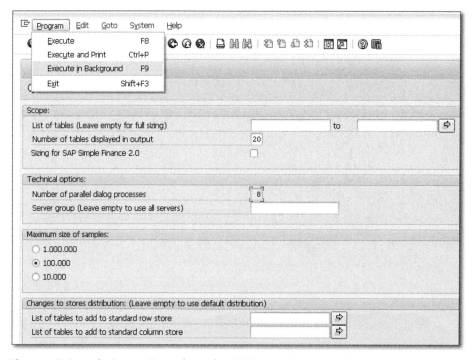

Figure 3.28 Example Options Entered into the SAP Business Suite on SAP HANA Sizing Report

7. After the background job completes, you'll see the created spool file.

8. In Figure 3.29, you can see the as-is requirement for this example system on SAP HANA will be 135GB of main memory. If we add in a 20% safety buffer, then we arrive at a requirement of 162GB of memory. That is about 40GB less than our ballpark estimate for the same system.

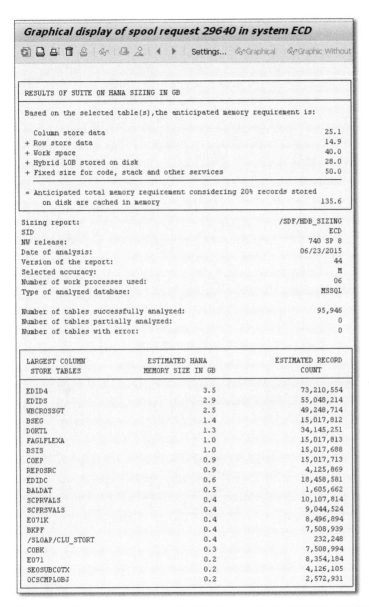

Figure 3.29 Example Output from the SAP Business Suite on SAP HANA Sizing Report

3.3.3   SAP Quick Sizer

The SAP Quick Sizer is another tool you can use to accurately size your SAP Business Suite on SAP HANA environment. There are two means of performing a sizing within the Quick Sizer: user-based sizing and throughput-based sizing. The latter requires more time and effort. User-based sizing is a count of users by activity type (more on that shortly). Throughput-based sizing focuses on the quantity of documents within your systems and the frequency at which they occur. Getting this information will take time, but it can provide an extremely accurate sizing estimate. However, as we've said before, the only way to mitigate the risk of a potentially bad sizing is to perform a performance test of the target landscape before go-live. If your team doesn't have the capacity to perform a throughput sizing, you can mitigate this risk with a performance test. Our goal with this section is to provide you with enough detail to understand the effort required and where to find more information on the Quick Sizer.

A user-based sizing will give you the quickest time to a number, which you can then provide to a hardware vendor. User-based sizing breaks down users into three categories by user activity type because not all users are created equal. The Quick Sizer also lets you enter user counts by time period. If your organization operates in multiple time zones, this feature will let you input user activity at varying times in the day. User-based sizing also has a field to capture data retention period by module. In the following examples, we entered a value of 84 months or 7 years. This is only an example, and ideally your organization has some data retention policy you can reference when completing these steps. Here's a summary of the user activity types you can use in user-based sizing:

▸ **Low-activity user**
This user is an informational or executive user in SAP ERP. These users perform 10 dialog steps within an hour.

▸ **Medium-activity user**
This user is someone whose daily job duties primarily occur in SAP ERP, for example, accountants, clerks, shop floor workers, and so on. These users perform 120 dialog steps an hour or one click in SAP ERP every 30 seconds during work hours.

▸ **High-activity user**
This is a heavy user of the system, for example, customer service agents, data entry users, or system administrators. These users perform 360 dialog steps in an hour or one click every 10 seconds in SAP ERP.

You can easily find the activity level of users within your system by following these steps:

1. Log on to SAP ERP with a valid user ID and password.

2. Run Transaction ST03N.

3. From the upper-left area, expand the node WORKLOAD • TOTAL • MONTH, and double-click the last full month of data.

4. Double-click WORKLOAD OVERVIEW under ANALYSIS VIEWS in the lower-left area.

5. Select the USER tab to see the user types by activity, as shown in Figure 3.30.

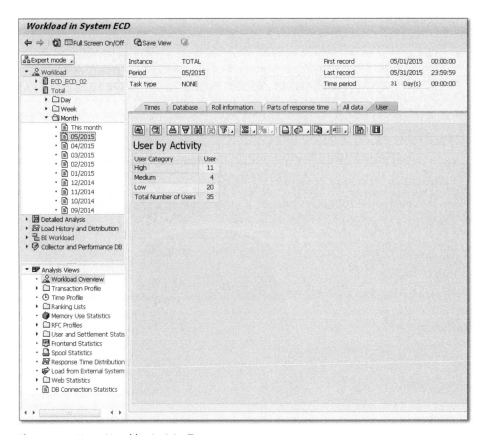

Figure 3.30 Users Listed by Activity Type

Now, you'll notice the rules give you the activity type by user but don't break it down by functional area. Your team will have to determine this. You can look at logons for the month analyzed to develop a list of users that you've assigned to a primary functional area. You know that users typically don't work within one module, so you need to identify the primary functional area they are responsible for.

When accessing the Quick Sizer, you'll notice your customer number and a project name displayed. These are important identifiers because after your sizing estimation is complete, you can share your Quick Sizer report directly with certified SAP hardware providers or other individuals in your company. The project name can be any text value that you associate with the project activity (i.e., SAP HANA Migration).

You'll also notice in the Quick Sizer that your project will have a status value. When setting your project to GoingLive, this will enable integration between your SAP Enterprise Support service called the GoingLive Analysis with the Quick Sizer project. SAP Support will essentially review your sizing project and then compare it to the actual hardware you've deployed. This ensures that your actual system will meet the needs of the sizing you estimated.

Accessing Quick Sizer

To access Quick Sizer, follow these steps:

1. Log on to the SAP Support Portal via the direct link to the SAP HANA version of the Quick Sizer at *http://service.sap.com/hanaqs*.

2. On the initial screen, enter a PROJECT NAME, and click CREATE PROJECT, as shown in Figure 3.31.

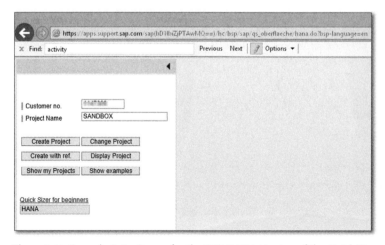

Figure 3.31 Example Entry Screen for the SAP HANA Version of the Quick Sizer

3. Initially, the PROJECT SANDBOX screen appears with several helpful items displayed (see Figure 3.32). Click HARDWARE VENDORS to get contact information for the SAP sizing competency center for each vendor.

4. Click QUICK SIZER TOOL DOCUMENTATION to access the guide to using the tool.

5. In the NEW SYSTEM/SYSTEM EXTENSION section, you must decide between NEW SAP BUSINESS SOLUTION/SOFTWARE COMPONENT and SAP BUSINESS SOLUTION/SOFTWARE COMPONENT EXTENSION. If you size as a new solution, your hardware can tell you what existing hardware will support what you've sized.

6. The PLATFORM AND COMMUNICATION, SYSTEM AVAILABILITY, and NETWORK INFRASTRUCTURE sections are optional. They help provide the hardware vendor and SAP with more background information.

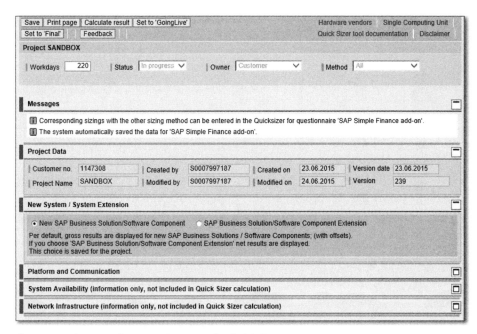

Figure 3.32 Project Information Screen in the Quick Sizer

7. If you look to the left of your screen, you can see a navigation tree with multiple components under SAP BUSINESS SUITE ON SAP HANA.

8. The items you select will depend on the scope within your organization's SAP ERP environment. In the example in Figure 3.33, there is data for a user-based

sizing with SAP S/4HANA Finance, Logistics Execution, Product Dev & Execution, and Sales & Service.

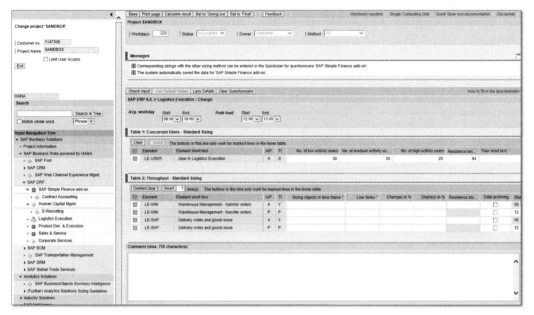

Figure 3.33 Example User-Based Sizing for SAP Business Suite on SAP HANA

9. In Figure 3.33, you can see that we entered a total of 100 Logistics users, with a data retention of 84 months for this example. We entered similar data for the other SAP ERP components to simulate a sizing for a system with 600 active users.

10. Click on Calculate result at the top of the screen to see a summary of the sizing (see Figure 3.34).

In Figure 3.34, we used the default of 220 workdays per year, with the average workday running from 9AM to 6PM, and peak load occurring from 9AM to 11AM and 1PM to 2PM. Based on the 600 users we entered, with a retention period of 84 months for SAP ERP, the Quick Sizer believes we'll need a SAP HANA appliance with essentially 1TB of capacity to support both our user load and data volumes. We also get a SAPS number for the application server in the sizing summary. The Quick Sizer doesn't know if our ABAP AS will be on the same hardware as SAP HANA or separate. We would add these values together if they will be installed on the same host.

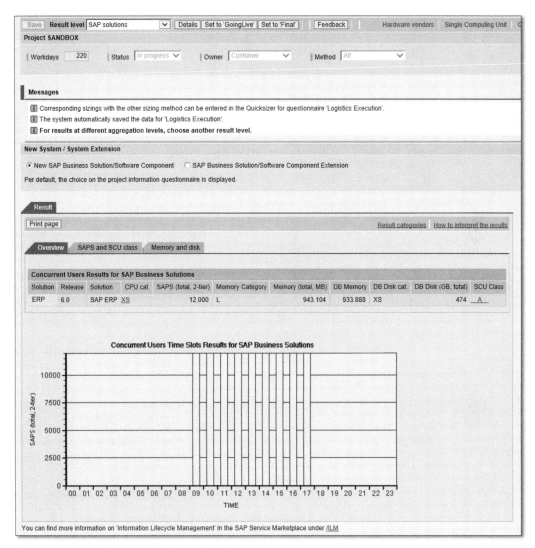

Figure 3.34 Example Sizing Results Displayed

Sizing your new SAP Business Suite on SAP HANA system using the Quick Sizer can get very complicated if you move into the throughput-based sizing method. Using this sizing method, you need to capture or estimate specific activity within your SAP ERP system. If you believe you require this level of sizing, we recommend engaging a certified SAP sizing professional either through SAP or one of its certified partners.

In this section, we described how to perform initial sizing estimations, how to execute the ABAP report for SAP Business Suite on SAP HANA sizing, and how to perform the user-based sizing method using the Quick Sizer. SAP and its certified hardware partners are available to support your organization through this process. Uncertainty as to what hardware you need to migrate SAP Business Suite on SAP HANA can be easily remedied by using the solutions described in this chapter and engaging your hardware partner early in the process. SAP sizing tools exist to ensure success at your go-live. This isn't a process you'll only execute once during the project. As you continue to learn during the upgrade and migration process, you'll need to add reminders throughout your project to revalidate the sizing that was completed. And, don't forget, you can mitigate risk due to a bad sizing by running a performance test during your project.

[»]

> **Note**
>
> For even more information on SAP sizing, training events, and how-to guides, see the SAP Service Marketplace at *https://service.sap.com/sizing*. Click on the SAP HANA QUICK SIZER link to access the SAP Business Suite on SAP HANA sizing tool.

3.4   Backup and Recovery

When SAP HANA was initially released and touted as an in-memory database, the IT person in all of us wondered how data in-memory is handled when the system crashes. Rest assured, SAP thought of this well before releasing SAP HANA to the public. SAP HANA is an in-memory database that also uses persistent storage. This allows you to backup and recover the database just like any other database on the market. You have graphical, command-line, and third-party backup tools that enable you to recover when the power is cut, a disk drive fails, or an entire data center has a catastrophe. Both data and log backups are completed online, with negligible impact to the users. Parameters in SAP HANA are set by default, but customers can change these to determine their own recovery point objective (RPO). Focusing on your SAP Business Suite on SAP HANA migration project, we'll cover the backup and recovery scenarios that are specific to a scale-up scenario or a single node. SAP Business Suite on SAP HANA isn't yet supported on a scale-out scenario, so we'll avoid the backup and recovery options for a multi-node environment. We'll also point out where you can enable third-party backup options, but we won't cover those vendor tools specifically. The concepts we'll cover apply to both SAP HANA-provided tools and third-party tools.

[«]

> **Note**
>
> Want to know more about available third-party certified backup options? Go to *http:// global.sap.com/community/ebook/2013_09_adpd/enEN/search.html*, and enter "hana-brint" into the search box. A list of currently certified partners will be displayed.

3.4.1 Backups

Your organization's backup strategy will be a combination of SAP recommendations, industry best practices, and lessons learned from operating an SAP ERP system in your environment. SAP supports data backups, storage snapshots, and log backups. These backups can be used to recover the system in the event of failure to the most recent point in time or a specific point in time, or they can be used as the source for a system copy. The backup and recovery function will be performed and set up by your SAP NetWeaver (Basis) administrators in coordination with the infrastructure team that supports the backup devices and storage solutions (ideally, the SAP NetWeaver administrator attended the HA200 class we talked about earlier). SAP recommends a backup strategy that leverages all types of backups available, specifically, a daily storage snapshot, automatic log backups, and a complete data backup once a week. In the event of a failure during the week, you can either restore from the nightly storage snapshot or from the complete data backup, and then read the logs from the automatic log backup. If you have a failure in your storage solution, the storage snapshot won't be available, but the complete data backup will be because you would have saved it to a location other than the local SAP HANA system. Leveraging all backup types mitigates risk and dependencies on a single component of the backup solution.

As you dig into the administration, backup, and recovery of SAP HANA, you'll see references to the savepoint. As we mentioned, SAP HANA persists data on disk. During normal operations, changed data is automatically saved from memory to disk at regular savepoints. The time period for the savepoint is set by default to every five minutes, but this value can be changed. So, every five minutes, the savepoint is defined, and data is written to disk. If you think about a system restart, the savepoint reduces the time to restart because it doesn't have to read all redo log files. Only those redo logs that occurred after the most recent savepoint need to be read after a system restart. It's important to know that savepoints are written asynchronously by each service within SAP HANA. A global savepoint is a consistent collection of savepoints for all services in the system. For example, a global savepoint is written when you start a complete data backup. The point here isn't to make you an expert at SAP HANA database backup and recovery, but instead to talk about critical components of the backup mechanisms. If during your SAP Business Suite on SAP HANA migration, you begin to see errors related to the savepoint, you now know this is related to the ability to recover or restore your system.

[»]

> **Note**
>
> Want to become an SAP HANA backup expert? Check out the *SAP HANA Administration* book (SAP PRESS, 2014). Or see more by going to *http://help.sap.com* and choosing TECHNOLOGY PLATFORM • SAP HANA PLATFORM • SYSTEM ADMINISTRATION AND MAINTENANCE INFORMATION • SAP HANA ADMINISTRATION GUIDE.

Now let's walk through a system backup using SAP HANA Studio:

1. Be sure to download and install SAP HANA Studio from the SAP Software Download Center at *https://support.sap.com/swdc.* Then choose SUPPORT PACKAGES & PATCHES • A-Z PRODUCTS • H • SAP HANA PLATFORM EDITION • SAP HANA PLATFORM EDIT. 1.0 • ENTRY BY COMPONENT • HANA STUDIO.

2. Launch the SAP HANA Studio, select FILE • NEW • FOLDER, and give the folder a name. The folder is a logical grouping of systems. You can have one folder for the entire landscape or one folder per Software Development Lifecycle (SDLC) phase (development, QA, production). The folder only exists locally.

3. Right-click the folder you created, and click ADD SYSTEM. Enter the server name, instance number, and a description. Click NEXT.

4. Choose AUTHENTICATION BY DATABASE USER, and enter the credentials given to you by your SAP HANA installer. Click FINISH after you've entered the user ID and password.

5. Right-click the system you added, and select LOGON.

6. Right-click the BACKUP folder, and select OPEN BACKUP CONSOLE, as shown in Figure 3.35.

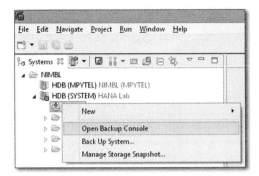

Figure 3.35 Opening the Backup Console to View Backup History

7. The initial screen displays backups in progress, if any, and the most recent successful backup. Click the BACKUP CATALOG tab to see the backup history detail.

8. If you want to run a backup now, then right-click the BACKUP folder and select BACK UP SYSTEM, as shown in Figure 3.36.

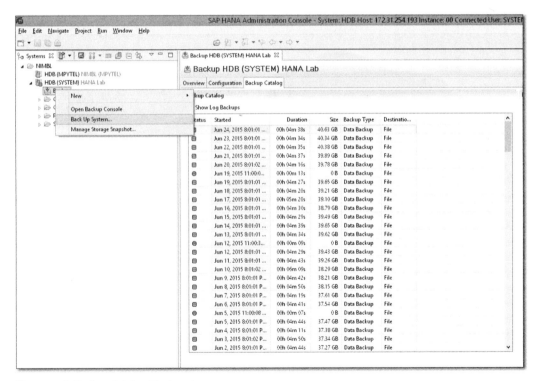

Figure 3.36 Backup Catalog Displayed

9. Review the parameters on the SPECIFY BACKUP SETTINGS screen. Adjust the BACKUP DESTINATION or BACKUP PREFIX if required (see Figure 3.37). Click NEXT.

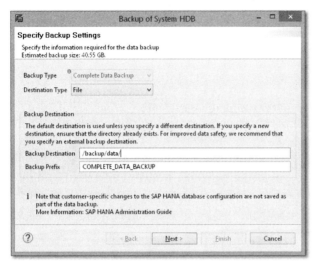

Figure 3.37 Default Backup Location and Description

10. On the next screen, confirm the settings, and then click FINISH.

11. You get a message that the backup is running (see Figure 3.38). Wait for the status to update, and then click CLOSE.

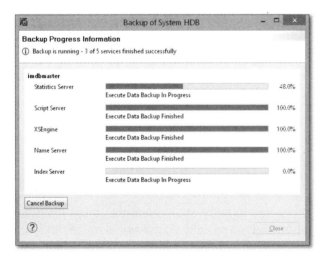

Figure 3.38 Backup Status Displayed during the Backup Execution

12. Confirm the results, and click Close.

What we've shown covers a system backup. The automatic log backup functionality will facilitate the log backups to the specified directories in the Global.ini. We've only covered the very basic backup scenario you would use during the initial phases of your project. Your backup strategy will need to be automated, which is supported by SAP HANA out of the box. All backups and restores can be run from the command line in addition to SAP HANA Studio, the Database Administration Cockpit (DBA Cockpit), or the SAP Database Control Center (DCC; more on this in Chapter 9). Thankfully, SAP has provided an excellent backup script and documentation on how to use that script with Cron in Linux. Attached to SAP Note 1651055 – Scheduling SAP HANA Database Backups in Linux, you'll find two files. One file is a compressed file with the script and configuration file. The second is a PDF document describing the usage of the backup script. The script can perform multiple functions related to backup paths, naming conventions, retention periods, backup catalog maintenance, and listing backups available. Figure 3.39 is an example from our lab environment. In this example, we keep two days of backups on a shared storage. For good measure, we move one backup to a cloud location daily. This ensures that we can restore in the event of an appliance or storage failure.

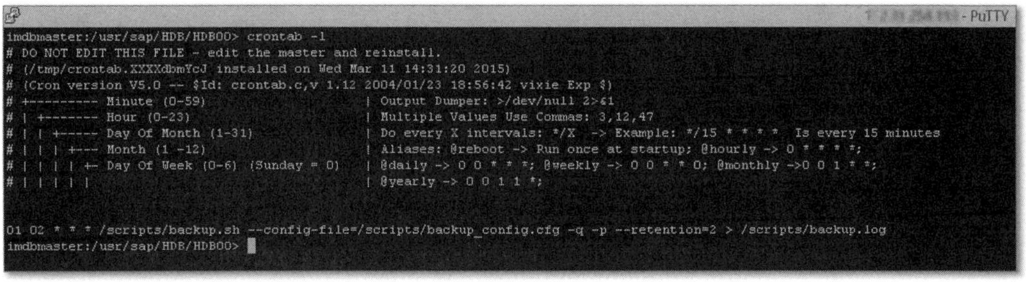

Figure 3.39 Retaining Backups for Two Days Using the Retention Parameter

3.4.2 Recovery

The recovery tools in SAP HANA include features you expect from a modern database. You can recover to the latest point in time or a specific point in time, and you can use the recovery tools to restore to a new system to create a copy of the database. Unlike backups that can be run while the database is operational, the recovery process must be done while the database is shut down. Here are some other restrictions that apply when attempting to recover a database:

- At the start of the recovery, all data and log backup files must be accessible in the system or via the third-party backup tool.

- To recover the database, you need at least one full database backup.

- The recovery must be executed on a system that is the same release or higher than the source system.

- You can't pause and resume a restore. After the restore starts, you can cancel; however, the database will be left in an inconsistent state.

- There are no restrictions on restores from multinode systems to single-node systems or the reverse.

- The permanent license is restored if the system ID and landscape ID haven't changed. If either has changed, a temporary license will be installed that is valid for 90 days.

In Figure 3.40, you can see three options to recover your SAP HANA database. During the SAP Business Suite on SAP HANA project, you may want to restore the database in multiple scenarios.

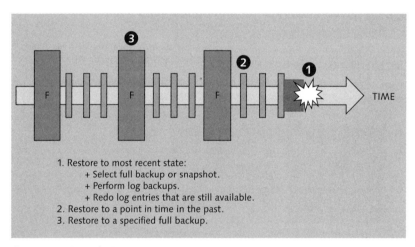

Figure 3.40 Example Restore Scenarios

In one example, you might want to run your cutover procedures multiple times to develop the shortest execution strategy. In this scenario, you complete an SAP Business Suite on SAP HANA migration, take a full backup, and then let your team execute the cutover plan. After they finish, you can validate the system. If the timing was too long, or something wasn't correct, you'll need to restore the database and try again. Without the backup and restore scenario, you would have to run the entire migration again. Another scenario includes a QA refresh after the production go-live. In this scenario, you execute your go-live cutover procedures and system validation, and right before you release the system to the end users, you take a backup. You then restore that backup to the QA system as a system copy to provide a working copy of production to support defect resolution.

Your SAP NetWeaver administrators will become very familiar with your backup and restore process. Now, let's walk through an example database restore using SAP HANA Studio. There are command-line options to perform the restore as well.

1. Log on to the SAP HANA database using SAP HANA Studio, which you downloaded and installed in Section 3.4.1.

2. Right-click the system, and select Backup and Recovery • Recover System (see Figure 3.41).

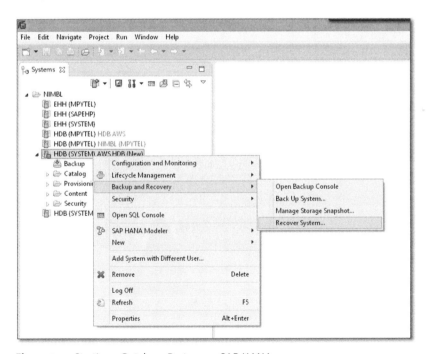

Figure 3.41 Starting a Database Restore on SAP HANA

3. Enter the <SID>ADM user ID and password if prompted.

4. Confirm that the database can be shut down.

5. Specify the recovery type by selecting RECOVER THE DATABASE TO THE FOLLOW-ING POINT IN TIME to simulate the restore you might run during the project (see Figure 3.42).

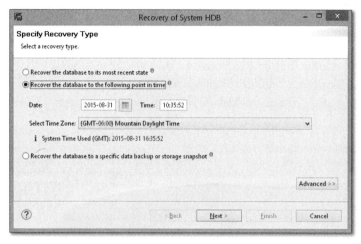

Figure 3.42 Selecting the Point in Time for Recovery

6. Click NEXT, and choose the LOCATIONS of the backups (see Figure 3.43). You can add multiple locations here, for example, the "cold" storage location.

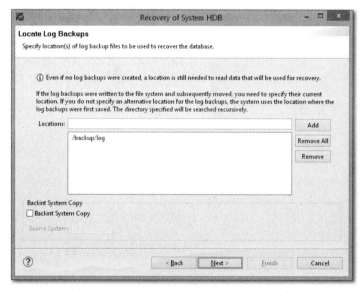

Figure 3.43 Selecting Locations for Backups

7. An overview of the data backups is displayed (see Figure 3.44). You can manually input an ALTERNATIVE LOCATION, and then click CHECK AVAILABILITY.

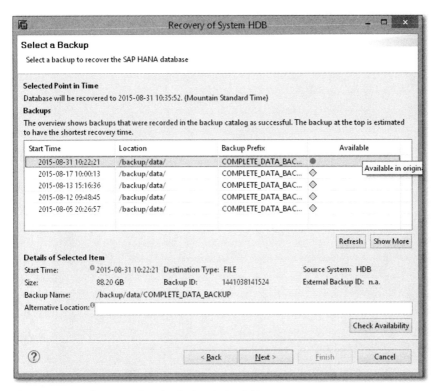

Figure 3.44 Confirmation that the Backup Is Available

8. Select the data backup, and choose NEXT.

9. The wizard now lets you choose some additional options. You can select USE DELTA BACKUPS to potentially shorten the restore time if they are available.

10. Click NEXT after you've confirmed your options (see Figure 3.45).

Figure 3.45 Additional Restore Options for SAP HANA

11. Review the summary screen, and click Finish to begin the restore. You should see a progress screen like the one shown in Figure 3.46.

12. If successful, you'll see the message System <SID> recovered (see Figure 3.47). Click the Close button, and confirm that SAP HANA services have been started.

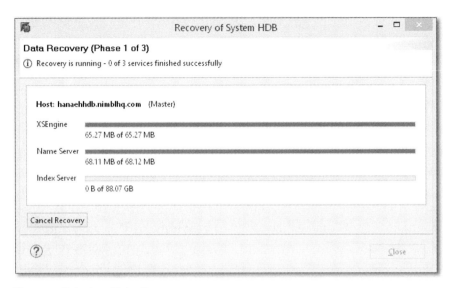

Figure 3.46 Restore Status Screen

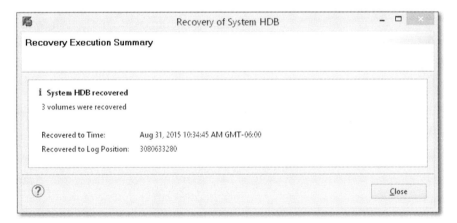

Figure 3.47 Summary Screen Confirming Restore Complete

3.5 Summary

In this chapter, we focused on some of the infrastructure requirements needed to prepare your landscape for the SAP Business Suite on SAP HANA migration. Your organization will need to manage multiple types of change during the project.

Your technical team will be managing a new hardware platform, learning to manage a new database, and potentially making changes to a landscape that has been stable for several months or years. These will be challenging times. However, you can mitigate risk by following the guidelines and best practices published by SAP. Performing the ABAP and Java stack split early on, in addition to the enqueue server split, will save time and reduce risk during the actual migration to SAP Business Suite on SAP HANA.

In the sizing section, you learned about the varied sizing activities you can perform. You can initially perform a rough sizing; however, the ABAP report provided by SAP is so simple to install there really isn't a need to guess. It estimates the required size of the SAP HANA appliance from your current production environment, to which you can add the SAP recommended 20% for safety purposes. Finally, in the sizing section, we talked about the user-based and throughput-based sizing. The user-based sizing requires more time than the ABAP report because you need to sort your users by functional area into activity types. The more accurate throughput-based sizing requires significantly more effort due to the extensive data you need to collect about your organization. Remember that bad sizing estimates can be mitigated by running a performance test during your project. Performance testing tools can now be purchased on a term basis (e.g., 60 days), utilized for the project, and then decommissioned after your project is complete. The performance test is the insurance policy for not collecting or focusing enough energy on a throughput sizing.

We ended the infrastructure topic on backup and recovery. While this section was merely an introduction to the options available with SAP HANA SP 09, you should now appreciate how important those tasks will be to your project. Depending on your landscape strategy (five-system or four-system), your team might be performing several restores or system copies over the life of the project. The features we covered in this chapter were focused on SAP HANA SP 09 and below. We know that SAP has planned innovations in SP 10 to include new backup types and capabilities, but your SAP Business Suite on SAP HANA backup and recovery strategy probably won't need to change unless the business is asking for higher Service Level Agreements (SLAs). You still have the ability to perform periodic weekly, monthly, and ad hoc full backups whenever required. The policy governing when and why SAP ERP is backed up won't change. However, the procedures and documentation of the tools will need updating.

Planning for security in your SAP landscape extends beyond SAP ERP roles and profiles. In this chapter, we'll highlight some key areas of new concern when implementing SAP Business Suite on SAP HANA.

4   Security Planning

When discussing system security and, in particular, SAP Business Suite on SAP HANA security, it's helpful to remember that an attacker only needs to find one way to compromise a system, but an organization and security practitioner must defend against all attacks. It's not necessarily fair, but it's helpful to remember. The goal of this chapter is to give you an understanding of the controls you should consider when implementing SAP Business Suite on SAP HANA in a way that covers the common attack vectors used to compromise the confidentiality, availability, and integrity of data within an SAP Business Suite on SAP HANA system post-migration.

That said, security for SAP NetWeaver AS ABAP and SAP NetWeaver AS Java with a SAP HANA backend is similar in scope to controls needed for other database platforms. Organizations that have spent the time investing in developing organizational security capabilities will be able to leverage much of the knowledge and skillsets they already have when it comes to securing their digital assets managed within SAP Business Suite on SAP HANA. Consider that authority check statements in ABAP code will remain the same during the upgrade process, which means that roles will still allow access to transaction codes, functions, Business Application Programming Interfaces (BAPIs), Business Add-Ins (BAdIs), and so on as expected; and user master records will perform as expected as well. System logging will essentially be the same, which means that mitigating controls relying on review of change documents, system logging, and the like will perform the same way they did before. For most SAP customers, this means SAP ERP audit controls should remain the same or only require minor tweaking.

The impact for customers migrating to SAP Business Suite on SAP HANA is similar to organizations migrating from one major database platform to another. For example, an organization migrating from the Oracle database platform to the Microsoft SQL Server, which has invested time in Oracle hardening procedures, in defining authorizations and roles within Oracle, and has patch and backup strategies in place for Oracle, will have to redevelop these controls for Microsoft SQL server. Similarly, an organization migrating to SAP HANA will need to spend the same time developing these controls for their SAP HANA systems.

In this chapter, we'll map the key security controls needed for SAP HANA against a risk-based framework, beginning with a discussion around security configuration specific to SAP Business Suite on SAP HANA and moving into some application-level security. We'll define some of the key controls needed, including authorizations needed for some common user types you'll need to create before, during, and after the migration of SAP Business Suite on SAP HANA. The SAP migration tools will create a schema in SAP HANA and the necessary service accounts, so we'll also talk about the accounts created by the tool, their use, and how to secure them. Due to the nature of SAP HANA and its capabilities, you may need direct access to the database to utilize data modeling capabilities. We won't focus on security for data modeling for analytics, but we'll provide details on how to enable secure access for ABAP developers to enable them access to the latest SAP HANA features.

We'll end this chapter with a discussion of long-term maintenance and planning for patch management of SAP Business Suite on SAP HANA as it relates to security. What can you do to stay ahead of and monitor your security risk? You'll end this chapter with a better understanding of the new responsibilities, controls, and resources your organization will need to apply for securing SAP Business Suite on SAP HANA.

4.1   Risk-Based Approach

A risk-based approach to SAP security is one that identifies the assets you're trying to protect, understands the threats, and assesses the vulnerabilities. For example, one asset you want to protect is SAP Business Suite on SAP HANA. A threat could be the destruction or theft of data, and the vulnerabilities can be both technical and social. Technical refers to known vulnerabilities documented by SAP at the application level or OS level as documented by your OS vendor, and social refers to the identification procedures your organization has in place for password resets and new user ID setup.

The chapter assumes that your organization actively uses a risk-based approach to assess risk within the organization networks and to prioritize the additional controls needed by your organization as it seeks to continuously improve its security posture to meet current threats. That said, the focus of an organization's risk assessment is often based on compliance mandates such as Sarbanes-Oxley (financial statements), HIPAA (personal health information [PHI]), data privacy regulations (personally identifiable information), and the like. In many cases, these are what many organizations think of protecting when assessing risk in the organization.

However, a lot of organizations undervalue the impact a loss of confidentiality on other types of data may have for the organization. Consider the following scenarios:

▶ One organization we've worked with saw customer attrition rates nearly double in one year and stay at that rate for a sustained period. Subsequent investigation revealed that a competing organization had obtained that organization's customer master list, allowing them to target and lure away their customers at a rapid pace.

▶ For manufacturing customers, the bills of materials (BOMs) for products maintained within customer SAP systems often contain proprietary data and are important components of the intellectual property of that organization.

▶ Data maintained in Project Systems (PS) may contain information about strategic initiatives and organization within the company, which could be useful to competitors.

In short, the long-term effort many organizations have undertaken to get rid of data silos and integrate data within SAP ERP, SAP ERP Human Capital Management (HCM), SAP Customer Relationship Management (SAP CRM), and SAP Supply Chain Management (SAP SCM) systems means that a lot of the critical data assets of that organization are often concentrated in a few key systems. When undergoing a risk assessment to prioritize control effectiveness, organizations undervalue the data within those systems at their peril.

4.2   Initial Security Implementation

We begin our discussion of the controls many organizations will need to consider when implementing SAP Business Suite on SAP HANA with those necessary for the initial security implementation. In this section, we'll cover controls and considerations for infrastructure security, security configuration, and encryption. While some of this information might seem the responsibility of others, we hope it starts a conversation many organizations don't have until it's too late. We often see the security function of an IT organization reside within the infrastructure group with SAP treated as "another" application. SAP ERP contains customer and partner data, yes, but it also often contains trade secret information about products and the manufacturing process. This section will help guide you on the path to securing SAP.

4.2.1 Infrastructure Security

Planning for security while architecting the SAP Business Suite on SAP HANA landscape allows an organization to future-proof the security of its SAP HANA investment. Minimizing which network services can be accessed by which systems allows an organization to implement an in-depth defense approach, making it more difficult for an attacker to access the digital assets maintained within the SAP Business Suite on SAP HANA systems.

The following guidelines are intended to give an organization design principles that can be used to design security into the network layer. Firewalls are a key component in implementing infrastructure security, so we'll address them specifically. Database access firewalls, web application firewalls, intrusion prevention systems, data loss prevention (DLP) systems, and data extrusion prevention systems all play supporting roles, but because all organizations have an investment in firewalls, it's our primary focus in this section.

The following are key infrastructure controls to consider implementing in your SAP Business Suite on SAP HANA landscape:

▸ Ensure that Internet Communication Framework (ICF) services in your SAP NetWeaver AS ABAP systems are enabled on a demonstrated need-to-have basis.

▸ If services in your SAP Business Suite on SAP HANA landscape are available to users outside of the corporate network, terminate those connections on a system in the demilitarized zone (DMZ). All data flows from your DMZ to your corporate network should be allowed on a demonstrated need-to-have basis and should be reviewed and evaluated on a regular basis.

▸ Set up firewall rules so that only clients with a demonstrated need to access SAP HANA can directly access SAP HANA services. Often, organizations allow access to SAP NetWeaver AS ABAP and SAP NetWeaver AS Java from all networks where clients accessing SAP services are located. However, the only people needing to access the SAP HANA services directly are typically IT personnel, that is, SAP HANA administrators, developers, and so on.

▶ Consider either (1) implementing two-factor authentication to machines with administrative access to SAP HANA, or (2) implementing two-factor authentication for all administrative access. If you look at SAP HANA vulnerabilities released in 2014 and 2015, the risk of all of these could have been mitigated to what most organizations would consider acceptable levels by implementing at least one of these two controls.

4.2.2   Security Configuration

As of the time of this writing, a significant percentage of the monthly security patches released by SAP on each patch Tuesday fix SAP HANA vulnerabilities. In fact, 2014 saw 11 vulnerabilities patched by SAP; in 2015, we've seen an increase in the rate (1.3 per month vs. 0.9 per month) of SAP HANA vulnerabilities released. All but one in 2015 has been released with high priority.

When migrating to any SAP HANA-based system, including SAP Business Suite on SAP HANA, it's important to ensure that organizational hardening processes are updated to include SAP HANA-specific hardening steps.

The following are key controls to consider in your hardening process for SAP HANA systems:

▶ **Develop standard hardening procedures for your SAP HANA systems.**
Your organization most likely has standard hardening procedures for the host OS; if not, this is a great time to develop hardening procedures for the host OS as well.

▶ **Ensure all OS patches and SAP HANA patches are applied prior to releasing to user acceptance testing (UAT).**
When executing your test cycles we will ideally have implemented a code freeze for all levels of the application stack to ensure a consistent, valid test cycle.

▶ **Ensure that password management policies within the SAP HANA system are consistent with organizational password policies.**
Password policies are controlled via parameters in the *indexserver.ini* configuration file, and they can be used to define the following:

- ▸ Minimum password length

- ▸ Required characters

- ▸ Number of allowed logon attempts

- ▸ Account lockout period

- ▸ Maximum and minimum password life

- ▸ Password expiration notification

The following files can be modified in Transaction ST04, in the DBA Cockpit (in the CONFIGURATION • INI files view), or in SAP HANA Studio under the ADMINISTRATION perspective in the CONFIGURATION view (SECURITY • SECURITY, under the PASSWORD POLICY tab):

- ▸ If you have a blacklisted set of passwords for your organizations, these can be replicated in table _SYS_PASSWORD_BLACKLIST in your SAP HANA system. Note that this table is empty by default.

- ▸ Change the Secure Storage in File System (SSFS) master key in SAP HANA. The SSFS master key is used to encrypt the root encryption keys of your SAP HANA database. If not changed, the master key is a known value that can be used to decrypt your root encryption keys. More information is available in SAP Note 2183624 (*http://service.sap.com/sap/support/notes/2183624*).

- ▸ Consider implementing two-factor authentication for administrative access to the SAP HANA system. Options for authentication are discussed in Section 4.4.2.

- ▸ Implement auditing policies so that significant security events are audited. SAP HANA-specific options for auditing are discussed in Section 4.5.2 of this chapter. A standardized auditing posture should be developed so that key security events are logged and proactively reviewed for suspicious activity.

▸ **Ensure that audit logs are replicated to a central location.**
An attacker compromising a SAP HANA instance could manipulate the logs to cover his tracks. Replicating audit logs to a central location makes the task of covering tracks significantly more difficult.

▸ **After creating named administrator accounts and a copy of the SYSTEM account, disable the SYSTEM account.**
If necessary, the SYSTEM account can be reactivated by a user with the privilege "USER ADMIN" using the statement ALTER USER SYSTEM ACTIVATE USER NOW. As of this writing, SYSTEM is the only account that needs to be disabled;

other default accounts include <SID>ADM, an OS service account used to authenticate to SAP HANA resources on behalf of the ABAP/Java instances, and technical users that can't be logged in directly. Technical users include SYS, _SYS_AFL, _SYS_DATAPROV, _SYS_EPM, _SYS_REPO, and _SYS_STATISTICS.

► **Execute Report HANA_Configuration_MiniChecks, and validate that no checks come back as critical.**
Keep in mind that multiple version of this report may be found (Report HANA_Configuration_MiniChecks_SSS, Report HANA_Configuration_Mini-Checks_Rev90+_ESS, etc.). A lot of these checks can indicate administration configuration issues as opposed to security issues, but as these may impact data availability, they can also be considered security issues! The following alerts in particular may indicate security problems:

  ► 57: SSFS consistency

  ► 62: Expiration of database user passwords

  ► 63: Granting of SAP_INTERNAL_HANA_SUPPORT role

  ► 64: Total memory usage of table-based audit log

Additional information can be found in SAP Note 1999993 at *http://service.sap.com/sap/support/notes/1999993*.

► **Implement SAP Note 1986645 to ensure nonadministrative users can't connect to the SAP HANA database.**
In Section 4.2.1, we discussed firewalling access to SAP HANA management services so that only specific systems can access SAP HANA administrative services. This note can also be implemented to augment this control and restrict access to the SAP HANA database to administrative users only via SAP HANA user permissions.

4.2.3 Encryption

Encryption allows sensitive data to be stored and transmitted in such a way that an attacker with full access to the conversation or stored data still won't be able to decipher the meaning of that data—it will be useless to them.

In the past, best practice has indicated that sensitive data transmitted over public networks should be encrypted. The most recent version (as of this writing) of the Payment Card Industry Data Security Standard (PCI DSS), version 3.1, still only requires that sensitive cardholder data be encrypted over open, public networks.

That said, organizations encrypting data over private, internal networks achieve two key capabilities: (1) staying ahead of compliance mandates around encrypted communication in the future, and (2) achieving a security posture that significantly reduces the risk of loss of data confidentiality via man-in-the-middle attacks.

Encryption can be used to protect data in motion (over the network), and data at rest (in persistent storage). Both should be considered when implementing encryption with your security controls framework. All SAP HANA installations include CommonCryptoLib, the update to SAPCRYPTOLIB. CommonCryptoLib is foundational to both data at rest and data in motion encryption. The OpenSSL library is also installed as part of the OS. In many case, it's possible (but not recommended) to use OpenSSL instead of CommonCryptoLib. However, some security features of SAP HANA are only supported by CommonCryptoLib, and Common-CryptoLib functionality is part of the strategic direction. If you need to migrate from OpenSSL to CommonCryptoLib, you can reference SAP Note 2093286.

Consider the following key controls when implementing cryptographic controls to ensure data confidentiality for data at rest and data in motion:

▸ **Implement data encryption at the persistence layer of your SAP HANA systems.**
Keep in mind that persistence layer encryption isn't a panacea and doesn't encrypt data in-memory, database redo log files, or database backups files. Information on implementing secure storage for AS ABAP systems is available at *http://help.sap.com/saphelp_nw74/helpdata/en/6e/1f87252fd5414eada6c6b4 8a26e440/content.htm*.

▸ **For redo logs and database backups, consider implementing security at the file system level.**
Database backups and redo logs often contain sensitive data; encrypting these at the file system level allows you to encrypt data in these locations.

▸ **Ensure that the SSFS master key has been changed in SAP HANA as part of the hardening process.**
Note that you should never change the SSFS master key after you've enabled data volume encryption. If data volume encryption is enabled, the data will need to be unencrypted, the SSFS master key changed, and then the data reencrypted by reimplementing data volume encryption. Additional information on changing the master key is available in SAP Note 2183624 (*http://service. sap.com/sap/support/notes/2183624*).

► **Encrypt network communication between your AS ABAP and AS Java systems and the SAP HANA system.**
SAP has provided the ability to encrypt RFC communication within ABAP systems using Transaction SM59. Within the JAVA stack we have the option to select a checkbox for JCO RFC encryption.

4.3 Application Security

Application security is a critical component of an organization's security posture. An incorrectly designed application can permit an attacker to bypass every organizational technical control, including firewalls, antivirus, and the like, allowing an attacker to execute database commands within the SAP HANA systems directly in the security context of the ABAP or Java system <SID>ADM OS accounts (which has, among other things, essentially full database access).

Application security for SAP Business Suite on SAP HANA is dependent on secure ABAP and Java application design. SAP as an entity has a mature secure software development program and utilizes the SAP Code Vulnerability Assessment (CVA) and SAP Fortify by HP static analysis tools to systematically find security defects in code. So for most SAP customers, the application security controls for that organization are focused on custom code developed in house or by a third party for that customer.

Note that for most SAP customers following SAP Best Practices for software development, program enhancements won't be necessary, and ABAP and Java code should execute correctly. However, a SAP HANA migration is a great opportunity for a customer to ensure that existing code follows SAP Best Practices to minimize the risk of problems during the upgrade, and CVA and SAP Fortify by HP can both be leveraged to find these types of defects (in addition to other software security defects).

4.3.1 Common ABAP Vulnerabilities

Because we're focusing this chapter on discussing SAP Business Suite on SAP HANA security, most application security vulnerabilities will be in ABAP code. Many or most ABAP security defects are commonly addressed by following ABAP development best practice. These are things that the global ABAP community has

awareness of, even though they may not understand some of the security impli-
cations. Examples of common ABAP development best practice include the following:

- **Verify that in-line SQL statements are allowed via the Exec SQL command.**
  Using EXEC SQL statements is problematic in two ways: it can make migrating
  to a new database platform problematic, and it can be used by a user to escape
  and pass multiple native SQL commands into a database platform. Because all
  SQL-compliant databases allow for both Data Markup Language (SELECT,
  INSERT, UPDATE, etc.) and Data Definition Language commands (such as CREATE
  TABLE), an attacker can take advantage of code using the EXEC SQL command to
  gain essentially full access to the database. This is an example of a SQL injection
  vulnerability, and the best practice is to avoid using EXEC SQL altogether.

- **Don't allow user input to be passed into dynamic ABAP code generated at
  runtime.**
  Passing user-defined variables into the statements GENERATE SUBROUTINE POOL,
  PERFORM, INSERT REPORT, or GENERATE REPORT can allow an attacker to execute
  arbitrary ABAP code dynamically, giving them full access to the resources managed by the ABAP instance. User input passed into these routines should be validated—typed, checked against blacklisted values and strings, and so on—prior
  to being passed into these statements. This is an example of a code injection
  vulnerability.

These are just two examples of types of security defects that can be used by an
attacker to escalate privileges within an SAP Business Suite on SAP HANA system.
Unfortunately, in our experience, this is an area many security practitioners fail
to take responsibility for. Many security team members make the assumption
that the ABAP developers are doing their job and following secure software
development practices, and while there are a lot of security-conscious developers
out there, there are also a lot of developers who are challenged to produce working code under tight deadlines who are willing to "find security issues in UAT."
Additionally, many ABAP developers will naturally become defensive when
asked if they are following secure software development practice and when they
are questioned on specific issues within their custom code. SAP customers need
to ensure that someone within the organization has the responsibility of ensuring
that security defects are tested, identified, and addressed—preferably early on
within the software development lifecycle because defects found early in the lifecycle are the least expensive to fix.

4.3.2   Recommendations for Managing Application Security

Fortunately, SAP has solutions available to address these concerns. Integrated into all SAP NetWeaver installs is Code Inspector, which gives developers the ability to perform static analysis on reports, BAPIs, and so on and receive information on security defects within the code. If a customer wants a holistic, project-based view of all ABAP security defects, SAP's Code Vulnerability Analyzer (CVA) is an additional license that gives a holistic view of defects in all objects within a project. And, if a customer has invested in Web Dynpro Java or Java applications on SAP NetWeaver, SAP Fortify by HP gives customers the ability to perform static analysis on Java (as well as other) code.

Following are key controls to consider when implementing secure applications:

▸ **Designate one person within the organization with the responsibility to ensure that application security vulnerabilities are addressed.**
  It's important that one person, and ideally one without development responsibilities, have responsibility to oversee that secure software development practices are incorporated into the SDLC process.

▸ **Train developers on common application vulnerabilities.**
  Some great resources SAP customers have available to base training on include SAP's guide "Protecting SAP Applications Based on Java and ABAP against Common Attacks," and the OWASP Top Ten – 2013 PDF document (available at *http://owasptop10.googlecode.com/files/OWASP%20Top%2010%20-%202013.pdf*).

▸ **Consider implementing static analysis tools within the unit test and UAT phases of a software development project.**
  Options available include Code Inspector (free), CVA, and SAP Fortify by HP.

4.4   User Security

Another important consideration in planning for security when implementing SAP Business Suite on SAP HANA is user-based security. In this section, we'll discuss the roles you can assign to users, the privileges these roles have, the available authentication options, and what to consider regarding endpoint security.

4.4.1   Access Control

Access control is what most SAP practitioners think about when they think of SAP security—roles assigned to users and the authorizations in those roles. Again, from the perspective of an SAP Business Suite on SAP HANA migration, within the ABAP instances (and within the Java instances as well), the security roles and authorizations shouldn't change much, if at all. UAT of the SAP Business Suite on SAP HANA solution should definitely include testing of security roles to identify potential issues, but for the most part, the same roles used pre-migration should perform as expected and designed post-migration.

However, there are roles that need to be defined within the SAP HANA platform itself to allow access for things such as the following:

- <SID>ADM account
- Administrative access
- Security access
- Developer access

Note that the first of these roles, the <SID>ADM account, is created as an OS user, and access is assigned during the migration process. The Software Update Manager (SUM) uses the SYSTEM account credentials to create the <SID>ADM SAP HANA user privileges needed for the SAP instances to access resources in the SAP HANA platform.

For all roles, you'll want to make sure that your organization plans and tests the SAP HANA access and users needed to support and maintain the SAP HANA-based solution within the SAP HANA platform.

Overview of Privileges within the SAP HANA Platform

A user's ability to perform activities within the SAP HANA platform is controlled by privileges. When a user tries to perform an activity within the SAP HANA platform, that user's privileges are evaluated to see if he has the necessary privileges to access the object. After the correct combination of privileges is identified, the SAP HANA user is allowed to access the resource. If no privilege is found, the user is denied access to the resource by default.

There are five types of privileges that can be granted to SAP HANA users:

- **System privileges**
  System privileges control administrative access for general system maintenance activities. Types of system privileges include DATA ADMIN, EXPORT/IMPORT, LOG ADMIN, and CREDENTIAL ADMIN.

▶ **Object privileges**
Object privileges allow access to specific tables, schemas, and views within the SAP HANA database platform.

▶ **Analytic privileges**
Analytic privileges are used to determine if a user is allowed to access data in SAP HANA information models (e.g., analytic views, and calculation views).

▶ **Package privileges**
Package privileges are used to grant access to packages in the SAP HANA repository.

▶ **Application privileges**
Application privileges are used to grant access to SAP HANA extended application services (XS) applications. Given most SAP Business Suite on SAP HANA customers won't use SAP HANA XS applications, in the context of SAP Business Suite on SAP HANA, these privileges aren't usually a consideration.

Role Design in SAP HANA

Within ABAP applications, authorizations can't be directly granted to end users; in the SAP HANA platform, privileges can be assigned directly to users. However, best practice is to assign users' privileges via roles. In the context of SAP HANA, roles are collections of privileges that can be assigned to a user and can include system, object, analytic, package, and application privileges.

Roles can be modeled in the SAP HANA platform one of two ways:

▶ As runtime objects
▶ As design-time objects

Creating roles created as design-time objects is recommended because these roles can be transported between SAP HANA systems; roles designed as runtime objects can't be transported between SAP HANA systems.

Design-time roles are assigned to users by executing the SAP HANA procedure GRANT_ACTIVATED_ROLE, and they are removed from users using procedure REVOKE_ACTIVATED_ROLE.

Defining Roles for Technical User Access

Multiple repository roles are available to use as a reference when creating technical system roles. However, these are repository objects and so aren't grantable after they are assigned to a user. Best practice is to create custom roles, using the repository roles as references to determine the relevant system, object, analytic, and so on privileges that need to be assigned to customer-defined roles.

A limitation of role administrators is that role administrators can't assign a privilege to a user or to a role that they themselves don't have. An administrator must have a privilege along with the GRANT option to assign that privilege to a role or user. Consequently, role administrators will need a superset of all privileges that they will be granting (with the associated GRANT privileges), at least at role design time, to design and assign the roles within the system.

Table 4.1 outlines reference repository roles and associated privileges needed for each. The user creating this role will need to have all of these privileges.

Function	Roles/Privileges
Security administrator	The following roles are available as references: ▸ sap.hana.ide.roles::SecurityAdmin ▸ sap.hana.ide.roles::SecurityTester ▸ sap.hana.xs.ide.roles::SecurityAdmin The following system privileges may be assigned as well: ▸ ROLE ADMIN ▸ USER ADMIN ▸ AUDIT ADMIN
SAP HANA administrator	The following roles are available as references: ▸ sap.hana.admin.roles::Administrator ▸ sap.hana.admin.roles::Monitoring ▸ sap.hana.backup.roles::Administrator ▸ sap.hana.backup.roles::Operator ▸ sap.hana.security.base.roles::HANACertificateAdmin ▸ sap.hana.admin.roles::* The following system privileges may be assigned as well: ▸ ADAPTER ADMIN ▸ AGENT ADMIN ▸ AUDIT ADMIN

Table 4.1 Example SAP HANA Roles by User Type

Function	Roles/Privileges
	▸ BACKUP ADMIN
	▸ CERTIFICATE ADMIN
	▸ CREATER SCRIPT
	▸ CREATE SCHEMA
	▸ DATA ADMIN
	▸ EXPORT
	▸ LICENSE ADMIN
	▸ LOG ADMIN
	▸ MONITOR ADMIN
	▸ OPTIMIZER ADMIN
	▸ RESOURCE ADMIN
	▸ SAVEPOINT ADMIN
	▸ SESSION ADMIN
	▸ SSL ADMIN
	▸ TABLE ADMIN
	▸ TRACE ADMIN
	▸ TRUST ADMIN
	▸ VERSION ADMIN
	▸ WORKLOAD ADMIN
SAP HANA developer	The SAP HANA developer is a special case. Developers may need granular object access to work with repository objects. They also need to be able to work with packages in the repository, as well as the appropriate system privileges.
	The following system privileges may be considered when developing SAP HANA developer roles:
	▸ REPO.CONFIGURE
	▸ REPO.EXPORT
	▸ REPO.IMPORT
	▸ REPO.MAINTAIN_DELIVERY_UNITS

Table 4.1 Example SAP HANA Roles by User Type (Cont.)

Function	Roles/Privileges
SAP HANA developer	▸ REPO.WORK_IN_FOREIGN_WORKSPACE REPO.MODIFY_CHANGE
	▸ REPO.MODIFY_OWN_CONTRIBUTION
	▸ REPO.MODIFY_FOREIGN_CONTRIBUTION
	The following package privileges are available for creating SAP HANA developer roles:
	▸ REPO.READ
	▸ REPO.EDIT_NATIVE_OBJECTS
	▸ REPO.ACTIVATE_NATIVE_OBJECTS
	▸ REPO.MAINTAIN_NATIVE_PACKAGES
	And finally, developers will need access to execute the database procedure SYS.REPOSITORY_REST.

Table 4.1 Example SAP HANA Roles by User Type (Cont.)

Assigning Roles to Users

After roles are created, they can be assigned to end users as long as the user granting the role has the GRANT option on the role. Roles should be assigned to the security administrator or SAP HANA administrator with the GRANT option selected. As security administrators assign these roles to end users, we recommend that they grant them without the GRANT option.

4.4.2 Authentication

Generally speaking, access to SAP HANA resources is handled at the application server layer. Direct access to the database should be limited to users with a demonstrated need to access, and those users should be authenticated with strong authentication procedures.

Out of the box, SAP HANA supports the following authentication options:

▸ **Username/password authentication**
Basic authentication with a userid and password. We have several options within SAP HANA to define the password complexity and history.

▸ **Kerberos authentication**
Users authenticating with Kerberos must have a database user defined in the SAP HANA database.

- **Security Assertion Markup Language (SAML)**
  Similar to Kerberos authentication, users authenticating via SAML must have a database user defined.

- **X.509 certificates**
  These can be used to authenticate users to XS applications via HTTP/HTTPS, but not to the SAP HANA database directly via SAP HANA Studio.

- **SAP logon and assertion tickets**
  Users authenticated to Portal and SAP Web Application Server systems can be authenticated to SAP HANA resources, provided a database user exists, and all relevant usernames are identical.

Managing Password Policies in SAP HANA

Password policy configuration was covered in Section 4.2.2 of this chapter and can be managed by modifying the INITSERVER.INI file. These files can be modified in Transaction ST04 or the DBA Cockpit in the CONFIGURATION • INI files view or in the SAP HANA Studio under the ADMINISTRATION perspective in the CONFIGURATION view (SECURITY • SECURITY, under the PASSWORD POLICY tab).

> **Note** [«]
>
> More detail about configurable SAP HANA parameters is available in SAP Note 2186744.

Recommendations for Authentication

When considering authentication, we recommend the following:

- Direct access to the SAP HANA database should be limited to users with a demonstrated need to access.

- Users authenticated to the SAP HANA database must be authenticated with strong authentication procedures. Consider implementing complex usernames and passwords, and only allowing access from terminals requiring two-factor authentication to access.

- If username/password authentication is used, implement strong password policies in the *initserver.ini* file. Note that users managing password complexity settings will need AUDIT ADMIN system privileges.

▸ OS users of the host SAP HANA OS must have password policies and procedures commensurate to those at the SAP HANA database level. Ensure the root
and <SID>ADM accounts are protected with strong passwords and distributed
on a need-to-know basis. Consider giving users with a need to access these
account pseudo access without the corresponding passwords to limit those
who have a demonstrated need to know those passwords.

4.4.3   Endpoint Security

Endpoint security is often outside the scope of responsibility for SAP security
practitioners and is usually considered something best left to the server team or
desktop administrators. Regardless, endpoint security is critical to the security of
the SAP system—after all, this is where users authenticate to their SAP applications, view the data, and update data. Endpoints with malicious software mean
that one of the key controls of any system, password-based authentication, can
easily be compromised by an attacker.

Client compromise remains a common theme of the most common attack patterns and thus remains one of the most likely attack vectors for SAP customers.
An organization needs to fully understand the security posture and current status
of its endpoint to assess the risk of its data assets.

The controls for endpoints are outside the scope of SAP controls, but a SAP HANA
upgrade is a great time to reassess the overall risk to data assets maintained in SAP
systems. Outside of stating that antivirus isn't as effective as most organizations
assume that it is and application whitelisting is a far more effective control, orga-
nizational-specific controls are left for each organization to assess. Our recommendations for client security include the following:

▸ **Extend SAP-focused risk assessments to include the connecting clients.**
Depending on the organization, this could include workstations, desktops,
mobile devices, and virtualized systems.

▸ **Log all outbound connections for clients.**
Many organizations don't police or monitor outbound connectivity, or they
have multiple exit points that effectively monitor outbound traffic differently.
Consider carefully logging all outbound activity to a central location.

▸ **Review outbound traffic for suspicious activity.**
Manually, this is a nearly impossible task; consider implementing tools such as

FireEye's suite of products for automating the analysis of outbound activity for anomalous activity.

4.5   Ongoing Security Management

Finally, we'll discuss the security steps you should take on an ongoing basis. It's important that you keep up to date with system patches and you track and monitor activity within your system. This is often referred to as "get secured, stay secured." You don't have the luxury of setting up systems with the latest vulnerabilities patched and then not patching them ever again. As new enhancements are released, you can expect more vulnerabilities to be identified. Even if you don't upgrade or enable new functionality, you still need to stay current. SAP and other enterprise software vendors remain a target of blackhat conventions and corporate espionage around the world. Identifying an ongoing process for patch and vulnerability management is the new normal.

4.5.1   Vulnerability and Patch Management

When migrating to any SAP HANA-based system, including SAP Business Suite on SAP HANA, it's important to ensure that patch and vulnerability management processes are updated to include SAP HANA-specific vulnerabilities and patches/notes. (Remember in 2015, all but one security path was marked High Priority.) As of this writing, the SAP-approved method of managing patches and vulnerabilities is via the security notes hotlink, that is, via *https://service.sap.com/securitynotes*. Make sure your filters are updated to include your SAP HANA-based installations.

Because Report RSECNOTE was deprecated in 2012, SAP customers haven't had an SAP-approved way of automatically validating whether or not a patch has been implemented in their environment. This means that for many SAP customers, patch and vulnerability management is a spreadsheet exercise. Whether or not a specific note has been implemented in any given system is manually tracked, which adds time to the process and introduces an error rate due to the potential for human error.

As of this writing, two non-SAP vendors have introduced products to identify vulnerabilities in SAP products: ERPScan and Onapsis. Both work in a manner similar to the Windows Update utility (and extend this to include Nessus and Metasploit-like functionality), looking for both missing patches and security misconfiguration in SAP systems. Customers seeking to automate their patch management process and reduce human error rate should consider implementing one of these tools.

The following are key recommendations for vulnerability and patch management:

▶ Modify your patch management processes to include SAP HANA systems. Processes should support policy, and you should designate responsibility for SAP HANA patch management, test procedures, and validation procedures.

▶ Modify your filters in your *http://support.sap.com/securitynotes* page to ensure you're notified of updates for SAP HANA-based systems. SAP HANA-specific patches will begin with the three character prefix "HAN" (e.g., HAN-AS-XS or HAN-DB)

▶ Maintain a system or process that allows you to track current status of notes in your SAP HANA-based landscapes.

▶ Implement a process which regularly validates that security notes are implemented correctly to reduce the potential for and correct for human error.

4.5.2 Tracking and Monitoring Security Activity

Monitoring security activity is a key component of an organization's information security program. A good monitoring program allows organizations to respond to changing threat conditions to detect unanticipated malicious activity on the system.

Auditing can be managed in SAP HANA Studio under the ADMINISTRATION perspective (under SECURITY • SECURITY, AUDITING tab). Auditing can also be set and managed via the *global.ini* file. Users making changes to audit levels must have the AUDIT ADMIN system privilege assigned to them (or the corresponding OS-level permissions to *global.ini*).

To enable auditing, navigate to the AUDITING tab in SAP HANA Studio, and select ENABLED. There are three log locations you can send audit events to:

▶ **Database table**
This allows for granular select capabilities, but adds the challenge of managing potentially significant data growth on a system where data storage is relatively expensive.

▸ **CSV file**
This isn't recommended for production systems because the log locations aren't as secure. Also, for multiple instances, the logs are distributed between SAP HANA systems, making centralized analysis more difficult.

▸ **Syslog**
This is recommended because standard OS security restricts access to syslog files. We recommend syslog because this offers your organization scalability and easily integrates into any centralized log management system you have.

There are three audit trail levels available to audit: CRITICAL events, EMERGENCY events, and ALERTS events. ALERTS covers the broadest level of events, EMERGENCY log only covers events classified as EMERGENCY or CRITICAL, and CRITICAL only logs critical EVENTS. Additional information on auditing levels and log formats is available in the "SAP HANA Security Guide" available by choosing SECURITY at *http://help.sap.com/hana_platform*.

When enabling auditing, consider the following recommendations:

▸ Enable auditing in SAP HANA to the syslog facility. The log level should be as high as possible while allowing the organization to retain 365 + 1 days of log data.

▸ Ensure SAP HANA audit logs are collected in a central location. An intelligent attacker will often seek to delete or alter audit logs to remove evidence of malicious activity. Storing log data in a separate system, preferably in a dedicated log management system, makes this task more difficult.

▸ Designate someone in the organization the responsibility to review the logs on a regular basis. Individuals reviewing the logs should look for anomalous activity, including a high rate of failed attempts by a user.

4.6   Summary

Organizations with a mature security program will find that incorporating SAP HANA into their security program can be achieved with an effort similar to that needed to incorporate any other database or application server platforms into their security program. It's not an insignificant process, but it shouldn't cause an undue burden to the information security program.

For all organizations, a SAP HANA migration or implementation provides an opportunity for that organization to reassess its security posture. The organization can take a look at procedures and technical controls that ensure the availability, integrity, and confidentiality of organizational data assets, and reassess security posture in often-overlooked areas such as secure software development, vulnerability and patch management, and security monitoring. You can review how you secure your ABAP application servers, grant access to your primary business system, and manage vulnerability notifications from software vendors. This chapter is meant to start a conversation that, in an ideal world, would have already begun. We do work in the real world, however, where report enhancements, configuration changes, and new functionality sometimes put security in the back seat. Use this migration project as an opportunity to improve and ensure a secure working environment.

Having said all that, the SAP Business Suite on SAP HANA migration won't greatly impact your project as it relates to security. If you choose to keep security controls as-is and not invest in a comprehensive security plan, your SAP ERP environment will operate as-is. Application-level security will migrate as-is, providing end users and administrators within SAP ERP the same access they had before the migration. The installation and deployment of SAP HANA within your landscape provides an opportunity for your organization to put new security controls in place that will help prevent disruptions of service or loss of data from your SAP ERP system as a result of a security-related event.

PART II

Migration

SAP provides the migration tools and applications for the migration to SAP Business Suite on SAP HANA. We'll explore both the planning required and utilities that will help you execute a successful migration.

5   Migration Tools and Options

As you continue your planning and move on to the execution of the SAP Business Suite on SAP HANA migration, you need to get more details on the available tools and options to perform the actual migration. Up to this point, you've defined how to plan for the scope of the upgrade, the team members involved, and how you'll plan for your new technical landscape. SAP has continually improved and enhanced the tools available to SAP customers to perform the migration, a trend which will no doubt continue. The core tools that perform the migration to SAP Business Suite on SAP HANA will remain part of the software logistics toolset (SL Toolset). You already know a little from previous chapters about the Software Update Manager (SUM) and the Software Provisioning Manager (SWPM) (which we'll cover in detail), but we'll also cover several utility type programs to help you plan and execute the migration, including the benchmark migration tool, which will help you estimate the time for the SAP Business Suite on SAP HANA migration without actually performing the migration, and the table comparison utility, which can be used before and after the migration to validate tables. Finally, we'll cover the various approaches supported by SAP. All of these tools make up the SL Toolset. Any enhancements or notification of changes are found under the dedicated SAP Support Portal page for SOFTWARE LOGISTICS TOOLS (*http://service.sap.com/sltoolset*) or under the SAP Community Network (SCN) content area for SOFTWARE LOGISTICS (*http://scn.sap.com/community/it-management/alm/softwarelogistics*).

At this point in the book, you should have a good idea of whether your organization will be able to use the SWPM to simply migrate to SAP Business Suite on SAP HANA or if your organization will need to both upgrade SAP ERP and migrate to SAP HANA using SUM. We assume most organizations will choose SUM even if they are already running the required version of SAP ERP EHP 6 or EHP 7. You'll be incurring business downtime during the migration to SAP HANA, so to make the best use of that downtime, you can use SUM to get your systems to the latest support package level, if not a new enhancement package version. Moving to a new enhancement package will install new components, and, by default, they will only be installed, not activated. Each Support Package Stack (SP Stack) provided by SAP for EHP 6 or EHP 7 will have a corresponding support package level for SAP ERP. At a technical level, your organization will need to decide if these additional components installed will create additional risk beyond the migration to SAP HANA.

5.1 Migration Tools

This section covers all the tools you'll use during the migration, including the SAP Solution Manager Maintenance Optimizer. The Maintenance Optimizer was introduced in SAP Solution Manager 7.0, and, as of July 2015, it can be replaced by the Maintenance Planner. Both tools are available for use as of August 2015. The primary purpose of these tools is to plan the update activity to be performed, prepare the media, and build an instructions file that will be used by SUM or SWPM during the SAP Business Suite on SAP HANA migration. As SAP landscapes have become more complex, these tools have proven to be invaluable in validating the decisions your administrators are making when choosing what software to install.

SWPM and SUM are the primary tools you'll use on the migration to SAP Business Suite on SAP HANA. We'll cover each tool's use case in detail as well as provide some more technical background. As you'll see, each tool performs a complex set of tasks by exporting your entire source database and reimporting it into the target SAP HANA database. In mid-2015, SAP added performance optimization capabilities within these tools so each subsequent migration learns from prior migrations. In essence, as you perform test migrations from sandbox systems, development, and other nonproduction systems, the migration tools will learn how to optimize the processing of data within your environment. So by the time you perform your production migration, you've optimized the process as much as possible.

Two other tools are also available as part of SUM and SWPM: the table comparison tool and the benchmarking tool. These will be essential to validate a migration as well as plan or simulate downtime for future migrations. In this section, we'll cover the installation and usage of these tools, and discuss how their output might affect decisions you make on the infrastructure required to perform the SAP Business Suite on SAP HANA migration. When we simulate the database migration with the benchmarking tool, we select a group of tables that the SAP tools will split into files during the migration. In prior releases of SAP tools, you could perform some table splitting modifications based on your own knowledge of your SAP systems. The tools available today somewhat limit your ability to override how the SAP tools split tables during the migration to SAP HANA. We'll discuss how the SAP tools perform the table analysis, how they determine what tables to load and when, and why table splits should be managed by the application instead of you. Finally, we'll discuss how to generate the migration key needed for a number of these tools, including the actual migration you complete in Chapter 6 and Chapter 7.

This section gives you a detailed understanding of the tools that will be used during your SAP Business Suite on SAP HANA migration. SAP ERP and its associated components can be configured in numerous scenarios. Following the screenshots included in this chapter will give you and your technical teams the guidance required to execute the actual migration. The decisions depicted here are specific to the scenario we built during the writing of this book. Our environment consists of an SAP ERP system will all core modules configured and functioning. We don't have any localizations or third-party add-ons installed. Your screens might look somewhat different; however, the process will remain the same. For example, you might have ABAP add-ons installed for SAP Governance, Risk, and Compliance (GRC), Mater Data Governance (MDG), or Employee Self-Service (ESS). The tools will recognize the components specific to your landscape and might ask for information specific to your organization's SAP ERP system. Regardless of the components you have installed, the phases and tools used in this book will remain the same.

5.1.1 Maintenance Optimizer

The Maintenance Optimizer has been included with SAP Solution Manager since version 7.0 and continues to receive updates in 7.1. It's meant to help organizations plan, track, and organize updates to its systems. The tool leads your administrators though a series of screens to select the updates you plan to apply, validate your selection criteria and dependencies, and then organizes a download basket for you when you're ready to retrieve the software. The Maintenance Optimizer is also meant to provide transparency across an organization so team members can understand how a system was patched previously, with what components, and when. After you create a transaction in the Maintenance Optimizer, it can only be withdrawn but never deleted. It becomes, in a sense, a record as to what software components were applied to your system. The output of the Maintenance Optimizer isn't only a set of files you need to download but also an XML file that will be used as input for SUM. SUM will use this information to set the target software versions during your SAP Business Suite on SAP HANA migration.

Let's walk through the execution of the Maintenance Optimizer for your SAP Business Suite on SAP HANA migration. You only need to execute the Maintenance Optimizer if your strategy is to upgrade and migrate to SAP Business Suite on SAP HANA with SUM.

Prerequisites

The prerequisites of the Maintenance Optimizer are as follows:

- ▸ Maintenance Optimizer can only be executed against systems that have been successfully defined and are managed by SAP Solution Manager.
- ▸ If you have an SAP EarlyWatch Report for the system to be migrated to SAP HANA, then the technical prerequisites have been met. If SAP EarlyWatch Reports aren't being generated for the system to be migrated, you must execute the managed system configuration for the system using Transaction SOLMAN_SETUP with SAP Solution Manager and by following these steps:
  - ▹ Navigate to MANAGED SYSTEM CONFIGURATION.
  - ▹ Highlight the row for the system to be migrated, and select CONFIGURE SYSTEM.
  - ▹ Select MINIMAL CONFIGURATION or FULL CONFIGURATION WITH EWA.
  - ▹ Completed the steps required.
- ▸ You'll need a super user ID (SUSER) associated to your SAP Solution Manager user. You can check this configuration by running Transaction AISUSER.
- ▸ Your SAP Solution Manager user ID will need access like the SAP-provided user SOLMAN_ADMIN.

Executing Maintenance Optimizer

To start executing the Maintenance Optimizer, follow these steps:

1. Log on to your SAP Solution Manager system with a valid user ID and password.

2. Run Transaction SM_WORKCENTER. This opens a browser window.

3. Navigate to the CHANGE MANAGEMENT work center, and select MAINTENANCE OPTIMIZER on the left (see Figure 5.1).

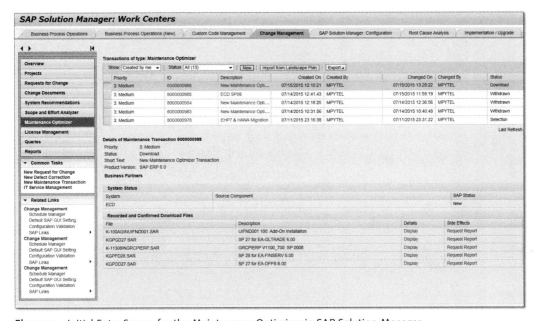

Figure 5.1 Initial Entry Screen for the Maintenance Optimizer in SAP Solution Manager

4. Click the NEW button. This launches another browser window.

5. In the DESCRIPTION field, enter a description for this task.

6. Enter the SYSTEM ID (SID) for the system to be migrated to SAP HANA with SUM, and press Enter.

7. In the PRODUCT VERSION field, select the dropdown for SAP ENHANCEMENT PACKAGE *X*, where *X* is your current version of SAP ERP (see Figure 5.2). If you're not running an enhancement package for SAP ERP, select SAP ERP 6.0 or your current SAP ERP version that is supported by SUM.

8. Click CONTINUE after you've selected your system.

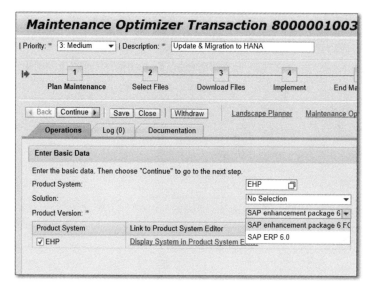

Figure 5.2 Settings to Upgrate and Migrate the System Enhancement Package

9. On the STEP 2 SELECT FILES screen, you can choose either automatic or manual file calculation. For this example, we choose CALCULATE FILES AUTOMATICALLY – RECOMMENDED (see Figure 5.3).

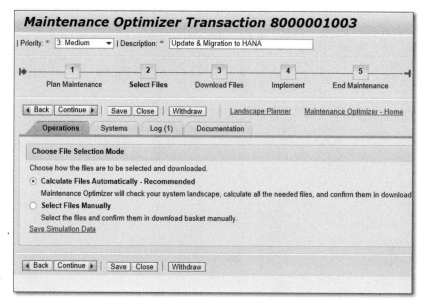

Figure 5.3 Choose How the Files Will Be Selected and Downloaded: Manually or Automatically

10. If you have any warnings at this stage in the Maintenance Optimizer transaction, resolve them now. Errors or warnings at this stage could impact the automated software selection for download.

11. Click CONTINUE after you've confirmed that there are no warnings.

12. The Maintenance Optimizer begins calculating what enhancement packages are available. You can close the window and return to the transaction later or wait for the transaction to complete (typically less than 10 minutes).

13. Next, you're presented with a screen to select the change type (see Figure 5.4). Because we're upgrading an SAP ERP system and migrating to SAP HANA, we select the option SAP ERP ENHANCEMENT PACKAGE FOR SAP ERP.

14. Click CONTINUE.

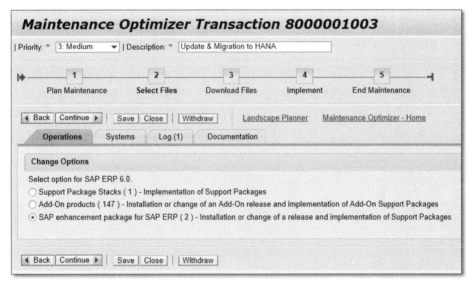

Figure 5.4 Selecting the Change Type in Maintenance Optimizer

15. On the next screen, define the target enhancement package and SP Stack level. SAP recommends selecting the latest available version for both.

16. This screen also displays the TECHNICAL USAGES of your SAP ERP system, which come directly from information stored in the Landscape Management Database (LMDB) in SAP Solution Manager (see Figure 5.5).

   ▶ Verify the information displayed here is correct because it impacts the patch selection process.

▷ If you feel the information is incorrect or missing, withdraw this transaction and resolve any issues using Transaction LMDB.

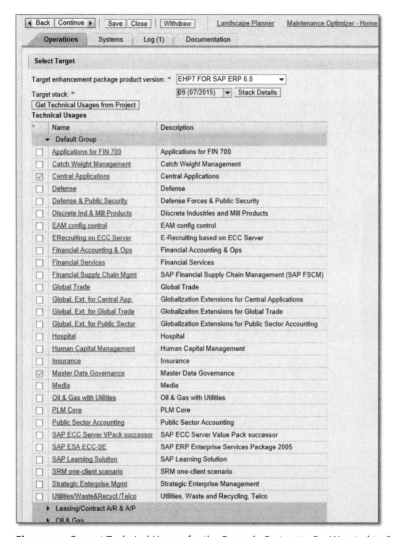

Figure 5.5 Current Technical Usages for the Example System to Be Migrated to SAP Business Suite on SAP HANA

[»] Note

For more information, see SAP's detailed Maintenance Planning Guide for SAP Solution Manager 7.1 SP 05 and Higher at *https://scn.sap.com/docs/DOC-35437*.

The information displayed in the SELECT TARGET screen is meant to describe the system as it stands today. If you plan on adding additional functions, you'll select that functionality later in the Maintenance Optimizer transactions.

If you plan on creating a foundation for the eventual move to SAP S/4HANA Finance, be sure to update applications for FIN 700 to the latest version available.

17. Click CONTINUE after you've verified the selection in Step 2.1.

18. Maintenance Optimizer processes some calculations. You have the option of closing this window and returning later or interactively waiting for the calculation to complete.

19. After Step 2.2 displays results, you'll confirm the target enhancement package and SP Stacks for both SAP ERP and SAP NetWeaver. Click CONTINUE after you've confirmed the target (see Figure 5.6).

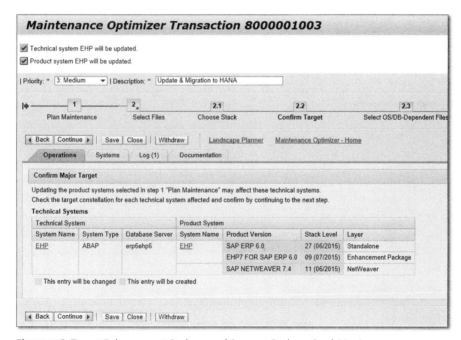

Figure 5.6 Target Enhancement Package and Support Package Stack Versions

20. In STEP 2.3 CHOOSE ADD-ON PRODUCTS, you can select the SAP ABAP add-on components to be included with your patching process. When migrating to SAP Business Suite on SAP HANA and eventually to SAP S/4HANA, you might

want to select multiple add-ons that will prepare your system and provide a solid foundation for functional enhancement teams.

21. In our example scenario, we want to migrate SAP ERP to SAP HANA and include an upgrade. We'll also include the following optional components:

   ▸ SAP SCREEN PERSONAS 3.0

   ▸ SAP SMART BUSINESS FOR ERP 1.0

   ▸ UI FOR EHP 7 FOR SAP ERP 6.0

22. These add-ons will enable your team to access SAP Screen Personas and SAP Fiori for SAP ERP after the upgrade and migration are complete.

23. Selecting additional add-ons is optional. Leave the checkboxes blank, and click CONTINUE (see Figure 5.7), or choose your add-ons to be included with the upgrade and migration, and click CONTINUE (see Figure 5.8).

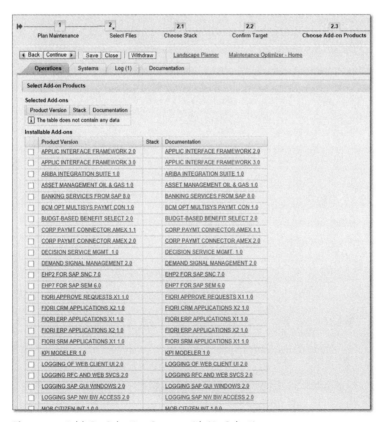

Figure 5.7 Add-On Selection Screen with No Selections

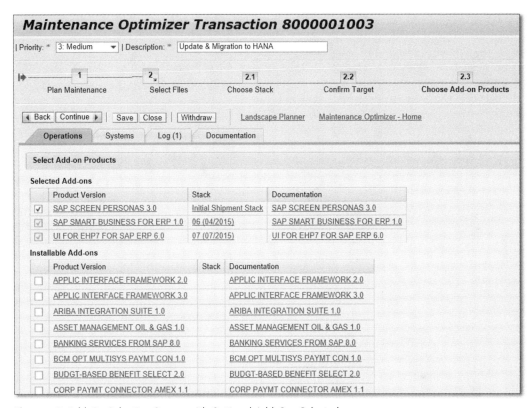

Figure 5.8 Add-On Selection Screen with Optional Add-Ons Selected

24. In STEP 2.4 SELECT OS/DB-DEPENDENT FILES, you need to choose the SAP NetWeaver kernels specific to your operating system (OS). You have the option at this point to also select the SAP HANA kernel.

25. In our example, we're running SAP ERP on Microsoft Windows and SQL, so we select the MS SQL SERVER and SAP HANA DATABASE kernels in Figure 5.9.

26. After selecting your kernel, click CONTINUE.

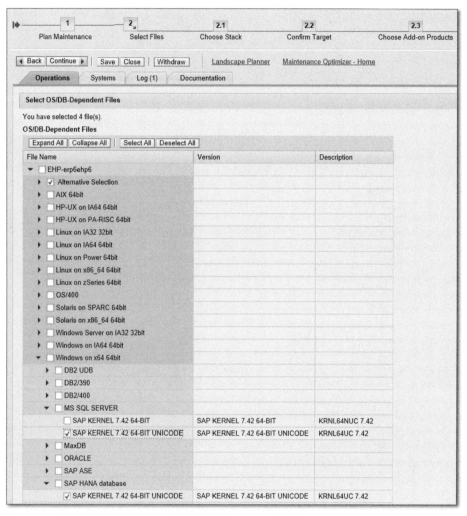

Figure 5.9 Selecting Multiple Kernels in the Maintenance Optimizer

27. In STEP 2.5 SELECT STACK-INDEPENDENT FILES, you see a list of content to be download that isn't dependent on the patching you've selected. Everyone will see updates for SAP Patch Manager (SPAM)/SAP Add-On Installation Tool (SAINT) and ST-A/PI; however, the other objects shown in Figure 5.10 exist because, in this example, we chose to include add-ons as part of the migration to SAP Business Suite on SAP HANA.

28. In STEP 2.6 SELECT STACK-DEPENDENT FILES, you can review and accept the defaults (see Figure 5.11). Click CONTINUE.

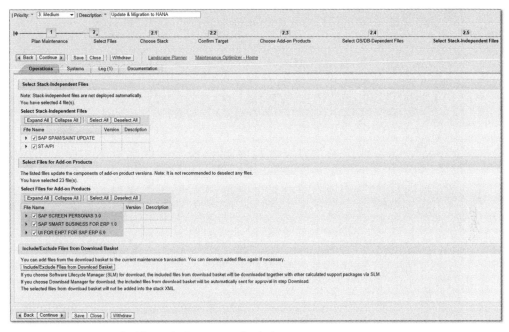

Figure 5.10 Summary of Additional Files to Downloaded

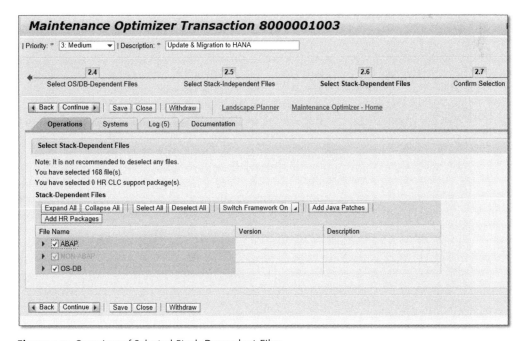

Figure 5.11 Overview of Selected Stack-Dependent Files

29. On STEP 2.7 CONFIRM SELECTION, you confirm that the files will be added to your download basket and click CONTINUE.

30. On STEP 3 DOWNLOAD FILES, you're given multiple status messages on the top of the screen (see Figure 5.12):

   ▸ The first two messages highlight that a text file and an XML file have been written to a directory on SAP Solution Manager within the EPS inbox (*/usr/sap/trans/EPS/in*). These two files will be used in the SUM process.

   ▸ The third line reads that an *X* number of files have been added to your download basket. The files can be downloaded with the SAP Download Manager.

[»]

> **Note**
>
> The SAP Download Manager is an application that can run on any platform to manage the download of files from SAP. It can be installed directly on a server to download the required files for the migration. If you need to know more about the SAP Download Manager or need to install it, go to the SAP Support Portal *http://support.sap.com/swdc*, and choose DOWNLOAD MANAGER • *<Select your Operating System>*.

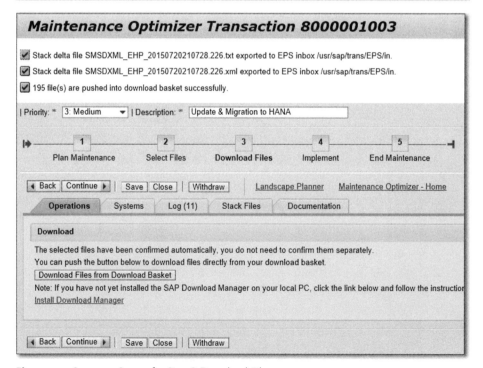

Figure 5.12 Summary Screen for Step 3 Download Files

The two files created on SAP Solution Manager are referred to as the *Stack.xml* or *Stack.txt*. The naming convention represents the SID, date, and time; however, the SAP documentation will simply read *stack.xml*.

31. By clicking on the STACK FILES tab, you can also download these files directly to your desktop (see Figure 5.13). Sometimes this is easier that trying to retrieve them from the SAP Solution Manager system.

32. Click the DOWNLOAD link next to the CROSS-SYSTEM STACK XML text, and save the file to your desktop for use later.

33. Click CLOSE when finished.

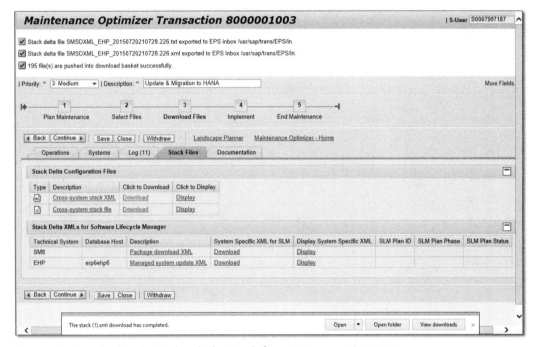

Figure 5.13 Downloading the Stack.xml File Directly from Maintenance Optimizer

34. At this point, you've now identified the target enhancement package and SP Stack version for the migration to SAP Business Suite on SAP HANA. You can begin downloading the files from SAP now, which can take some time. The content of what was selected and downloaded has been documented in Maintenance Optimizer. One common technical mistake on projects is downloading the wrong components when moving from sandbox to development to QA. Your team must execute the Maintenance Optimizer for each system to be

migrated to SAP HANA. It's important that each system to be migrated in SAP Solution Manager has consistent information about that system defined within the LMDB in SAP Solution Manager. To validate the data in the LMDB, you'll use the reporting feature to list the systems you plan on updating to ensure that they are correctly configured.

LMDB Reporting

Use the steps below to quickly report on a system in the LMDB. With multiple output options, this LMDB report is the easiest tool to use.

1. Log on to your SAP Solution Manager with a valid user ID and password.

2. Run Transaction LMDB, which will open a browser.

3. Select the LANDSCAPE REPORTING link (see Figure 5.14).

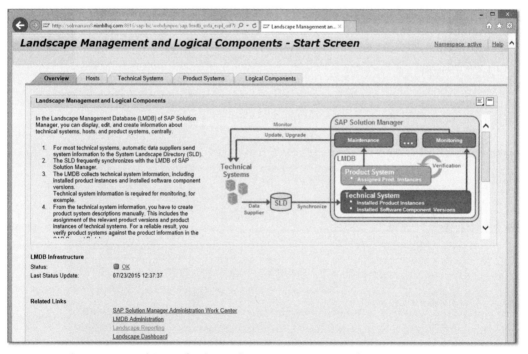

Figure 5.14 Initial Screen for the Landscape Management Database

4. On the next screen, select SAP: PRODUCT SYSTEM from the REPORT dropdown, and click SEARCH.

5. A list of systems and their Assigned Product Versions are displayed. From this screen, you can compare the systems to be migrated to ensure that they are consistently maintained.

6. In Figure 5.15, the two systems ECD and ED1 are in the same landscape, but they are assigned different product versions. You need to resolve these assignment inconsistencies within the Technical System Editor accessed via the LMDB.

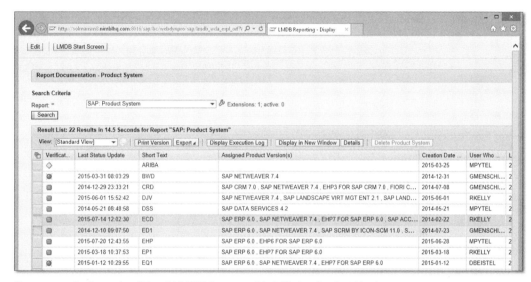

Figure 5.15 An Example of Two SAP ERP Systems with Differing Product Versions

---

Note **[«]**

To learn more about LMDB and how to maintain product assignments, as well as access guides and blogs on editing systems and maintaining consistency, check out the continually updated documentation blog on SCN at *http://scn.sap.com/docs/DOC-29495*.

5.1.2 Maintenance Planner

The next tool we'll discuss is the future replacement of the Maintenance Optimizer. As of August 2015, there is no firm date for the changeover, but the Maintenance Planner can be used today to define your upgrade and migration to SAP Business Suite on SAP HANA. With Maintenance Planner, you still rely on information from the LMDB, so some of the content from Section 5.1.1 will still apply. The Maintenance Planner is an online application hosted by SAP and accessed with your SAP Service Marketplace ID specific to your SAP customer and installation number. SAP Solution Manager shares data with the SAP Service Marketplace. Specifically, it shares with SAP the components you've installed, their patch levels, OS/DB versions, and information stored within the SAP EarlyWatch Reports. This is the same information the Maintenance Optimizer uses to calculate the target system version.

<table>
<tr><td>[»]</td><td>Note</td></tr>
</table>

For a detailed description of all the Maintenance Planner features and functions, navigate to the SCN Wiki for SAP Solution Manager 7.1 at *http://wiki.scn.sap.com/wiki/ display/SM/Solution+Manager+7.1*, and choose MAINTENANCE TOOLS: MAINTENANCE PLANNER AND MAINTENANCE OPTIMIZER near the bottom of the screen.

To use the Maintenance Planner, follow these steps:

1. Log on to the SAP Maintenance Planner (*https://apps.support.sap.com/sap/support/mp*) with a valid SAP Service Marketplace ID and password.

2. Click EXPLORE SYSTEMS (see Figure 5.16).

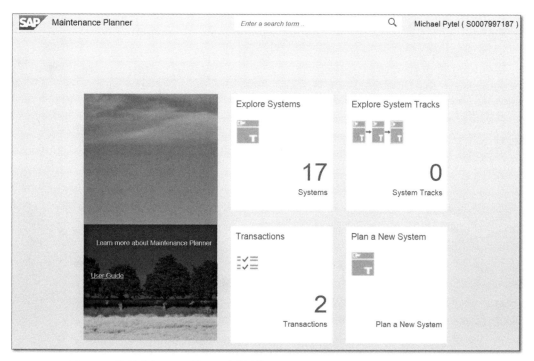

Figure 5.16 Maintenance Planner Initial Screen

3. A list of systems is displayed that have been synchronized to the SAP Support Portal. If you don't see your system, install SAP Note 2002546, and follow the instructions to manually sync your system to the SAP Support Portal.

4. Select the system to be upgraded and migrated to SAP Business Suite on SAP HANA by clicking the System ID. For example, in Figure 5.17, we selected the system EHP.

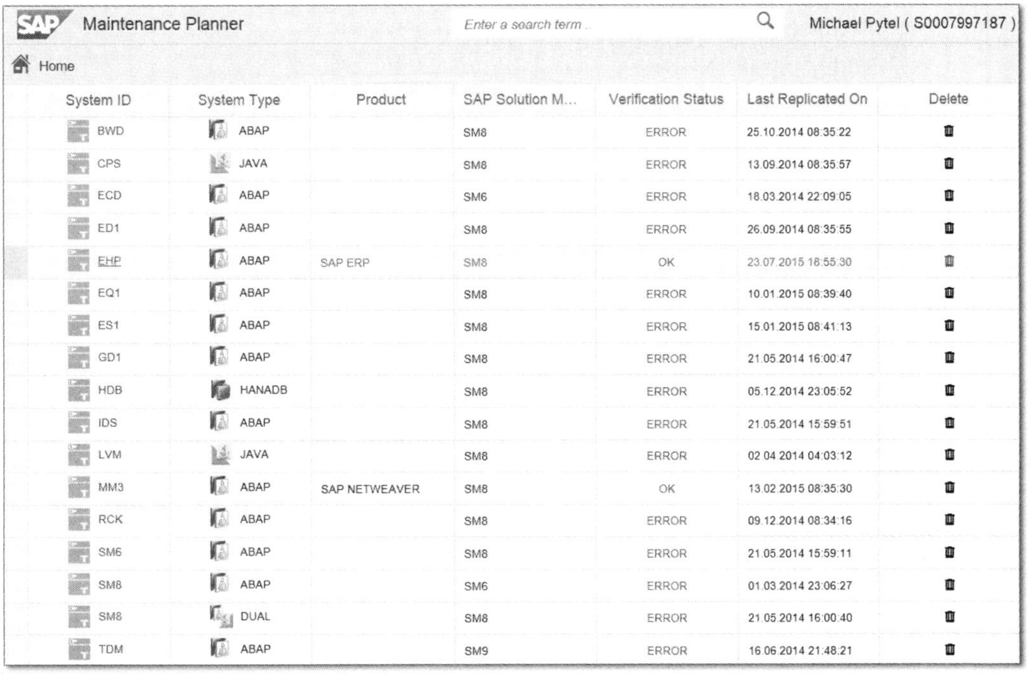

System ID	System Type	Product	SAP Solution M...	Verification Status	Last Replicated On	Delete
BWD	ABAP		SM8	ERROR	25.10.2014 08:35:22	🗑
CPS	JAVA		SM8	ERROR	13.09.2014 08:35:57	🗑
ECD	ABAP		SM6	ERROR	18.03.2014 22:09:05	🗑
ED1	ABAP		SM8	ERROR	26.09.2014 08:35:55	🗑
EHP	ABAP	SAP ERP	SM8	OK	23.07.2015 18:55:30	🗑
EQ1	ABAP		SM8	ERROR	10.01.2015 08:39:40	🗑
ES1	ABAP		SM8	ERROR	15.01.2015 08:41:13	🗑
GD1	ABAP		SM8	ERROR	21.05.2014 16:00:47	🗑
HDB	HANADB		SM8	ERROR	05.12.2014 23:05:52	🗑
IDS	ABAP		SM8	ERROR	21.05.2014 15:59:51	🗑
LVM	JAVA		SM8	ERROR	02.04.2014 04:03:12	🗑
MM3	ABAP	SAP NETWEAVER	SM8	OK	13.02.2015 08:35:30	🗑
RCK	ABAP		SM8	ERROR	09.12.2014 08:34:16	🗑
SM6	ABAP		SM8	ERROR	21.05.2014 15:59:11	🗑
SM8	ABAP		SM6	ERROR	01.03.2014 23:06:27	🗑
SM8	DUAL		SM8	ERROR	21.05.2014 16:00:40	🗑
TDM	ABAP		SM9	ERROR	16.06.2014 21:48:21	🗑

Figure 5.17 Selecting the EHP System for Upgrading and Migrating to SAP Business Suite on SAP HANA

5. After selecting the system, a screen appears that displays four steps required to plan for system maintenance:

▶ Sync

This task should be highlighted in green, which signifies the system was recently synchronized with your on-premise SAP Solution Manager. If not, you can click the Sync button and find more details on the error.

▶ Verify

This task defines the product versions that are assigned to this system. If the button is highlighted in green, then the task is complete based on the data from SAP Solution Manager. If red, click the button and manually verify the assigned product versions. After you click Save, the button will turn green.

▶ Plan
This task walks you through selecting the target enhancement package and SP Stack for the system to be migrated to SAP Business Suite on SAP HANA. This button is essentially the same as running Maintenance Optimizer.

▶ Schedule
This task allows you to set a planned date for the maintenance. This scheduled date is only reflected within the Maintenance Planner application.

6. Click the Plan button after you've verified that Sync and Verify are green (see Figure 5.18).

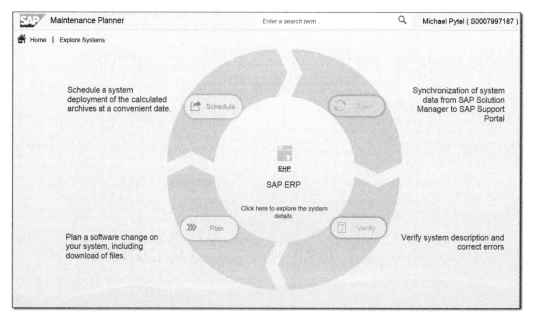

Figure 5.18 Completed Sync and Verify Tasks

7. The first step in the Maintenance Planner, Define Change, allows you to select from two options. In this example scenario, we select Install or Maintain an Enhancement Package to upgrade and migrate this system to EHP 7 on SAP HANA.

8. Next we select the EHP 7 FOR SAP ERP 6.0 radio button and the SP Stack from the dropdown (see Figure 5.19).

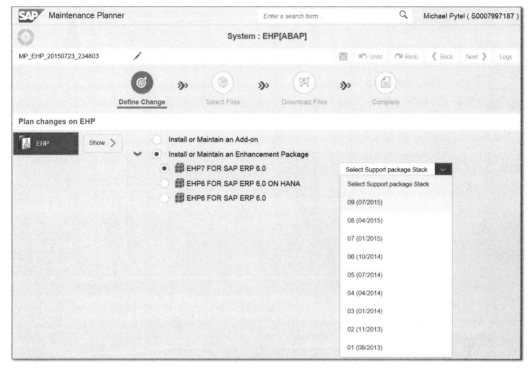

Figure 5.19 Maintenance Planner Displaying Available Support Package Stacks

After selecting the stack level, the PROCESSING message appears.

9. Select the TECHNICAL USAGES that should be defined by default (see Figure 5.20). Click CONFIRM SELECTION when you're done.

10. If you plan on updating your system to the highest level available for a future SAP S/4HANA Finance implementation, then check the APPLICATION FOR FIN 700 box as shown in Figure 5.20. This screenshot covers the upgrade and migration to HANA without preparing components for SAP S/4HANA Finance. Click NEXT in the upper-right corner.

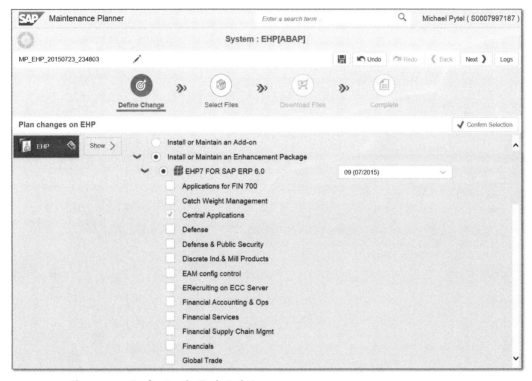

Figure 5.20 Confirming the Technical Usages

11. In the SELECT FILES step, you select the kernel for your OS and DB version (see Figure 5.21). You can also select the SAP HANA kernel at this step.

12. Click CONFIRM SELECTION.

13. Review the files selected for download. Click NEXT after you've confirmed the selections.

14. In the DOWNLOAD FILES step, you have multiple selection options (see Figure 5.22):

   ▸ DOWNLOAD STACK XML: Enables you to download the *stack.xml* file needed by SUM.

   ▸ PUSH TO DOWNLOAD BASKET: Populates your download basket with the files required to upgrade and migrate.

   ▸ DOWNLOAD PDF: Provides a summary PDF document describing the source and target versions for your maintenance activity.

Figure 5.21 Kernel Selection for Your Environment in the Maintenance Planner

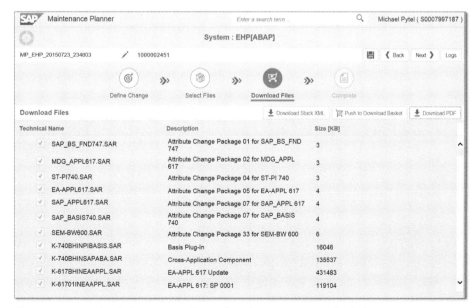

Figure 5.22 Download Files Step Displaying the Objects to Be Downloaded

15. To complete the process to enable future maintenance plans for the same system, click NEXT and then click COMPLETE. Leaving this Maintenance Planner task open prevents new tasks from being created for the same system.

5.1.3 Software Update Manager

Software Update Manager (SUM) evolved from the SAP Enhancement Package Installer and the SAP upgrade tools. We even still see references to the binary SAPup tool in log files and on specific upgrade screens. SUM now has its own product support team and dedicated subsites on *http://help.sap.com* and *http://support.sap.com*, and it receives planned updates multiple times per year. When you begin your project, you'll have a specific SUM release level available. Even though a new release level may become available during your SAP Business Suite on SAP HANA migration, we recommend that you use one version of the SUM tools throughout the life of your project unless told otherwise by SAP Support. By the time you complete your second and third nonproduction migration to SAP Business Suite on SAP HANA, you'll have worked out any bugs or nuances with that specific SUM release. SUM is comprised of multiple tools that might require specific updates to resolve issues. You (typically) won't update to an entire new SUM release during your project.

You only use SUM with the Database Migration Option (DMO) when you want to both upgrade and migrate to SAP Business Suite on SAP HANA in one step. If you're going to migrate to SAP HANA as-is without patching, then move to Chapter 7, which discusses migration using SWPM. SWPM will update your system using, essentially, a system copy and switch procedure. Keep in mind that the procedure defined in Chapter 7 only applies if you're running SAP ERP EHP 6 or above. SUM introduces the concept of a shadow system and can be run for any version of SAP ERP 6. The shadow system is a copy of your system and is installed alongside it. The shadow system receives the planned updates while your original system is still operational. As you might imagine, this requires additional resources (CPU, memory, disk) during the uptime phases. During these initial phases of the SUM update, you'll be running two copies of your SAP system. You need to take this into account as you look at your existing landscape and plan for this additional workload. Adding additional application servers, disk space, and CPU will help the process. You also have the option of running the shadow instance on a remote host when selecting export mode in the UI (more on that in

Chapter 6). In this section we'll talk about the performance-related settings you can modify and explain their impact on system resources.

As mentioned earlier, SUM and SWPM include the table comparison tool and the benchmark migration tool, which we'll cover in Section 5.1.5 and Section 5.1.6, respectively. These tools are included in the SL Toolset when you download SUM. These tools will help you plan and validate the migration to SAP Business Suite on SAP HANA. The preparation for SUM with DMO includes steps that are also required to support the execution of the table comparison and benchmark migration tools. We'll discuss these preparation steps in addition to the startup of the Software Logistics Common UI (SL Common UI). Traditionally, when you execute SUM, you run the STARTUP script and connect to a specific port that opens a Java application on your desktop. The SL Common UI introduces a new UI based on SAPUI5, which depends on the local SAP Host Agent. Updating the SAP Host Agent is one of the several steps you'll execute in preparing your system for the use of SUM.

Downloading Software

First you need to download the latest version of the SUM tools from the SAP Support Portal by following these steps:

1. Log on to the Software Download Center (*http://support.sap.com/swdc*) with a valid ID and password.

2. Navigate to SUPPORT PACKAGES & PATCHES • ALPHABETICAL LIST OF PRODUCTS • S • SL TOOLSET • SL TOOLSET 1.0 • ENTRY BY COMPONENT • SOFTWARE UPDATE MANAGER (SUM) • SOFTWARE UPDATE MANAGER 1.0 • SUPPORT PACKAGE PATCHES • <YOUR OS VERSION>.

3. Download the latest patch level for SUM available in the display to your primary application server (PAS). Save the file in a new empty directory (see Figure 5.23).

4. You also need to download the latest SAP Host Agent for your PAS (see Figure 5.24). The SAP Host Agent can be upgraded with no downtime on your PAS. It doesn't require a server restart or any interruption in service for the SAP application server.

5. Return to the SOFTWARE DOWNLOAD CENTER main page, and navigate to SUPPORT PACKAGES & PATCHES • BROWSE DOWNLOAD CATALOG • SAP TECHNOLOGY

COMPONENTS • SAP HOST AGENT • SAP HOST AGENT 7.21 (or latest available version) • <YOUR OS VERSION>.

6. Download the latest available version, and save to a new empty directory on your PAS.

Figure 5.23 Downloading the SUM Tools from the Software Download Center

Figure 5.24 SAP Host Agent Download from the SAP Software Distribution Center

7. You'll also need a copy of SAPCAR to extract the files on your PAS. SAPCAR can be downloaded from SUPPORT PACKAGES & PATCHES • BROWSE DOWNLOAD CATALOG • SAP TECHNOLOGY COMPONENTS • SAPCAR • SAPCAR 7.21 • <YOUR OS VERSION>.

Updating the SAP Host Agent

To update the SAP Host Agent, follow these steps:

1. Using the SAPCAR utility, extract the contents of the downloaded SAR files for the SAP Host Agent (`SAPCAR -xvf SAPHOSTAGENT<PatchNr>.SAR`).

2. Because this is an upgrade and migration, you can execute the following command as <SID>ADM within the directory where the SAR file was extracted: `saphostexec -upgrade`.

3. After the process completes, navigate to the SAP Host Agent directory to check the version. An example output is displayed in Figure 5.25.

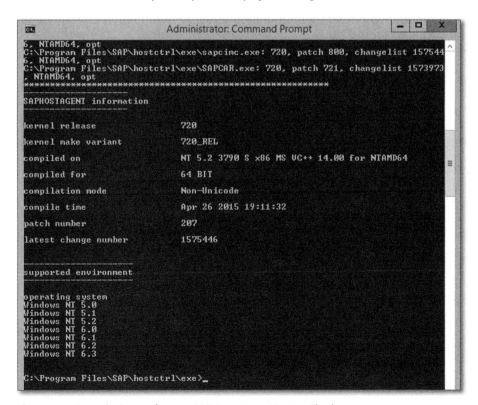

Figure 5.25 Example Output from an SAP Host Agent Version Check

You can execute one of the following commands to verify:

▸ Windows: `%ProgramFiles%\SAP\hostctrl\exe\saphostexec.exe -version`

▸ Unix: `/usr/sap/hostctrl/exe/saphostexec -version`

4. As of August 2015, SUM requires an SAP Host Agent version higher than 203.

Configure SAP Host Agent and Software Update Manager

After you update the SAP Host on the PAS and any application servers you plan on distributing processes to, you need to configure SUM to use the SAP Host Agent for the SL Common UI. Follow these steps:

1. Navigate to the directory where you downloaded the SUM SAR file on the PAS.

2. Execute SAPCAR to extract the files into the current directory or into the */usr/sap/<sid>* directory.

   ▸ SAP recommends extracting SUM into the */usr/sap/<sid>* directory to ensure directory permissions are correct.

   ▸ You may not always have the file space available in */usr/sap/<sid>*, so we've used a directory on a different mount point. If you use a different directory, ensure that the permissions are the same as */usr/sap/<sid>*.

3. Extract the files using the following command:

```
SAPCAR -xvf <download directory>\<path>\<Archive>.SAR -R <DRIVE>:\
usr\sap\<sapsid>
```

4. Navigate to *<SUM Directory>\ABAP*, and run the following command:

```
SUMSTART confighostagent
```

5. Confirm the results on screen. An example is shown in Figure 5.26.

6. At this point, SUM is ready for use. You can test it's availability by accessing the following URL using a web browser:

   http://<hostname>:1128/lmsl/sumabap/<SID>/doc/sluigui/ (where *<SID>* is the SID of the system to be migrated).

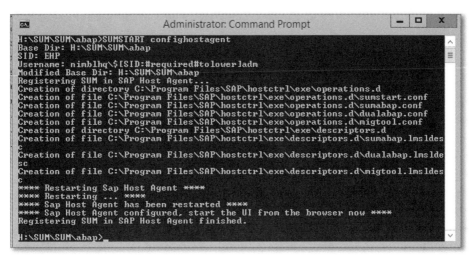

Figure 5.26 Output from the Registration of the SL Common UI with the SAP Host Agent

Advanced Functions

You've got SUM downloaded, installed, and running. Before you start the update procedure, let's cover some of the options you'll be able to select when running the utility. SAP can't predict a specific amount time for uptime and downtime phases of the update process. Every customer system is different. You have variations in your data, the add-ons installed, languages installed, hardware, and so on. You'll find that your initial executions of the update and migration will generally be the slowest. These are typically systems that don't match the production hardware specification; however, they should ideally have a most recent copy of production to begin validating the procedure against. Here are two additional factors that might affect performance:

▶ **Clients**

The number of clients has a substantial impact on the SUM runtime. There are specific phases where client-specific data is imported. If you have multiple clients then the process cascades. Remove any unnecessary clients before starting the procedure.

▶ **Background processes**
The number of background processes in the source system can impact processing. SAP recommends three available background processes during the uptime phases. Monitor your daily background process utilization to ensure that enough processes are configured.

SUM typically offers three preconfigured modes for the execution of the update and migration: single system, standard, and Advanced. We won't cover single system because it's not available when migrating to SAP HANA. The standard configuration will create a shadow instance and is generally a good option to minimize downtime. Your first one or two executions of SUM within your environment should be executed using the standard mode. Using this mode, you'll develop a baseline for performance of the tools and then can determine whether the advanced configuration is required. The advanced preconfigured mode enables more granular control of processing and includes the option of Near Zero Downtime (nZDM). nZDM includes the capabilities to record and replay business transactions, which further reduces the downtime phase. This will require additional hardware resources; however, the cost benefit of the few hours saved in downtime might make sense for your business.

You can also select the SWITCH EXPERT MODE ON option to obtain even more control over the update and migration process. With this option, you can do the following:

▶ Override the support package level originated by the *stack.xml*.

▶ Modify the instance number for the shadow instance.

▶ Use the remote shadow instance.

▶ Remove installed languages.

▶ Use saved profiles from prior SUM executions.

In prior version of SUM, you had RESOURCE MINIMIZED and DOWNTIME MINIMIZED update options. It's assumed with both the standard and advanced modes that DOWNTIME MINIMIZED is used. This method refers to the usage of a shadow instance to perform updates while keeping business users operating in the system.

Near Zero Downtime

nZDM has been available since SUM 1.0 SP 07 and continues to be enhanced. You can use this feature when applying a support package, installing an enhancement package, or performing an upgrade. Relevant source and target releases are defined in Table 5.1 and Table 5.2 along with minimum supported database versions.

Type	Target	Source
Support package	Apply SP 8 or higher (SAP NetWeaver 7.02 SP 8)	SAP NetWeaver 7.0 EHP 2
	Apply SP 5 or higher	SAP ERP 6.0 EHP 5 System
Enhancement package	Install SAP EHP 5+	SAP ERP 6.0 system with SAP EHP 4+
	Install SAP EHP 2	SAP NetWeaver 7.0
Upgrade	SAP ERP 6.0 EHP 7	SAP R/3 4.6C

Table 5.1 Supported Target and Source Releases for nZDM.

Database	Version
Oracle	10g
DB2 LUW	9.7 FP4
DB2 for IBM i	IBM i 7.1 (see SAP Note 1809339)
DB2 for Z/OS	10.1
MaxDB	7.9
SAP HANA	1.00.52
MS SQL Server	2005
SAP Application Server Enterprise (ASE)	15.7.0.122 (see SAP Notes 1926697 and 1990192)

Table 5.2 Supported Minimum Database Versions for nZDM

Note	[«]
See SAP Notes 1678564 and 1678565 for the latest information on nZDM. These SAP Notes provide solutions to known issues with nZDM and provide critical information on how to monitor replication of data.	

Remember, nZDM enables the execution of downtime phase activities during system uptime to preserve the system for business users. This advanced function will increase system utilization and reduce the amount of downtime required. nZDM introduces a new functionality called the Change Recording and Replication (CRR) framework. This framework captures database changes at the table level on the production instance and replays those changes to the shadow instance after table structures have been adjusted. The process is managed by SUM and can be monitored directly in the shadow instance using Transaction CRR_CONTROL. Within this transaction, you stop, start, and restart table replication. You're provided a list of tables with errors that can be restarted individually (see Figure 5.27).

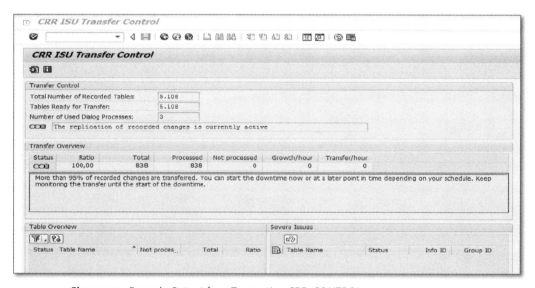

Figure 5.27 Example Output from Transaction CRR_CONTROL

Background Processes and Parameters

When you select standard or advanced mode, you'll have the opportunity to input several performance-related parameters that define the number of processes to be used during the uptime and downtime phases of the migration. When increasing the number of processes for the uptime phases, keep in mind these are resources that will be shared with your production users. Here are some additional details and recommendations for each of the options you can input:

▶ **BATCH PROCESSES (UPTIME and DOWNTIME)**
Number of parallel background processes and activation processes used by `tp` (transport control). SAP has noted a value larger than 8 rarely decreases runtime.

▶ **SQL PROCESSES (UPTIME and DOWNTIME)**
Number of database-level SQL processes to be used. SAP and most database vendors recommend one per CPU core. If you increase this parameter, keep an eye on transaction logging space.

▶ **R3TRANS PROCESSES (UPTIME and DOWNTIME)**
Number of parallel import processes used by Program R3trans to import data into the database. SAP says values larger than 8 rarely improve performance in the SUM guide.

▶ **R3LOAD PROCESSES**
Number of parallel processes used for Program R3Load and table comparisons. In general, you should set the value equal to the number of cores on the application server multiplied by two.

▶ **PARALLEL PHASES (UPTIME and DOWNTIME**
Number of parallel processes used by SAPup during specific subphases of the update and migration. The default of 6 has been useful. Increasing this parameter hasn't significantly reduced runtime.

> **Note** [«]
>
> There is a lot of confusing information within the SAP community and online regarding setting the number of parallel processes. Officially, SAP has posted its recommendations as part of SAP Note 2040118 – SAP HANA: Additional Information - Software Update Manager 1.0 SP 13. This SAP Note is also important because it details known issues and resolutions.

▶ With recent versions of SUM, you can now dynamically change some of these parameters during the uptime phases. When using the SL Common UI, you can connect to *http://<hostname>:1128/lmsl/sumabap/<SID>/set/procpar.* and adjust any parameter displayed as shown in Figure 5.28. When prompted for a login, use the <SID>ADM account and password.

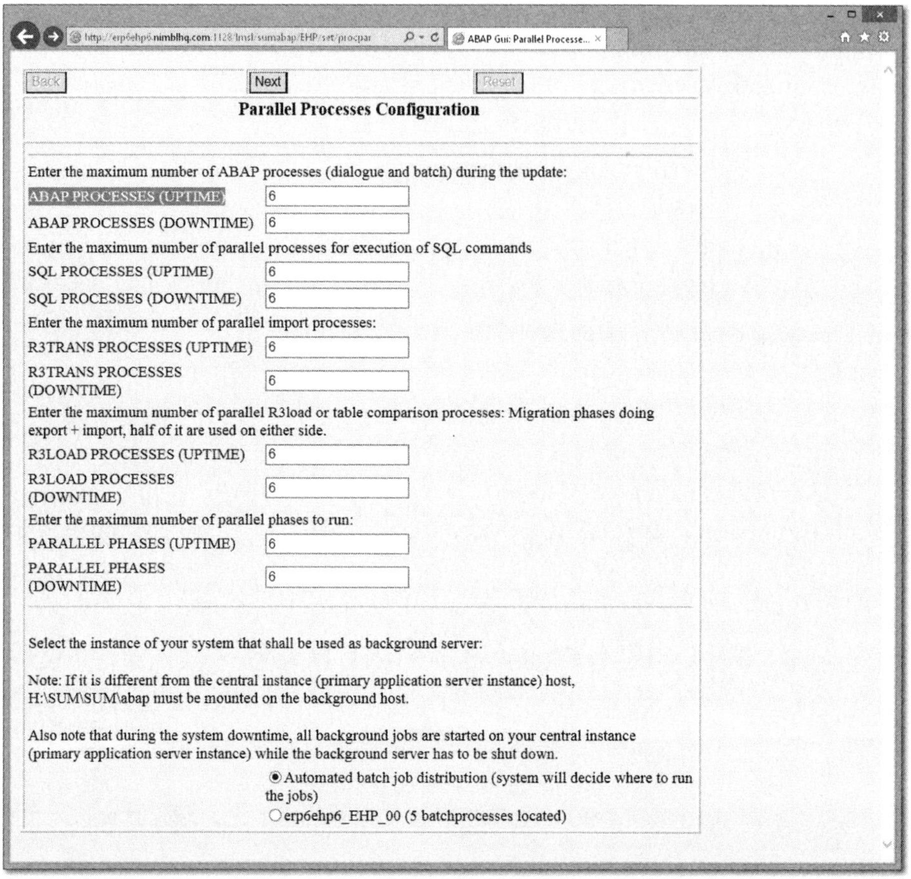

Figure 5.28 Dynamically adjusting parallel processes in the Software Update Manager

Restarting or Resetting the Software Update Manager

You may want to reset or restart SUM with DMO processes at some point. SAP has built in a reset function that can be run at any point in the uptime or down-time processing as long as the source database is still available and as long as you haven't modified or cleaned up the SUM directory. The reset function within the SL Common UI doesn't delete the target database if it was created, restore BRTOOLS, or delete any users created during the process. The feature essentially lets your return your source system to normal operation, but you have to manually adjust anything new created by SUM. For obvious reasons, SUM can't execute the reset function after the migration is complete and the cleanup phase has started. If you need to restart at this point in the migration, a full database and file system restore is required. After you run the reset and confirm the cleanup step, you can replace your SUM directory by extracting a fresh copy of the SUM tools download from the SAP Support Portal.

To reset SUM, follow these steps:

1. On any step prior to the execution step, click the Reset button shown in Figure 5.29.

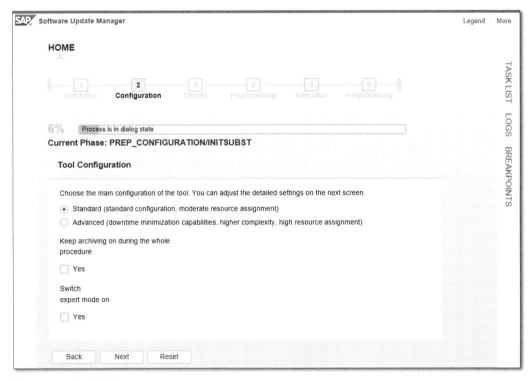

Figure 5.29 Reset Button

2. Confirm that you want to reset the procedure by selecting the Yes radio button and clicking Next (Figure 5.30).

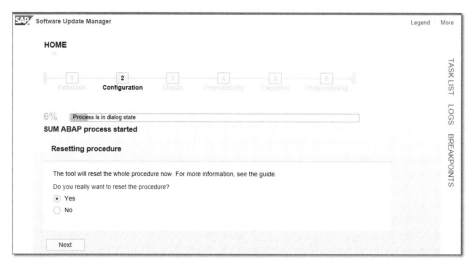

Figure 5.30 Confirming the Reset Procedure

3. You receive a confirmation that the reset procedure completed as shown in Figure 5.31. Click the CLEANUP button to remove any temporary and log files from the SUM directory.

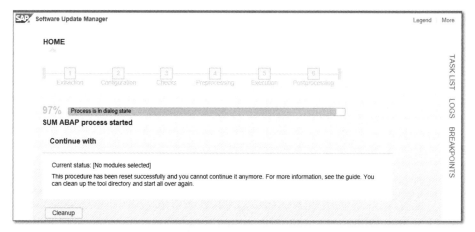

Figure 5.31 Final Confirmation That the Reset Process Is Completed

Logs and Troubleshooting

Within the SL Common UI, there is some additional functionality to display logs while the update is running. You can generate a support file for SAP Support directly from the MORE button within the UI (shown in Figure 5.32), and you can tail specific logs to view updates, errors, or warnings (see Figure 5.33). The underlying SUM directory structure is the same as previous versions. When troubleshooting issues, you'll first navigate to the *<sum directory>\ABAP\log* to view the latest logs file from the update process. It might also be helpful to view logs within the *<sum directory>\ABAP\tmp* directory. Let's review some of the log types within the log directory:

▸ **SAPupchk.log**
General overview of the preparation roadmap steps.

▸ **SAPup.log**
Another general overview file during the update roadmap steps.

▸ **TP log files**
Files beginning with *SLOG <rel>*, *ALOG<rel>*, and *ULOG<YY_Q>* are related to procedures called by `tp`. You can tail these files but should never open them for editing.

▸ **<Phase>.ELG**
These files contain errors or warnings specific to a certain phase. Error codes less than 8 can be ignored. Error codes 8 or 12 and larger will cause the SUM tool to stop.

▸ **SAPup_troubleticket.log and SAPup_troubleticket_logs.sar**
These files are created when the SUM tool has stopped processing. You should upload these files to SAP Support when reporting an issue with SUM.

▸ **dev_SAPup**
This file is located in the *<sum directory>\ABAP\tmp* and provides information related to internal errors to the SUM tools. SAP Support might request this information when debugging issues related to the update and migration tools.

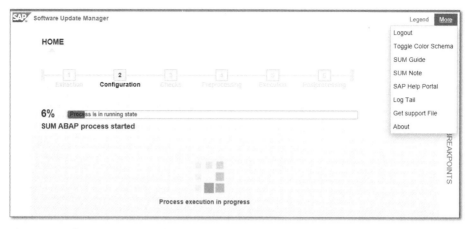

Figure 5.32 Clicking More the Software Update Manager to Generate Support File or Select Log Tail

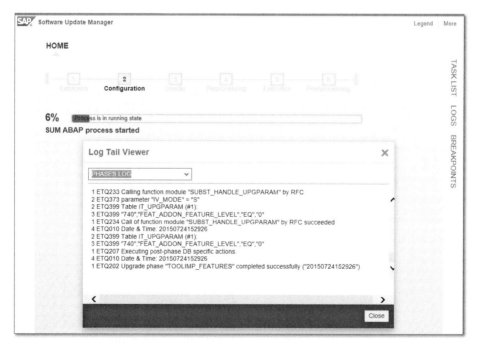

Figure 5.33 Example Log Tail Viewer from within the Software Update Manager

5.1.4 Software Provisioning Manager

The Software Provisioning Manager (SWPM) is the successor to the SAPINST tool you might have used in the past. SWPM is a component of SL Toolset 1.0 and can be found in the same location as SUM (*http://service.sap.com/sltoolset*, and choose SOFTWARE LOGISTICS TOOLSET 1.0). SAP recommends you download the latest version of SWPM when starting your project. When migrating to SAP Business Suite on SAP HANA using SWPM, you've confirmed your source SAP ERP and SAP NetWeaver versions meet the minimum requirement for SAP Business Suite on SAP HANA. Using SWPM, you can migrate an SP ERP system as-is without including additional support packages or enhancement packages. SWPM enables you to change the underlying database to SAP HANA, but you can also migrate the application server to a different OS as well. In the examples, included in this book, you'll only be changing the underlying database. However, the process to switch an application server during the database migration will follow a similar path.

The process of migrating SAP Business Suite on SAP HANA using SWPM has traditionally been called a heterogeneous system copy. The tools supporting this copy type have been available for numerous years so the process has been well defined. In addition to the standard system copy guides provided by SAP, SAP has made available specific system copy guides with the SAP HANA database as the target. Those guides can be found by navigating to *http://service.sap.com/sltoolset*and choosing SOFTWARE LOGISTICS TOOLSET 1.0 • DOCUMENTATION (scroll down) • SYSTEM PROVISIONING • SYSTEM COPY: SYSTEMS BASED ON SAP NETWEAVER 7.1 AND HIGHER. Within Figure 5.34, you'll see a section titled DATABASE OF THE TARGET SYSTEM: SAP HANA DATABASE. Click on the ABAP link next to the OS of your source application server.

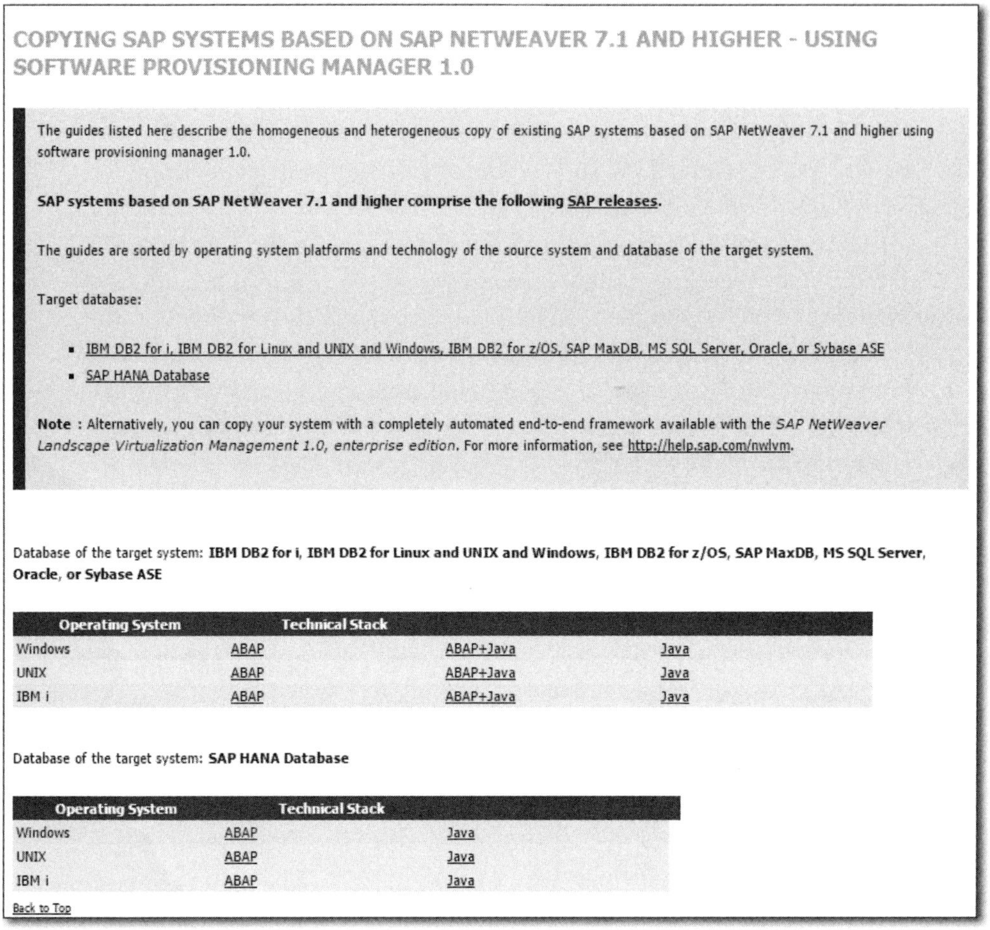

**COPYING SAP SYSTEMS BASED ON SAP NETWEAVER 7.1 AND HIGHER - USING
SOFTWARE PROVISIONING MANAGER 1.0**

The guides listed here describe the homogeneous and heterogeneous copy of existing SAP systems based on SAP NetWeaver 7.1 and higher using
software provisioning manager 1.0.

SAP systems based on SAP NetWeaver 7.1 and higher comprise the following SAP releases.

The guides are sorted by operating system platforms and technology of the source system and database of the target system.

Target database:

- IBM DB2 for i, IBM DB2 for Linux and UNIX and Windows, IBM DB2 for z/OS, SAP MaxDB, MS SQL Server, Oracle, or Sybase ASE
- SAP HANA Database

Note : Alternatively, you can copy your system with a completely automated end-to-end framework available with the *SAP NetWeaver
Landscape Virtualization Management 1.0, enterprise edition*. For more information, see http://help.sap.com/nwlvm.

Database of the target system: **IBM DB2 for i, IBM DB2 for Linux and UNIX and Windows, IBM DB2 for z/OS, SAP MaxDB, MS SQL Server,
Oracle, or Sybase ASE**

Operating System	Technical Stack		
Windows	ABAP	ABAP+Java	Java
UNIX	ABAP	ABAP+Java	Java
IBM i	ABAP	ABAP+Java	Java

Database of the target system: **SAP HANA Database**

Operating System	Technical Stack	
Windows	ABAP	Java
UNIX	ABAP	Java
IBM i	ABAP	Java

Back to Top

Figure 5.34 System Copy Guides Provided When SAP HANA Is the Target Database

Downloading Software

To download SWPM, follow these steps:

1. Log on to *http://support.sap.com/swdc* with a valid user and password.

2. Click on Support Packages & Patches • Alphabetical List of Products • S • SL
   Toolset • SL Toolset 1.0 • Entry by Component • Software Provisioning
   Manager • SOFTWARE PROVISIONING MGR 1.0 • Support Package Patches •
   <Your OS Version>.

3. You'll notice two versions of the SWPM available for download. The *70SWPM <release>* file is only used for maintenance activities on SAP NetWeaver 7.0 and below.

4. When migrating SAP ERP to SAP HANA, you need to download the *SWPM <release>.SAR* version of SWPM. In the screen shown in Figure 5.35, select the *SWPM10SP08_4-20009707.SAR* file.

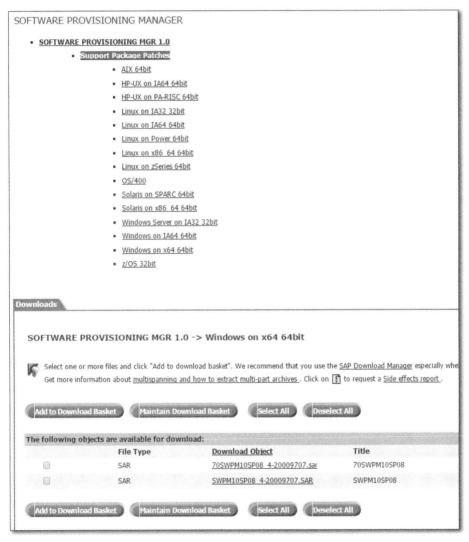

Figure 5.35 Downloading the Most Recent Version of SWPM<release>.SAR

5. Save the SAR file to a directory on your application server.

6. Extract the SWPM file contents using the command `<path to sapcar>\ sapcar.exe -xvf SWPM<release>.SAR`.

7. Within the extracted contents of the root directory of the SWPM, you should see a file named *sapinst*. This will launch the SWPM.

<table>
<tr><td>[»]</td><td>**Note**</td></tr>
</table>

> On Windows, you need to right-click and select RUN AS ADMINISTRATOR.
>
> On UNIX, you need to export the display to an X Windows Server. We've used Xming (*http://sourceforge.net/projects/xming/*), which is provided as open source. Exceed is a commercially available X Windows Server provided by OpenText and can be purchased online (*http://connectivity.opentext.com/products/exceed.aspx*).

8. You need to download two more applications in preparation for the migration: the latest version of SAPCAR and the SAP Host Agent for your OS.

9. Return to the SOFTWARE DOWNLOAD CENTER main page, and navigate to SUPPORT PACKAGES & PATCHES • BROWSE DOWNLOAD CATALOG • SAP TECHNOLOGY COMPONENTS • SAP HOST AGENT • SAP HOST AGENT 7.21 (or latest available version) • <YOUR OS VERSION>.

10. Download the latest available version, and save it to a new empty directory on your PAS.

11. SAPCAR can be downloaded from SUPPORT PACKAGES & PATCHES • BROWSE DOWNLOAD CATALOG • SAP TECHNOLOGY COMPONENTS • SAPCAR • SAPCAR 7.21 • <YOUR OS VERSION>.

12. Save SAPCAR in a central location that can be accessed to extract the downloaded files.

Updating SAP Host Agent

Follow these steps to update the SAP Host Agent:

1. Using SAPCAR, extract the contents of the downloaded SAR files for the SAP Host Agent:

```
SAPCAR -xvf SAPHOSTAGENT<PatchNr>.SAR
```

2. Because this is a migration of an existing system, you can execute the following command as <SID>ADM within the directory where the SAP Host Agent downloaded SAR file was extracted:

```
saphostexec -upgrade
```

3. After the process completes, navigate to the SAP Host Agent directory to check the version. You can execute one of the following commands to verify (see Figure 5.36):

▶ **Windows:** `%ProgramFiles%\SAP\hostctrl\exe\saphostexec.exe -version`

▶ **UNIX:** `/usr/sap/hostctrl/exe/saphostexec -version`

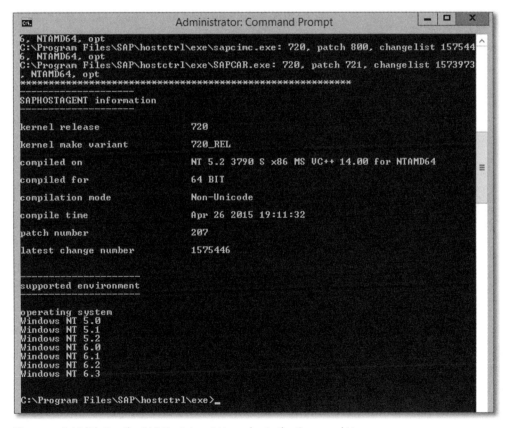

Figure 5.36 Validating the SAP Host Agent Upgrade via the Command Line

Preparing the Software Provisioning Manager

Before executing SWPM for the SAP Business Suite on SAP HANA migration, SAP recommends updating the source kernel to the latest available version. This means updating to the 7.40+ kernel if possible. Updating to the latest patch level for the 7.20 or 7.21 is required if a move to the 7.40+ kernel isn't possible (see SAP Note 1990894 for details on corrupt tables with older kernels). There are multiple components of the source system kernel that will be used during the migration to SAP HANA. Let's explore some of the binaries executed during the migration and how they will be used:

▶ **R3ldctl**
This executable will be responsible for generating files with the extensions STR and TPL to be used by the R3LOAD processes. These files contain information about tables, indexes, views, and database-specific patterns in the source system.

▶ **R3ta**
SWPM will access this binary during the table splitting processes. This process creates multiple files with the extension WHR.

▶ **R3szchk**
This executable will generate multiple EXT files that contain information about the size of tables in the source database.

▶ **R3Load**
SWPM will call R3Load during the export of the database. This process also creates files. Files with the TOC extension will be created that store information about rows exported and dump files. R3Load will create cmd and TSK files as well. The TSK file lists the work to be completed by R3Load.

To validate the version of these components, navigate to the *exe* directory within your SAP instance (*/usr/sap/<SID>/<instance>/exe*) and execute the following command as <SID>ADM:

```
<binary name> -version
```

For example, r3ldctl -version displays the information in Figure 5.37.

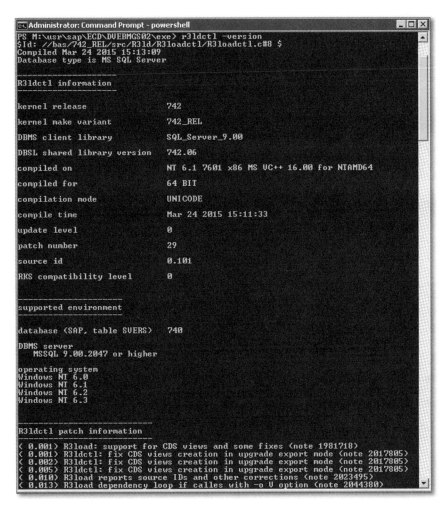

Figure 5.37 Kernel Version 742 Patch 29

When SWPM builds the target database, you'll require the latest kernel version for the SAP HANA database in addition to the SAP HANA client software. First let's download the kernel version by following these steps:

1. For the SAP KERNEL, go to *http://support.sap.com/swdc*, and select SUPPORT PACKAGES AND PATCHES • A-Z INDEX • E • SAP ERP • SAP ERP ENHANCE PACKAGE • EHP 7 FOR SAP ERP 6.0 • ENTRY BY COMPONENT • ABAP TECHNOLOGY FOR ERP EHP 7 • SAP KERNEL 7.42 64-BIT UNICODE.

2. Select the OS for your PAS.

3. Select #DATABASE INDEPENDENT. Navigate the grid rows to download the latest kernel available. The file name will be *SAPEXE_<Patch No>_<file number>.SAR*.

4. Note the patch version you downloaded, and click the database version for your source database. Select the SAPEXEDB_<PATCH NO> file that matches the database-independent file you downloaded.

5. Select SAP HANA DATABASE, and select the file SAPEXEDB_<PATCH NO> that matches the previously selected kernel files.

6. When downloading the selected files, be sure to keep the source database kernel in a separate directory from the target SAP HANA database kernel (see Figure 5.38). Placing these files in the same directory might lead to confusion.

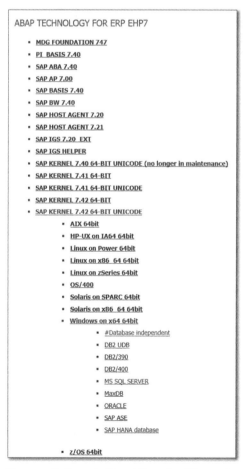

Figure 5.38 Example Kernel Download Screen from the Software Distribution Center

Next, you need to download the SAP HANA client that matches your SAP HANA database version by following these steps:

1. Navigate to *http://support.sap.com/swdc*, and select SUPPORT PACKAGES AND PATCHES • A-Z INDEX • H • SAP HANA PLATFORM EDITION • SAP HANA PLATFORM EDIT. 1.0 • ENTRY BY COMPONENT • HANA CLIENT • SAP HANA CLIENT 1.00 • <YOUR OS VERSION>.

2. Scroll down and select the SAP HANA client SAR file that matches your SAP HANA database release.

3. In our example here, the SAP HANA database is SP 10 (100), so we would download the *IMDB_CLIENT100_101_0-10009664.SAR* file (see Figure 5.39).

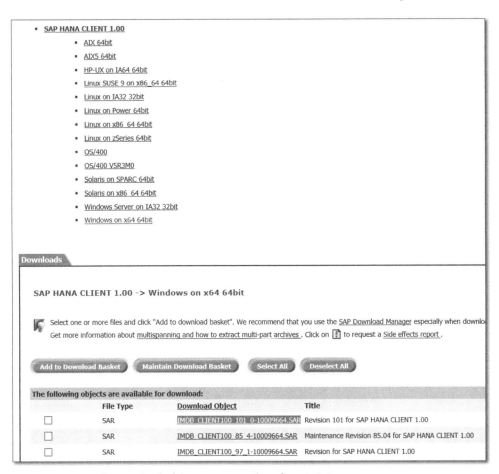

Figure 5.39 Example Download of the SAP HANA Client from SAP Support

4. Save the SAR file into its own directory, and extract using SAPCAR. You'll point SWPM to this folder during the execution of the migration.

Improving Software Provisioning Manager Performance

Many factors will impact the performance of SWPM, much like we discussed in Section 5.1.3 regarding SUM. Your current database size, customer driven enhancements, hardware resource availability, languages, and the number of client within the system to be migrated will all have an effect. Fortunately, SAP has provided several enhancements within SWPM to improve performance during the heterogeneous system copy of SAP ERP to SAP HANA. The most impactful improvement has been the ability to leverage additional hosts for the database export. If you think about the application servers you'll have available during your migration (refer to the landscape plan you created and the SAP HANA architecture options in Chapter 1), you should have additional SAP HANA database servers available for temporary use during the migration to increase throughput. After all, you won't be running a single appliance in production. Ideally, you'll have a standby or failover node that can be used to offload some work during the export. We'll talk about that more in Chapter 7 when you execute the migration using SWPM.

The Migration Monitor and Migration Time utilities can be used to measure the performance of the migration both during the process and afterwards. Some of you may remember the Migration Monitor from prior OS/DB migrations. The utility has been enhanced and now includes a feature called the Dynamic Controller of the Import Migration Monitor. The tool will access the *Order_by.txt* file during the import where you can make adjustments. The *Order_by.txt* files is checked by the SWPM processes every 30 seconds so you have some ability to make changes during the migration process based on CPU and I/O utilization. The Time Analyzer (migtime) utility is run post-migration to identify settings for improvement. Both tools will be covered in this book with screenshots.

Lastly, on the hardware side, SAP recommends that the export be directly created on a separate disk with its own controller. This is especially important when performing the export and import in parallel, which will drive I/O utilization. Avoid placing the export directory on the same disk as the database data file, log files, and tempdb. The export directory will contain files that need to be shared with the SAP HANA host. You have two options to move data between the source and target system: Network File System (NFS) and File Transport Protocol (FTP). The examples in this book use NFS. Note that FTP can be slower than NFS. Preserving the SWPM directory after your first migration is essential to enable the analysis required to improve migration performance. It contains the log files with time-stamps required for analysis.

Logs and Troubleshooting

SWPM provides similar functionality to SUM when it comes to logs and bundling information for SAP Support. From within the SWPM GUI, you can select SAP-INST • LOG BROWSER to view basic log information. After you start the migration, you'll no doubt become more familiar with the SWPM file system. By default, in Windows, the SWPM will create a directory called *sapinst_instdir* under *%Program Files%*. In UNIX, it will create the same directory under */tmp*. Within the *sapinst_instdir*, you can find most of the logs required for troubleshooting SWPM. Let's review some of the import log files available:

▸ *Sapinst.log*
This is the main log file for SWPM. When opening this file, the most recent entries are located on the bottom. You should look for the word "ERROR" when troubleshooting.

▸ *Sapinst_dev.log*
This file contains more details about warning and error situations. This file is also one of the first log files that should be reviewed. SWPM should be stopped when reviewing this log file. If the SWPM is running, then not all entries will have been written to this file.

▸ *export_monitor_cmd.properties/import_monitor_cmd.properties*
These files contain information about the configuration of the Migration Monitor.

▸ *export_state.properties/import_state.properties*
This set of files contains the status of the current R3Load jobs. The symbols within the file translate as follows (see Figure 5.40 for an example):

  ▸ 0 = To be executed

  ▸ ? = In process

  ▸ + = Execution successful

  ▸ - = Execution aborted

▸ *ExportMonitor.console.log/ImportMonitor.console.log*
These log files show output from the Migration Monitor but more importantly show status messages related to the jobs processing, for example, EXPORT MONITOR JOBS: RUNNING 2, WAITING 7, COMPLETED 11, FAILED 0, TOTAL 20.

```
deverp:/tmp/sapinst_instdir/NW740SR2/DB6/COPY/EXP/AS-ABAP/EXP # more export_state.properties
#Tue Dec 30 14:59:54 MST 2014
SAP0000=+
SAPAPPL0=+
SAPAPPL1=+
SAPAPPL2=+
SAPCLUST=+
SAPDDIM=+
SAPDFACT=+
SAPDODS=+
SAPNTAB=+
SAPPOOL=+
SAPSDIC=+
SAPSDOCU=+
SAPSLEXC=+
SAPSLOAD=+
SAPSPROT=+
SAPSSEXC=+
SAPSSRC=+
SAPUSER=+
SAPUSER1=+
SAPVIEW=+
```

Figure 5.40 Example Log File for the R3LOAD Export Jobs

▸ *export_monitor.log/import_monitor.log*
Think of the console log as the summary information. These logs provide additional detail about the individual R3Load jobs.

▸ *export_monitor.java.log/import_monitor.java.log*
These logs are somewhat duplicative and provide similar information to the *ExportMonitor.console.log*.

▸ *migmonctrl_cmd.properties*
This file contains configuration for `migmonctrl` and is read by the `migmon` at runtime. You can make changes to parameters in this file and see the immediate impact.

▸ *order_by.txt*
This file is created by the Migration Monitor and contains a listing of tables with two sort orders: sorted by size and sorted by last runtime.

▸ *order_by_visual.txt*
This is a log file for the *order_by.txt* file, which reports the size or runtime of the object.

▸ *R3LOAD_JOBS.csv*
This is an export of information that can be loaded into Excel and used to create graphs displaying the performance of the migration (see Figure 5.41). SWPM will also create the files *CPU_USAGE.csv*, *SAVEPOINT_STATISTIC.csv*, and *FREE_MEMORY.csv*.

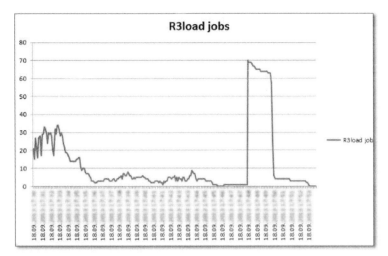

Figure 5.41 Example Graphical Representation of the R3load Job Runtime

[«]

> **Note**
>
> For the most up-to-date information about SWPM, check out the SAP Support Portal. For more information on the installation, execution, and troubleshooting of SWPM, navigate to *http://service.sap.com/sltoolset*, and choose SOFTWARE LOGISTICS TOOLSET 1.0 • DOCUMENTATION (scroll down) • SYSTEM PROVISIONING • SYSTEM COPY: SYSTEMS BASED ON SAP NETWEAVER 7.1 AND HIGHER. The Software Logistics Central SAP Note 1563579 will link to the latest information about SWPM and how to resolve known problems.

5.1.5 Benchmark Migration

The benchmark migration tool is delivered as part of the SL Common UI included with SUM 1.0 SP 13. Its primary purpose is to help customers estimate the time required for the migration to SAP HANA from the source database. You can execute the benchmark tool while the source system is operational, and you can select a specific number or percentage of tables to be used for the migration sample. It also helps you simulate the load from the PAS or another host. It's very helpful in determining which hardware to use during the export and import into SAP HANA.

In addition to having the latest SUM installed, you also need to ensure that no active SUM DMO process is running. When you start the benchmark tool, it checks the SUM DMO directories. If you need assistance resetting the SUM DMO, see subsection "Restarting or Resetting SUM" in Section 5.1.3. The benchmark tool is accessed via the browser. Because this tool is only delivered with SUM, you can't access the tool when using SWPM. You can also install SUM with the new SL Common UI to perform a benchmark to get an estimate for your SWPM executions. This isn't an official SAP documented use case but can be executed at your discretion. The benchmark tool won't change source system data, and the target system is cleaned up before the tool completes.

Now, let's explore the tool's usage:

1. After you've completed the steps to install SUM and configured the SAP Host Agent defined in Section 5.1.3, log on to *http://<host>:1128/lmsl/migtool/<SID>/doc/sluigui*.

2. If prompted, login as the <SID>ADM user for the host on which SUM has been installed.

3. In this example, we'll benchmark both the export and import (see Figure 5.42). Under BENCHMARKING MODE, select BENCHMARK EXPORT AND IMPORT, and then click NEXT.

Figure 5.42 Initial Migration Tool Screen

4. On the MIGRATION PARAMETERS screen (see Figure 5.43), select the OPERATE ON ALL TABLES radio button, enter "20" in the PERCENTAGE OF DB SIZE FOR SAMPLE field, and enter "1" in the SIZE OF LARGEST TABLE IN SAMPLE field.

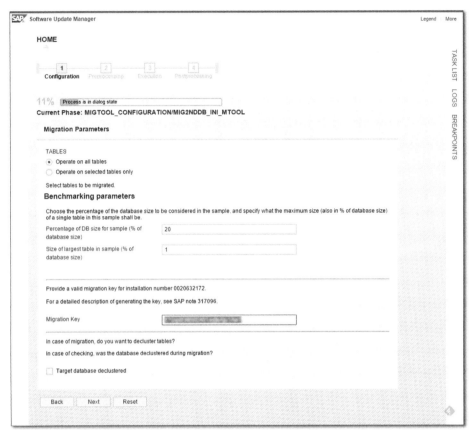

Figure 5.43 Entering Paramters to Benchmark the Software Update Manager Database Migration Option

5. On this same screen, enter your MIGRATION KEY, and deselect TARGET DATABASE DECLUSTERED.

Note   [«]

Need your migration key? Log on to the SAP Support Portal with a valid user ID and password at *https://support.sap.com/keys-systems-installations/keys/migration.html*. Follow the prompts to retrieve your license key specific to your system versions. We cover the process in detail in Section 5.1.7.

---

6. Confirm your entries, and click NEXT.

7. The next screen will prompt you for a download directory. This directory should contain the files downloaded as a result of your Maintenance Optimizer (or Maintenance Planner). The tool will be looking for copies of both the source and target database kernels. Enter the directory with the files, and click NEXT (see Figure 5.44).

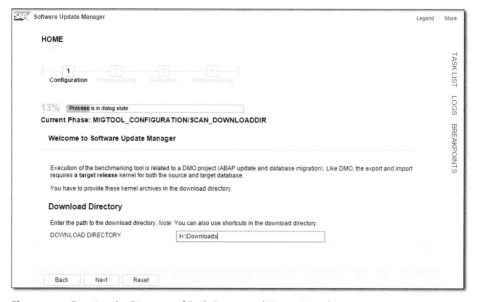

Figure 5.44 Entering the Directory of Both Source and Target Kernels

8. On the TARGET DATABASE CLIENT screen, enter the path to the extracted SAP HANA client you downloaded in Section 5.1.3 (see Figure 5.45). Click NEXT. The benchmark tool will validate the path and download before continuing.

[»] **Note**

Avoid any spaces with folder names in the path to the SAP HANA client. Remove spaces in directory names, or use underscores.

9. Next you'll be prompted for the <SID>ADM password. Enter the password, and click NEXT.

10. On the PARALLEL PROCESSES CONFIGURATION screen, define the number of processes to be used during the benchmark execution. In our example, the PAS has six cores assigned:

▶ SQL PROCESSES: 6 (1 × CPU cores)

▶ R3LOAD PROCESSES: 12 (2 × CPU cores)

Figure 5.45 Entering the Path to the SAP HANA Client in the Benchmark Tool

11. The benchmark tool can be reexecuted to fine-tune the number of processes you utilize. Click NEXT after you've entered the values (see Figure 5.46).

Figure 5.46 Determining the Parallel Processes by Our Current Hardware

12. On the DATABASE MIGRATION INITIALIZATION screen, you enter the information given to you by the certified SAP HANA installer(s) (see Figure 5.47):

   ▶ TARGET HOSTNAME: Hostname of the SAP HANA database server

   ▶ SID OF THE TARGET DATABASE: SID of the database created during installation

   ▶ TARGET INSTANCE NUMBER: Instance number created during installation

   ▶ TARGET DB SCHEMA: The schema to be created

13. Click NEXT after you've entered the required information.

Figure 5.47 Entering the Target SAP HANA Database Information

14. Next you're prompted for the SYSTEM account password. This would have been provided by the SAP HANA system installer(s). Enter the password, and click NEXT.

15. The benchmark tool prompts you to create a password for the DBA Cockpit user if one doesn't already exist. Enter a new password, and click NEXT.

16. Next you're prompted to create a new password for the target SAPSID user. Enter the password, and click NEXT.

17. Confirm that the configuration step is complete, and then click NEXT (see Figure 5.48).

Figure 5.48 The Completed Configuration Step for the Benchmark Tool

18. At this point (see Figure 5.49), the benchmark tool is creating the list of tables to be migrated and validating configuration information you entered. You can monitor log files in the *<path to SUM>\ABAP\log* directory.

19. You're then prompted to continue with the execution step. Click NEXT to confirm (see Figure 5.50).

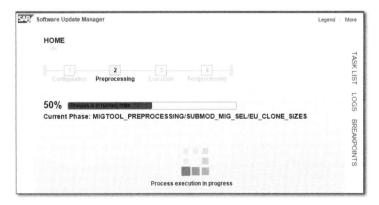

Figure 5.49 Standard Processing Screen Displaying the Current Status

Figure 5.50 Continuing with the Execution Step

20. The processing screen displays the current status until the phase is complete. Click Next to complete postprocessing as shown in Figure 5.51.

21. Click Next (as shown in Figure 5.52) until you see the Reset and Cleanup buttons. At this point, you want to review the benchmark migration logs before clicking Cleanup.

Figure 5.51 Benchmark Tool Completing Execution

22. Navigate to the *<SUM directory>\ABAP\log,* and open the *EUMIGRATERUN.LOG* file.

Figure 5.52 Confirmation That the Benchmark Tool Is Complete

23. Scroll to the bottom of the file and review the results. In this example, the benchmark took 2 hours to complete with a predicted 23 hours to complete the actual migration.

24. You can also see that it processed an average of 16.89/GB per hour. For a 1TB system, you would extrapolate out to 64 hours of runtime. Obviously, this isn't acceptable, so you can rerun the benchmark tool to fine-tune the number of processes (see Figure 5.53).

```
EUMIGRATERUN.LOG - Notepad                                      _ □ X
File  Edit  Format  View  Help
3 ETQ399 ============= 2015/07/27 19:57:31, Progress 6459 MB/6616 MB (97.63%) ====================
3 ETQ123 20150727195733 (3): PID 4960 exited with status 0 (time 0.000 real)
3 ETQ123 20150727195733 (2): PID 3256 exited with status 0 (time 0.000 real)
3 ETQ399 ============= 2015/07/27 19:57:33, Progress 6463 MB/6616 MB (97.68%) ====================
3 ETQ123 20150727195808 (1): PID 3764 exited with status 0 (time 0.000 real)
3 ETQ123 20150727195810 (0): PID 2168 exited with status 0 (time 0.000 real)
3 ETQ399 ============= 2015/07/27 19:58:10, Progress 6616 MB/6616 MB (100.00%) ====================
1 ETQ000 ================================================
4 ETQ010 Date & Time: 20150727195810
2 ETQ102 Finished execution of 242 process(es).
3 ETQ128 Interval: 20150727193440-20150727195810, time 0.000 real
2 ETQ108 Analyzing logs for errors.
3 ETQ114 Analyzed 242 log files.
1 ETQ399 Finished execution of buckets with rc = 0.
1 ETQ000 ================================================
4 ETQ010 Date & Time: 20150727195812
3 ETQ399 Bucket evaluation (decreasing import speed, more than 300s import time):
4 ETQ399 Bucket #00016: exp:    6:54,  0.64 MB/sec imp:    6:54,  0.64 MB/sec
4 ETQ399 Bucket #00012: exp:    5:16,  0.51 MB/sec imp:    5:13,  0.52 MB/sec
4 ETQ399 Bucket #00005: exp:    9:27,  0.47 MB/sec imp:    9:27,  0.47 MB/sec
4 ETQ399 Bucket #00002: exp:   12:12,  0.20 MB/sec imp:   12:12,  0.20 MB/sec
4 ETQ399 Bucket #00003: exp:   23:08,  0.11 MB/sec imp:   23:10,  0.11 MB/sec
2 ETQ399 Total import time: 2:13:37, maximum run time: 23:10.
2 ETQ399 Total export time: 2:15:29, maximum run time: 23:08.
2 ETQ399 Average exp/imp/total load: 5.0/5.8/10.8 of 12 processes.
2 ETQ399 Summary (export+import): time elapsed 23:30, total size 6616 MB,  4.69 MB/sec (16.89 GB/hour).
1 ETQ207 Executing post-phase DB specific actions.
4 ETQ010 Date & Time: 20150727195815
1 ETQ202 Upgrade phase "EU_CLONE_RUN" completed successfully ("20150727195815")
```

Figure 5.53 Example Output from the Benchmark Tool

25. Click CLEANUP after you've reviewed the log files to reexecute the migration tool with new parameters (see Figure 5.54 and Figure 5.55).

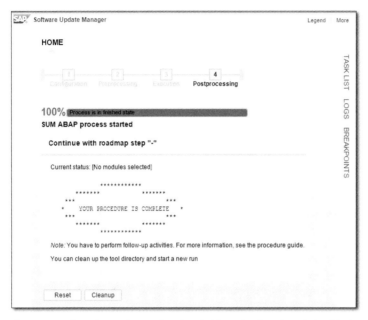

Figure 5.54 Completion Screen Displayed When the Benchmark Tool Is Complete

Figure 5.55 Clicking Cleanup to Remove Log Files and Reset the Procedure

5.1.6   Table Comparison

Much like the benchmark migration tool just described in Section 5.1.5, SAP included a table comparison tool within SUM. In Section 5.1.5 on the MIGRATION TOOL start page, you'll have noticed two selection options: the BENCHMARK MIGRATION and TABLE COMPARISON. In this section, we're going to talk about the table comparison tool (which can be run as a standalone tool). Much like the benchmark tool, you also must run this tool either after or before SUM because it can't be executed while a SUM processes is running. You can also run the table comparison tool when using the SWPM migration procedure. This can be helpful because it allows you to run a comparison just before the database export and then again on database import. The utility is accessed via the same URL as the migration tool.

Let's walk through a scenario where you want to execute a comparison on several critical functional-related tables in your system. We want to avoid comparing IDoc tables, SAP Business Workflow tables, or system log tables, so we created a table list as described in the tool to compare specific tables related to Finances (FI) in SAP ERP.

Executing Table Comparison on Export

To execute the table comparison tool, follow these steps:

1. After you've completed the steps to install SUM and configure the SAP Host Agent defined in Section 5.1.3, log on to *http://<host>:1128/lmsl/migtool/ <SID>/doc/sluigui.*

   If prompted, log in as the <SID>ADM user for the host on which SUM has been installed.

2. Select the TABLE COMPARISON option with the target database SAP HANA.

3. Select the EXPORT TO FILE SYSTEM radio button.

4. Click NEXT (see Figure 5.56).

5. For this analysis, select OPERATE ON SELECTED TABLES ONLY, and provide a path to a text file with the table names you want to compare. There can be multiple strategies here to decide which tables to compare. (Later in Chapter 6 when executing SUM, we show how you can compare all tables, but this does slow down the update process.) In our example system, we know the FI tables are the most critical, so we add those tables to a list (Figure 5.57) with one table represented on a line in the text file.

Figure 5.56 Initial Selection Screen for the Migration Tool

Figure 5.57 Your Text List of Tables to Be Compared

6. Leave the TARGET DATABASE DECLUSTERED box deselected, and click NEXT (see Figure 5.58).

7. Referring to Figure 5.57, we selected tables that require roughly 40GB of storage.

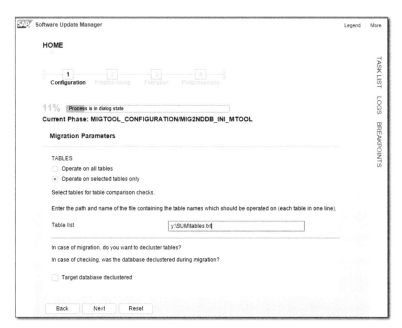

Figure 5.58 Determining whether to Compare All Tables or Tables That Are Part of a List

8. Next, select the number of processes used to execute the comparison (see Figure 5.59). Because you're executing SUM on your PAS, be aware of system resource availability.

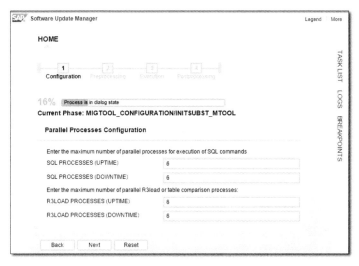

Figure 5.59 Determining the Number of Processes to be Utilized for the Compare

9. Confirm the end of the configuration step, and click NEXT after validating the *CHECKS.LOG* in the *<SUM Directory>\abap\log* (see Figure 5.60 and Figure 5.61).

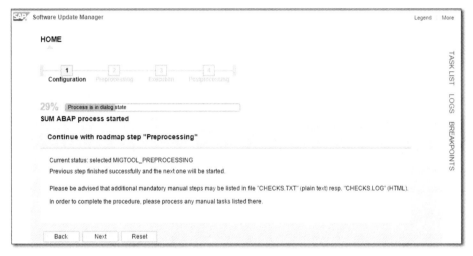

Figure 5.60 Confirming That This Phase Is Complete

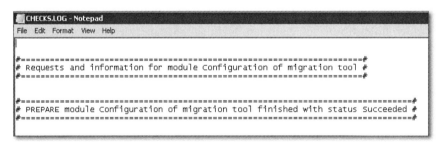

Figure 5.61 Validating That the CHECKS.LOG Is Free from Error

The preprocessing phase doesn't require interactive input. It should complete without interruption.

10. Confirm the start of the execution phase by clicking NEXT (see Figure 5.62).

11. Within the *<SUM Directory>\ABAP\log* directory, you'll see several log files being updated during the execution phase.

12. If you open the *EUMIGRATETABCHKEXP.LOG*, you'll see an updated status of the executables being called in the background.

Figure 5.62 Starting the Execution Phase within the Table Compare Tool

13. In Figure 5.63, you can see the tables to be compared and the current status of the table comparison at 13.01%.

```
EUMIGRATETABCHKEXP.LOG - Notepad
File  Edit  Format  View  Help
1 ETQ399 Getting all tables/views supposed to be cloned.
2 ETQ399 Read 8 entries from 'y:\SUM\SUM\abap\mem\MIGTABLES.LST'.
2 ETQ399 Read 4 entries from 'y:\SUM\SUM\abap\bin\EUCLONEDEFS.LST'.
1 ETQ000 ========================================================
2 ETQ399 List of cloned tables:
4 ETQ165 Clone COEPL                    to COEPL
4 ETQ165 Clone FAGLFLEXA               to FAGLFLEXA
4 ETQ165 Clone BKPF                    to BKPF
4 ETQ165 Clone COBK                    to COBK
4 ETQ165 Clone COEP                    to COEP
4 ETQ165 Clone COIX #3                 to COIX
4 ETQ165 Clone COSS                    to COSS
4 ETQ165 Clone BSIS                    to BSIS
2 ETQ399 Statistics of different clone types:
3 ETQ399      8 x ' '.
1 ETQ000 ========================================================
4 ETQ010 Date & Time: 20150805194829
1 ETQ399 Read 17 tasks from 'MIGRATE_CHECK_CHK.BUC' in directory 'migrate_check', now running export side only.
2 ETQ399 Using dynamically number of R3load processes.
2 ETQ000 ========================================================
2 ETQ100 Executing 17 processes in total - will run 6 in parallel.
3 ETQ121 20150805194830 #1 (1): PID 9596 execute 'y:\SUM\SUM\abap\bin\SAPuptool crctable y:\SUM\SUM\abap\migrate_check\MIGR
3 ETQ121 20150805194830 #2 (2): PID 5760 execute 'y:\SUM\SUM\abap\bin\SAPuptool crctable y:\SUM\SUM\abap\migrate_check\MIGR
3 ETQ121 20150805194830 #3 (3): PID 9400 execute 'y:\SUM\SUM\abap\bin\SAPuptool crctable y:\SUM\SUM\abap\migrate_check\MIGR
3 ETQ121 20150805194830 #4 (4): PID 8308 execute 'y:\SUM\SUM\abap\bin\SAPuptool crctable y:\SUM\SUM\abap\migrate_check\MIGR
3 ETQ121 20150805194830 #5 (5): PID 8184 execute 'y:\SUM\SUM\abap\bin\SAPuptool crctable y:\SUM\SUM\abap\migrate_check\MIGR
3 ETQ121 20150805194830 #6 (6): PID 7888 execute 'y:\SUM\SUM\abap\bin\SAPuptool crctable y:\SUM\SUM\abap\migrate_check\MIGR
3 ETQ123 20150805195312 (5): PID 9400 exited with status 3 (time 0.000 real)
2 ETQ399 Need to check for more, user should schedule task #1 for '00003_COEP' on import side.
3 ETQ399 ============= 2015/08/05 19:53:12, Progress 1615 MB/20080 MB (8.04%) ==================
3 ETQ121 20150805195312 #7 (6): PID 2452 execute 'y:\SUM\SUM\abap\bin\SAPuptool crctable y:\SUM\SUM\abap\migrate_check\MIGR
3 ETQ123 20150805195545 (5): PID 8308 exited with status 3 (time 0.000 real)
2 ETQ399 Need to check for more, user should schedule task #1 for '00004_COEP' on import side.
3 ETQ399 ============= 2015/08/05 19:55:45, Progress 2561 MB/20080 MB (12.75%) ==================
3 ETQ121 20150805195545 #8 (6): PID 5280 execute 'y:\SUM\SUM\abap\bin\SAPuptool crctable y:\SUM\SUM\abap\migrate_check\MIGR
3 ETQ123 20150805195602 (5): PID 5280 exited with status 3 (time 0.000 real)
2 ETQ399 Need to check for more, user should schedule task #1 for '00008_BSIS' on import side.
3 ETQ399 ============= 2015/08/05 19:56:02, Progress 2613 MB/20080 MD (13.01%) ==================
3 ETQ121 20150805195602 #9 (6): PID 1872 execute 'y:\SUM\SUM\abap\bin\SAPuptool crctable y:\SUM\SUM\abap\migrate_check\MIGR
```

Figure 5.63 Log File Created during the Table Comparison Process

14. After the execution phase completes, you need to save the directory specified on screen. In this case, it's *<SUM Directory>\abap\migrate_check*. This directory contains the checksums for the tables identified previously to be used in the comparison.

15. Move this directory to the target system, and execute the TABLE COMPARISON ON IMPORT.

16. After you've saved the migration directory, click NEXT (see Figure 5.64).

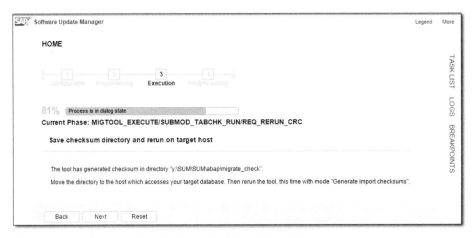

Figure 5.64 Confirmation That the Execution Phase Is Complete

17. Click NEXT to confirm the start of postprocessing.

18. If prompted, complete the EVALUATION FORM, click SUBMIT, and then click CLOSE (see Figure 5.65).

19. On the completion screen, click CLEANUP and verify the results. You've now completed the first step in the table comparison (see Figure 5.66).

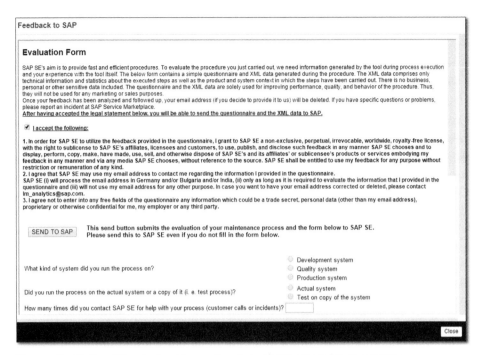

Figure 5.65 Optional Step to Send Survey Results to SAP for the Table Comparison

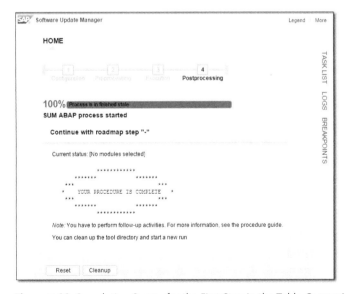

Figure 5.66 Completion Screen for the First Step in the Table Comparison

Executing Table Comparison on Import

The procedure we've just detailed creates several cyclical redundancy check (CRC) files within the directory you specified in the procedure. You'll use these files on the target system to perform the table comparison. Let's explore the steps:

1. After you've completed the steps to install SUM and configure the SAP Host Agent defined in Section 5.1.3, log on to *http://<host>:1128/lmsl/migtool/<SID>/doc/sluigui.*

   If prompted, log in as the <SID>ADM user for the host on which SUM has been installed.

2. Choose TABLE COMPARISON and IMPORT FROM FILE SYSTEM. Specify the directory with the CRC files created in the previous procedure.

3. Click NEXT (see Figure 5.67).

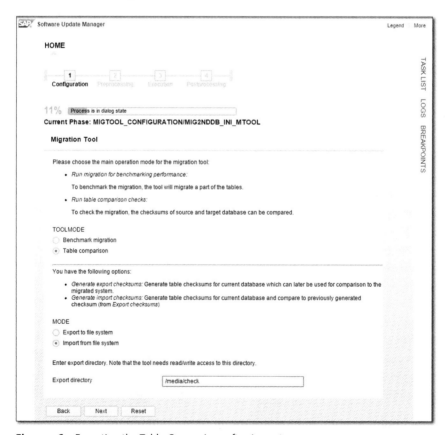

Figure 5.67 Executing the Table Comparison after Import

4. Specify the number of processes to be utilized. Be conscious of the number of processes if your system is currently in use (see Figure 5.68).

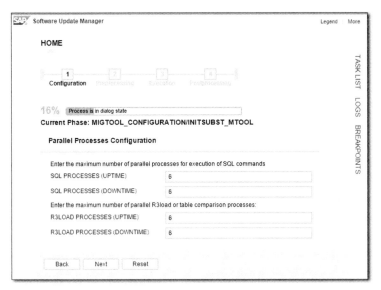

Figure 5.68 Entering the Number of Processes to Be Used during the Table Comparison

5. On the next two screens, you confirm exit and entry to the next phases of the table comparison (see Figure 5.69).

Figure 5.69 Confirmation Screen to Begin the Table Comparison

6. When you click NEXT, the table comparison will be executed (see Figure 5.70).

Figure 5.70 Example Execution Status Screen from the Table Comparison

7. If the process stops at this point, you have a table checksum that doesn't match between the source and target systems. If you see the completion screen, then the checksums matched between source and target systems.

8. Review the *EUMIGRATETABCHKIMP.LOG* to validate checksum entries for all tables checked. You can see the log within the UI by clicking LOGS on the right side as shown in Figure 5.71.

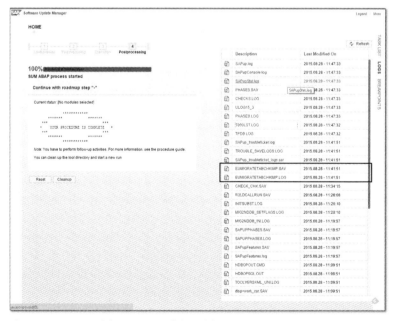

Figure 5.71 Successful Execution of the Table Comparison on the Import System

5.1.7 Generating a Migration Key

Many of the tools related to the migration to SAP Business Suite on SAP HANA require a migration key. This key is generated from the SAP Support Portal. It depends on good information from SAP Solution Manager and the system data previously entered by the system administrator who installed the initial license key. Let's walk through the steps of generating your migration key:

1. Log on to the SAP Support Portal (*http://support.sap.com*) with a valid user ID and password.

2. Click on KEYS, SYSTEMS, & INSTALLATIONS, and then click MIGRATION KEYS (see Figure 5.72).

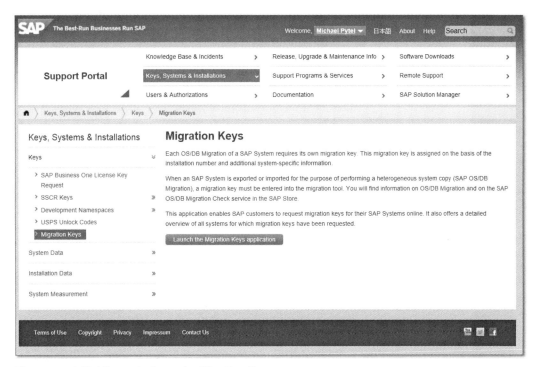

Figure 5.72 Initial Screen to Request a Migration Key

3. Click on REQUEST MIGRATION KEY (see Figure 5.73).

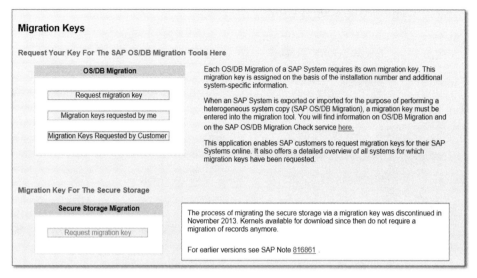

Figure 5.73 Clicking Request Migration Key

4. Read and accept the declaration.

5. Select the installation number specific to your SAP Business Suite on SAP HANA migration source system (see Figure 5.74). You can see your installation in any SAP GUI screen by selecting SYSTEM • STATUS from the toolbar.

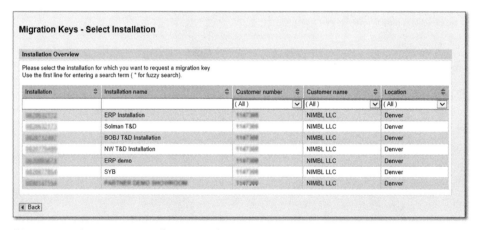

Figure 5.74 Selecting Your Installation Number

6. In the Source System area, follow these steps (see Figure 5.75):

   ▸ System ID: Enter the SID of the system to be migrated.

   ▸ Release: Select your source release level.

   ▸ Operating system: Select your OS for the PAS.

   ▸ Database: Select your source database.

   ▸ DB Server Hostname: Enter the hostname for the source database.

7. In the Target System area, follow these steps:

   ▸ System ID: Enter the same SID as before

   ▸ Operating system: Select the same OS as before.

   ▸ Database: Select SAP HANA database.

   ▸ DB Server Hostname: Enter the hostname for SAP HANA.

8. Click Submit when completed.

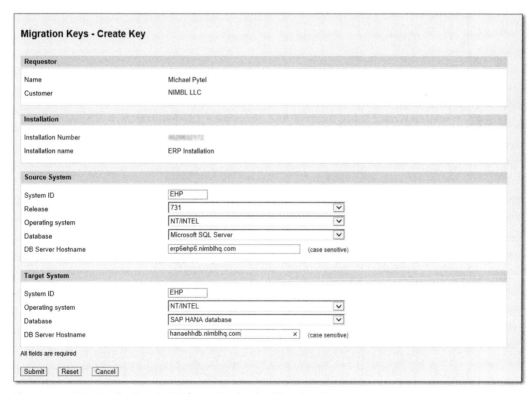

Figure 5.75 Entering the Required Information for the Migration Key

9. Your migration key is displayed on the next screen. Save this to a text file for later user (see Figure 5.76). You can also return to this screen to retrieve this key if required.

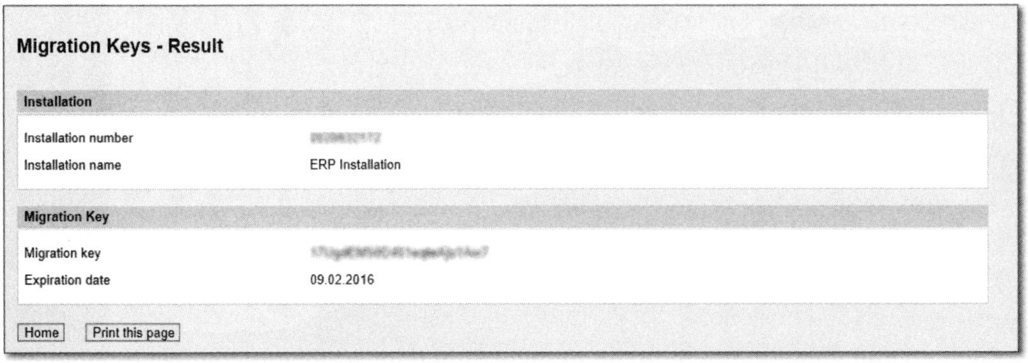

Migration Keys - Result

Installation	
Installation number	ꞏꞏꞏ
Installation name	ERP Installation

Migration Key	
Migration key	ꞏꞏꞏ
Expiration date	09.02.2016

Home   Print this page

Figure 5.76 Your Migration Key

5.2   Migration Options

In this section, we cover in more detail the migration options for SAP Business Suite on SAP HANA. At this point in the book, you've got a good understanding of how to determine the project scope and some more details on preparing the tools for the upgrade. By the end of this section, you'll have a solid understanding of the migration options and ideally will have chosen the approach you'll execute (if you haven't already). One of the many advantages to the migration to SAP HANA is that you have options, although multiple options can sometimes mean more complexity. With the infinite hardware and software variations between SAP customers, SAP has provided a platform (SL Toolset 1.0) that accounts for these variations and can adapt to each customer's unique environment. In Chapter 6 and Chapter 7, we'll execute the migration step by step using SUM and SWPM, respectively, and providing you with a technical overview of the process.

In our scenario, we have a standalone SAP ERP system. In your organization, you might have a different scenario that involves portals and other SAP NetWeaver components. The upgrade tools, phases, and process will remain the same regardless of your landscape complexity. The tools may present information specific to your landscape that you don't see in the screenshots within the subsequent chapters. Our goal isn't to explain every possible migration scenario but to arm you with the information and resources to run your SAP Business Suite on SAP HANA migration effectively (and error free). This section will provide more detail on the approach to the migration for each tool, how it's executed, and the resources used to complete the task. We'll explore the phases in depth and provide insight into monitoring the processes, where to check for errors, and how to find support should you encounter an error.

You already know that there are two primary tools you can use to migrate to SAP HANA. SUM and SWPM are both components of the larger SL Toolset 1.0 suite of solutions. Both applications are initiated from the PAS and provide a GUI to provide instructions. They both share a similar approach to a migration with similar phases, phase descriptions, and tasks, and they both provide a similar framework for error handling and resolutions. After your resources learn one tool, it won't take long for them to adapt to the other. Let's first explore SUM because we know most SAP customers will need (or would like) to upgrade and migrate to SAP HANA in one step. After we cover SUM, we'll move onto SWPM, which can be used by those customers already running a supported version of SAP ERP for SAP HANA.

5.2.1 Software Update Manager with Database Migration Option

SUM with DMO was created to simplify the migration from lower releases of SAP ERP directly to SAP Business Suite on SAP HANA. In addition to supporting your migration to SAP HANA, the SUM DMO also supports a conversion to Unicode when updating your SAP ERP system as it migrates from any source database to SAP HANA. This is a wonderful tool that greatly simplifies the maintenance your teams would have had to execute using the classical database migrations options. In Figure 5.77, you can see the approach on top represents the classical database migration, in which you would need to first upgrade to a supported version of SAP ERP for the SAP HANA database, and then execute the migration from your source database to SAP HANA. Using the SUM DMO, the processes are combined, resulting in less downtime for your business users and a reduction of risk. How does this reduce risk? When you think about the two separate projects you would have to run to accomplish the tasks SUM DMO completes, you'll soon realize this not only saves time but also reduces the risk of resource turnover between projects, decreases the opportunity for resources to make technical mistakes, and increases the value of testing on one project versus two.

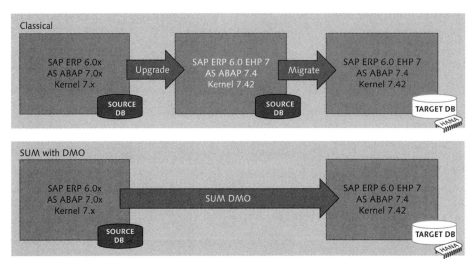

Figure 5.77 Example Process Comparison between Classical and Software Update Manager Database Migration Option

SUM DMO keeps the same SID and PAS. Only the underlying database is changed, so you don't need to update end-user connections, interfaces, or programs (as long as they follow common SAP design standards). If you have any outlier interfaces and programs that use specific file system paths on the database or make direct database calls, those programs will need to be remediated. SAP doesn't support direct database access for SAP ERP, and everything should be done via the application layer. If something breaks, it might be a good time to rewrite that interface! Joking aside, SUM DMO will leave your application server infrastructure in place. It will also leave the source database in place, which enables a fast recovery if you need to roll back. We won't cover the criteria for removing the source database in this book; however, it's a risk-based decision specific to your environment after you're live with SAP Business Suite on SAP HANA.

SUM DMO completes the upgrade and migration to SAP Business Suite on SAP HANA by leveraging the same downtime minimization concept that was introduced with the SUM years ago. A copy of your repository is created as a shadow instance within your source database (see Figure 5.78). This shadow instance has its own instance ID, its own tables, and is updated first when upgrading to SAP ERP EHP 7. This is all done while the primary instance remains active and available for users. This concept is the core component to SAP's approach to reducing downtime for upgrades and patching.

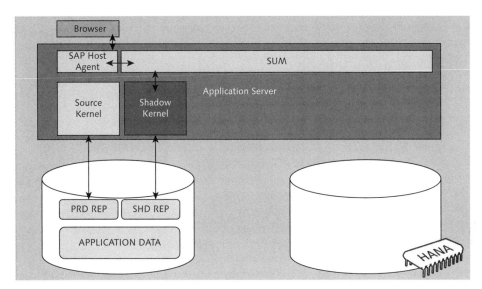

Figure 5.78 Creation of the Shadow Instance

In Figure 5.79, the shadow repository (SHD REP) is upgraded and migrated to the SAP HANA database. When you execute the SUM DMO, you'll provide it with updated kernels for both the source database (on the left) and target SAP HANA database (on the right). This enables the primary application to communicate with both databases while keeping users connected to the primary instance. After the shadow repository has been migrated, you can enter the downtime phase, which migrates the application data to SAP HANA.

During the downtime phase, the SUM DMO leverages the table-splitting functionality to best determine how to migrate tables to SAP HANA. In the prior sections of this chapter, we discussed the benchmark migration tool, which can be used to refine your work process count and distribution. At this point, you've determined the optimal number of processes specific to your environment. The SUM DMO leverages the resources available to migrate application data efficiently. You can then use the table comparison tool to validate the tables between systems. After the application data has been migrated, the shadow repository and kernels are switched (see Figure 5.80). The system is returned to an operating state that your teams will validate.

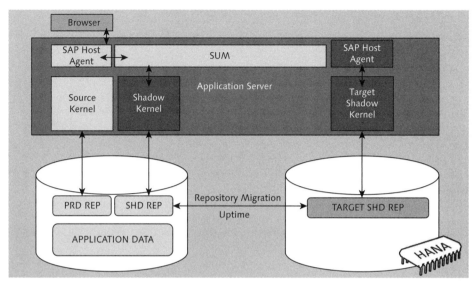

Figure 5.79 Repository Migrated during Uptime

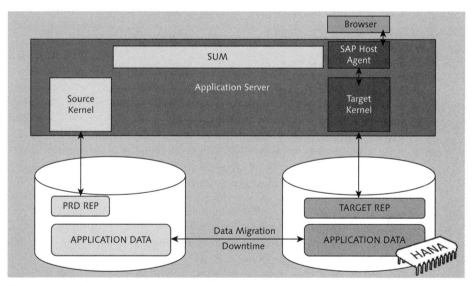

Figure 5.80 Aplication Data Migrated and the Kernel and Repository Switched

At the end of the process, SUM DMO performs several cleanup activities, including cleaning up the directories used on the PAS and removing the shadow instance; however, it leaves the source database as-is. The SUM DMO unlocks transports and creates several summary files that can be shared internally with your team members and sent to SAP. We recommend sending all summary files to SAP as a contribution to the SAP community. Sharing this information provides SAP with more information with which it can make decisions on adoption and tool innovation, and share anonymized information with other SAP customers regarding migration performance.

As part of SUM DMO SP 13+, SAP introduced an additional feature to the toolset that will help improve future executions of SUM DMO within your landscape. The SUM DMO tool collects information about the table-splitting and migration runtimes. Then it stores this information in two files within the *<SUM Directory>\ABAP\htdoc*:

▶ *MIGRATE_UT_DUR.XML* for the uptime migration

▶ *MIGRATE_DT_DUR.XML* for the downtime migration

These files should be saved before running cleanup and placed into the download directory of the next SAP ERP instance before the next migration. On the next SUM DMO execution, the information within the XML files will be used to make decisions on how to split tables for that system's DMO execution. During your project lifecycle, you'll have to perform three or more executions before reaching your production system. The information within these files is used by SUM for the production migration, which helps ensure that the processes execute as efficiently as possible. Never reuse XML files from a failed SUM DMO migration.

> **Note** [«]
>
> Need to know more about the SUM DMO? Check out the SAP Product Manager's SL Toolset space on the SAP Community Network at *http://scn.sap.com/docs/DOC-49580*. Recent news and enhancements are frequently posted there. It's also an excellent space to ask questions and get support from others in the SAP community.

5.2.2 Update with Software Update Manager and then Migrate with Software Provisioning Manager

The second option SAP offers customers is to first update your SAP instances to a supported SAP ERP release for SAP HANA and then migrate to SAP HANA using SWPM. This is often referred to as the classical migration option. There are specific use cases where this option is required. For example, if your source release is SAP ECC 5.0 with a lower support package level than that which is supported by SUM, you must use this option to migrate. Another use case is if your source release is SAP R/3 4.7. SUM supports a one-step upgrade, Unicode conversion, and migration to SAP HANA from SAP R/3 4.6C but not 4.7. Here again, the SAP customer would require a multiphase project with an upgrade first and then a migration. Depending on the size of the system and the hardware involved, you wouldn't be able guarantee a weekend cutover for this type of environment.

[»] **Note**

SAP continues to enhance the SL Toolset. Always check SAP Note 1563579 – Central Release Note for Software Logistics Toolset 1.0 for links to the updated versions of the tool. You'll also find out if your source release is supported in a one-step upgrade and migration.

SAP has stated the preferred approach to an SAP Business Suite on SAP HANA migration is the SUM DMO (see *http://scn.sap.com/docs/DOC-49743*); however, the classical migration tools are proven. The underlying OS/DB migration tools have been available for more than 15 years; they're known, and well documented. SWPM breaks down the migration to SAP HANA into multiple tasks selected from the UI as shown in Figure 5.81. Each task executes a series of phases (which you'll run step by step in Chapter 7).

SUM DMO does have one disadvantage when compared to SWPM. As of August 2015, SWPM can perform an SAP Business Suite on SAP HANA migration to a SAP HANA database using multitenant database containers. SUM DMO can only migrate SAP ERP systems to SAP HANA without multitenant configuration. During post-migration to SAP Business Suite on SAP HANA, you can perform the one-way switch from single tenant to multitenant.

[»] **Note**

SAP multitenant database containers enable multiple SAP components to use one instance of SAP HANA with separation of resources, security, and data. If you want to know more, take a look at SAP Note 2096000 – SAP HANA Multitenant Database Containers Additional Information. This SAP Note provides links to SAP Help, SAP HANA Administration Guides, and notes specific to multitenancy in SAP HANA.

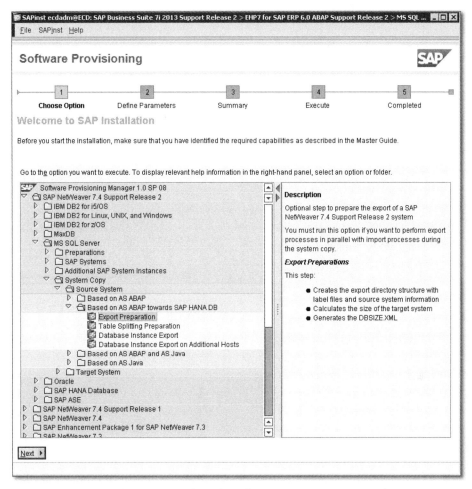

Figure 5.81 Example Selection Screen from the Software Provisioning Manager for Migration to SAP HANA

When executing the migration using SWPM, you have multiple options for the actual movement of data. When performing the export and import as two distinct separate tasks, you have the option of moving files been the source and target database using NFS or FTP. When using the option in SWPM for parallel export and import, you have another option of Network Socket Mode, which stores export data in temporary files that are then removed when the import is complete. The first option of performing an export and import as two distinct tasks has its use cases. If you're moving systems to a new geographic location or between on-premise and cloud, then the option to export and then import might be useful. Parallel export and import is the most widely leveraged use case.

Multiple tools are involved in the migration process. You already know the primary tool—SWPM. Let's explore the additional tools in use during this process:

- **Migration Monitor (migmon)**
  Migration Monitor is part of SWPM and controls export and import of data. It include the following tasks:
  - Create R3Load command files.
  - Create R3Load task files.
  - Start R3Load processes.
  - Transfer data files from source to target.
  - Manage the parallel export/import processes.
  - Provide detailed error handling.
- **R3Load**
  Performs all load tasks for the databases involved and is part of the kernel.
- **R3ldctl**
  Reads the ABAP Dictionary and creates source files to be used by R3Load.
- **R3ta**
  Serves as the table splitter tool provided by SAP for large tables.
- **Package Splitter**
  Distributes packages between processes to maximize throughput.
- **Time Analyzer (migtime)**
  Helps analyze the runtime of the processes.

All of these tools are included with the kernel in SWPM as well as the ABAP AS. It's important that you always start your project with the latest available kernel, which includes the latest versions of the tools. Downloading and installing these updates ensures that known issues are avoided. In addition to downloading the latest versions of the tools, you'll also want to download the latest version of SUM. In Section 5.1.6, we talked about the table comparison tool, which can be run standalone to support the validation of the SWPM system copy and migration processes. You'll need to prepare SUM following the steps defined in Section 5.1.3 as if you were going to execute the SUM DMO. However, you'll only use the table comparison tools. SWPM and SUM DMO can coexist on the same system without issue.

5.3 Summary

In this chapter, we covered a variety of tools your team will leverage during the SAP Business Suite on SAP HANA migration, including the Maintenance Planner, which provides details on the components and target versions, and the stand-alone benchmark tools to estimate migration runtimes. We also covered the SL Toolset, which performs the actual migration. Each one of these tools is dependent upon another, and it all begins with good source information within your SAP Solution Manager. We've covered SAP Solution Manager in various portions of this book, and it will continue to be an important part of your landscape. Each SAP ERP system in your landscape needs to both report information and be correctly assigned product systems within SAP Solution Manager's LMDB.

In the subsequent chapters, we'll execute the SAP ERP migration to SAP HANA using each option: SUM DMO and SWPM. By now you understand the approach for each tool and the process at a technical level, and you're ready to dive deep into the technical activities required during the SAP Business Suite on SAP HANA migration. Each chapter will include detailed screenshots and an explanation of the parameters on screen. We'll cover not only the execution of the tasks but also how to troubleshoot issues if they appear. These chapters will act as your guide through the update and migration process.

An upgrade and migration to SAP Business Suite on SAP HANA is the preferred approach for most customers. You can maximize the value of testing, limit downtime, and move your business to the latest SAP Business Suite on SAP HANA platform before the migration to SAP S/4HANA.

6 Migration Using the Software Update Manager with the Database Migration Option

The Software Update Manager with Database Migration Option (SUM DMO) will be your guide through the migration process. It controls all aspects of the migration, including the pre-migration checks, importing upgrade-related objects, migrating the data, and starting production operations on your newly upgraded (patched) and migrated SAP Business Suite on SAP HANA system. In Chapter 5, we talked about the download, installation, and basic setup of the Software Logistics Common UI (SL Common UI). In the past, you accessed SUM using a Java frontend, which most SAP administrators are aware of. The SUM DMO interface can only be accessed via the new SL Common UI, which is a SAPUI5 application. In this chapter, we'll show you step by step how to execute the SUM DMO processes on a system that requires an enhancement package, support package, and database migration to SAP HANA. Every SAP customer environment is unique, not only from the hardware perspective but also from the components installed, customizations, interfaces, and enhancements. In this chapter, we provide examples of an actual migration from one platform to another using the same tools you have available in the SAP Service Marketplace.

6.1 Prerequisites

Although we covered all the prerequisites in Chapter 5, we'll list them again here to ensure that you're ready to get started. Be sure to check for updates on the

SOFTWARE LOGISTICS TOOLSET 1.0 page on the SAP Support Portal at *http://support.sap.com/sltoolset*.

1. You've used the Maintenance Optimizer (Maintenance Planner) to identify your target enhancement and Support Package Stack (SP stack). The content has been downloaded from the SAP Support Portal and put into a single directory on the server with the *stack.xml*.

2. SUM has been extracted into a directory with 50GB–100GB of free space. The size of the directory will depend on the number of support packages applied.

3. You've configured the SAP Host Agent and SUM for the SL Common UI.

4. The following target SAP HANA database information is available:
   ▶ Hostname
   ▶ Port
   ▶ SAP HANA <SID>ADM account and password
   ▶ SAP HANA SYSTEM account password

5. You've downloaded and extracted the SAP HANA client to a directory on the primary application server (PAS).

6. You've determined what additional hosts (if any) will be used for the shadow instance and/or data migration.

7. The migration key is available that is specific to this SID being migrated.

6.2 Executing the Software Update Manager with Database Migration Option

At this point you are ready to execute the update and migration of an ERP system to SAP HANA. The instructions below will guide you step by step through a migration scenario where the database is migrated to SAP HANA but the application server remains on MS Windows.

1. Connect to *http://<hostname>:1128/lmsl/sumabap/<SID>/doc/sluigui/*, and log on as the <SID>ADM account for the PAS.

2. Enter the path to the *stack.xml* file, and click NEXT (see Figure 6.1).

Figure 6.1 Initial Software Update Manager Screen

3. Enter the passwords for the Data Dictionary (DDIC) and the <SID>ADM account for the PAS.

4. You now have the option of importing a SAP Patch Manager (SPAM) update. In this system SPAM/SAINT (SAP Add-On Installation Tool) is already running the latest version. Check the SAP Support Portal for the latest version specific to your landscape. Import that newer version, or click SKIP SPAM UPDATE.

5. When prompted to enter the target database type, select SAP HANA.

6. On the next screen, you have two selection items. The first option enables you to select the table comparison options. For the first migration you complete, you'll select OPERATE ON ALL TABLES. The following are a few things to keep in mind here:

   ▸ SAP doesn't recommend running the comparison during the production migration because it adds processing time.

   ▸ You can start the table comparison tool as a standalone component.

   ▸ You can also input a list of critical tables to be checked.

7. Enter your MIGRATION KEY (see Figure 6.2). (See Chapter 5, Section 5.1.7 for additional details on generating your migration key.) Click NEXT.

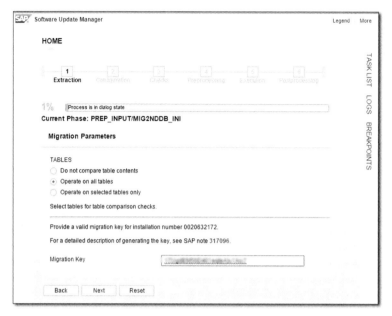

Figure 6.2 Entering the Migration Key and Deciding Whether to Compare Tables

8. Next you get confirmation that the extraction step is complete (see Figure 6.3). You also see a reference to two files for more information. *CHECK.TXT* and *CHECKS.LOG* contain the same information, and one should be checked when you move between phases.

Figure 6.3 Confirmation That the Extraction Step Is Complete

SAP provides additional information within these files, and they could ask you to install notes or review another log file. You'll find the files under *<SUM Directory>\ABAP\log*.

9. Review one of the files, and click NEXT.

10. At the beginning of the configuration step, you need to select the method with which you will proceed:

   ▶ STANDARD: Provides a shadow system and standard downtime minimization features.

   ▶ ADVANCED: Leverages a shadow system but enables you to select more advanced downtime minimization features such as Near Zero Downtime (nZDM).

11. Choose not to keep archiving on during the upgrade process. Database log file management can be cumbersome during updates. Given the amount of support packages and the enhancement package to be installed, leave this option deselected.

12. Check the SWITCH EXPERT MODE ON option, which allows you to do the following:

   ▶ Choose the instance number for the shadow instance.

   ▶ Use a remote shadow instance on another host.

   ▶ Leverage a saved profile.

13. After you've made your selection, click NEXT.

14. Input the number of processes specific to the process types for the uptime and downtime phases (see Figure 6.4 and Figure 6.5). Ideally, you would have already used the benchmark migration in Chapter 5, Section 5.1.5 to develop a plan for these processes.

15. Enter the number of processes based on the number of cores on the server and the results from the benchmark migration.

16. Under the section CHOOSE AN EXECUTION STRATEGY FOR TRANSACTION SGEN select DO NOT START ABAP LOAD GENERATION AS PART OF THE UPDATE. After the system is available, you can schedule SGEN manually. Running SGEN manually later will reduce the total processing time of the SUM execution but increase your post processing time. In most scenarios we want the system returned to an operational state quickly even if that means the very first users on the system will see transactions compiling at runtime.

17. Chose AUTOMATED BATCH JOB DISTRIBUTION as well to let the PAS and SUM decide to use multiple application servers. Ideally, you have a background job group defined in your system if multiple application servers are present.

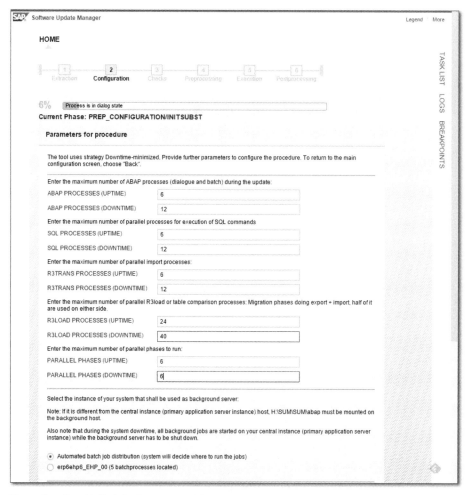

Figure 6.4 First Half of the Parameters Selection Screen

18. In this example scenario, we didn't choose to use a remote shadow instance due to hardware availability. Using this option will decrease the workload on the PAS and distribute work across multiple servers.

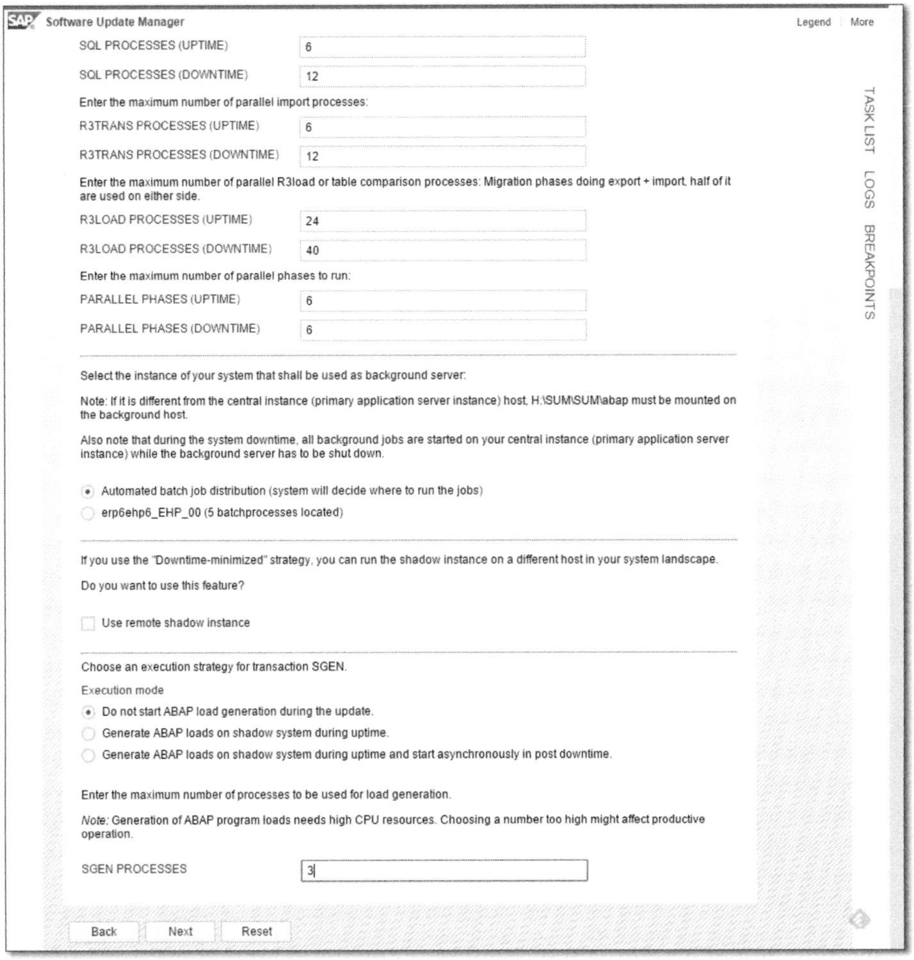

Figure 6.5 Second Half of the Parameters Selection Screen

19. When prompted, give the <SID>ADM password. This enables SUM to install the SAP HANA client.

20. Enter some parameters for the target SAP HANA database, and provide the file path to the permanent SAP license key. Enter the SAP HANA TARGET HOST-NAME, SID OF THE TARGET DATABASE, and TARGET INSTANCE NUMBER.

21. In the TARGET SYSTEM LICENSE field, enter the path to the license file for your SAP system.

▷ You can retrieve your existing system's license by logging on to *http://support.sap.com/system-data* and select VIEW AND EDIT YOUR SYSTEM DATA and search for your system. Select it.

▷ Click on the LICENSE KEY tab, and then click DISPLAY LICENSE SCRIPT. Save the content to a file accessible by SUM.

22. Enter the path to your license file, and click NEXT (see Figure 6.6).

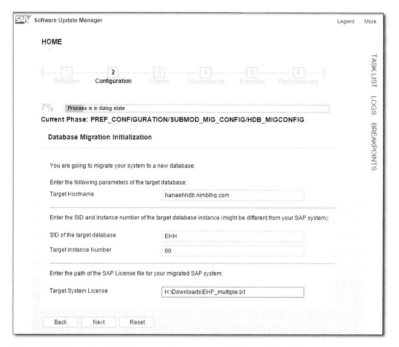

Figure 6.6 Entering SAP HANA Information and the Path to the License Key

23. Next, you're prompted for the SYSTEM user's password within the SAP HANA database. Enter the password, and click NEXT.

24. After you click NEXT, you should move to the next step. In our test case, however, an error appears (see Figure 6.7) and directs you to the *<SUM Directory>\ABAP\log\CHECKS.TXT* file.

25. Within the log file (see Figure 6.8), you can see that an SAP Note is missing that is required for the process to continue. To rectify this, download and install the note. Then click NEXT.

Figure 6.7 Error Message and Need to Check Log Files

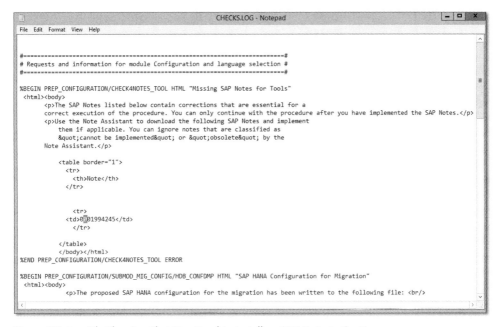

Figure 6.8 Log File Showing That You Need to Install an SAP Note to Continue

[»] **Note**

You may or may not receive an error at this step. Your system might require dozens of notes or none at all. What this highlights is the SUM tool's capability to support different environments. The *CHECKS.TXT* file is used throughout the process. Be sure to check this file for errors between screens.

26. Now you get the option to change the target version for several add-ons (see Figure 6.9).

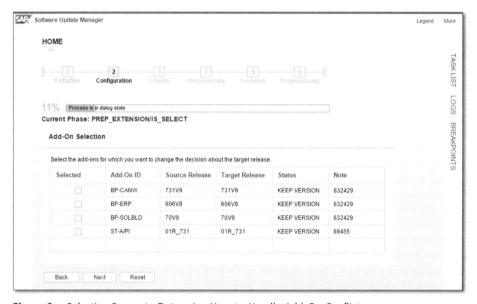

Figure 6.9 Selection Screen to Determine How to Handle Add-On Conflicts

27. Using the SAP Notes provided in the table in Figure 6.9, you can follow a process that allows you to enter a key to have these add-ons removed. Without going into too much detail for the sample environment (which will be different than yours), there were three ABAP add-ons that were specific to EHP 6 and not supported in EHP 7, which were related to the SAP Best Practices package installation. You may never see the screen shown in Figure 6.9, or you may see different objects. View the notes provided in the table much like the one displayed in Figure 6.9, and follow the procedure defined.

28. If your ABAP add-ons are third-party add-ons that SUM doesn't know how to handle, you'll see a screen like the one in Figure 6.10.

Figure 6.10 SUM Providing Multiple Options to Handle Add-On Conflicts

29. In this example scenario, we entered a vendor key (provided by SAP) to move forward. This may or may not be the solution in your system.

30. After resolving add-on conflicts, click NEXT.

31. In the SELECT SUPPORT PACKAGES YOU WANT TO INCLUDE screen, you can override the settings provided by *stack.xml*.

32. The screen shown in Figure 6.11 is displayed because you selected SWITCH EXPORT MODE ON earlier. Accept the defaults, and click NEXT.

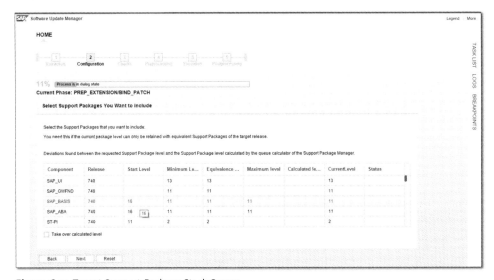

Figure 6.11 Target Support Package Stack Screen

33. On the INCLUDE CHANGE REQUEST screen, you have the option of including a transport or group of transports as part of the upgrade processes. If this is your first upgrade, it's likely you won't have anything to include here.

34. Enter transports, or leave it blank. Click NEXT.

35. On MODIFICATION ADJUSTMENT screen, you can choose to include a Transaction SPAU and Transaction SPDD transport. After your development team has completed Transaction SPAU/Transaction SPDD activities in a development system, you can include their transport at this point.

36. As this is the first migration, leave the fields blank, and click NEXT.

37. On the SHADOW INSTANCE NUMBERS screen (see Figure 6.12), you can change the instance ID for the shadow instance. This option is displayed because you selected SWITCH EXPERT MODE ON earlier in the process. For this example, accept the default port, and click NEXT.

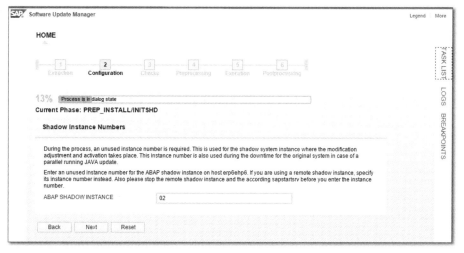

Figure 6.12 Shadow Instance Settings

38. Next you can use previously saved profiles generated for the shadow system. If this is your first migration, select NO, and then click NEXT.

The profiles are saved under the *<SUM Directory>\ABAP\save* directory. After a migration, you can save these profiles before selecting CLEANUP at the end of the processing.

You've now completed the configuration step (see Figure 6.13), so you can now move on to the checks step:

1. You're now prompted to review the *CHECKS.TXT* file. Navigate to *<SUM Directory>\ABAP\log* to review, and click NEXT.

Figure 6.13 Completion Message for the Configuration Step

2. Review the *CHECKS.TXT* file (see Figure 6.14) to find a reference to an SAP Note that contains release information about EHP 7. Continue with the SUM process.

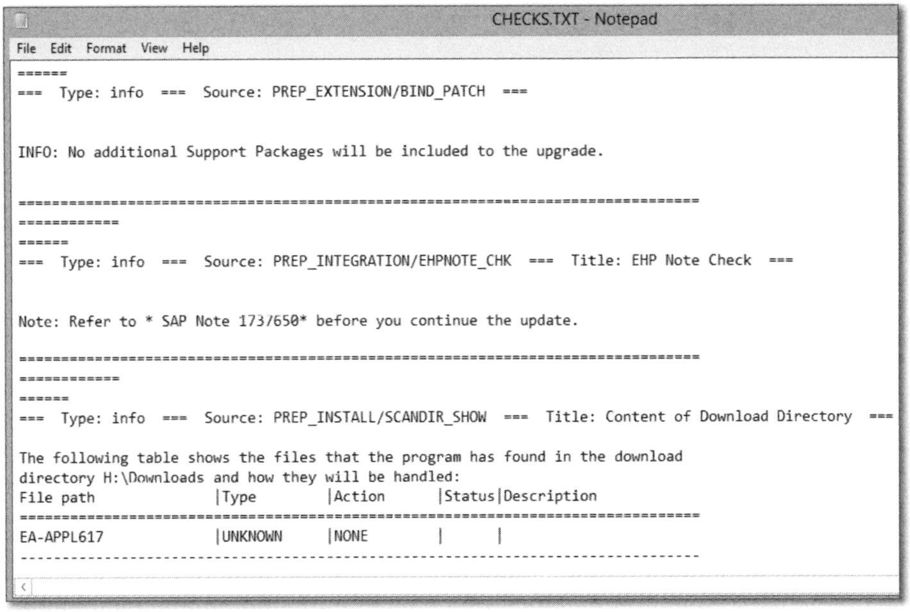

```
                                    CHECKS.TXT - Notepad
File  Edit  Format  View  Help
======
===  Type: info  ===  Source: PREP_EXTENSION/BIND_PATCH  ===


INFO: No additional Support Packages will be included to the upgrade.


=================================================================================
============
======
===  Type: info  ===  Source: PREP_INTEGRATION/EHPNOTE_CHK  ===  Title: EHP Note Check  ===


Note: Refer to * SAP Note 173/650* before you continue the update.

=================================================================================
============
======
===  Type: info  ===  Source: PREP_INSTALL/SCANDIR_SHOW  ===  Title: Content of Download Directory  ===

The following table shows the files that the program has found in the download
directory H:\Downloads and how they will be handled:
File path              |Type        |Action      |Status|Description
=================================================================================
EA-APPL617             |UNKNOWN     |NONE        |      |
---------------------------------------------------------------------------------
```

Figure 6.14 Example CHECKS.TXT Log File from the Software Udate Manager Process

3. Next you're prompted to start the Application Specific Upgrade (ASU) Toolbox. The ASU Toolbox provides a list of standard SAP Notes, background jobs, or programs that are required as part of the upgrade.

4. The content displayed in the ASU Toolbox is specific to your landscape.

   ▸ Log on to your SAP ERP instance with a valid user ID and password.

   ▸ Run Transaction /n/ASU/UPGRADE.

5. In this example migration scenario, all the ASU tasks are related to SAP Notes. You select each task, review the SAP Note, and then select the green question mark button to set the task complete as shown in Figure 6.15 and Figure 6.16.

6. Complete all tasks within the ASU Toolbox, then return to the SUM UI, and click NEXT.

7. After completing all tasks within Transaction /n/ASU/UPGRADE as shown in Figure 6.17, you return to the SUM UI. Click NEXT.

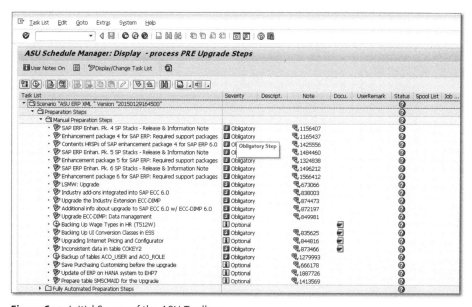

Figure 6.15 Initial Screen of the ASU Toolbox

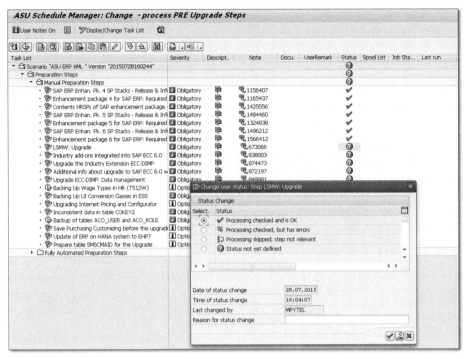

Figure 6.16 Selecting the Question Marks to Change the Task Status

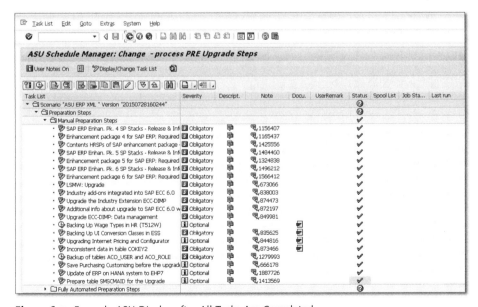

Figure 6.17 Example ASU Display after All Tasks Are Completed

8. The checks step is now complete. Once again, you review the *CHECKS.TXT* log file in the *<SUM Directory>\ABAP\log* directory as shown in Figure 6.18.

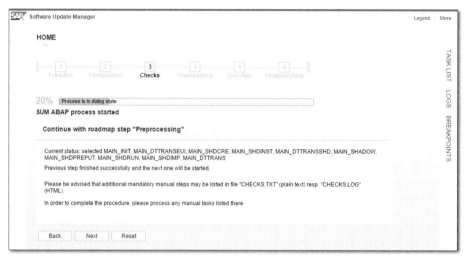

Figure 6.18 Completion Screen for the Checks Step in the Software Update Manager

9. After reviewing the *CHECKS.TXT* file for this example scenario, we're made aware of open updates on the source system. This issue is specific to this migration.

10. Log on to the system, and execute Transaction SM13 to delete or reprocess any updates displayed.

[»] **Note**

The error in our *CHECKS.TXT* related to open updates was specific to our system in our upgrade scenario. The important takeaway here is that SUM runs the required system checks to ensure that future processes complete correctly.

11. Click NEXT, and move onto the next step.

You're now in the preprocessing phase, which prompts you to lock development. This disables the creation of transports in your system and effectively disables any configuration or development in your system.

1. Confirm that your team is ready to lock development, and click NEXT.

2. The SUM tool prompts us to release two open transports. This is specific to our system and this example upgrade scenario. SUM is completing the required checks before continuing.

3. Release the transports, and click NEXT (see Figure 6.19).

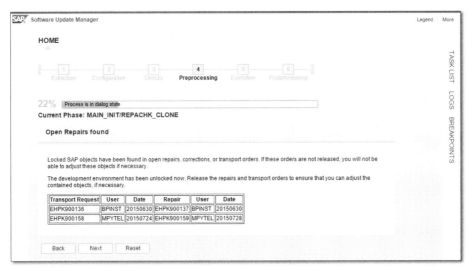

Figure 6.19 Displayed Open Transports That Need to Be Released

4. The preprocessing phase will complete two main activities:

   ▶ Create the shadow instance.

   ▶ Perform the migration of the repository.

5. After the migration of the repository is complete, you'll be presented with a screen to prepare for downtime.

6. At this point, you need to ensure that all users are logged off the system.

7. You can hold all background jobs using the ABAP Program BTCTRNS1.

8. When SUM says you need to "isolate the central instance" in Figure 6.20, this refers to multiple potential scenarios:

   ▶ Unschedule any Cron utility tasks or scheduled tasks at the operating system (OS) level. Essentially, SUM needs to be able to process uninterrupted.

   ▶ Validate the operation modes to ensure that nothing will change in the middle of the processes. You can use Transaction SM63.

▸ Validate Transaction SM13 again for any unprocessed update transactions.

▸ Shut down all application servers except for the PAS (and the remote shadow instance server).

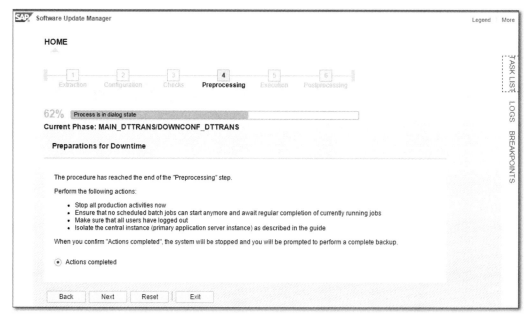

Figure 6.20 Preparations for Downtime Screen

9. You also need to validate the *CHECKS.TXT* file (see Figure 6.21).

10. When you receive a message that the preprocessing phase is complete, click NEXT to enter the downtime phase.

11. At this point you need to back up both your source database and the SUM directory.

12. After the backups are complete, click NEXT to enter downtime processing. After entering the downtime phase, your screen will continue to update with the various subtasks.

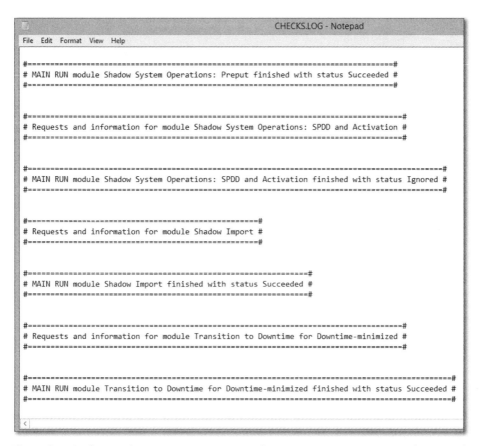

Figure 6.21 Confirming That Your CHECKS.TXT Log File Has No Errors, Warnings, or Informational Messages

The execution phase will include the following activities:

► Migration of SAP ERP data to the target SAP HANA database

► Repository and kernel switch

► Main import of objects

To begin this phase, consider the following:

1. You can dynamically increase or decrease the number of processes using the following URL: *http://<hostname>:1128/lmsl/sumabap/<SID>/set/procpar.*

2. As shown in Figure 6.22, you can modify the number of processes based on your system utilization during runtime.

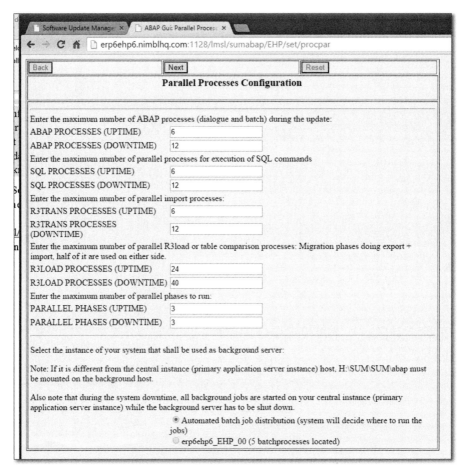

Figure 6.22 Modifying Parallel Process Counts during Execution

3. In this example scenario, we were able to see consistent 90–100% CPU utilization, so our settings remained unchanged.

4. You also can view a log file provided by SAP that attempts to predict the completion time of the SUM processes.

5. From the PAS, navigate to the *<SUMDirectory>\ABAP\log* directory, and display the *SAPupStat.log*. Scroll to the bottom, and the times displayed next to END are your predicted end times (see Figure 6.23).

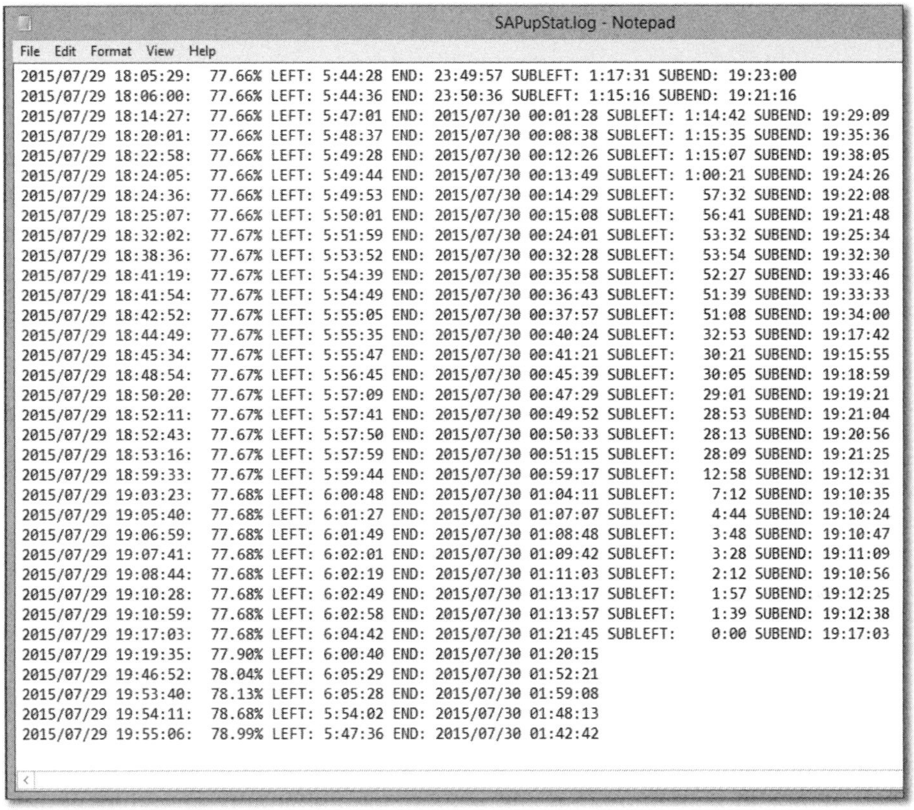

```
                                    SAPupStat.log - Notepad
File  Edit  Format  View  Help
2015/07/29 18:05:29:  77.66% LEFT: 5:44:28 END: 23:49:57 SUBLEFT: 1:17:31 SUBEND: 19:23:00
2015/07/29 18:06:00:  77.66% LEFT: 5:44:36 END: 23:50:36 SUBLEFT: 1:15:16 SUBEND: 19:21:16
2015/07/29 18:14:27:  77.66% LEFT: 5:47:01 END: 2015/07/30 00:01:28 SUBLEFT: 1:14:42 SUBEND: 19:29:09
2015/07/29 18:20:01:  77.66% LEFT: 5:48:37 END: 2015/07/30 00:08:38 SUBLEFT: 1:15:35 SUBEND: 19:35:36
2015/07/29 18:22:58:  77.66% LEFT: 5:49:28 END: 2015/07/30 00:12:26 SUBLEFT: 1:15:07 SUBEND: 19:38:05
2015/07/29 18:24:05:  77.66% LEFT: 5:49:44 END: 2015/07/30 00:13:49 SUBLEFT: 1:00:21 SUBEND: 19:24:26
2015/07/29 18:24:36:  77.66% LEFT: 5:49:53 END: 2015/07/30 00:14:29 SUBLEFT:   57:32 SUBEND: 19:22:08
2015/07/29 18:25:07:  77.66% LEFT: 5:50:01 END: 2015/07/30 00:15:08 SUBLEFT:   56:41 SUBEND: 19:21:48
2015/07/29 18:32:02:  77.67% LEFT: 5:51:59 END: 2015/07/30 00:24:01 SUBLEFT:   53:32 SUBEND: 19:25:34
2015/07/29 18:38:36:  77.67% LEFT: 5:53:52 END: 2015/07/30 00:32:28 SUBLEFT:   53:54 SUBEND: 19:32:30
2015/07/29 18:41:19:  77.67% LEFT: 5:54:39 END: 2015/07/30 00:35:58 SUBLEFT:   52:27 SUBEND: 19:33:46
2015/07/29 18:41:54:  77.67% LEFT: 5:54:49 END: 2015/07/30 00:36:43 SUBLEFT:   51:39 SUBEND: 19:33:33
2015/07/29 18:42:52:  77.67% LEFT: 5:55:05 END: 2015/07/30 00:37:57 SUBLEFT:   51:08 SUBEND: 19:34:00
2015/07/29 18:44:49:  77.67% LEFT: 5:55:35 END: 2015/07/30 00:40:24 SUBLEFT:   32:53 SUBEND: 19:17:42
2015/07/29 18:45:34:  77.67% LEFT: 5:55:47 END: 2015/07/30 00:41:21 SUBLEFT:   30:21 SUBEND: 19:15:55
2015/07/29 18:48:54:  77.67% LEFT: 5:56:45 END: 2015/07/30 00:45:39 SUBLEFT:   30:05 SUBEND: 19:18:59
2015/07/29 18:50:20:  77.67% LEFT: 5:57:09 END: 2015/07/30 00:47:29 SUBLEFT:   29:01 SUBEND: 19:19:21
2015/07/29 18:52:11:  77.67% LEFT: 5:57:41 END: 2015/07/30 00:49:52 SUBLEFT:   28:53 SUBEND: 19:21:04
2015/07/29 18:52:43:  77.67% LEFT: 5:57:50 END: 2015/07/30 00:50:33 SUBLEFT:   28:13 SUBEND: 19:20:56
2015/07/29 18:53:16:  77.67% LEFT: 5:57:59 END: 2015/07/30 00:51:15 SUBLEFT:   28:09 SUBEND: 19:21:25
2015/07/29 18:59:33:  77.67% LEFT: 5:59:44 END: 2015/07/30 00:59:17 SUBLEFT:   12:58 SUBEND: 19:12:31
2015/07/29 19:03:23:  77.68% LEFT: 6:00:48 END: 2015/07/30 01:04:11 SUBLEFT:    7:12 SUBEND: 19:10:35
2015/07/29 19:05:40:  77.68% LEFT: 6:01:27 END: 2015/07/30 01:07:07 SUBLEFT:    4:44 SUBEND: 19:10:24
2015/07/29 19:06:59:  77.68% LEFT: 6:01:49 END: 2015/07/30 01:08:48 SUBLEFT:    3:48 SUBEND: 19:10:47
2015/07/29 19:07:41:  77.68% LEFT: 6:02:01 END: 2015/07/30 01:09:42 SUBLEFT:    3:28 SUBEND: 19:11:09
2015/07/29 19:08:44:  77.68% LEFT: 6:02:19 END: 2015/07/30 01:11:03 SUBLEFT:    2:12 SUBEND: 19:10:56
2015/07/29 19:10:28:  77.68% LEFT: 6:02:49 END: 2015/07/30 01:13:17 SUBLEFT:    1:57 SUBEND: 19:12:25
2015/07/29 19:10:59:  77.68% LEFT: 6:02:58 END: 2015/07/30 01:13:57 SUBLEFT:    1:39 SUBEND: 19:12:38
2015/07/29 19:17:03:  77.68% LEFT: 6:04:42 END: 2015/07/30 01:21:45 SUBLEFT:    0:00 SUBEND: 19:17:03
2015/07/29 19:19:35:  77.90% LEFT: 6:00:40 END: 2015/07/30 01:20:15
2015/07/29 19:46:52:  78.04% LEFT: 6:05:29 END: 2015/07/30 01:52:21
2015/07/29 19:53:40:  78.13% LEFT: 6:05:28 END: 2015/07/30 01:59:08
2015/07/29 19:54:11:  78.68% LEFT: 5:54:02 END: 2015/07/30 01:48:13
2015/07/29 19:55:06:  78.99% LEFT: 5:47:36 END: 2015/07/30 01:42:42
```

Figure 6.23 Varied End Times in the Example Scenario

6. As the execution phase continues, you should see the status changes on screen. You can close the browser and access it again at any point.

7. When the execution phase is complete, you'll see the message shown in Figure 6.24. Click Next.

8. At this point, the system is running and unlocked. Users can now access the system. The phase completion message reminds you to view *CHECKS.TXT*.

9. Open the *CHECKS.TXT* file to look for errors or warnings. Confirm that none exist and continue (see Figure 6.25).

Figure 6.24 Completion Message for the Execution Phase

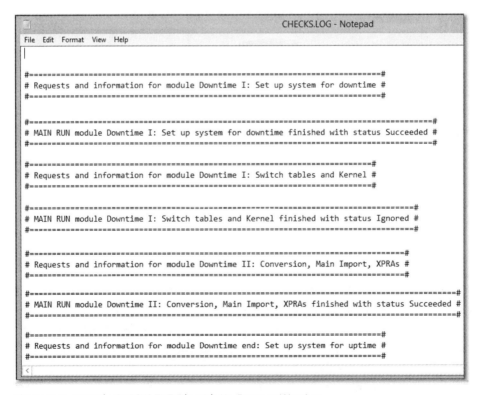

Figure 6.25 Example CHECKS.TXT File with No Errors or Warnings

10. The next screen reminds you to check Transaction SPAU and Transaction SPAU_ENH (see Figure 6.26).

   ▹ At this point, the development team uses the transactions previously described to either accept SAP updates of objects or remediate the objects manually.

   ▹ Transaction SPAU also prompts you to reimplement, update, or remove specific SAP Notes.

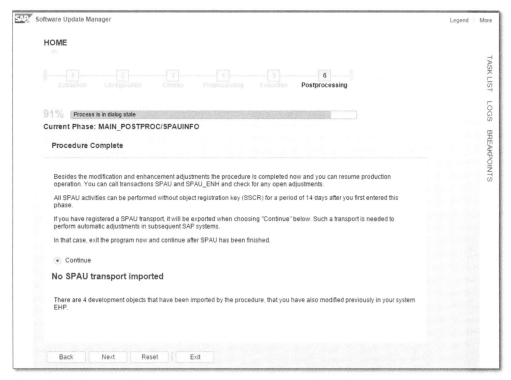

Figure 6.26 Software Update Manager Prompting You to Remediate Objects in Transaction SPAU

11. You don't need to wait for the development team to complete the tasks before clicking Next. You can progress through the transaction.

12. The Evaluation Form appears, which can be sent to SAP (see Figure 6.27). You can disregard this step or complete the form and submit. We recommend completing it because this supports the information exchange between customers and SAP. SAP uses this information to report against and enhance its solutions based on the results of customer executions.

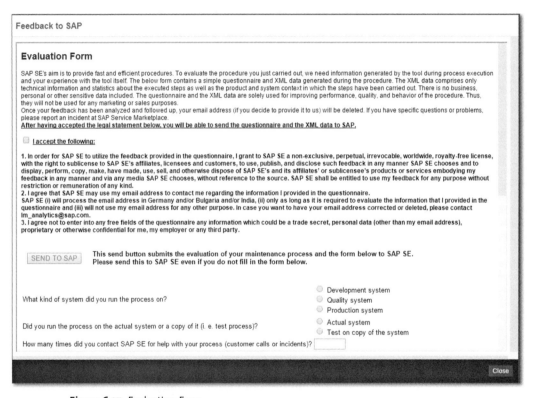

Figure 6.27 Evaluation Form

At this point, the SUM DMO processing is complete (see Figure 6.28). Before clicking the Cleanup button, however, you have some postprocessing items to complete, which we'll discuss in the following section.

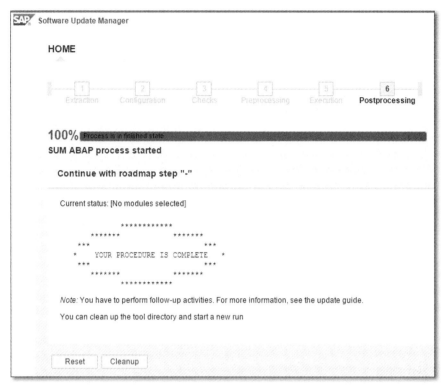

Figure 6.28 Complete Message for the Software Update Manager Database Migration Option Process

6.3 Postprocessing

You've completed your SAP Business Suite on SAP HANA migration with SUM—congratulations! Now you have some post-processing activities that need to be completed. You can release the system to your users at this point for validation, testing, or additional post-migration tasks. The following tasks can be run while the system is online and available:

1. Save two files within the SUM directory for future use. Before executing the cleanup step in the SUM UI, copy the *<SUM Directory>\ABAP\htdoc* directory to a central location.

2. The folder contains the following two files you'll place within the same directory on the next execution of SUM:

- ► ..\htdoc\MIGRATE_UT_DUR.XML: Uptime migration stats.
- ► ..\htdoc\MIGRATE_DT_DUR.XML: Downtime migration stats.

3. Log on to the SAP ERP system with a valid user ID and password.

4. Run Transaction SICK, and confirm no errors or warnings (see Figure 6.29).

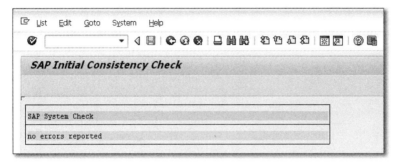

Figure 6.29 Results from the SAP Consistency Check

5. Import profiles from the OS. The SUM process edited the profiles at the file system, but they haven't been written to the database.

6. Run Transaction RZ10, and select UTILITIES • IMPORT PROFILES • OF ACTIVE SERVERS (see Figure 6.30).

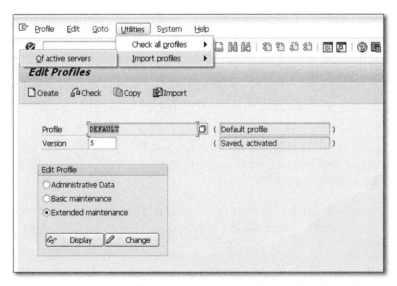

Figure 6.30 Importing Profiles from the Operating System and Inserting Them into the Database

7. Confirm the results of the import, and click BACK (see Figure 6.31).

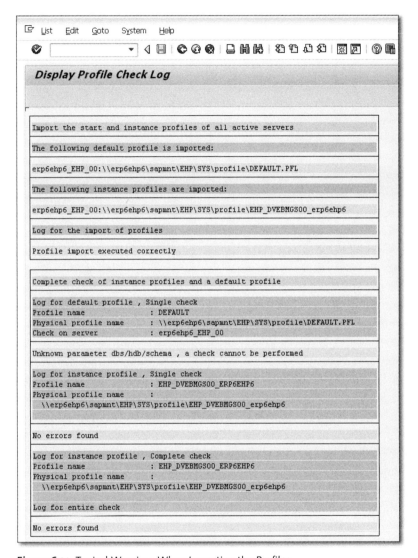

Figure 6.31 Typical Warnings When Importing the Profiles

8. To validate the changes (or to restore changes to the profiles before the execution of SUM), select DEFAULT in the PROFILE field, select the EXTENDED MAINTENANCE radio button, and click DISPLAY (see Figure 6.32).

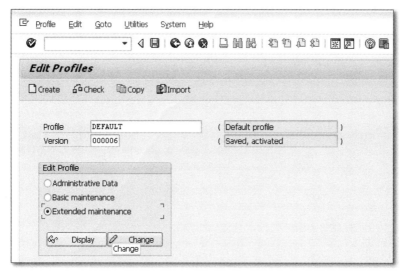

Figure 6.32 Validating the Profiles Loaded into the Database

9. After the profile is displayed, validate that the values for the following parameters are specific to the target SAP HANA database (see Figure 6.33):

  ▸ SAPDBHOST

  ▸ DBMS/TYPE

  ▸ DBS/HDB/SCHEMA

  ▸ RSDB/DBID

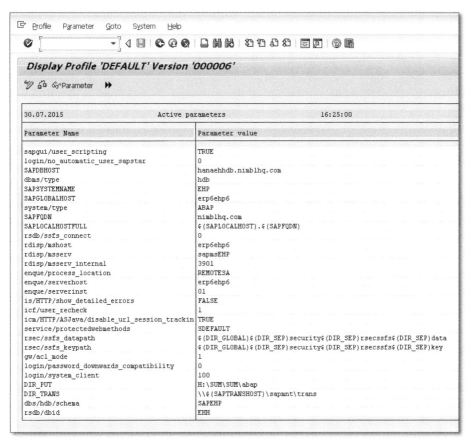

Figure 6.33 Validating the Updated Values Specific to the SAP HANA Database

10. Click BACK until you return to the main menu.

11. Run Transaction SM36 to schedule standard SAP jobs.

12. Click the STANDARD JOBS button, and confirm any new background jobs to be scheduled (see Figure 6.34).

13. Click the DEFAULT SCHEDULING button (see Figure 6.35). When you see the message DEFAULT JOBS SCHEDULED, click BACK to get to the main menu.

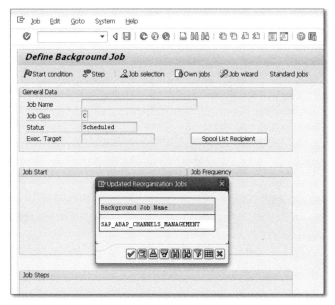

Figure 6.34 Scheduling Default SAP Jobs

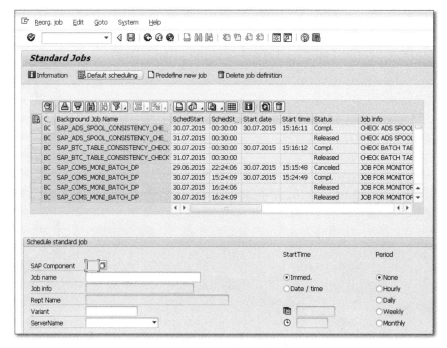

Figure 6.35 Summary Screen Displaying the Default SAP Jobs

14. Update the Transport Management System (TMS) if this system is a transport domain controller.

15. Run Transaction STMS, and select SYSTEM OVERVIEW (see Figure 6.36).

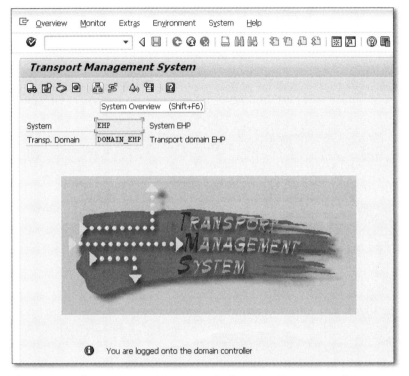

Figure 6.36 Selecting System Overview in the Transport Management System

16. Highlight the migrated system in the grid row, and select SAP SYSTEM • CHANGE.

17. Click on the TRANSPORT TOOL tab, and update the following parameters (see Figure 6.37).

   ▸ DBHOST: <your SAP HANA DB Hostname>

   ▸ DBTYPE: "hdb"

18. Click SAVE, and then click BACK.

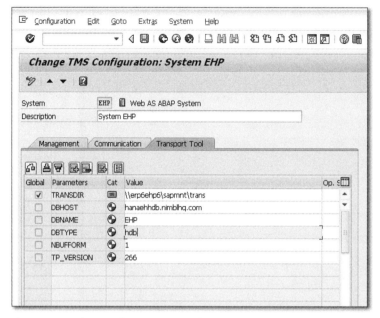

Figure 6.37 Adjusting the Transport Tool Settings Post-SAP HANA Migration

19. Click the DISTRIBUTE AND ACTIVATE button.

20. Select DISTRIBUTE CONFIGURATION TO ALL SYSTEMS, and click OK (see Figure 6.38).

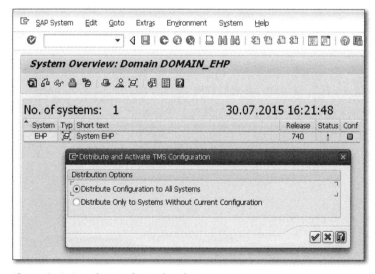

Figure 6.38 Distributing the Updated Transportation Management System Configuration

21. Log off and log back on to Client 000 of the system.

22. Run Transaction SA38, and input program "BTCTRNS2".

23. Press the EXECUTE, button and confirm the results.

24. Log off and back on to the production client.

25. Call Transaction SGEN to generate objects if you chose to skip SGEN during the update. Schedule the job for a future date and time if required.

26. Check for unused indexes. Run Transaction DB02.

27. Navigate to DIAGNOSTICS • MISSING TABLES AND INDEXES (see Figure 6.39).

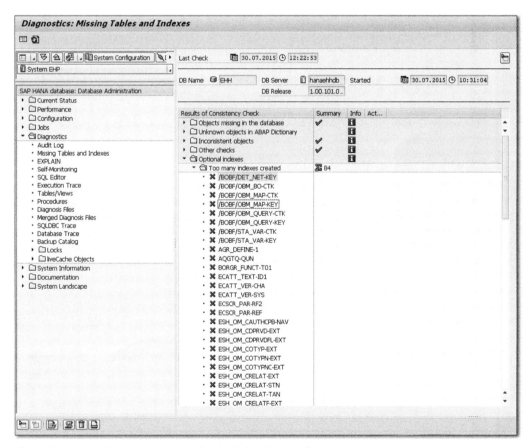

Figure 6.39 Example Indexes That Need to be Deleted Manually

28. If you see indexes under the Too many indexes created node, you need to delete them manually using Transaction SE14 or Transaction SE11. The list of indexes will be different for each environment depending on kernel version or system usage.

[»] **Note**

For more information on why you need to remove these indexes, see SAP Notes 1227270 and 2127815.

29. Run Transaction RZ70. Validate the System Landscape Directory (SLD) information.

   ▶ This should be an SLD that feeds information to SAP Solution Manager.

   ▶ Reporting updated information to SAP Solution Manager is required to complete postprocesses in SAP Solution Manager.

30. Click the Execute button and validate results as shown in Figure 6.40 and Figure 6.41.

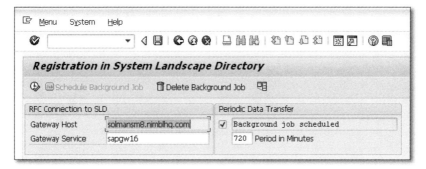

Figure 6.40 Validating System Landscape Directory Target Information

31. The SAP-specific post-processing is complete. Your specific landscape or migration scenario might require customer-specific configuration to be completed.

[»] **Note**

SAP continually updates SUM documentation, specifically, the tasks you need to complete before, during, and after a SUM execution. See SAP's up-to-date guide on the SAP Support Portal at *http://service.sap.com/sltoolset*. Choose SL Toolset 1.0 • Documentation • System Maintenance • DMO of SUM 1.0 up to SP 13 with Target DB: SAP HANA.

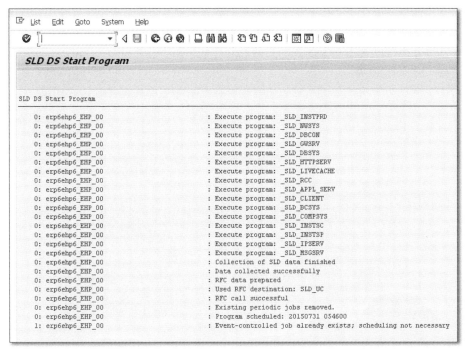

Figure 6.41 Sending Updated System Information to the System Landscape Directory

6.4   Troubleshooting and Tips

Throughout the procedure in the previous section, we discussed the logs and directories that can provide critical information to resolving errors during the SUM DMO processing. Within the SUM tool, the right side navigation panel displays the current TASK LIST and LOGS. When selecting LOGS (see Figure 6.42), you receive an HTML-formatted display of the *<SUM Directory>\ABAP\Log*. From within SUM, you can sort logs descending and view log content directly. Performance within the HTML view can be slow when viewing large logs files.

If you encounter problems that extend beyond those already identified in the SUM SAP notes and SUM documentation, you can report an incident to SAP Support. When submitting an incident to SAP, it's important that you share specific files and information with SAP to speed up the resolution process. Here are a few tips on categorizing incidents and content to share:

▶ Use the category BC-EHP-INS-TLA or BC-UPG-TLS-TLA (enhancement package or upgrade).

▶ Attach the *supportFile.xml* file generated by the SUM UI when selecting MORE • GET SUPPORT FILE.

▶ Attach the *SAPup_troubleticket_logs.sar* field from *<SUM Directory>\ABAP\Log*.

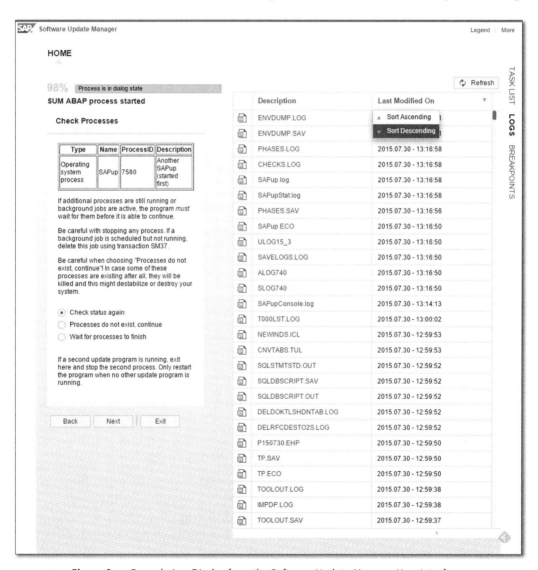

Figure 6.42 Example Log Display from the Software Update Manager User Interface

> **Tip** [+]
>
> The single logon to the SUM UI is the only logon available, which means any person who knows the account and password can potentially impact the execution of the tools. Keep this account and password secure during the migration process. If you encounter issues displaying content with the SUM UI, be sure to check your browser settings to disable any caching. If you encounter errors, be sure to check the directories we described in this chapter. Often when you receive errors in SUM, it's related to disk space, database availability, or application server availability. Be sure to check these more obvious but sometimes forgotten areas if you're unable to find information in the logs. And, as always, share your experiences not only with SAP but with the SAP community either through the SAP Community Network or Americas' SAP Users' Group (ASUG).

As a final reminder, at this point, the backup schema for SAP HANA should be in place. Your backup schema for SAP HANA should not only include data and log backups but also a procedure to back up the INI configuration files as part of SAP HANA. If you need to restore or rebuild your SAP HANA appliance, the configuration files might be required along with the mandatory data and log backups.

> **Note** [«]
>
> For more tips and procedures related to troubleshooting, see the official SUM guides from SAP. Navigate to *http://service.sap.com/sltoolset*, and choose SL TOOLSET 1.0 • DOCUMENTATION • SYSTEM MAINTENANCE • UPDATING SAP SYSTEMS USING SOFTWARE UPDATE MANAGER 1.0 SP 13.

6.5   Summary

You've now completed a migration using SAP's recommended approach. Congratulations! However, we know the work doesn't stop here, and there will be tasks you need to complete specific to your environment. We've covered the SAP system-level tasks to ensure your newly migrated SAP Business Suite on SAP HANA system is operational. From here, you would release the system to project team members for validation and testing, and inform the developers of the modifications and adjustments needed.

The migration tools and process are standardized and well documented. We've covered most screens within the SUM tool, but keep in mind certain steps might differ based on the components installed and source release. The overall phases within the SUM tool will remain the same. As of August 2015, the SUM DMO tools don't provide a view only mode like the previous versions of SUM. Another feature missing as of August 2015 is the ability to call a command line function when the SUM UI is waiting for input. In the past, we could invoke an SMTP script to send us an email when SUM was waiting for a response. After communicating with the SL Toolset product manager at SAP—we can expect multiple enhancements in the next few months to support view only and some type of command line to SMTP notification.

At this point you should have a good idea on the use of SUM DMO and its processes at the various stages of the migration. You've learned how to use the SL Common UI to find logs to troubleshoot any errors that might occur. We have provided suggestions on pre- and post-processing tasks; these tasks are not specific to your environment, but can be used as a baseline for developing your own set of tasks. You will have multiple executions of the SUM DMO processes prior to your production migration to do so. In the next chapter we will move to a different migration strategy: the heterogonous system copy using the Software Provisioning Manager.

The classical migration to SAP Business Suite on SAP HANA uses proven technology to migrate a system as-is. In this chapter, we'll explore the parallel export and import of a system using the Software Provisioning Manager.

7 Migration Using the Software Provisioning Manager

You've now reached the second option for the migration to SAP Business Suite on SAP HANA. At this point, you've already updated your SAP ERP and current database system to a supported version for the migration to SAP HANA and are ready for the migration. In Chapter 6, we covered the Software Update Manager (SUM), which enables you to upgrade, convert to Unicode if required, and migrate to SAP HANA. Using the Software Provisioning Manager (SWPM) process, you can convert to Unicode and migrate to SAP HANA, but you don't have the option of installing a support package or enhancement package. The SAP ERP system will be converted as-is with no application-level changes; only the underlying database is changed. This method has its benefits, as it reduces the test scope during the project, but it requires some of the same data validation you executed when using the SUM tool. Migrating to SAP Business Suite on SAP HANA using SWPM will sometimes be referred to as an OS/DB migration or the classical migration. The tools used within this process have been available for years and use some of the same functionality to migrate to any other database as they do to migrate to SAP HANA.

In this chapter, we'll cover some additional prerequisite steps that need to be completed when using SWPM. It's a good idea to install both the SWPM and SUM tools on the PAS because the SUM tool is the only one that contains the benchmark migration tool and the table comparison tool. Although you won't be executing SUM when using SWPM, you might find the two utilities beneficial in planning and validating your migration. SWPM can be described by two main phases: export and import. These two phases can be run independently or in parallel with the latter, providing a shorter runtime. The parallel method is a more real-world scenario, so we've chosen to use it in this chapter. When running the export and import as two separate tasks, you'll actually select fewer options, which greatly simplifies the processes.

[»] **Note**

Whenever you perform a migration using SWPM, check the release notes listed at *http:// service.sap.com/sltoolset* Choose SOFTWARE LOGISTICS TOOLSET 1.0 • SYSTEM PROVISIONING • SOFTWARE PROVISIONING MANAGER 1.0 SP<RELEASE>.

This book assumes a migration to SAP Business Suite on SAP HANA using the SAP HANA scale-up option only. SAP Business Suite on SAP HANA with the scale-out scenario isn't supported as of August 2015. For more details, see SAP Note 1781986 Business Suite on SAP HANA Scale Out.

7.1   Prerequisites

In Chapter 5, we talked about general preparations of the tools involved in the migration to SAP HANA. All of the preparation work there is still required. In this chapter, we'll focus on content specific to SWPM. Unlike with the SUM Database Migration Option (DMO), when using SWPM for the SAP Business Suite on SAP HANA migration, you have to maintain versions of the SWPM tools on both the source and target systems. When you download SWPM, you also need to download the updated kernel for SWPM, which differs from the SAP NetWeaver kernel on your source system. We'll walk through the downloads required, the background jobs to be executed in preparation, and the parallel export/import of your system. First, let's take a moment to review the migration scenario.

SWPM supports the move of the database only, leaving the application servers in place, or the move of both the application server and the database server. In the subsequent screenshots, we'll be migrating a Windows Server 2012 application server and Microsoft SQL database to a new application server on a SAP HANA appliance with the SAP HANA database (shown in Figure 7.1.) This scenario has been supported since 2013 with SAP HANA SP 07+. When performing sizing for the ABAP application server and the SAP HANA database, you use additive sizing with the following formula:

(OS CPU and Memory) + (SAP NetWeaver AS ABAP CPU and Memory) + (SAP HANA DB CPU and Memory) = Total CPU and Memory Requirements

This is a simplification of the IT landscape by combining the two functions onto one system. Of course, this scenario won't work for every SAP customer, so take into account your own SAP sizing requirements when planning your SAP Business Suite on SAP HANA migration.

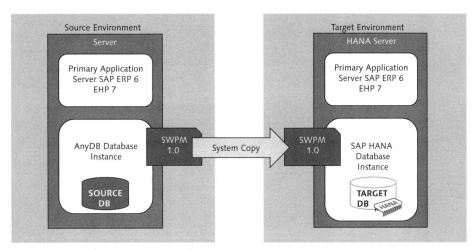

Figure 7.1 Example Scenario Using Software Provisioning Manager to Migrate to SAP Business Suite on SAP HANA

Note [«]

Find out more about ABAP and SAP HANA on one server by checking out the blog article "SAP HANA and SAP NetWeaver AS ABAP Deployed on One Server Is Available" at *https://blogs.saphana.com/2013/12/31/*. Also, see SAP Note 1953429 – SAP HANA and SAP NetWeaver AS ABAP on One Server.

7.1.1 Preparing the Source System

On the source system, you need to perform several tasks in ABAP before you can start the migration. These tasks should become part of your cutover task list (see Chapter 11). Some of the tasks can be performed in the days or weeks before the migration. Others will need to be performed just before the migration execution. We'll highlight both in the following.

Time-Independent Tasks

The tasks listed in this section can be performed in the days or weeks before the migration starts.

Cluster tables and pool tables within SAP ERP will be converted to transparent tables during the migration to SAP HANA. To prevent errors during the conversion or during the insert portion of the import phase, SAP has provided a series of utility reports that can be run in your production environment while it's available to business users.

Follow these steps to run the utility reports:

1. Using Transaction SNOTE, ensure that the latest version of the following SAP Notes have been downloaded and installed in the source system:
    ▸ 1077403 – Cluster Table Check Using SDBI_CLUSTER_CHECK
    ▸ 1807959 – Improved Versions of Reports SDBI_POOL_CHECK and SDBI_CHECK_BCD_NUMBERS
    ▸ 1921023 – SMIGR_CREATE_DDL: Corrections and Enhancements for SAP HANA

2. Using Transaction SA38, enter "SDBI_CLUSTER_CHECK" in the PROGRAM field, and click EXECUTE (see Figure 7.2).

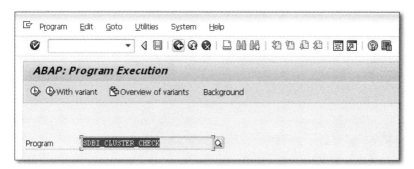

Figure 7.2 Checking Cluster Tables with the Utility Report from SAP

3. Select the DISPLAY OVERALL STATUS radio button, and click EXECUTE. If the check hasn't been run before, you should see the message NOT YET CHECKED (see Figure 7.3).

4. Click the BACK button. Then select the EXECUTE CLUSTER CHECK radio button.

5. Select PROGRAM • EXECUTE IN BACKGROUND from the toolbar. The program can take several hours to process.

6. After the program completes, return to Transaction SA38, and execute Program SDBI_CLUSTER_CHECK. Select the DISPLAY OVERALL STATUS radio button.

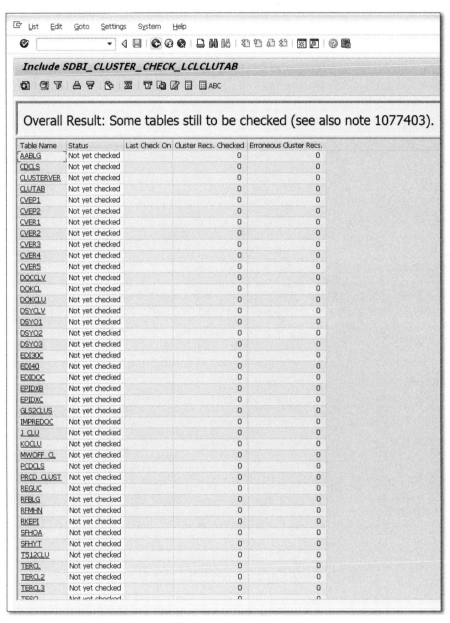

Figure 7.3 Results of the Cluster Table Check Showing No Analysis Has Been Run

7. Validate the results. If all items are green, you can proceed with the migration to SAP HANA.

In parallel to Program SDBI_CLUSTER_CHECK, you also need to execute the pool table check:

1. Use Transaction SA38 to execute Report SDBI_POOL_CHECK.

2. Verify that the SELECT dropdown has ALL POOL TABLES OF ALL TABLE POOLS selected. Click PROGRAM • EXECUTE IN BACKGROUND.

3. After the background job completes, view the spool file. It will display the results (see Figure 7.4).

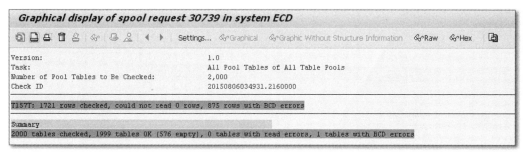

Figure 7.4 Example Output from the Pool Table Check

4. In our example system, one table failed the check with BCD errors (related to numbers with decimals stored in the pool table). To resolve errors such as these, you need to execute the next utility report.

5. Using Transaction SA38, execute Program SDBI_CHECK_BCD_NUMBERS (see Figure 7.5).

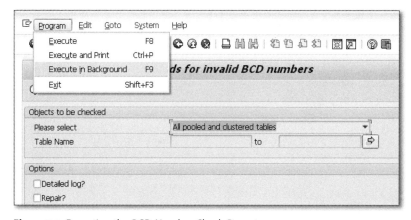

Figure 7.5 Executing the BCD Number Check Report

6. The utility can be executed in a display only mode by selecting ALL POOLED AND CLUSTERED TABLES.

7. If you have the table name that reported errors in Report SDBI_POOL_CHECK, you can select INDIVIDUALLY SELECTED TABLES and then input the table name.

8. Select the REPAIR checkbox, and then choose PROGRAM • EXECUTE IN BACK-GROUND.

9. Validate the results by viewing the spool file (see Figure 7.6).

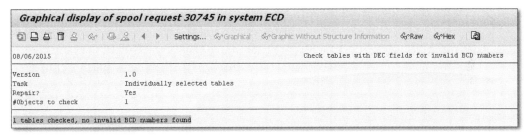

Figure 7.6 RESULTS of the BCD Table Repair Utility

Next you need to prepare a list of tables to be split if this is your first migration. You can either gather a list of tables to be split for the first migration or execute the first migration as-is and then determine which tables to split. Let's assume that you want to make your best effort for performance on the first execution, so you'll need to define a list of tables and the number of splits by following these steps:

1. Run Transaction DBACOCKPIT in your SAP ERP system to be migrated.

2. Navigate to SPACE • LARGEST TABLES, and export the grid to an Excel file by click-ing the EXPORT button and selecting SPREADSHEET. Using some simple formulas, you can define how many splits you want to perform on the largest tables. Here are a few things to keep in mind:

   ▹ Table size isn't always an indicator of tables to be split.

   ▹ Consider splitting tables into 2GB files or keeping them under 10 million rows.

   ▹ The following tables can't be split:

      – Table DDNTF

      – Table DDNTF_CONV_UC

      – Table DDNTT

- Table DDNTT_CONV_UC

- Table DDLOG (is never copied, but created empty in the target system)

- Table REPOLOAD (is never copied, but created empty in the target system)

3. After you've identified the tables to be split and the number of splits, write them to a text file accessible by SUM using the following format:

   <Table>%<Number of Splits> (e.g., *BSEG%6*)

4. In Figure 7.7, the largest tables are displayed, and the table splits are calculated for those tables with more than 10 million rows. Because this is your first migration, you don't have historical data to analyze how to most efficiently split the table. After the first execution of SWPM, you'll have the opportunity to further analyze table load performance to identify future splits.

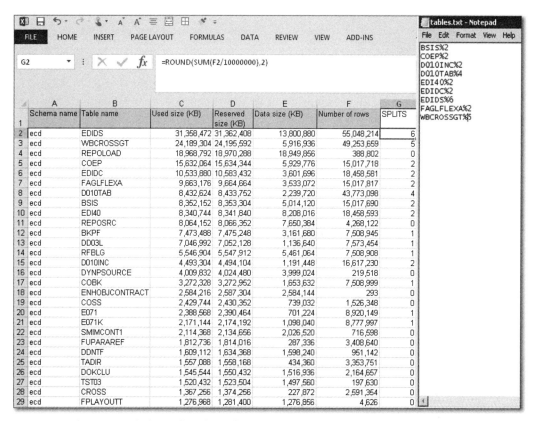

Figure 7.7 Calculating the Table Splits and Then Manually Transferring Them to a Text File

5. Save the text file *tables.txt* to a location accessible by the SWPM process (preferably the directory planned for the export data).

Time-Dependent Tasks

You should execute the task in this section in the days or hours before the migration to SAP HANA using SWPM. These tasks can have various functional impacts when executing them; we'll highlight the specific steps that could have an impact on your end users.

Follow these steps to execute time-dependent tasks:

1. Check for unprocessed updates or updates in error using Transaction SM13.

2. Figure 7.8 shows one unprocessed update from a service account. This entry can be deleted in our example scenario. You have the option of reprocessing the update if required. All unprocessed updates must be removed prior to starting SWPM. Unprocessed updates could be related to erroneous BDC sessions executed by end users. You can check this transaction periodically throughout the year as a best practice.

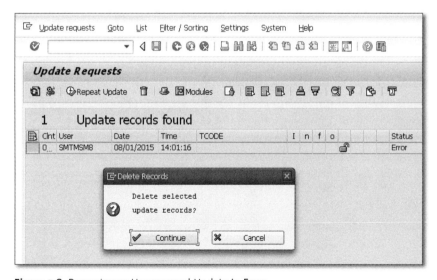

Figure 7.8 Removing an Unprocessed Update in Error

3. To validate that the work modes will remain consistent before and after the migration, run Transaction SM63, and click DISPLAY. Validate that the operation mode will remain consistent (see Figure 7.9).

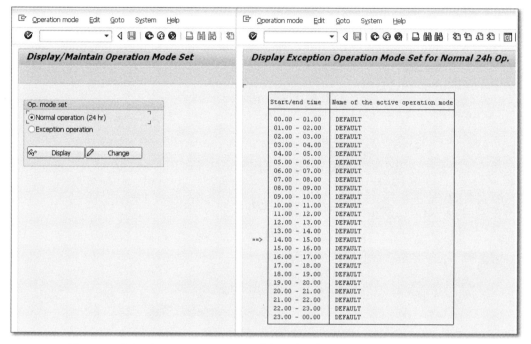

Figure 7.9 Using Transaction SM63 to Validate That the Work Mode Won't Change

4. If not, use the CHANGE button to make the appropriate changes.

5. To review any unfinished table conversions, run Transaction SE14, and then select EXTRAS • INVALID TEMP. TABLE.

6. Select any tables displayed, and then click the DELETE SELECTED button (see Figure 7.10).

7. To delete any delta queues related to SAP Business Warehouse (SAP BW) or SAP Supply Chain Management (SAP SCM) extraction, execute Transaction RSA7.

8. Review the information displayed, and delete the data in the delta queue (see Figure 7.11). Note that this could impact the target system that the data was supposed to be delivered to. You can also work with those teams to complete the data extraction before starting the SWPM downtime.

Figure 7.10 Confirming Deletion of Temporary Table Objects

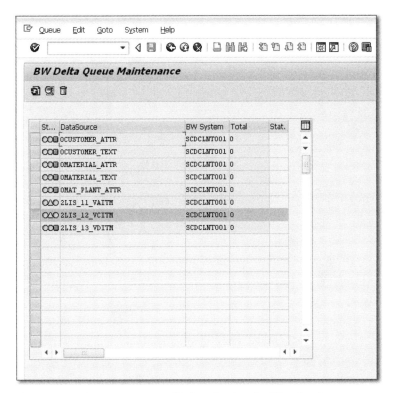

Figure 7.11 Delta Queues Emptied before Starting the Migration Process

Predowntime Nonproductive Tasks

You should execute the tasks in this section immediately before the SWPM execution. You need to lock all user accounts except for Data Dictionary (DDIC) and system administrators, hold background jobs, and then execute two utility programs that will provide input files for the migration.

To execute these tasks, follow these steps:

1. Lock all non-administrative users using Transaction SU10.

2. Prevent background jobs from processing by executing Program BTCTRNS1 in Transaction SA38 (see Figure 7.12).

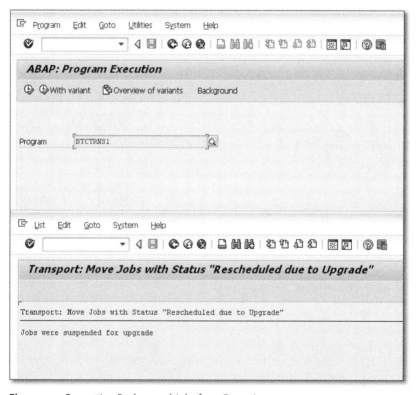

Figure 7.12 Preventing Background Jobs from Executing

3. In Transaction SA38, execute Program SHDB_GROUP_TABLES_LOAD_BASED. This program is technically only required when migrating to a scale-out SAP

HANA instance. If you don't run the program now, you could see warnings during the export.

4. Leave all options default, and select PROGRAM • EXECUTE IN BACKGROUND.

5. After the job completes, you need to generate Data Definition Language (DDL) statements used during the migration. Run Transaction SA38, and execute Program SMIGR_CREATE_DDL.

6. In the TARGET DATABASE area, select the SAP HANA DATABASE radio button (see Figure 7.13).

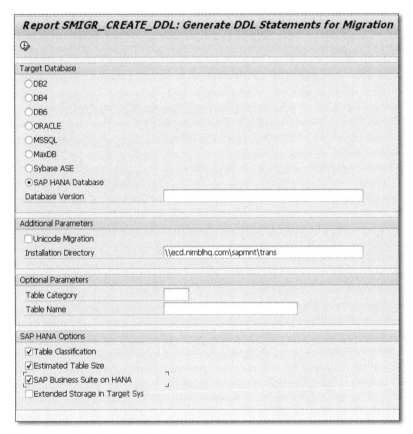

Figure 7.13 Entering Parameters

7. In the ADDITIONAL PARAMETERS area, only select UNICODE MIGRATION if you're converting to Unicode. Enter the path to a folder reachable by the application server in the INSTALLATION DIRECTORY field.

8. In the SAP HANA OPTIONS area, select the following checkboxes

   ▶ TABLE CLASSIFICATION

   ▶ ESTIMATED TABLE SIZE

   ▶ SAP BUSINESS SUITE ON HANA

9. Click PROGRAM • EXECUTE IN BACKGROUND.

10. Validate the program's completion using Transaction SM37.

11. Check the directory specified for the files generated (see Figure 7.14). Save those files to a directory accessible by SWPM.

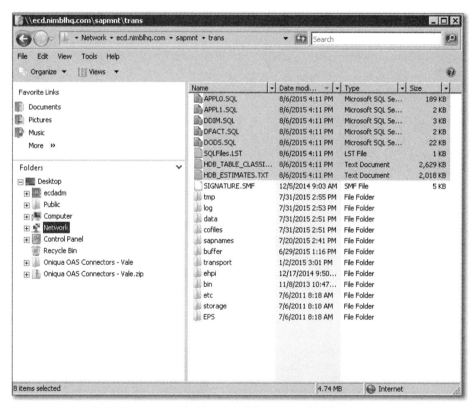

Figure 7.14 Data Definition Library Files Generated by the ABAP Utility

7.1.2 Preparing the Target System

In this section, we assume you've already determined your target system, performed the SAP sizing, and prepared the operating system (OS) for an SAP installation. These tasks are specific to your landscape. In our scenario, the target system will be both the application server and SAP HANA database.

To change the log mode in SAP HANA to "overwrite", follow these steps:

1. Open SAP HANA Studio and log on to the target database.

2. Right-click the system, and select CONFIGURATION AND MONITORING • OPEN ADMINISTRATION.

3. Click on the CONFIGURATION tab.

4. In the filter, search for "log_mode".

5. Under GLOBAL.INI • PERSISTENCE • LOG_MODE, double-click the parameter.

6. Set the new value to "overwrite", and click SAVE (see Figure 7.15).

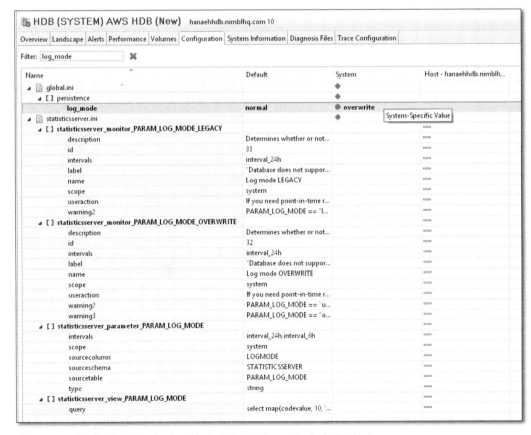

Figure 7.15 Confirming That the Log Mode Is Set to Overwrite in SAP HANA

Next, you need to download SWPM and the latest kernel for SWPM from the SAP Support Portal by following these steps:

1. Navigate to *http://support.sap.com/swdc*, and log on with a valid user ID and password.

2. Continue navigating to SUPPORT PACKAGES AND PATCHES • A–Z INDEX • S • SL TOOLSET • SL TOOLSET 1.0 • ENTRY BY COMPONENT • SOFTWARE PROVISIONING MANAGER • SOFTWARE PROVISIONING MGR 1.0 • SUPPORT PACKAGE PATCHES • <YOUR PLATFORM>.

3. Select the latest version of SWPM10SPXX...SAR (see Figure 7.16).

Figure 7.16 Downloading the Latest Version of Software Provisioning Manager from SAP

4. Next, return to *http://support.sap.com/swdc*.

5. Navigate to INSTALLATIONS AND UPGRADES • A–Z INDEX • S • SL TOOLSET • SL TOOLSET 1.0 • KERNEL FOR INSTALLATION/SWPM • SAP KERNEL 7.42 64-BIT UNICODE • INSTALLATION • <YOUR OS>.

6. Extract the contents of *SWPM10SPXX.SAR* on the target server: *<SAPCAR Path>/SAPCAR –xvf SWPM10SPXX.SAR*.

7. Verify that you can open SWPM using the executable *SAPINST*.

8. In our example scenario, we're logged on to the Linux SAP HANA server. Export the display and then run ./sapinst.

7.2   Preparation

In this section, we describe the process that prepares the source system for export. We'll show you how to execute SWPM to create the export folder with required files that describe the system, export files, and target database size. We'll then step through the tasks required to manually define table splitting for the export to increase processing and performance. As you saw in an earlier chapter, table splitting is an opportunity to decrease the overall processing time by breaking large tables into smaller, more manageable files that can be processed in parallel using multiple processes. The next two subsections will create files within the export directory that will be used throughout the migration process.

7.2.1 Export Preparation

In this section, we're going to start the export process on the source system. After the export process has started, you can immediately start the import process on the target system. You can also prepare the target system first if you've defined the export directory ahead of time. The import processes will wait for files to import while you prepare the export. In our experience, starting the import processes immediately after starting the export process enables the export process to create content to be processed by the import server. Either approach will work. You'll be using the export and import in parallel. Whereas Section 7.2.1 and Section 7.2.2 are linear within the book, you can execute these tasks in parallel.

Follow these steps:

1. Log on to the source system primary application server (PAS) where you installed SWPM.

2. Navigate to the SWPM directory, and execute SAPINST for your platform:
   ▸ Windows: Right-click SAPINST.EXE, and select RUN AS ADMINISTRATOR.
   ▸ Linux: Export your display and then run `./sapinst`.

3. On startup, navigate to SAP BUSINESS SUITE <YOUR RELEASE>. In our example scenario, the system is already at EHP 7.

4. Select your source database, and then choose SYSTEM COPY • SOURCE SYSTEM • BASED ON AS ABAP TOWARDS SAP HANA DB • EXPORT PREPARATION (see Figure 7.17).

5. Next validate the path to the profile directory for the instance you plan to migrate, and click NEXT.

6. Enter the password for the <SID>ADM account on the PAS.

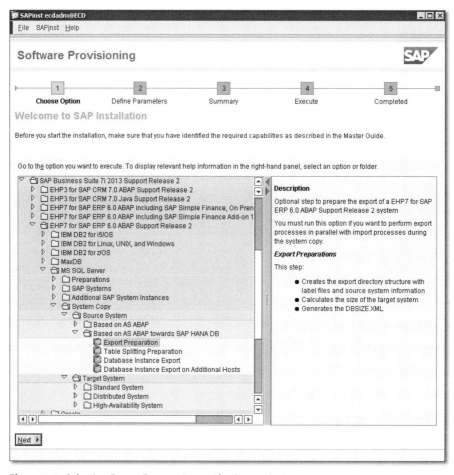

Figure 7.17 Selecting Export Preparation on the Source System

7. Select the DATABASE ID (DBSID) to be migrated as shown in Figure 7.18.

8. Select the export directory to be used for the migration, which should ideally reside on its own disk and controller. Following are a few notes about this step:

   ▹ You have the option to use the Network File System (NFS) between two systems for the data export. If using multiple hosts for export/import, then this directory will need to be mounted on all systems.

   ▹ Alternatively, you can select SOCKETS (FTP) to move data between systems.

   ▹ The directory should be sized to 15%–20% of your total used database size. SAP documentation defines 10% as the requirement for export disk space.

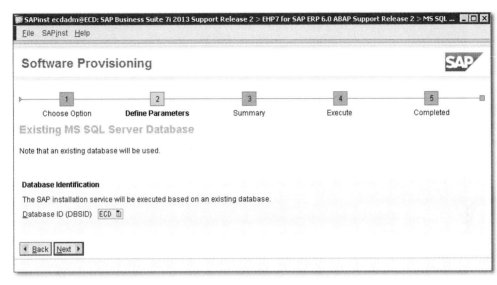

Figure 7.18 Default Database Selected by Default

9. Define the target database, and click NEXT (Figure 7.19).

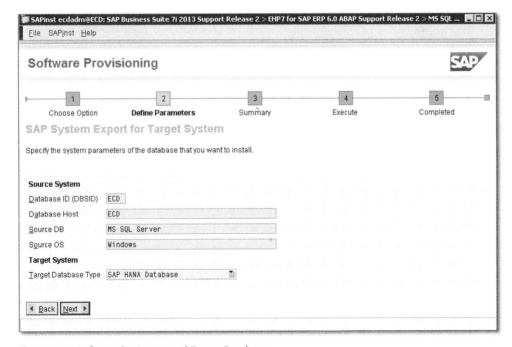

Figure 7.19 Defining the Source and Target Databases

10. On the SUMMARY step, validate your entries, and click NEXT.

11. When the process completes, you'll see the confirmation screen shown in Figure 7.20. Click OK to close SWPM.

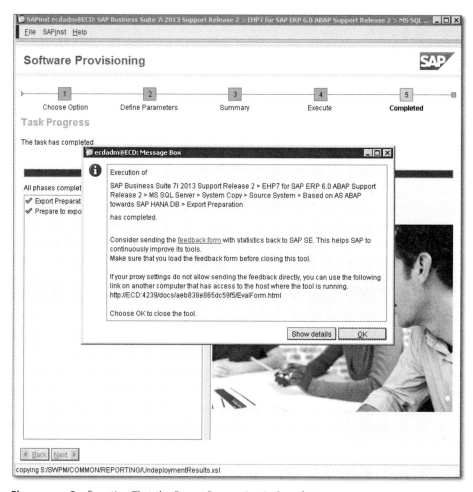

Figure 7.20 Confirmation That the Export Preparation Is Complete

7.2.2 Table Splitting Preparation

Next you need to prepare for table splitting. In this step, we'll use the text file we built in Section 7.1.1 to define the tables to be split during your first system migration to SAP HANA using SWPM. You'll run this step for future migrations with the data you've collected postmigration on the performance of table splits completed by SWPM.

To prepare for table splitting, follow these steps:

1. Log on to the source system PAS where you installed SWPM.

2. Navigate to the SWPM directory, and execute SAPINST for your platform:

    ▸ Windows: Right-click SAPINST.EXE, and select RUN AS ADMINISTRATOR.

    ▸ Linux: Export your display, and then run `./sapinst`.

3. On startup, navigate to SAP BUSINESS SUITE <YOUR RELEASE>. In our example scenario, the system is already at EHP 7.

4. Select your source database, and then choose SYSTEM COPY • SOURCE SYSTEMS • BASED ON AS ABAP TOWARDS SAP HANA DB • TABLE SPLITTING PREPARATION.

5. Specify the profile directory of the system to be migrated, and click NEXT (see Figure 7.21).

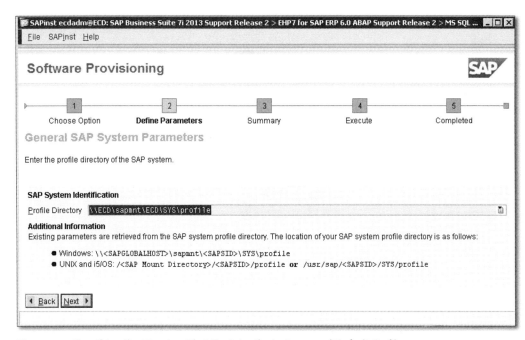

Figure 7.21 Specifying the Directory That Contains the Instance and Default Profiles

6. Enter the password for the <SID>ADM account, and click NEXT.

7. Select the DATABASE ID (DBSID) (which corresponds to the SID you're migrating to SAP HANA) to be migrated, and click NEXT.

8. On the next screen, enter or select data in four fields (Figure 7.22):

   ▶ EXPORT LOCATION: Enter the path to the export directory you defined during the export preparation.

   ▶ TARGET DATABASE TYPE: Select SAP HANA DATABASE.

   ▶ TABLE INPUT FILE: Input the path to the text file that contains the list of tables and the number of splits. The information in the text file will be read to define the table splits.

   ▶ NUMBER OF PARALLEL R3TA JOBS: Enter the number of parallel R3ta jobs to be executed. We recommend two to three jobs per processor core. Our example source system here has four virtualized cores.

Figure 7.22 Defining Parameters for Table Splitting

9. For your first migration with SWPM, we recommend you choose USE R3TA_HINTS.TXT FROM DIRECTORY COMMON\INSTALL OF THE INSTALLATION MEDIA (see Figure 7.23).

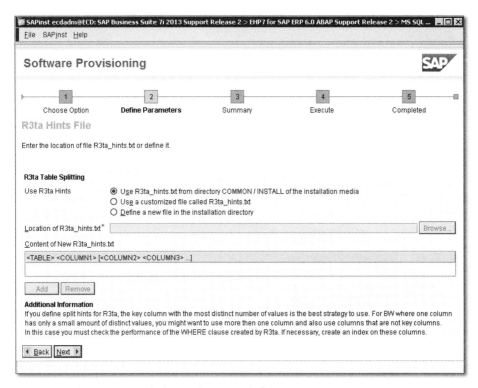

Figure 7.23 Choosing the Default R3ta_hints.txt File from SAP

10. Leave the default selection, and click NEXT.

11. Click NEXT on the SUMMARY screen, which is displayed before the execution of table splitting preparation, to start the process.

7.3 Execution

At this point, you've prepared the source system and defined the table splitting to be executed during the export processing. You can now move forward with the export of the source system and then begin the import into the target system. As we mentioned before, you can start the target system preparation before the source system if you have the export directory defined beforehand. After the instance import is started, it will check for files to import every minute or so. When the export begins, the import processes will pick up the files for import.

SAP has done a good job with SWPM in recent releases. Always let the application start the Migration Monitor for you unless you have an advanced use case where the manual start of the Migration Monitor is required. As a point of reference, we haven't had a use case manually start the Migration Monitor when using the parallel export and import procedure.

7.3.1 Database Export: Source System

At this point, the SAP ERP system can still be operational, but you should have the users locked out and predowntime tasks in process or completed. You'll start the database export in the following steps. SWPM will prompt you to stop the SAP ERP instance when the export begins. You have the option of starting the export and then immediately moving to the import steps on the target system. Our goal is to leverage the parallel export and import capabilities to reduce system downtime.

To perform the database export, follow these steps:

1. Log on to the source system where you installed SWPM. In our example scenario, this system will have the database and application server migrated to a new host.

2. Navigate to the SWPM directory, and execute SAPINST for your platform:

   ▸ Windows: Right-click SAPINST.EXE, and select RUN AS ADMINISTRATOR.

   ▸ Linux: Export your display, and then run ./sapinst.

3. On startup, navigate to SAP BUSINESS SUITE <YOUR RELEASE>. In our example scenario, the system is already at EHP 7.

4. Select your source database, and then choose SYSTEM COPY • SOURCE SYSTEM • BASED ON AS ABAP TOWARDS SAP HANA DB • DATABASE INSTANCE EXPORT (see Figure 7.24). Click NEXT.

5. Enter the password for the <SID>ADM account.

6. Select the DATABASE ID to be exported.

7. Next you input the directory to be used for the export. This is the same directory you used previously for export preparation and table splitting preparation.

8. On the SAP SYSTEM EXPORT FOR TARGET SYSTEM screen (see Figure 7.25), select the TARGET DATABASE TYPE as SAP HANA DATABASE.

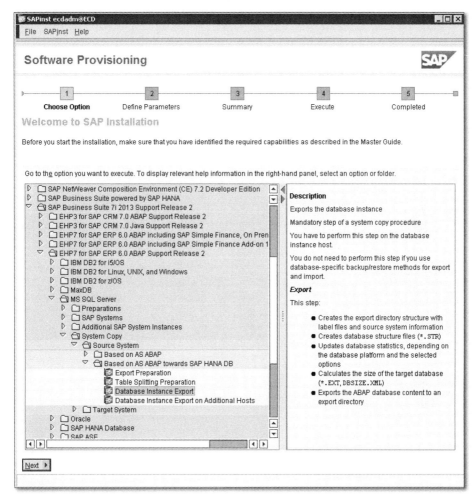

Figure 7.24 Navigating the SWPM Directory to Complete the SAP Business Suite on SAP HANA Export

9. Leave the SPLIT STR FILES option checked, and keep START MIGRATION MONITOR MANUALLY unchecked. Then click NEXT.

10. On the next screen, select the YES, USE THE GENERATED SQL FILES FOR SYSTEM COPY EXPORT radio button to use the SQL files generated by the ABAP Program SMIGR_CREATE_DDL (Figure 7.26). Enter the directory with the SQL files in the SQL FILE DIRECTORY field. You had previously placed these files in the export directory.

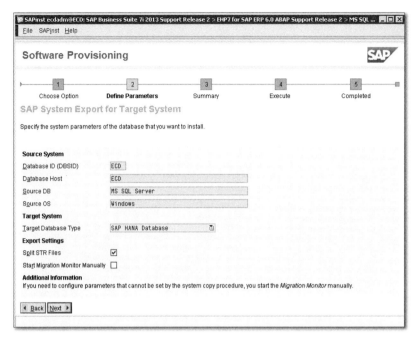

Figure 7.25 Setting to Have the Migration Monitor Automatically Started

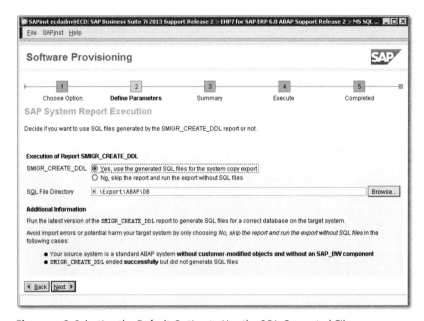

Figure 7.26 Selecting the Default Option to Use the SQL Generated Files

11. On the check step for the generated files, SWPM checks the export directory for the output of the ABAP Program SMIGR_CREATE_DDL. You should see FILE EXISTS for each file displayed (see Figure 7.27).

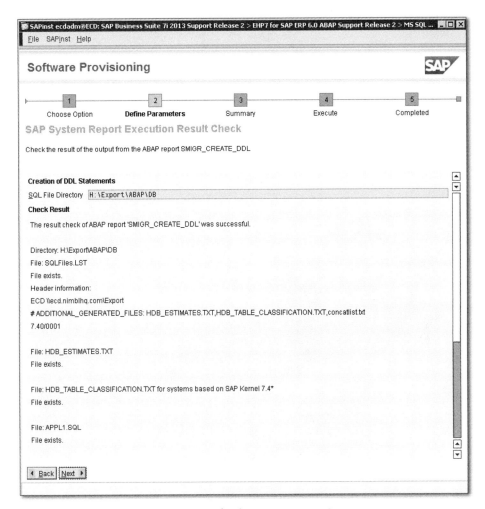

Figure 7.27 Checking the Export Directory for the ABAP Program Output

12. On the SAP SYSTEMS EXTENDED EXPORT OPTIONS screen (Figure 7.28), you select the specific option for your scenario, and click NEXT:

▹ NEW EXPORT FROM SCRATCH: Runs the R3szchk tool again.

▹ REPEAT EXPORT: Restarts an export using existing files in the export directory.

▷ NEW EXPORT, REUSE *.STR, *.EXT, *.WHR FILES: Uses files created in the table splitting preparation or from a previous export.

13. For DETERMINE SIZE OF SOURCE DATA, you want to select USE DATA DICTIONARY INFORMATION (R3SZCHK PARAMETER –S DD) because this is a heterogeneous system copy.

14. Check the box for PARALLEL EXECUTION, and enter the NUMBER OF PARALLEL JOBS. Click NEXT.

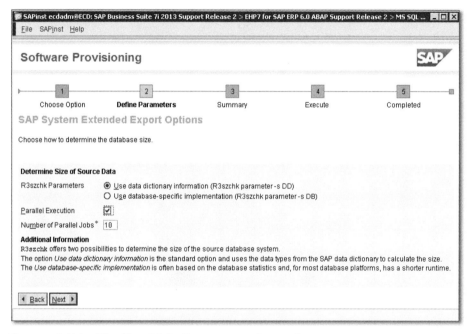

Figure 7.28 Using R3szchk –s DD for Heterogeneous System Copies

15. For SPLITTING TOOL PARAMETERS, select the following options (Figure 7.29):

▷ LARGEST TABLES IN SEPARATE PACKAGES: Checked

▷ NUMBER OF TABLES TO BE EXTRACTED: "10"

▷ SPLIT PACKAGES WITH SIZE MORE THAN LIMIT: Checked

▷ PACKAGE SIZE LIMIT (MB): Default is 1000

▷ EXTRACT TABLES WITH SIZE MORE THAN LIMIT: Checked

▷ TABLE SIZE LIMIT (MB): "300"

▶ SPLIT PREDEFINED TABLES: Checked

▶ TABLE INPUT FILE: Path to the file created during table splitting preparation. This should be the export directory.

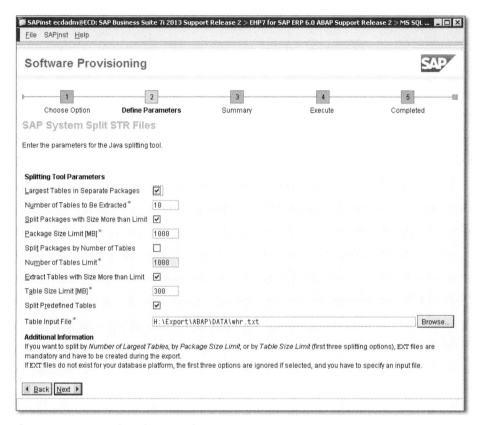

Figure 7.29 Entering the Splitting Tool Parameters

16. For the GENERAL UNLOAD SETTINGS area, leave the default settings. Here again, for this example, we chose not to start the Migration Monitor manually. The NUMBER OF PARALLEL JOBS can be changed at runtime.

17. For the EXPORT OPTIONS area, choose UNLOAD ORDER BY SIZE. After your first or second execution, you can choose to change this option to see if performance is impacted.

18. For the NUMBER OF JOBS IN GROUP area, the default is 5. This option can be changed dynamically during runtime. Also, you don't have a CUSTOM SORT ORDER FILE for the first migration (Figure 7.30).

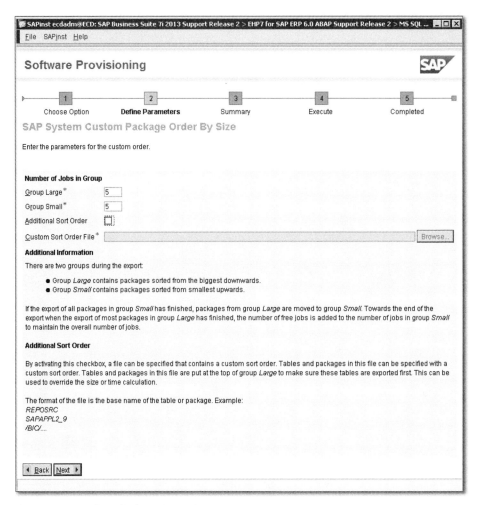

Figure 7.30 Number of Jobs in Group Parameters

19. For the DATA TRANSFER area, for the TRANSFER TYPE, select USE NETWORK SHARE. You have the option of using FTP if your scenario requires this option.

20. For the COMMUNICATION FOR EXPORT area, select USE EXCHANGE DIRECTORY. Then input the local export directory you defined earlier in this process in the NETWORK EXCHANGE DIRECTORY field (see Figure 7.31).

21. Validate the parameters on the PARAMETER SUMMARY screen, and click NEXT to start the process (Figure 7.32).

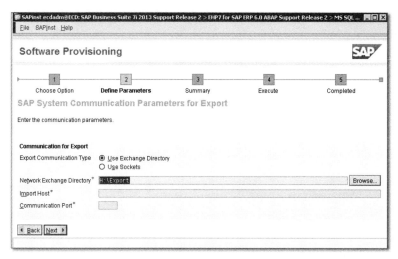

Figure 7.31 Entering the Local Export Directory as the Network Exchange Directory

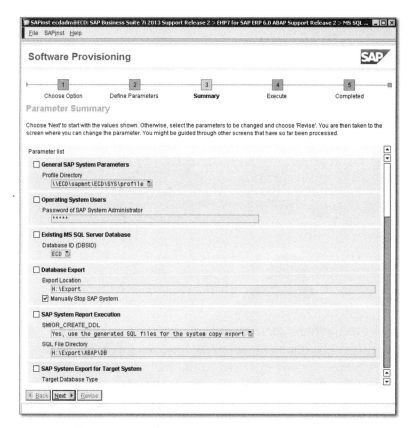

Figure 7.32 Summary Screen for the Export

22. SWPM prompts you to stop the SAP system to begin the export. Stop the SAP system, and click OK.

23. After the Export Monitor is started, you'll see a confirmation on the number of jobs completed in the lower status bar (see Figure 7.33).

Figure 7.33 Migration Monitor – Automatic Start

24. As you monitor the performance of the export system, if you determine that more processes could be run on the source system, you can open the *export_ monitor_cmd.properties* file and dynamically add more jobs by changing the `jobNumLarge` and `jobNumSmall` parameters (Figure 7.34). The properties file is reread every 30 seconds.

Figure 7.34 Modifying the Properties File

After the export completes, you'll see the confirmation message as shown in Figure 7.35.

Figure 7.35 Confirmation That the Export Processes Have Completed

At this point, you should have the import processes running on the target host, which enables the parallel export and import. To understand better how to start the import processes, see Section 7.3.2. If you want to analyze your export processing further, you have three options. The first is the *LogAnalyzer.html* , which is located in the SWPM working directory. This HTML file provides a great high-level summary of the export process. In Figure 7.36, the export completed in just under three hours for the entire process.

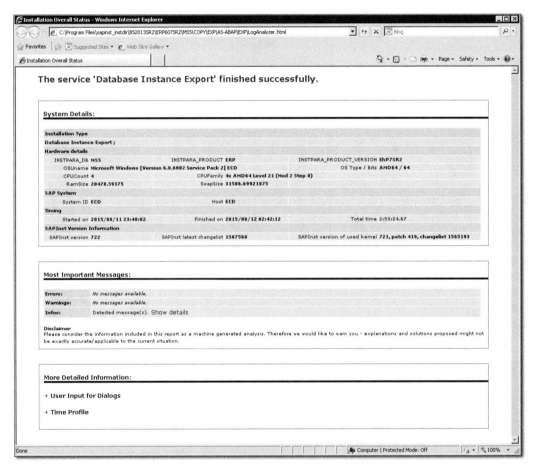

Figure 7.36 Example LogAnalyzer.html Displaying High-Level Export Performance

Next, you can load *R3LOAD_JOBS.CSV* into Excel to graph the number of R3Load jobs by timestamp. You want to see the process ramp up and then ramp down quickly. Ideally, you don't want big swings in the number of active jobs in the middle of the export. Figure 7.37 shows an example of an efficient export.

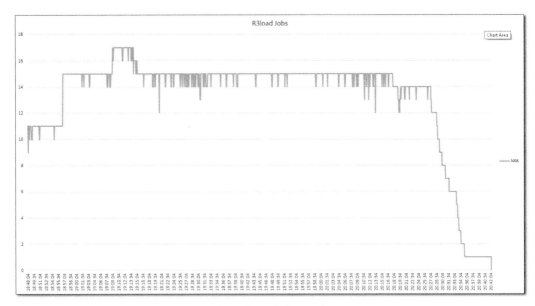

Figure 7.37 Quick Ramp Down Indicating That Jobs Ended Near the Same Time

Next you have a utility from SAP called Migtime or Time Analyzer. This utility is delivered with SWPM within the *COMMON/INSTALL* directory. Follow these steps to create both a text and graphical display of the export processing time by package:

1. Copy the *MIGTIME.SAR* file from the *<SWPM Directory>COMMON\INSTALL* to the SWPM working directory:

    ▸ On Windows, this is *C:\Program Files\sapinst_instdir\....*

    ▸ On UNIX, this is usually */tmp/sapinst_instdir/....*

2. Extract the contents of *MIGTIME.SAR* directly into the working directory of the recently completed export:

    ▸ *<SAPCAR Patch>SAPCAR –xvf MIGTIME.SAR*

3. From the command line, run the following command (Figure 7.38):

    ▸ **On Windows:** `export_time.bat -html`

    ▸ **On UNIX:** `export_time.sh -html`

Figure 7.38 Example Running the Utility from Windows

4. After the command completes, open the following files. The text file displays the runtime for each package.

- ▸ *export_time.txt*
- ▸ *export_time.html*

In Figure 7.39, you can see the packages SAPNTAB, REPOSRC, RFBLG, and EDIDS-3 all had significant runtimes. Originally, we split all tables over 10 million lines, which these tables did not exceed, so we might need to find another metric to key off of to split these tables for the next export.

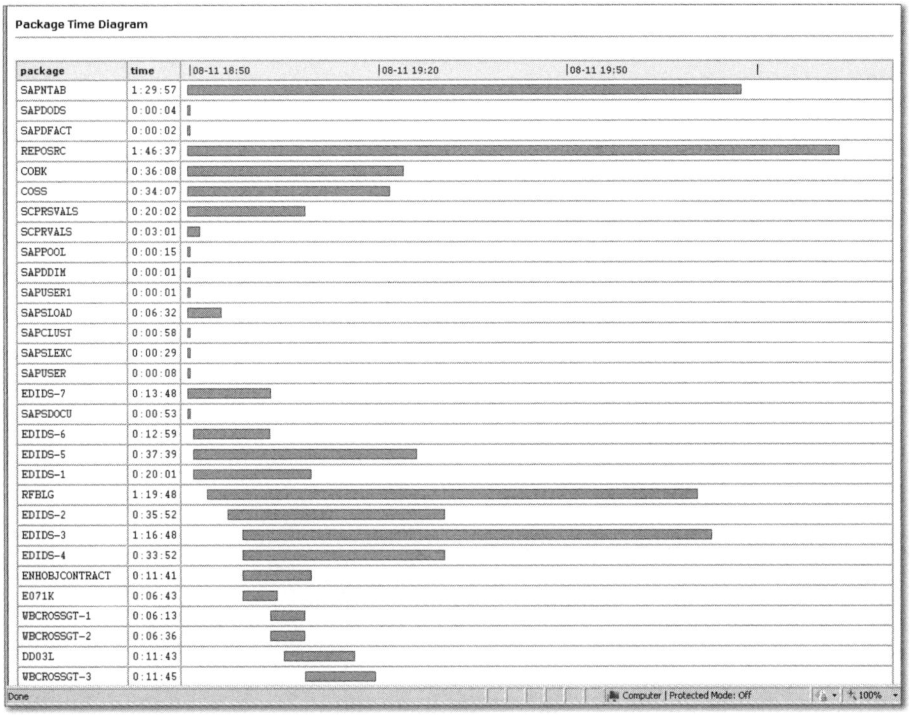

Figure 7.39 Example HTML File Created by the Time Analyzer Utility

7.3.2   System Import: Target System

This step can be executed immediately after the database export has started or can be started concurrently with the database export. The import process essentially waits for files to import once started and continues to wait until tables from the export become available. In our example scenario, we're installing a standard system because our scenario includes moving the SAP ERP ABAP AS and database to the SAP HANA appliance.

Follow these steps for the import process:

1. Before running SWPM, you need to set an environment variable to be used by the installer. This variable should be used for any SAP HANA database SP 08+ and SAP NetWeaver 7.40+. See SAP Note 1806935 – SAP HANA: Corrupt Database after R3Load Import.

2. Our target application server for this example scenario is Linux, so we run the following command within the BASH shell: export HDB_MASSIMPORT=YES (Figure 7.40).

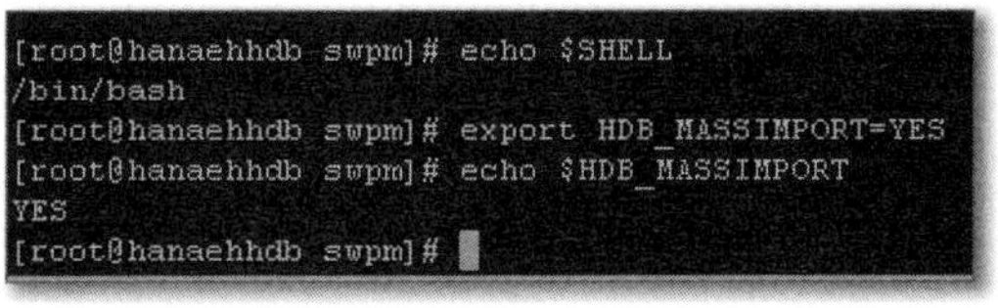

```
[root@hanaehhdb swpm]# echo $SHELL
/bin/bash
[root@hanaehhdb swpm]# export HDB_MASSIMPORT=YES
[root@hanaehhdb swpm]# echo $HDB_MASSIMPORT
YES
[root@hanaehhdb swpm]#
```

Figure 7.40 Setting the Environment Variable to Improve Data Load Performance

3. In Windows, you set the variable in the System Properties. Navigate to CONTROL PANEL • SYSTEM • ADVANCED SYSTEM SETTINGS • ADVANCED • ENVIRONMENT VARIABLES.

4. Log on to the target system where you installed SWPM. In our example scenario, this system will function as the new PAS and database.

5. Navigate to the SWPM directory, and execute SAPINST for your platform:
   ▶ Windows: Right-click SAPINST.EXE, and select RUN AS ADMINISTRATOR.
   ▶ Linux: Export your display, and then run ./sapinst.

6. On startup, navigate to SAP BUSINESS SUITE <YOUR RELEASE>. In our example scenario, the system is already at EHP 7.

7. Select your source database, and then choose SYSTEM COPY • TARGET SYSTEM • STANDARD SYSTEM • BASED ON AS ABAP • STANDARD SYSTEM.

8. Select CUSTOM for the PARAMETER SETTINGS step. Selecting TYPICAL won't provide you with the parameter options you need to complete your SAP Business Suite on SAP HANA migration.

9. Input the SAP SYSTEM ID (SAPSID) and SAP MOUNT DIRECTORY to be used by the installer. You don't want users to change their log on information, so you use the same SID as the source system (Figure 7.41).

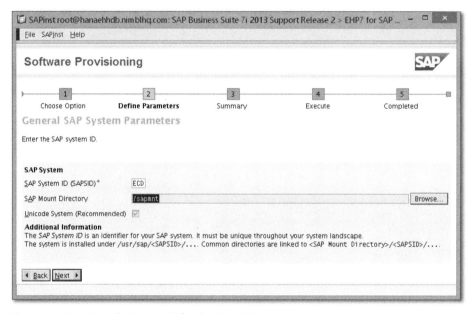

Figure 7.41 Inputting the System ID for the Target System

10. Verify that you want to use the full qualified domain name (FQDN), and enter the Domain Name Server (DNS) domain (Figure 7.42). Click NEXT.

11. Input the path to the latest available extracted kernel for SAP NetWeaver 7.40. As of August 2015, the 7.42 kernel was available. Extract the SAR file to a directory on the server.

12. Enter the master password for all system users. This will default the PASSWORD field on future screens. You can update passwords in subsequent steps manually if required.

13. Next, you have the option to edit parameters for the <SID>ADM user account (Figure 7.43). In our example scenario, we left the defaults. Click NEXT.

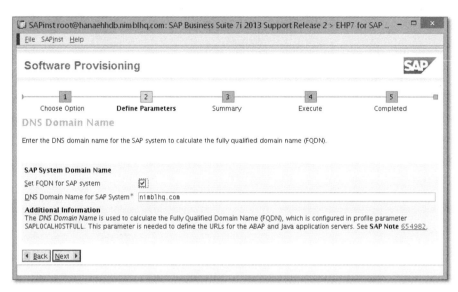

Figure 7.42 Entering the Correct Domain Name Server Information

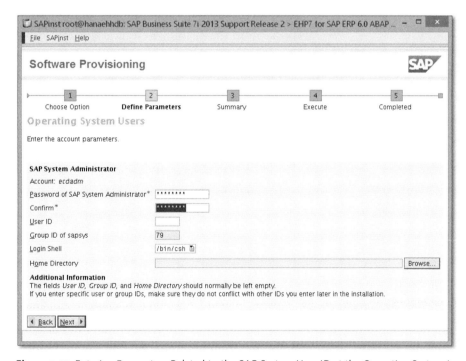

Figure 7.43 Entering Parameters Related to the SAP System User ID at the Operating System Level

14. In the TARGET DATABASE area, select STANDARD SYSTEM COPY/MIGRATION (LOAD-BASED).

15. Don't select START MIGRATION/RESTORE MANUALLY because you want SWPM to start the Migration Monitor automatically.

16. In the SAP HANA DATABASE OR DATABASE TENANT area, enter the parameters of your target SAP HANA database (Figure 7.44). The DATABASE ID (DBSID) in this case is the SID for the SAP HANA instance, which will be the target for your database migration.

17. Enter the password for the SYSTEM account.

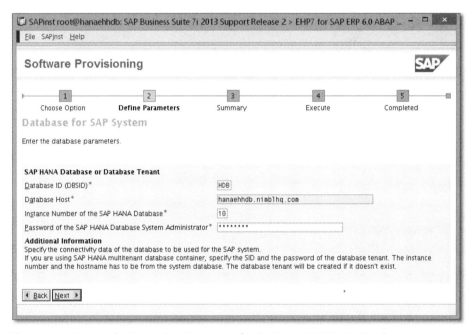

Figure 7.44 Entering the Connection Parameters for the Target SAP HANA Database

18. Next you have the option to choose a local or shared copy of the SAP HANA database client. Our example scenario requires the use of the local client directory. Click NEXT after your selection.

19. On the MEDIA BROWSER screen, enter the path to the SAP HANA database client software (Figure 7.45). This can be downloaded from the SAP Software Download Center. The client software version must match the target database version.

Figure 7.45 Entering the File Path to the SAP HANA Client Installation Software

20. In the next step, enter the path to the export directory you've identified for the location of the database export files.

   ▶ In our example scenario, we've mounted the Windows share from the source application server to the target Linux application server.

   ▶ If you had selected the FTP method, then this directory would be the location where database export files were placed.

21. On the next screen, you have the option to initialize the SAP HANA database. If you're using a new installation of SAP HANA, you can leave INITIALIZE DATA-BASE OR DATABASE TENANT deselected and click NEXT (Figure 7.46).

22. Enter the password for the DBA Cockpit user who will create a schema within the SAP HANA database. This is a required step.

23. The master password you entered early in the process will be defaulted here. Accept the password, or override with a new password (Figure 7.47). Click NEXT.

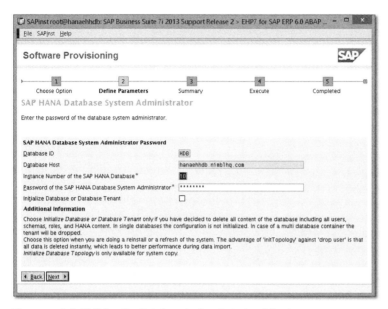

Figure 7.46 Initializing the Database before Data Load Option

Figure 7.47 Enter the Database Schema Password Screen

24. Provide a name for the SAP ERP database schema. Use the format SAP<SID>, and confirm the schema password. Then click NEXT.

25. The SAP HANA IMPORT PARAMETERS screen will be displayed. Accept the defaults, and click NEXT (Figure 7.48).

Figure 7.48 Accepting the Default Selections When Prompted for SAP HANA Import Parameters

26. The next step checks for the existence of the files generated when you generated the DDL statements in Section 7.1.1 (Figure 7.49). These files should be located in your export directory.

The following files should exist in the directory *<Export Directory>* \ABAP\DB:

▸ *HDB_ESTIMATES.TXT*

▸ *HDB_TABLE_CLASSIFICATION.TXT*

▸ *SQLFiles.LST*

The following files should exist in the directory *<Export Directory>* \ABAP\DB\ *HANA:*

▸ *APPL0.SQL*

▸ *APPL1.SQL*

▶ *DDIM.SQL*

▶ *DFACT.SQL*

▶ *DODS.SQL*

▶ *Rowstorelist.txt*

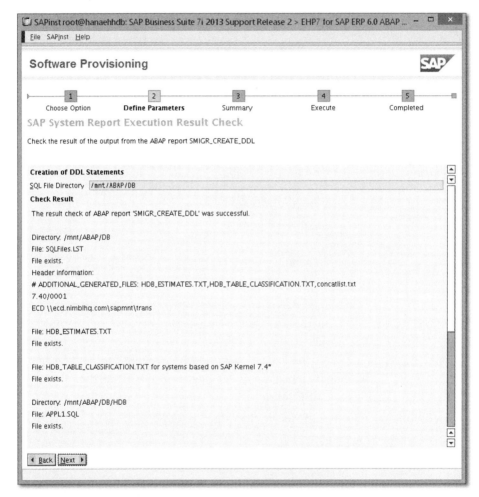

Figure 7.49 Software Provisioning Manager Checking for the Files Generated during the Preparation Tasks

27. In the TABLE PLACEMENT PARAMETERS area, select DO NOT USE A PARAMETER FILE.

[«]

> **Note**
>
> As of August 2015, SAP ERP is recommended only for the scale-up scenario. As a result, you don't need a table placement file. In the future, SAP ERP for the scale-out scenario will likely be supported, and this step will change. For the latest information, see SAP Note 1900822 – Using SAP HANA Landscape Reorg from SWPM.

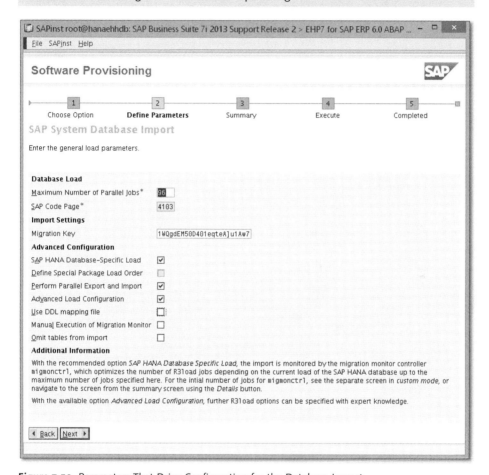

Figure 7.50 Parameters That Drive Configuration for the Database Import

28. For the database import settings, you have multiple options to select (Figure 7.50):

   ▸ MAXIMUM NUMBER OF PARALLEL JOBS: 3 jobs per processor core

   ▸ MIGRATION KEY: Can be retrieved from the SAP Support Portal (go to *http://support.sap.com/licensekey*, select MIGRATION KEYS, and click LAUNCH THE MIGRATION KEYS APPLICATION)

- ▷ SAP HANA Database-Specific Load: Checked

- ▷ Perform Parallel Export and Import: Checked

- ▷ Advanced Load Configuration: Checked

- ▷ Use DDL mapping file: Unchecked

- ▷ Manual Execution of Migration Monitor: Unchecked

- ▷ Omit tables from import: Unchecked

29. Next you have the option to further modify the usage of the Migration Monitor Controller. Settings written here will be input to the file named *migmonctrl_cmd.properties* within the SWPM working directory (*/tmp/sapinst_instdir/…*).

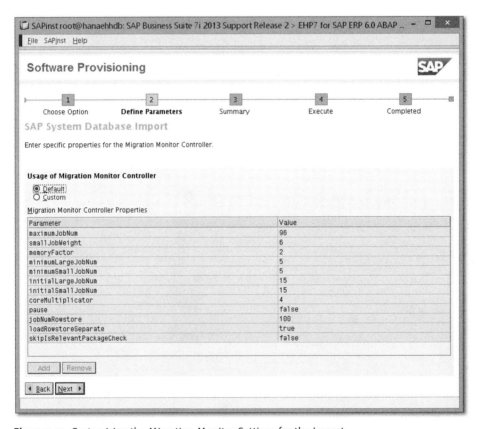

Figure 7.51 Customizing the Migration Monitor Settings for the Import

You can modify the properties file at runtime because it's read every 30 seconds. This enables you to monitor the performance of the import and make dynamic adjustments to the number of jobs. Here are some important settings you might want to modify (Figure 7.51):

- INITIALLARGEJOBNUM: Initial and minimum number of R3Load jobs for the group Large. The default is 5.

- INITIALSMALLJOBNUM: Initial and minimum number of R3Load jobs for the group Small. Again the default is 5.

- MAXIMUMJOBNUM: The maximum number of jobs is 95 by default.

- COREMULTIPLICATOR: This setting has been deprecated.

30. On the SAP SYSTEM COMMUNICATION PARAMETERS FOR IMPORT settings screen, you define the communication method for the import files (Figure 7.52). We can select USE EXCHANGE DIRECTORY or USE SOCKETS. In our example we are using a shared directory between Windows and Linux so we select USE EXCHANGE DIRECTORY. Earlier in the export, you defined the directory that would be shared between the export and import hosts.

31. For this example scenario, we leave MULTIPLE HOSTS unchecked. If you have multiple export hosts, then you would check this box.

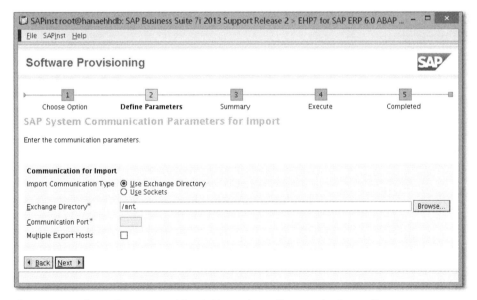

Figure 7.52 Defining the Directory That Is Mapped to a Share on the Export Host

32. In the ADVANCED LOAD CONFIGURATION area, accept the defaults and click NEXT.

33. In the PAS AND ACSC INSTANCE area, you see a list of instances currently installed on the host (Figure 7.53). For our example scenario, we select a new set of instance IDs. Click NEXT.

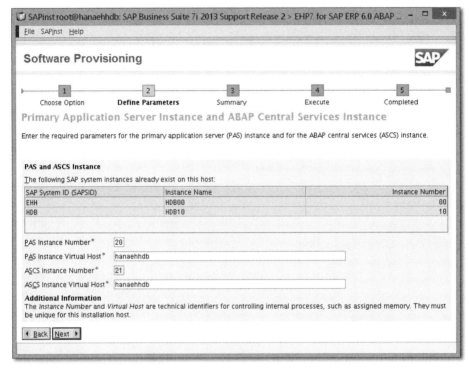

Figure 7.53 Choosing Instance IDs

34. Confirm your port selection based on the instance ID, and click NEXT.

35. The master password you defined earlier will be populated on the next screen as the password for webadm. Confirm the password, and click NEXT.

36. Register the new system with a System Landscape Directory (SLD). You should take advantage of this opportunity to register to an SLD that can be read from SAP Solution Manager.

37. In our example scenario, we're using the SLD local to a SAP Solution Manager system. Enter the SLD HOST, SLD HTTP(S) PORT, SLD DATA SUPPLIER USER, and PASSWORD OF SLD DATA SUPPLIER USER (Figure 7.54). Click NEXT.

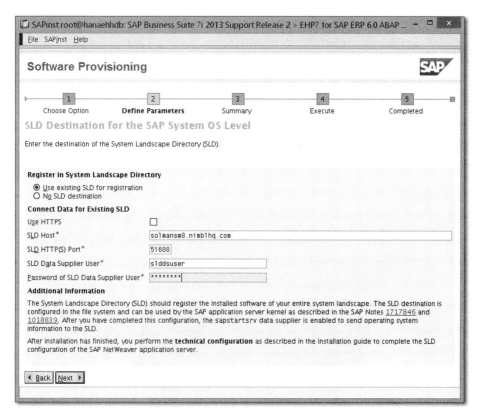

Figure 7.54 Registering an SLD to Ensure That Your System Is Displayed Correctly in SAP Solution Manager

38. Because this is a new installation, you have the option to define a Message Server Access Control List (ACL). This is an opportunity to introduce an additional layer of security for unauthorized access to your SAP Business Suite on SAP HANA system. (Refer to Chapter 4 for more on security.)

39. Select CREATE MESSAGE SERVER ACCESS CONTROL LIST, and click NEXT. For more information on ACLs, see SAP Note 1495075 – Access Control Lists (ACL).

40. Next you have the option to choose not to start the SAP system after the import is complete. This could be useful in scenarios where the source system is still operational (nonproduction). For our example scenario, we left the option unchecked. Click NEXT.

41. Enter the password for the DDIC user from the source system. Click NEXT.

42. On the SECURE STORAGE KEY GENERATION screen, you have two options:

    ▷ INDIVIDUAL KEY: Generate an individual key for the secure storage. This is the most secure option.

    ▷ DEFAULT KEY: Use the default key, which is insecure but typically used in nonproduction systems.

    If you chose INDIVIDUAL KEY you'll be presented with the key for safekeeping (shown in Figure 7.55.) This key will be needed if you copy the system in the future.

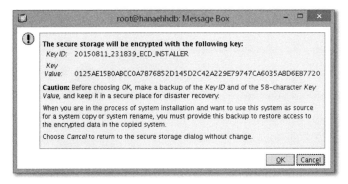

Figure 7.55 Warning to Save the Encryption Key to a Secure Location

43. On the UNPACK ARCHIVES screen (Figure 7.56), accept the defaults, and click NEXT.

44. On the next screen, confirm that you want to install a diagnostic agent.

45. Enter the HOST NAME to be used by the diagnostic agent (Figure 7.57).

46. Accept the default SAP System ID, and click NEXT.

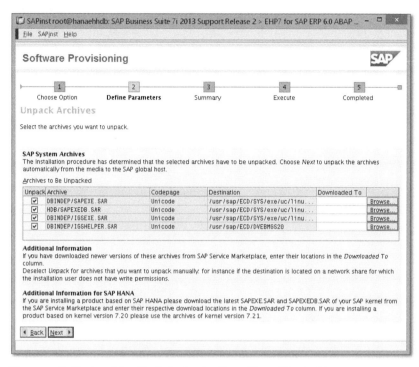

Figure 7.56 Display of the File Paths for the Unpacking of the Archives

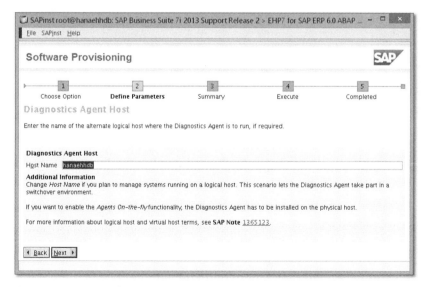

Figure 7.57 Entering the Host Name to Be Used by the Diagnostic Agent

47. Next you have the opportunity to change OS-related settings for the DAA adm user account (Figure 7.58). Accept the defaults, and CLICK Next.

48. When prompted, click YES to continue with the installation.

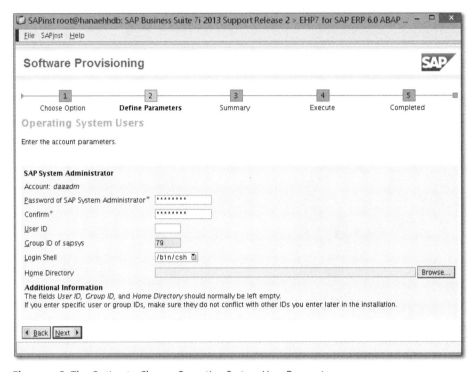

Figure 7.58 The Option to Change Operating System User Parameters

49. Accept the default INSTANCE NUMBER of 98, and click NEXT (Figure 7.59).

50. Select the option to register the diagnostic agent to the SLD, which enables SAP Solution Manager to assign this agent to the SAP ERP system for diagnostics.

51. Enter the SLD HTTP HOST, SLD HTTP PORT, SLD DATA SUPPLIER USER, and PASSWORD OF SLD DATA SUPPLIER USER (Figure 7.60). The default user ID is "SLDDSUSER".

52. In our example scenario, we choose to skip the configure connection to SAP Solution Manager. Because you've registered the agent to the SLD, you can assign the agent within the managed system configuration in SAP Solution Manager. You can choose to skip or enter the parameters (Figure 7.61).

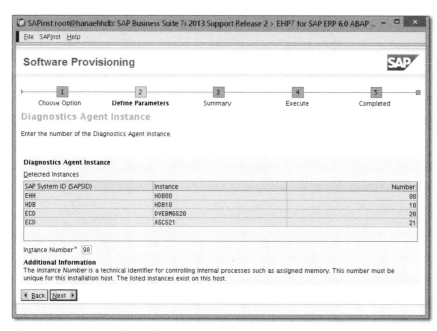

Figure 7.59 Accepting the Default Instance Number for Diagnostic Agents

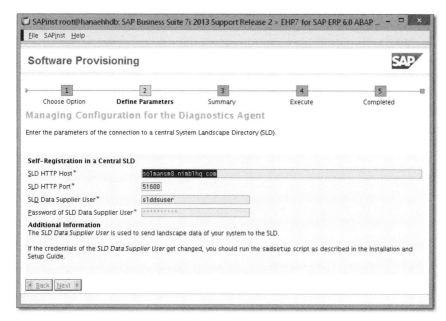

Figure 7.60 System Landscape Directory Registration Parameters

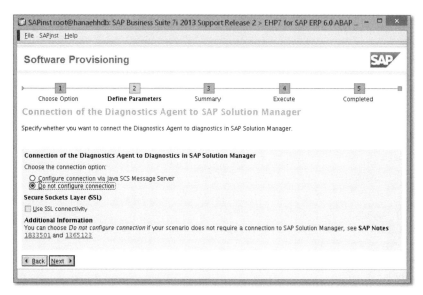

Figure 7.61 Skipping the Direct Connection Configuration

Figure 7.62 Confirming the Archives for the Agent Runtime Objects

53. The archives for the agent runtime objects are displayed and their extraction path (Figure 7.62). Confirm the entries, and click NEXT.

54. On the PARAMETER SUMMARY screen, confirm your entries, and click NEXT to begin the import. Ideally the export has already started or will be started soon.

55. Figure 7.63 shows the IMPORT ABAP step being run. This is the step that will read files from the export directory. In our example scenario, this directory is a file share between Windows and Linux.

Figure 7.63 Import ABAP Step Where the Export Directory Is Read

56. As jobs process, you can monitor the system to determine if you should increase or decrease the number of running jobs. If necessary, you can edit the *export_monitor_cmd.properties* file within the working directory.

57. After the import completes, the remaining installation steps for the application server are completed (Figure 7.64).

Figure 7.64 Completed Installation Process Following the Database Import

58. On the completion of the database import, you'll receive the confirmation message shown in Figure 7.65.

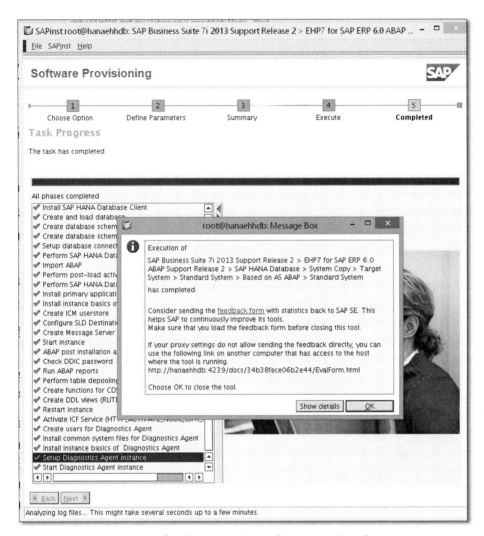

Figure 7.65 Success Message after the System Copy and Import Are Complete

At this point, you've completed both the export and import of the SAP ERP database, which now resides on SAP HANA. Because this is your first migration, you'll want to utilize the Migtime (Time Analyzer) utility to analyze the log files for the import processes much like you did in Section 7.3.1. From here, you can analyze the number of jobs executed by time to determine how to more efficiently execute the data load. As for the target system, you now need to execute your postsystem copy procedures: reimport profiles, resolve Transport Management System (TMS) changes, and so on. Congratulations! You're running SAP Business Suite on SAP HANA using the SWPM classical migration.

7.4   Troubleshooting

Throughout the process defined in this chapter, we tried to explain troubleshooting steps for each phase or process. The first level of error handling within SWPM provides you with a summary screen that includes a description of the error, the current phase, and then typically four options to choose from:

▶ RETRY

   ▶ The SWMP will repeat the previous task without attempting to restart the entire phase.

   ▶ If you see the WITH INIT checkbox, then you have the option of restarting the entire phase not just the task in error.

▶ STOP
   This won't only stop the SWPM UI but will stop all SWPM processes. It records the progress in the *keydb.xml* file within the SWPM directory.

▶ CONTINUE
   When a warning is presented instead of an error, you can select CONTINUE to advance the installer.

▶ VIEW LOG
   This will open a dialog window you can use to navigate log files located in *<SWPM Directory>\abap\log*.

When restarting SWPM after clicking STOP as described in the preceding list or in the event of a system or power failure, you'll have two options to choose from:

▶ **Run a new option**
   This disregards the previously interrupted migration and starts a new migration.

▶ **Continue with the old option**
   This continues with the previously interrupted migration at the point of failure.

SWPM will read from the following locations on startup to check for previously failed or incomplete processes. In the event you want to start over, you can manually remove the subdirectories within the following directories:

▸ Windows: *C:\<program files>\sapinst_instdir*

▸ UNIX: */tmp/sapinst_instdir*

There are three primary notes you can reference for known errors related to the SAP Business Suite on SAP HANA migration process. SAP provides updates to these notes on a regular basis. We recommend reviewing them before the migration and if you encounter any errors.

▸ SAP Note 1722395 (SAP HANA: Known problems) lists known issues that may occur during a migration to SAP HANA.

▸ SAP Note 1860493 (Out of Memory during Import Migration to SAP HANA) is helpful if you're facing an out-of-memory error during the migration to SAP HANA.

▸ SAP Note 1641210 (SAP HANA Database: Checking for Suspected Problems) provides a checklist of how to investigate a potential problem in the SAP HANA database.

We also recommend involving SAP early in your troubleshooting process. After you've eliminated errors that can be easily resolved (disk space, passwords, connectivity, etc.), use the following categories to expedite processing of your SAP support request:

▸ **BC-INS-MIG-TLA**
Migration tool issues.

▸ **BC-INS-MIG**
General migration issues.

▸ **BC-DB-HDB-INS**
General SAP HANA database issues during the migration.

7.5 Summary

In this chapter, we covered both the preparation and execution tasks to perform an SAP Business Suite on SAP HANA migration using SWPM. Using this procedure, you defined the number of table splits by table, prepared both the source and target systems, and completed a parallel export and import of your system. You'll notice a collection of CSV files within the SWPM directories that can be used to graph and report on the export and import process. With each migration you complete, you can improve and optimize your table splitting and processing to minimize the downtime required for the procedure. The SWPM functionality is also best suited for migrating systems between data centers or from on-premise to cloud environments. These tools can be used with SAP HANA Enterprise Cloud migrations in addition to system copies and system refreshes within your own data center.

If you compare the runtime and the number of screens requiring between SUM DMO and SWPM, you'll notice the SWPM process is significantly longer. If you're already running EHP 7 with no plans to upgrade to the next SP Stack, then SWPM might be the tool for you. Using SWPM, you eliminate the need for some application-level testing because the migration is only changing the underlying database. The application layer remains the same between databases. SWPM gives you as the customer more control over the export and import processing. You can distribute processing to multiple hosts. You have the option of migrating your application server and database to SAP HANA when using SWPM, as opposed to just migrating your database.

We'll argue that most customers can benefit from using SUM DMO instead of SWPM because a majority of environments won't be running the latest SP Stack from SAP. SUM DMO will enable you to include an SP Stack in the migration. When using SWPM on a version of SAP ERP 6 EHP 7 supported on SAP HANA, your application team might find themselves applying multiple notes to resolve defects. Staying current with support packages not only provides your organization with the latest fixes from SAP, but it also provides the latest security patches. As discussed in Chapter 4, these technical fixes will be required to secure your SAP landscapes.

PART III
Go-Live

Establishing a test scope and driving efficient test cycles will be one of the greatest challenges on your SAP Business Suite on SAP HANA migration project. We'll explore the available tools to ensure you only test what is impacted during the migration.

8   Test and Change Management Strategy

A key component to your SAP Business Suite on SAP HANA migration will be the test and change management strategy you define for your project. The test strategy has significant impact on the project time line because this is typically the phase of the project that requires the greatest collective effort from the project team members. It's also usually the most expensive phase of the project in terms of labor cost and directly impacts the success of your go-live. How can you help define the test scope? Can you tell the business users and testers exactly what to test? When and how long will you need business users for test support? SAP has provided its customers with several options for defining a test strategy. In this chapter, we'll dive deep into the Business Process Change Analyzer (BPCA), including step-by-step instructions on the tool's execution, which helps you define impacted objects at the transaction code and program level. This will serve as input to your test plan, ensuring that you only test what is impacted.

When it comes time to execute your test cycles, you no longer need to test based on tribal knowledge or a Microsoft Excel spreadsheet. Using the output from the BPCA, you utilize the test management tools in SAP Solution Manager or leverage third-party applications from HP and IBM. Based on project experience, we know a majority of SAP customers don't realize they own a test planning, execution, reporting, and defect management tool in SAP Solution Manager. It has the capability to organize test scripts by test cycle or phase. You can enable email notifications to testers and provide text cycle reporting to your stakeholders. And, it's a solution you already have installed today.

Software change management, control of changes within your SAP landscape, will require a higher level of focus and attention during your project because you need to support the movement of production support items while also running your SAP Business Suite on SAP HANA migration project. How can you support the production environment while running multiple databases? Do you own any tools to help track, manage, and execute change management for SAP landscapes? As part of SAP Enterprise and SAP Standard maintenance, SAP customers are entitled to the usage of SAP Solution Manager for Change Request Management. In this chapter, we'll discuss SAP Solution Manager's Change Request Management and how it can be used to control transports during your project. We'll also touch on a lesser-known tool called Quality Gate Management. It's a solution for those who want transport control without the user interface (UI) in Change Request Management. And we'll end this chapter with a discussion on the Retrofit tool. This is the only SAP-supported tool that enables cross-version imports, which supports the movement of your production support transports to the new SAP Business Suite on SAP HANA landscape.

8.1   Regression Test Strategy

When you need to define an approach to testing during your SAP Business Suite on SAP HANA migration project, you must reference your migration strategy defined earlier in the book. Are you simply migrating the underlying database with Software Provisioning Manager (SWPM)? Alternatively, are you applying an Enhancement package, Support Package Stack (SP Stack), or upgrading releases using the Software Update Manager (SUM) with the Database Migration Option (DMO)? Each migration strategy will drive the test strategy for the project because each migration option is fundamentally different. When migrating using SWPM, you're performing a database migration without update to the repository objects in SAP ERP. Think of this as a replacement of the engine in your car. When you migrate using SWPM, you're replacing the engine of your car, but the exterior and interior of the car remain unchanged. You have the same look and feel with similar functionality inside the car, except more power! Do you need to test the turn signals because the engine is replaced? Conversely, when migrating SAP ERP to SAP HANA using SUM, which includes an enhancement package or SP Stack, you're essentially migrating to a whole new model car—new engine, new exterior, and new interior. Repository objects are changed when migrating SAP Business Suite on SAP HANA when using SUM DMO.

A regression test strategy defines the how, who, when, and where for testing during your SAP Business Suite on SAP HANA migration. It should define the following test-relevant items:

▶ **Test level**
To what level are you testing during your project? Because you're changing the underlying database and potentially the application code, your focus will be regression testing. You might also define performance testing as part of your test strategy.

▶ **Roles and responsibilities**
Clearly define the roles and responsibilities of the test leader, project manager, individual testers, and technical support resources.

▶ **Risk plan**
A well-run project will define potential risks to the project and how you can mitigate those risks. For the test strategy, you define risks to a successful test project. This section of the test strategy defines scenarios such as determining how you will handle test data or test user availability.

▶ **Test tools**
The two types of testing are manual and automated. Within the test strategy, you need to define what methods will be used and the tools that will support them. We'll talk about test tools later in this chapter.

▶ **Test priorities**
Not all tests are created equal. You must define test priorities that will be associated to test cases later. If your project is time fenced, you must be able to plan for the test execution from critical to lowest priority.

▶ **Test plan maintenance**
Here you define where the test plan will be stored and how you'll report on test execution status. The test plan will define the test script execution order, define the test cycles, and provide the data required for test cycle status reporting.

▶ **Test reporting**
Next you need to define what type of reporting will be required and who will be recipients. Let's assume you would provide a dashboard of test execution status to project sponsors—what other type of reporting is required?

▶ **Exit criteria**
Lastly, you define the exit criteria for your migration testing. In an ideal world,

you resolve all defects before exiting the test phase, although this is unlikely. You need to define the acceptable types of defects that still allow the project to move forward.

Your organization's test strategy might include more or less content, but these items should provide enough content to lay the foundation for a successful regression test during your SAP Business Suite on SAP HANA migration. Now let's discuss how each migration tool might affect your test strategy.

8.1.1 Software Provisioning Manager

When using SWPM, you're leveraging capabilities similar to a heterogeneous system copy. Functionality within SAP ERP will remain unchanged during the migration, but you still need to define some sort of test scope for the project. Because repository objects will be unchanged, you won't be able to use test scope identification tools such as BPCA or Scope and Effort Analyzer (SEA) included with SAP Solution Manager. Instead, you must rely on other sources of information to determine what to test.

For some organizations, the most conservative approach, and most costly, is to perform a full regression test. When you think about how SAP has certified specific releases of SAP ERP and SAP NetWeaver for the migration without upgrade, you can to assume base SAP functionality will work as-is due to SAP's rigorous release management processes. You don't need to test every SAP-delivered transaction code and program that your users execute in production. You should only need to test those SAP-delivered objects that you've enhanced, modified, or deemed critical to your business operations. If you haven't modified or enhanced Transaction VA01 (Sales Order Entry), it will function the same after as it did before the SAP HANA migration using SWPM.

When using SWPM, where do you focus your testing? Based on information you collected using the Solution Documentation Assistant (SDA; discussed in Chapter 2, Section 2.3), you know what transactions, both SAP and customer created, are being executed within your environment. In addition to knowing what transactions and programs are executed in production, you also know how often they are being executed within the SDA results.

Ideally, this list of transactions will help you define the custom transactions that will be tested because you won't know specifically how those programs are interacting with the database and file system (we mention the file system because the migration from Microsoft Windows or iSeries systems means a change in file systems on the database server). In Figure 8.1, you'll note that both SAP and customer transactions are displayed. (If you don't remember how to access this screen, refer to Section 2.3 of Chapter 2.) Again, you're operating under the assumption that SAP has certified the application code on SAP HANA. You must focus only on those areas where you've created new objects or enhanced SAP objects. You do test SAP-delivered objects with customer user exits because you can't know for sure how the developer of that custom program is interacting with the database. If all custom development was completed using common industry and SAP standards, you should be fine.

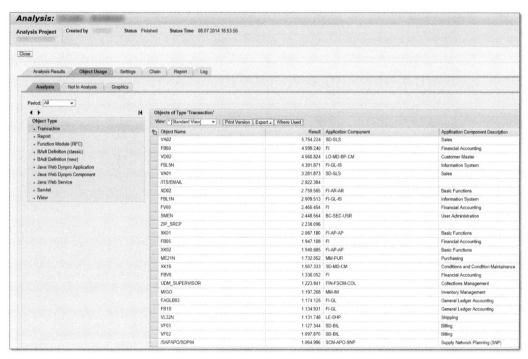

Figure 8.1 Solution Documentation Assistant Analysis Displaying Production SAP ERP Transactions and Their Respective Usage

Migrating SAP ERP to SAP HANA using SWPM is a change to the underlying database. After you've identified the customer created and enhanced objects, you also need to perform some data validation. Remember, the migration to SAP HANA is a full export and import of your database into flat text files potentially across multiple systems. Although SAP does it's best to ensure proper error handling and processing, errors can occur. Example data validation procedures will vary from customer to customer based on functionality in scope, criticality of business processes, and potential financial impact. Table 8.1 defines common areas you can validate using standard SAP reports and transaction codes. Execute these validation steps before and after the database migration.

Area	Item	Report
Financials	Open GL Balances	FAGLB03
		FBL3N
Financials	Open AR	FBL5N
Financials	Open AP	FBL1N
Material Management	Open PO Amounts	ME2N
		ME2L
Inventory Management	Inventory Balances	MB5B
Sales	Customer Balances	FD10N

Table 8.1 Data Validation Areas and Reports

Service and interface testing should also be considered as potentially in scope when using SWPM. If your interfaces are executed at the application layer only, you might limit your test scope to only those interfaces that are critical to daily operation. Interfaces at the application layer include interfaces leveraging IDocs, remote function calls (RFCs), Gateway services, or web services calls directly to SAP ERP. Because the application server is typically not changing, and the repository isn't changing with SWPM, these interfaces at the application layer are considered lower risk. If, for example, you have an interface that interacts at the database level or database server file system, then these interfaces are absolutely included in the regression test scope. A common challenge is finding those interfaces that exist outside of SAP. Standard SAP functionality doesn't include the ability to monitor OS-level connections from interfacing systems. The Gateway Monitor delivered with SAP NetWeaver enables the monitoring of interfacing systems at the application layer.

Transaction SMGW (see Figure 8.2) in SAP ERP displays active connections from interfacing systems and clients. Using this transaction, you can view the interfacing systems that are connected to SAP ERP. This data can be stored in trace files for later analysis to determine which systems are connecting to SAP ERP over a period of time.

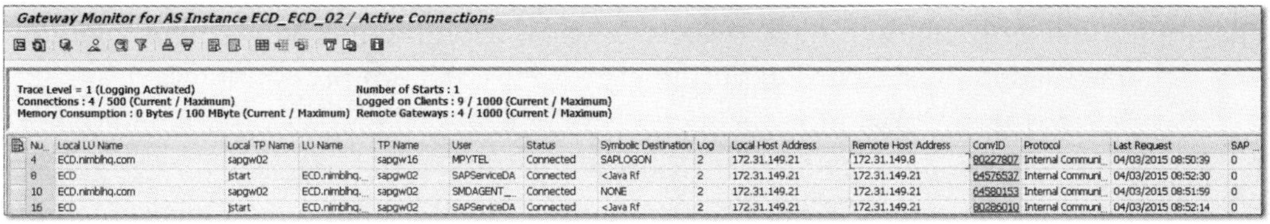

Figure 8.2 Transaction SMGW: Active Connections

8.1.2 Software Update Manager

When migrating to SAP Business Suite on SAP HANA using the Software Update Manager (SUM), you must now consider all items from the previous section and include changes to the repository within SAP ERP. SUM DMO gives customers the option of including an SP Stack or enhancement package with the migration to SAP HANA. Your test strategy must change because the scope of change has increased. SAP delivers updates to standard transactions and programs that you reference within your customer-created objects. There are several tools you can use to help define what to test. We covered one of these tools—Scope and Effort Analyzer (SEA)—earlier in Chapter 2, Section 2.3.2. The other tool, Business Process Change Analyzer (BPCA), will be discussed later in Section 8.2.2. These tools are provided by SAP to help customers focus testing on only those objects being impacted by the upgrade activities during the migration with SUM.

Now that you understand at a high level how SUM is different from SWPM, let's move onto the BPCA, which will help you define the impact of the update included with your migration to SAP HANA.

8.2 SAP Solution Manager Business Process Change Analysis

As of SAP Solution Manager 7.01 SP 18, SAP has delivered a tool for use by customers that can more narrowly define the transactions and programs to be tested related to a specific change event. BPCA has been greatly enhanced in SAP Solution Manager 7.1 with enhancements in SP 10 and above that provide even more flexibility and ease of use. In addition to defining the objects impacted by a change event, BPCA can optimize test scope, further reducing the test scope, which can save time. If you're a customer whose current test strategy includes a full regression test during enhancement package projects, BPCA will likely decrease your test effort and duration. However, if you're a customer who doesn't test regularly or have formalized testing during an enhancement package installation, then BPCA will likely increase the amount of testing your team executes with the goal of reducing potential defects when you upgrade during the SAP Business Suite on SAP HANA migration. BPCA will be used when upgrading or changing your SAP ERP release level using SUM. BPCA won't be used for the SAP Business Suite on SAP HANA migration using SWPM.

BPCA is available to those customers with an SAP Enterprise Support or SAP Max-Attention Agreement. Customers with a SAP Standard Support Agreement can only access those SAP Solution Manager tools defined as part of the functional baseline, which doesn't include access to BPCA. To learn more about SAP Solution Manager usage rights, speak to your SAP account executive or check the SAP Support Portal (*https://support.sap.com/solution-manager/usage-rights.html*).

8.2.1 Prerequisites

BPCA can be implemented fairly quickly and doesn't require extensive effort to support. The first prerequisite is to have a business process blueprint defined within SAP Solution Manager (as discussed in Chapter 2, Section 2.3.2). At this point, you should be able to run Transaction SOLAR01 to see the business processes and transactions codes currently used by your organization. Next, you need to build a technical bill of materials (TBOM) for each of the transactions and programs defined in your business process blueprint. A TBOM defines all of the technical objects used by a specific transaction code or program. For example, Transaction VA01 can access any one of 3000+ tables in SAP ERP at runtime. How do you know what tables Transaction VA01 uses in your environment based on how your users use the production systems? And how do you know if an enhancement package or SP Stack will update one of those 3000+ tables? TBOM provides the details required for the BPCA to measure the impact of a change.

There are multiple types of TBOMs that can be generated (see Table 8.2). The most desirable type of TBOM is the semi-dynamic TBOM, which is generated from Usage and Procedure Logging (UPLs) of ABAP objects from the kernel. Semi-dynamic TBOMs have specific release requirements on both the SAP ERP system and SAP Solution Manager. Static TBOMs can be implemented on any release of SAP ERP and SAP Solution Manager 7.1. Dynamic TBOMs are the third type of

TBOM and most accurate because they are generated via frontend recording of a user's transaction. Dynamic TBOMs require the most effort to support and won't be realistically generated for all SAP ERP transactions. Each customer's strategy for TBOMs will vary and will include a mixture of two or more types of TBOMs.

	Static	Semi-Dynamic	Dynamic
Build Effort	Low	Low	High
Covered objects	All objects potentially used by the transaction	All objects used by the transaction during observed period	Exact list of objects used by transaction specific to business process recorded
UPL required	No	Yes	No
Dynamic calls	No Supported	Not Supported	Supported
SAP Solution Manager release	SAP Solution Manager 7.1 SP 1+	SAP Solution Manager 7.1 SP 11+	SAP Solution Manager 7.1 SP 1+
SAP ERP release	SAP NetWeaver 6.40 or higher Kernel 7.00 patch 264+ or Kernel 7.01 patch 116+ ST-PI 2008_1_XXX SP 06	SAP NetWeaver 7.01 SP 10+ or SAP NetWeaver 7.02 SP 09+ or SAP NetWeaver 7.31 SP 03+ Kernel 7.20 patch 430+ or Kernel 7.21 patch 120+ ST-PI 2008_1_XXX SP 06	SAP NetWeaver 6.40 or higher Kernel 7.00 patch 264+ or Kernel 7.01 patch 116+ ST-PI 2008_1_XXX SP 06

Table 8.2 Technical Bill of Material Types and Specific Release Requirements

Setup Usage and Procedure Logging

If your SAP Solution Manager and SAP ERP release levels supports UPL for semi-dynamic TBOMs, you can set up UPL from SAP Solution Manager. Follow these steps:

1. Log on to SAP Solution Manager via SAP GUI with the SOLMAN_ADMIN user ID or a user ID with like access.

2. Execute Transaction SOLMAN_SETUP, which opens your default web browser. Navigate to BUSINESS PROCESS CHANGE ANALYZER on the left side menu (see Figure 8.3).

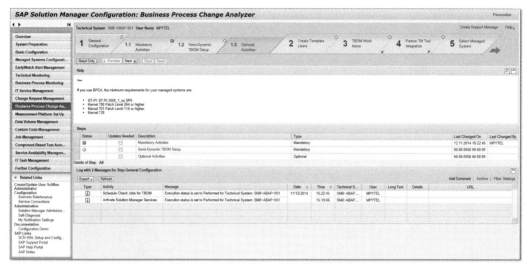

Figure 8.3 SAP Solution Manager Configuration to Define UPL Settings for a Specific System

3. Click the EDIT button and then the NEXT button. For each activity under Step 1.1 MANDATORY ACTIVITIES, you must click START TRANSACTION under the NAVIGATION column for each row under the MANUAL ACTIVITIES area (see Figure 8.4).

Figure 8.4 Manual Activities to Be Executed

4. For ACTIVATE SOLUTION MANAGER SERVICES in the ACTIVITY column, click START TRANSACTION. This opens a new browser window for the SAP GUI for HTML. Ensure all green lights are reported, and click BACK • EXIT SESSION (see Figure 8.5).

5. Back on the SAP SOLUTION MANAGER CONFIGURATION: BUSINESS PROCESS CHANGE ANALYZER screen, you'll be prompted to schedule two background jobs for the activity SCHEDULE CHECK JOBS FOR TBOM. To view the details of the background jobs to be scheduled, click DISPLAY under DOCUMENTATION for that activity (see Figure 8.6).

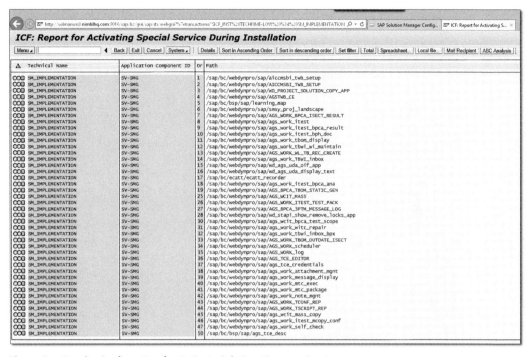

Figure 8.5 Results Confirmation for Activate Solution Manager Services

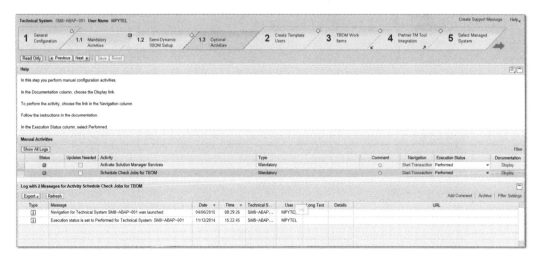

Figure 8.6 Clicking Display to View the Details of the Background Job

6. Click OPEN IN A NEW WINDOW to display the necessary background job details.

7. The details for the two background jobs to be scheduled are displayed (see Figure 8.7). Be sure to schedule these jobs with a user ID that won't expire and has similar authorizations to the SOLMAN_ADMIN account.

Figure 8.7 Background Job Details to Be Scheduled When Executing the Activity

8. Return to the initial screen, and click START TRANSACTION for the SCHEDULE CHECK JOBS FOR TBOM activity. The SAP GUI for HTML is launched. Define the background jobs using the information shown earlier in Figure 8.7. Click the JOB WIZARD button, and enter the JOB NAME as "AGS_BPCA_TBOM_OUT-DATE_CHECKER2".

9. In SPECIFY JOB STEP, choose ABAP PROGRAM STEP.

10. Enter the ABAP PROGRAM NAME as "AGS_BPCA_TBOM_OUTDATE_CHECKER2" and enter the VARIANT as "SAP&STANDARD".

11. Don't add any more steps.

12. Choose DATE/TIME as the start condition.

13. Schedule the job daily, at a time with low system load.

14. Choose COMPLETE to schedule the job.

15. Repeat the Job Wizard for the background job AGS_BPCA_TBOM_REFER-ENCE_CHECK described earlier in Figure 8.7. Make all the same selections as you just did for AGS_BPCA_TBOM_OUTDATE_CHECKER2, except enter the JOB NAME as "AGS_BPCA_TBOM_REFERENCE_CHECK" and enter the ABAP PROGRAM NAME as "AGS_BPCA_TBOM_REFERENCE_CHECK". The VARIANT remains "SAP&STANDARD".

16. Choose COMPLETE to schedule the job as shown in Figure 8.8.

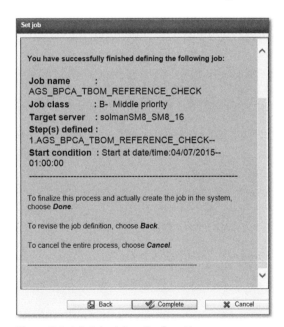

Figure 8.8 Job Scheduling Confirmation

17. Click EXIT • EXIT SESSION, and return to the initial screen showing Step 1.1 MANDATORY ACTIVITIES.

18. Click Next to advance to Step 1.2 Semi-Dynamic TBOM Setup.

19. Click Start Web Dynpro for the first activity Setup UPL in Managed System (Figure 8.9). This launches another browser tab.

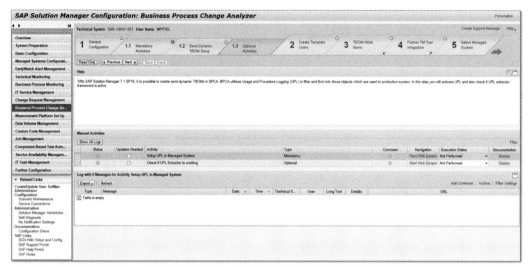

Figure 8.9 Clicking Start Web Dynpro for the Setup UPL in Managed System Activity

20. On the screen displayed, you see a list of systems where you can enable UPL. The RFC Status and Auto. Conf. Status columns should show green lights (Figure 8.10). The Preparation Check Status light can be red or green.

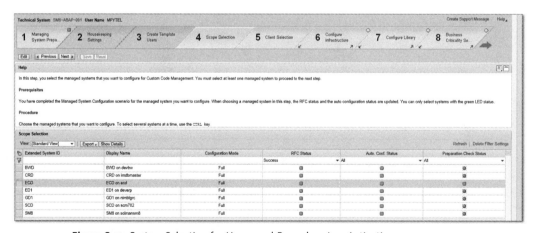

Figure 8.10 System Selection for Usage and Procedure Log Activation

> **Note** [«]
>
> If the RFC STATUS or AUTO. CONF. STATUS lights are red, then there is potentially a problem with your baseline SAP Solution Manager configuration. For additional details on how to resolve these problems, see the SAP Solution Manager Configuration Guide at *http://service.sap.com/rkt-solman*. Once there, choose SAP SOLUTION MANAGER 7.1 SP 12 • SAP SOLUTION MANAGER SETUP AND OPERATIONS • CONFIGURATION OF SOLUTION MANAGER.

21. Select the production system you want to activate UPL on, and click NEXT.

22. In Figure 8.11, you'll select the client to activate UPL against. Because this is your production system, you'll typically only have one client. Click NEXT after you've selected the client from the CLIENTS CONFIGURED FOR RFC dropdown.

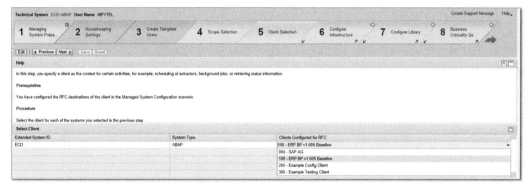

Figure 8.11 Selecting the Client for the System You Activate the Usage and Procedure Log Against

23. In Step 6 CONFIGURE INFRASTRUCTURE, you get a summary of the activities to be completed to activate UPL. First, you'll activate extractors, which is essentially the extract of data from the target system into the local SAP Business Warehouse (SAP BW) instance within SAP Solution Manager. The tool will then check the target system to ensure all SAP Notes for UPL have been installed followed by a cleanup of tasks related to older SAP Solution Manager Custom Code Management configuration. On the summary screen for Step 6, click NEXT (Figure 8.12).

24. In Step 6.1 ACTIVATE EXTRACTORS, you should see a description of the extractors to be activated. By default, all columns should be checked. Click the ACTIVATE button and confirm results on screen under the LOG section on the bottom of the screen. Click NEXT (Figure 8.13).

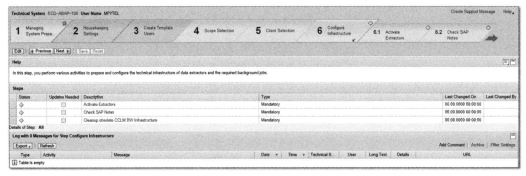

Figure 8.12 Summary Screen Showing Activities to Be Completed

Figure 8.13 Results Displayed after Activating Extractors

25. In Step 6.2 CHECK SAP NOTES, the SAP Solution Manager system uses the READ RFC to connect to the target system to ensure all appropriate SAP Notes have been installed to support UPL extraction. Highlight the row on screen, and select EXECUTE ALL (Figure 8.14). Click NEXT after you've confirmed results in the LOG section.

26. For Step 6.3 SCHEDULE ANALYSIS JOBS, you'll schedule several background jobs required for UPL extraction. The background job creates the corresponding data in the target system and stores it in temporary tables. The SAP Solution Manager Extractor Framework (EFWK) triggers the data extractor automatically

every day and checks for new data in the target system. If new data is available, the framework retrieves the data and uploads it to the local SAP BW in SAP Solution Manager. Define the date and times in the grid (Figure 8.15), and click SCHEDULE ALL JOBS. Confirm all jobs have been scheduled in the LOG section, and click NEXT

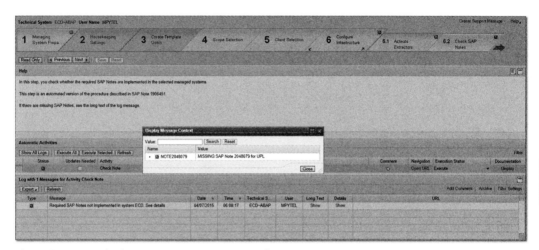

Figure 8.14 Example Showing Missing SAP Notes in the Target System

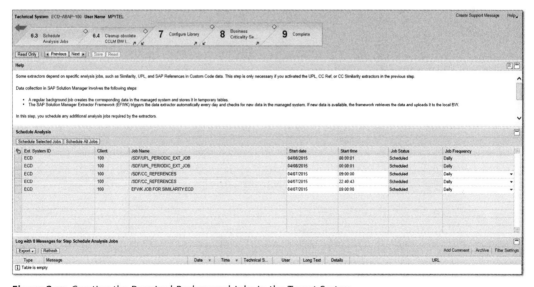

Figure 8.15 Creating the Required Background Jobs in the Target System

387

27. In Step 6.4 CLEANUP OBSOLETE CCLM BW, you execute some cleanup tasks defined by SAP. This step is required if you had previously connected the target system to a SAP Solution Manager system prior to SP Stack 12. Under AUTOMATIC ACTIVITIES, click the EXECUTE ALL button, and confirm results in the LOG section (Figure 8.16).

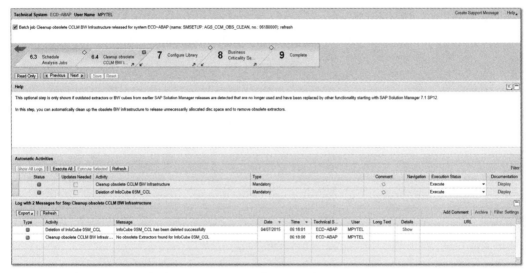

Figure 8.16 Results from Executing SAP Cleanup Tasks

28. At this point, you can click the READ ONLY button and return to the Business Process Change Analyzer Wizard. Advancing to Step 7 CONFIGURE LIBRARY and beyond in this specific setup wizard isn't required for UPL activation.

29. In Step 1.2 SEMI-DYNAMIC TBOM SETUP, you can confirm completion of the SETUP UPL IN MANAGED SYSTEM activity. Click the START WEB DYNPRO link for the CHECK IF UPL EXTRACTOR IS WORKING activity (Figure 8.17).

30. Clicking the START WEB DYNPRO link launches the SAP SOLUTION MANAGER: SAP SOLUTION MANAGER ADMINISTRATION work center.

31. To verify that the UPL extractors are active, navigate to the EXTRACTOR ADMINISTRATION page. From the work center, click INFRASTRUCTURE. Then select the FRAMEWORK button and select EXTRACTOR FRAMEWORK, as shown in Figure 8.18.

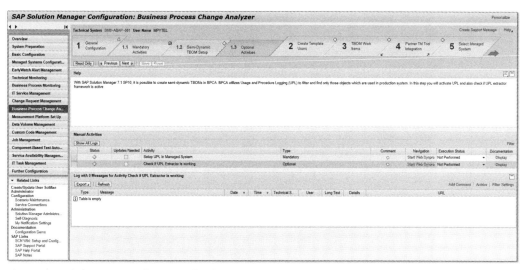

Figure 8.17 Clicking Start Web Dynpro for the Activity

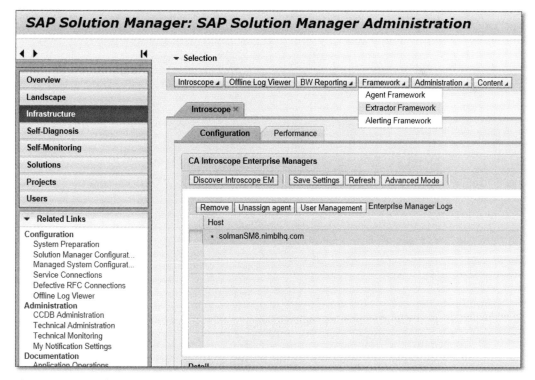

Figure 8.18 SAP Solution Manager Administrator Work Center

The EXTRACTOR ADMINISTRATION page is displayed. From here, you need to validate that the UPL extractor you activated is working for the specific production system you selected. There will be several rows displayed on screen to scroll through, or you can create a filter for the specific object you're looking for.

32. Click the FILTER link on the right side of the table display to enter the following values:

   ▸ NAME: "*UPL*".

   ▸ SYSTEM ID: Enter the target System ID (e.g., "ECD").

33. Press ⎡Enter⎤, and the extractor specific to UPL for the target system defined is displayed. Select the row, and the extractor history is displayed. You can view the number of records extracted, when, and if the process completed successfully (Figure 8.19).

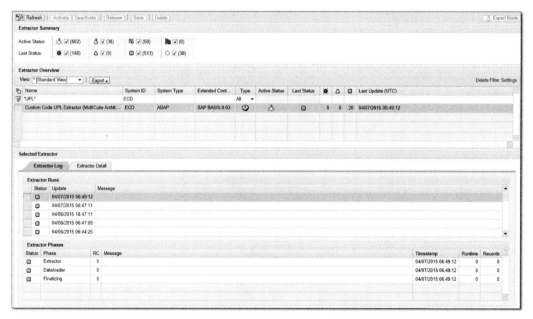

Figure 8.19 Viewing the Usage and Procedure Log Extractor Status

Technical Bill of Material Generation

You've now completed the one of the prerequisites to executing BPCA to identify the test scope for your SAP Business Suite on SAP HANA migration using SUM. After you've activated UPL data collection within SAP Solution Manager, you must regularly update the TBOMs using a background job in SAP Solution Manager. The TBOMs are generated based on the project you created in Chapter 2, Section 2.3. The project contains the transactions and programs used within your production environment. By generating TBOMs against these transaction codes and programs, you can measure the impact of updates delivered by SAP to your system.

Follow these steps:

1. Log on to your SAP Solution Manager system to access the TEST MANAGEMENT work center using Transaction SM_WORKCENTER. When the browser opens, select the TEST MANAGEMENT tab.

2. Select the ADMINISTRATION link from the left side navigation bar (Figure 8.20).

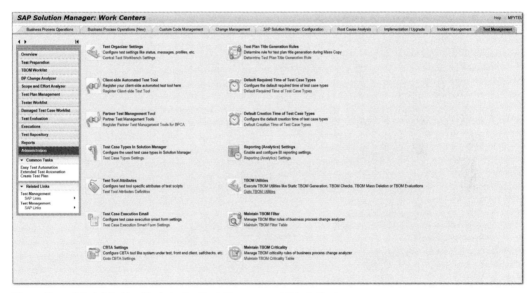

Figure 8.20 Administrative Tools in the Test Management Work Center

3. Select the TBOM UTILITIES option, which launches an ABAP transaction within SAP GUI. Click GENERATION OF STATIC AND SEMI DYNAMIC TBOMs from the screen that appears.

   The browser launches a transaction that enables you to execute an immediate generation of semi-dynamic TBOMs or schedule a periodic background job. Ideally, you schedule the background on a daily basis to support the changes within your landscape.

4. In the Project ID field, use the project created in Chapter 2, Section 2.3, and select the CREATE SEMI-DYNAMIC TBOMs checkbox (Figure 8.21).

5. In the USAGE AND PROCEDURE LOGGING UPL area, choose PRODUCTION SYSTEM from the SYSTEM ROLE dropdown. Leave all other fields default.

6. Click SCHEDULE to define a periodic job, which would run daily. The background job isn't resource intensive and won't interfere with normal system operations. Once scheduled, verify the job completion using Transaction SM37.

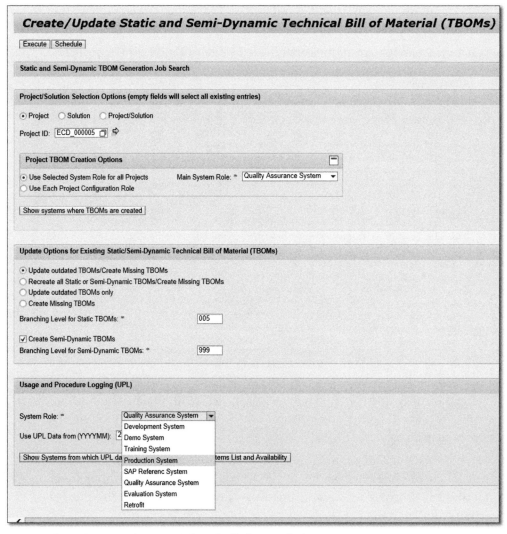

Figure 8.21 Semi-Dynamic Technical Bill of Materials Generation Settings

8.2.2   Executing the Business Process Change Analyzer

After completing the prerequisites within the previous pages, you're now ready to execute BPCA for the updates planned to your production SAP Business Suite on SAP HANA migration using SUM. At this point in the project, you've already updated and migrated your sandbox or development environment to SAP HANA. You can leverage the tools in SAP Solution Manager to measure the impact of those updates against your production SAP ERP business processes. The output of BPCA will be a listing of transaction codes and programs that were impacted by the SUM activities, giving your team the opportunity to narrowly define the test scope for your project. This is especially valuable given the time and cost associated with regression testing of SAP solutions.

How does this relate to the SEA you executed in Chapter 2, Section 2.3.2? A BPCA analysis was executed behind the scenes by SEA. In the beginning of the book, you executed the analysis prior to installing or migrating to SAP Business Suite on SAP HANA. After your system has been upgraded, you can run the analysis yourself in BPCA.

Another use case for BPCA might be defining the impact of multiple transports you created during your project. This transports might contain bug fixes or minor enhancements that you want to know the impact of. In the following steps we will analyze the impact of an Enhancement Package. You could, however, select the TRANSPORT REQUESTS radio button and run the analysis just for objects in a specific group of transports. BPCA is extremely useful on projects and during normal change management.

To execute BPCA, follow these steps:

1. Log on to your SAP Solution Manager system using SAP GUI, and run Transaction SM_WORKCENTER.

2. Navigate to the TEST MANAGEMENT work center using the top-level navigation. Then select the BP CHANGE ANALYZER from the left hand navigation menu (Figure 8.22).

3. Input the PROJECT ID created by SEA in Chapter 2, Section 2.3.2. Enter a description for the ANALYSIS DESCRIPTION field.

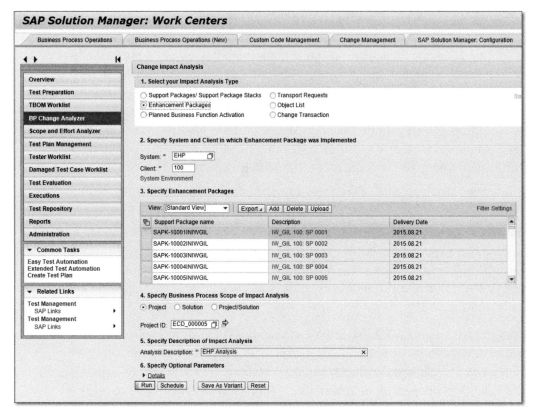

Figure 8.22 Business Process Change Analyzer within the Test Management Work Center in SAP Solution Manager

4. Then select RUN or SCHEDULE. Selecting RUN runs the job immediately in the background. Selecting SCHEDULE allows you to select a time in the future to run the program in the background.

5. After the job is scheduled, you can return to the work center to check the status by scrolling to the ACTIVE QUERIES area.

6. Select the row for your analysis when it completes.

7. Figure 8.23 shows the analysis selected under RESULTS – CURRENT. In the DETAILS OF <PROJECT NAME>, you see a list of transactions.

8. This list contains the transactions and programs that will be impacted by the enhancement package, support package, or group of transport requests you chose to analyze.

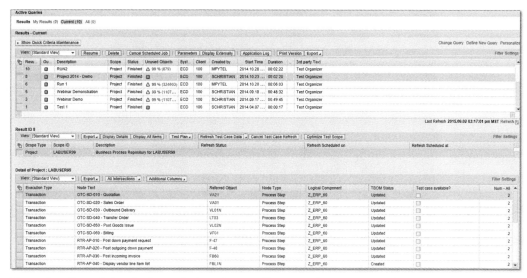

Figure 8.23 Example Results from a Business Process Change Analyzer Impact Analysis

The result set created by BPCA can be exported to Excel, used to create a test plan in SAP Solution Manager Test Workbench, integrated with HP Application Lifecycle Management (ALM), or sent to IBM Rational. Now that you have a result set to be tested, let's explore your test planning and execution options in the next section.

8.3 SAP Solution Manager Testing Tools

SAP Solution Manager Test Management is included with the suite of tools that SAP describes as tools that support Build SAP like a Factory. SAP provides its customers with the software tools needed to define, document, build, test, and deploy SAP components. SAP Solution Manager, delivered as part of a customers' SAP Enterprise or SAP Standard Maintenance Agreement, has become a critical component of an SAP customer's overall landscape. Whether implementing a new SAP solution or performing an SAP Business Suite on SAP HANA migration, the tools delivered in SAP Solution Manager Test Management will meet any organization's basic test management requirements. We'll discuss the SAP Solution Manager tools provided for both Test Management and test execution.

In Chapter 2, Section 2.3, you defined a business blueprint based on the usage of your production system analyzed over a period of time. This blueprint defines the transactions and programs your business users execute in the production environment. In the previous chapter, you used this information to measure the impact of change on your system. After the impact has been measured, this information can then be fed into a test plan. A test plan can best be described as those objects (transactions, programs, interfaces, or manual processes) that need to be tested to confirm the successful implementation of your updates during the migration to SAP HANA. The test plan defines what business processes will be tested, by whom, and by what method (manual or automated). Test execution covers the activities and tools required to meet the requirements of the test plan in addition to the test status reporting.

SAP refers to three supported test options when discussing Test Management within SAP Solution Manager 7.1 (shown in Figure 8.24). Test Option #2 and Test Option #3 require you to purchase additional software, which will be discussed further in Section 8.3.3 and Section 8.3.4, respectively.

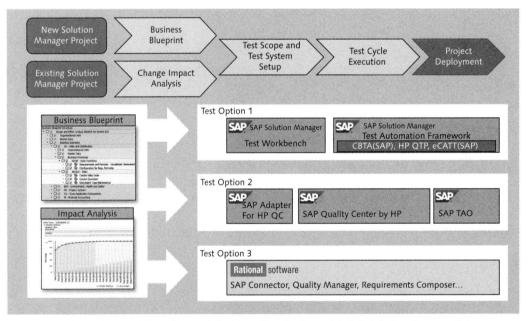

Figure 8.24 SAP Description of the Three Test Options with SAP Solution Manager 7.1

8.3.1 Test Option 1: Test Workbench

In Test Option 1, you can use the Test Workbench to generate a test plan based on the business processes defined within a blueprint. Test scripts, both manual and automated, can be assigned to specific testers or groups of testers. The solution includes standard SAP Business Workflow with email notifications to streamline the process of testing, which is especially useful for geographically dispersed teams. The solution also provides real-time reporting for the status of test execution in addition to integration with SAP Solution Manager IT Service Management (ITSM) for defect tracking and resolution. It's an end-to-end Test Management solution provided as part of your SAP Enterprise Maintenance Agreement.

The test plan defines the scope of business processes to be included in the regression test. These business processes can then be divided into different test packages that you can assign to different teams or potentially different testing streams. The release of test packages can be controlled by a test manager to control the pace of the test cycles. Within a test package, you manually sequence test scripts and then assign them to a specific tester or group of testers. This sequencing will then drive email notifications after each tester completes his test script. In the example shown in Figure 8.25, the test manager has defined three test packages with testers assigned to each package.

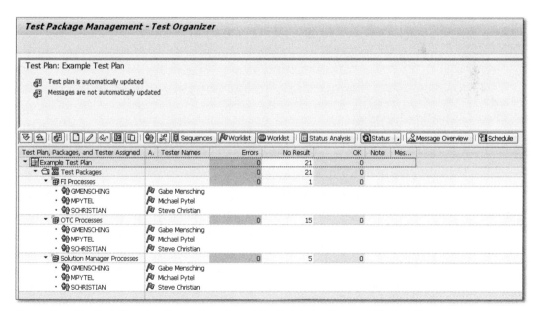

Figure 8.25 The Test Organizer Screen Overview of the Test Script Status within Each Test Package

The same tester can be assigned to one or more packages at the same time. This gives the test manager the flexibility to organize the flow of testing during the regression test.

When the testers receive an email notification, they are provided with a link that directs them to the tester worklist. The browser-based view of the test plan limits the information displayed to only those test cases relevant to that tester (Figure 8.26). The tester can quickly interpret which test cases are ready for test, which test cases have been completed, and which test cases are waiting to be released by the test manager.

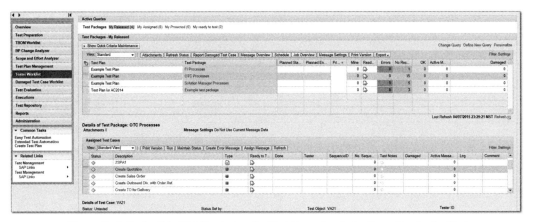

Figure 8.26 Tester Worklist Displaying the Test Cases Ready for Execution by the Tester

Generating Test Plans

You can generate test plans from the TEST MANAGEMENT work center accessed using the Transaction SM_WORKCENTER:

1. Log on to your SAP Solution Manager, and run Transaction SM_WORKCEN-TER. Then navigate to the TEST MANAGEMENT tab.

2. Select TEST PLAN MANAGEMENT from the left side navigation pane.

3. Click the TEST PLAN button, and select CREATE TEST PLAN (Figure 8.27). This launches a transaction within the SAP GUI.

4. When prompted, select the PROJECT you created in Chapter 2, Section 2.3.

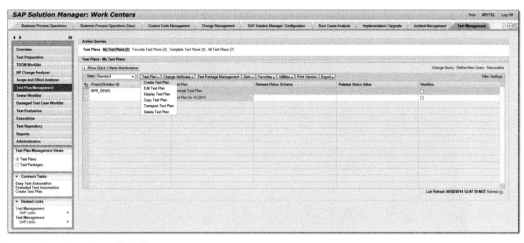

Figure 8.27 Creating a Test Plan

5. Enter a TITLE for your test plan, and select DEFAULT as your RELEASE STATUS
   SCHEMA (Figure 8.28). All other fields can remain.

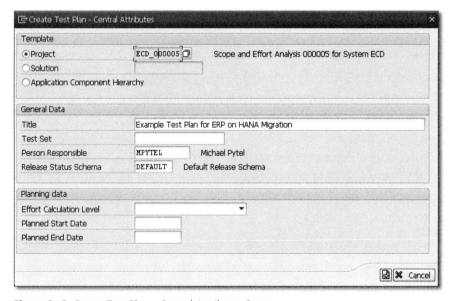

Figure 8.28 Create Test Plan – Central Attributes Screen

6. Click NEXT (or press F5).

7. Click the WITH TRANSACTIONS checkbox (Figure 8.29).

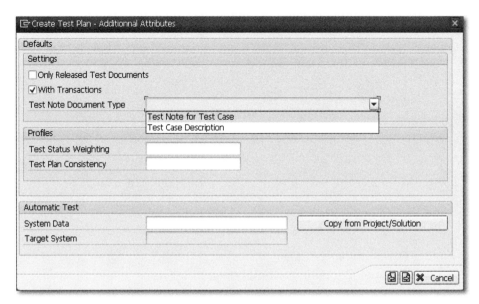

Figure 8.29 Defining the Document Used by Testers for Test Notes

8. In the TEST NOTE FOR DOCUMENT TYPE field, select TEST NOTE FOR TEST CASE. Leave all other fields blank, and click NEXT F5 .

9. When the TEST PLAN generation screen appears, select the transactions to be included in your test plan.

10. Navigate to BUSINESS SCENARIOS to select which transactions you want included in this test plan. A test plan can represent an entire test cycle or individual streams of testing within a test cycle.

11. Select the checkbox next to the individual transactions to include them within the test plan (Figure 8.30).

[+] **Tip**

You can click the EXPAND ALL button to quickly see all transactions within a business process.

12. After you select the required transactions or business processes, click the TEST PLAN button.

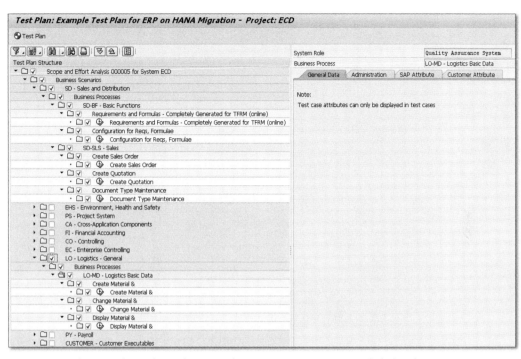

Figure 8.30 Selecting Sales and Distribution and Logistics Processes to Be Included in the Test Plan

13. When prompted to CREATE OBJECT DIRECTORY ENTRY, click LOCAL OBJECT (Figure 8.31).

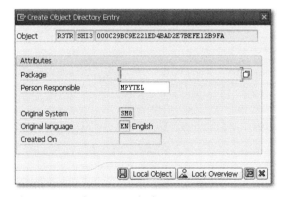

Figure 8.31 Selecting Local Object

14. Next you should see the message from Figure 8.32 displayed in the SAP GUI.

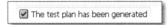

Figure 8.32 Test Plan Generation Confirmation Message

15. Return to the TEST MANAGEMENT work center in your browser. Click the Refresh link on the lower-right corner of the grid row (Figure 8.33).

16. Confirm that you see your test plan within the view.

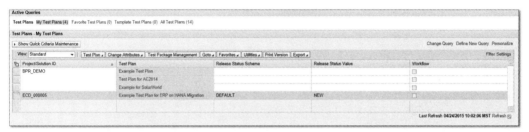

Figure 8.33 The Test Plan You Created

You've now successfully created a test plan and can move on to assigning testers to it. When users are setup in SAP Solution Manager with an email address, you can enable tester workflow to generate notifications to testers when a test plan is released.

Assigning Testers

After creating the test plan, you'll need to assign testers to the test plan to release the test plan for use during your test cycle. Testers are assigned to a test package, which is a logical breakdown of the processes to be tested during the test cycle. You can define a one-to-one relationship between test plan and test package, or you can define multiple test packages for each test plan. Because testers are assigned at the package level, you might want to organize the test packages in a way that more closely relates to those involved. In the example scenario here, two test packages are defined: one for the Sales and Distribution (SD) team and another for the Logistics team.

To assign testers, follow these steps:

1. From the TEST MANAGEMENT work center, select TEST PLAN MANAGEMENT, and then choose the test plan you created earlier.

2. Click the TEST PACKAGE MANAGEMENT button. This will open a transaction within the SAP GUI.

3. Click the CREATE TEST PACKAGE button, as shown in Figure 8.34.

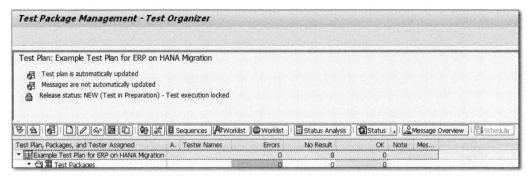

Figure 8.34 Initial Test Package Management Screen

4. Select the BUSINESS SCENARIOS to be included with this test package. As mentioned previously, you'll create one test package for Sales and Distribution (SD), and another package for Logistics.

5. Click the TEST PACKAGE button (Figure 8.35).

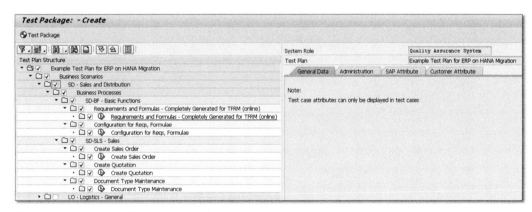

Figure 8.35 Selection of Sales Processes for the Test Package

6. Enter a TITLE for the test package. You also have the option of defining the test package PRIORITY (we all know not all test scripts are created equal), as shown in Figure 8.36.

403

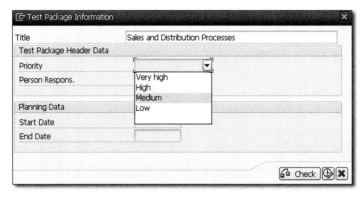

Figure 8.36 Entering a Test Package Title and Priority

7. Click the EXECUTE button, and then select LOCAL OBJECT if prompted to CREATE OBJECT DIRECTORY ENTRY.

8. You can now see one test package defined. Repeat the preceding steps for each additional test package you'll create. (In this example scenario, we've created an additional test package for Logistics.)

9. Next you need to define testers for each test package. These testers will be the recipients of the email notifications for the test plans. Select the test package you created, and click the ASSIGN TESTER button (Figure 8.37).

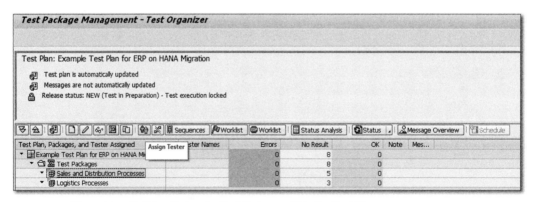

Figure 8.37 Defining Testers by Test Package within the Test Plan

10. You're prompted with a search screen to select the testers for the test package. Use the criteria to find your tester users.

11. Check the box next to each tester, and click the green checkmark button (Figure 8.38).

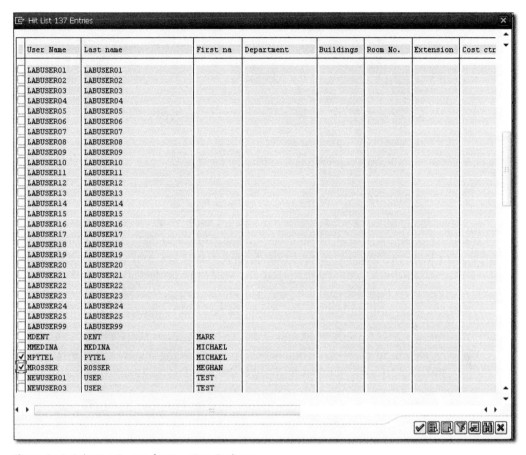

Figure 8.38 Selecting Testers for Your Test Package

12. Now that you've selected your testers, you can release the assignment that is required for the test plan to be used. Click the WORKLIST button (green flag), as shown in Figure 8.39.

13. Click BACK to return to the main menu.

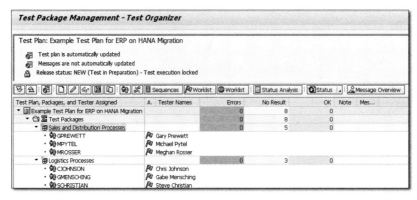

Figure 8.39 Released Assignments by Test Package

Test Plan Release

Now that you've created the test packages and assigned the testers, you can release your test plan to begin the test cycle. This is an important feature because you can stage your test plans prior to your actual test execution. Test plans are also reusable within the same project and on future projects. For now, let's define what is to be tested specific to your SAP Business Suite on SAP HANA migration today. Later, you can use the same tools to test future updates and upgrades.

1. From your SAP Solution Manager TEST MANAGEMENT work center, select TEST PLAN MANAGEMENT on the left side, and then highlight your test plan. Click the CHANGE ATTRIBUTES button, and select CHANGE SINGLE TEST PLAN (Figure 8.40).

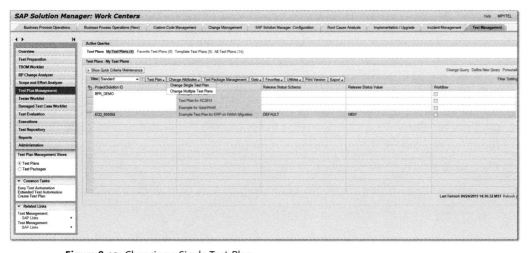

Figure 8.40 Changing a Single Test Plan

2. On the TEST PLAN ATTRIBUTES screen, change the STATUS to RELEASED, and ensure that the WORKFLOW ACTIVE checkbox is checked.

3. Click SAVE, and verify the confirmation message.

4. Click BACK to go to the main menu.

Summary

You've now created the test plan, which defines the transactions and programs to be tested during your project. You've also defined who will be responsible for testing those transactions. Testers will receive an email (see Figure 8.41) from the system informing them of the test cases assigned to them.

Figure 8.41 Example Email from SAP Solution Manager Test Management Workflow

This section defines the minimum steps required to define a test plan for your SAP Business Suite on SAP HANA migration; however, this doesn't include all features and functions available to customers within SAP Solution Manager. For a more detailed description of test capabilities within SAP Solution Manager, see *Testing SAP Solutions* (SAP PRESS, 2011) by Markus Helfen and Hans Martin Trauthwein.

8.3.2   Test Option 1: Test Automation Framework

Test Option 1 supports two types of test automation that are available to SAP customers as part of their SAP Enterprise Support Agreements. Test automation can significantly reduce a customer's test cycle duration and effort (which drives cost). The purpose of this section isn't to describe in detail how to automate all test scripts for your SAP Business Suite on SAP HANA migration, but to inform you of the capabilities within SAP Solution Manager. Regression testing your SAP Business Suite on SAP HANA migration is required, and manual testing and the test planning described earlier in the chapter will meet those test requirements. However, if you choose to also include test automation as part of your SAP Business Suite on SAP HANA migration project, note that this will increase the project duration. Building automated scripts while executing manual test cases is an excellent strategy, but it will require additional resources and time.

Component-Based Test Assistant

Component-Based Test Automation (CBTA) was provided by SAP with SAP Solution Manager 7.1 SP 07. It includes both server-side components and an installable component on the tester workstation that enables the tester to record SAP ERP (ABAP), SAP Customer Relationship Management (SAP CRM) UI, SAP Fiori, or SAP Enterprise Portal transactions as automated test scripts. These test scripts can then be centrally stored in SAP Solution Manager and managed. The SAP Solution Managers Test Automation Framework also enables the use of a test data container. This container essentially stores sets of data to be used by the CBTA scripts, such as multiple sales order types with varied materials and customers. As long as sales order entry process steps remain the same, you can store multiple sets of records to be used by the automated script.

One concept that many customers miss is that test automation can't be achieved with one person building the automated test scripts, that is, business analysts recording scripts in silos. Whether using CBTA, SAP Test Acceleration and Optimization (SAP TAO), HP Unified Functional Testing (UFT), or even a third-party product such as Worksoft, you need two separate functions to be successful. What does this mean? In the ideal world, a business analyst would be able to record a transaction in SAP ERP and then easily play it back later during test cycles. While automated testing technology has improved drastically over the years, it's not an easy button. To successfully build and leverage test automation, you must pair business analysts with test engineers. Marry the business process knowledge with the technical expertise specific to whatever toolset you choose. With CBTA, SAP provides customers with the ability to record unit tests and then string multiple unit test scripts together as an end-to-end functional test. Wonderful technology, but it does require a technical skillset to adapt the unit test recorded by the business analyst. Ideally, you can maintain a one-to-many relationship between test engineer and business analysts to realize the value of test automation. There are two important lessons to take away from this section: only SAP customers with SAP Enterprise Support can use CBTA within SAP Solution Manager 7.1, and a successful test automation strategy includes business analysts executing test script recordings with test engineers refining and organizing automated test scripts.

Test Automation with HP QuickTest Professional

Every customer's SAP Enterprise Support contract includes two HP QuickTest Professional (HP QTP) 11 seat licenses, which can be downloaded one time via the SAP Service Marketplace (*https://support.sap.com/solution-manager/integrated-tools/hp-qtp.html*). The same offering is also available to SAP Product Support for Large Enterprises (PSLE) and SAP MaxAttention customers. Because these licenses are seat licenses, we recommend installing them on a workstation that can be shared by multiple people. These licenses come at no additional charge and can be used to begin building out your test automation environment. You can increase the number of licenses by contacting your SAP or HP sales representative. This specific license for HP QTP will enable your organization to use HP QTP for test automation working directly with SAP Solution Manager. The test script and test data are stored in SAP Solution Manager which has integration to the installation of HP QTP on the desktop. An overview of this process is shown in Figure 8.42.

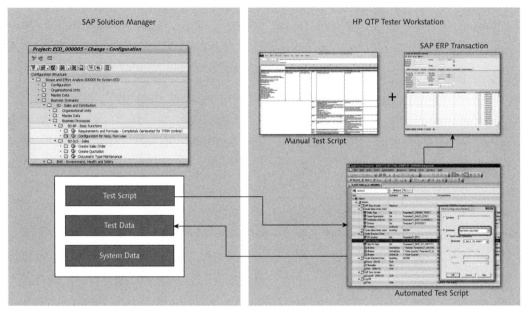

Figure 8.42 HP QTP Integration Overview

To begin using these HP QTP 11 licenses, you have to register the users who will be using them. The user IDs can be switched based on requirements ad hoc. To avoid having to switch user IDs, you would need to purchase more HP QTP 11 licenses.

Follow these steps to register your users:

1. Log on to your SAP Solution Manager system, and run Transaction SPRO .

2. Select SAP REFERENCE IMG.

3. Navigate to SAP SOLUTION MANAGER • CAPABILITIES (OPTIONAL) • TEST MANAGE-MENT • EXTERNAL INTEGRATION • EXTERNAL TEST TOOL WITH eCATT • REGISTER HP QUICKTEST PROFESSIONAL USERS (Figure 8.43).

4. Click the EXECUTE button next to REGISTER HP QUICKTEST PROFESSIONAL USERS.

5. Enter the User IDs of the users who will record automated test scripts using HP QTP 11 (Figure 8.44).

6. Click SAVE. When prompted for a transport, choose an existing transport to save configuration or create a new one.

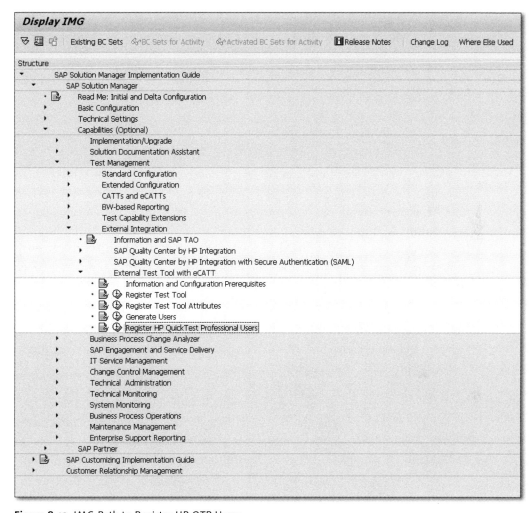

Figure 8.43 IMG Path to Register HP QTP Users

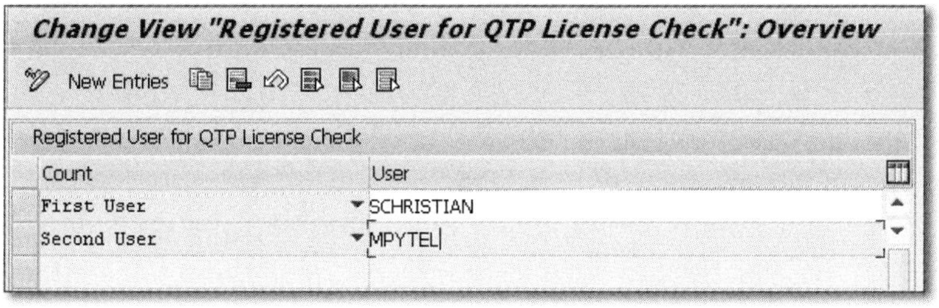

Figure 8.44 Users Authorized to Use HP QTP 11 Licenses

There is value in using HP QTP directly with SAP Solution Manager. As we move to the next section, you'll get even more value by using SAP Solution Manager with HP ALM and HP QTP. The tight integration between HP QTP and HP ALM enables test managers to efficiently know where test automation has been completed and what is outstanding.

8.3.3 Test Option 2: Integration between HP Application Lifecycle Management and SAP Solution Manager

To leverage Test Option 2, you must have licensed the SAP Adapter for HP Quality Center (HP QC) from SAP and potentially licensed SAP TAO as well. The two products are related but operate independently of each other. Both are developed and sold by SAP, but they rely on software from HP. HP ALM can be licensed from SAP or HP and used with the products created by SAP. In this section, we'll explore how they all work together and why you would want to own these tools, given the additional cost.

To start, the Test Management tools included in Option 1 will meet most organizations' requirements during an SAP Business Suite on SAP HANA migration. Using Test Option 1, you'll be able to plan your test cycles, manage the execution, report on progress, and reuse the test plans between test cycles. However, the tools in SAP Solution Manager will require ownership and additional project team training to deploy. If your organization already leverages HP ALM for SAP or non-SAP testing, you may prefer to continue the use of tools your team already knows. This could reduce project team training and potentially increase license cost (due to the purchase of SAP QC by HP) but overall streamline the SAP Business Suite on SAP HANA migration testing by leveraging an enterprise-class testing tool.

SAP Adapter for HP Quality Center

The SAP Adapter for HP QC is an ABAP add-on that is installed in SAP Solution Manager 7.1. The adapter enables two-way communication with HP ALM QC. HP QC is a requirements-based testing tool, which simply means that test scripts are associated to a test requirement. Because SAP Solution Manager already knows what needs to be tested (think back to Chapter 2, Section 2.3.1, on the Solution Documentation toolset), SAP has provided an interface to send those transactions and programs to HP QC as test requirements. This functionality has been available to SAP customers since 2007, and the current downloadable component, SAP ADAPTER FOR QC 1.0, is supported until December 2020.

[«]

> **Note**
>
> For the latest information and installation guides on the SAP Solution Manager adapter for HP QC, see SAP Note 2090856 – Collective Note for SAP Solution Manager Adapter.

The adapter enables two-way communication with HP ALM QC. The first communication path sends business processes from Solution Documentation to HP ALM as test requirements (shown in Figure 8.45). The second communication path enables HP ALM Defect Management (DM) to send test plan and defect stats to SAP Solution Manager for test reporting. In real-world scenarios, we don't see too many customers leveraging this functionality. If you're running test cycles in HP ALM, it's easier to complete reporting from a single tool. HP ALM also delivers several out-of-the-box reports you can use to communicate to stakeholders.

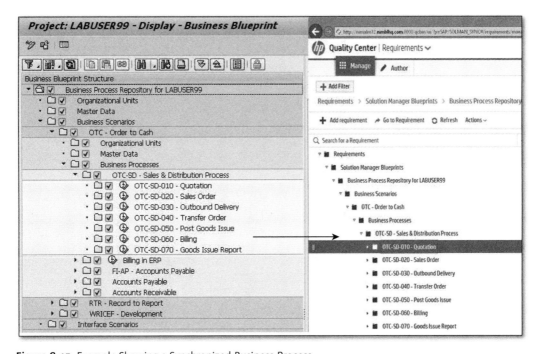

Figure 8.45 Example Showing a Synchronized Business Process

SAP Test Acceleration and Optimization

SAP TAO is another licensed product from SAP that simplifies the UI for auto-mated test script development. The installation process for SAP TAO includes the installation of HP QTP on the test script developers' workstations. This SAP-designed application provides a link between SAP Solution Manager for business process information, transportable object information, and the automated test script, which is eventually stored and executed from HP ALM QC. SAP TAO is intended to simplify the creation of automated test scripts by enabling business analysts to use the tool to record simple unit test scripts (see Figure 8.46). These unit test scripts can later be modified by a test script engineer to enable end-to-end process tests. Because SAP TAO is built on top of HP QTP, you can enable input and output variables to string multiple scripts together. For example, you can enter an invoice and pass the invoice number to the next script, which will perform a goods receipt and eventual invoice posting.

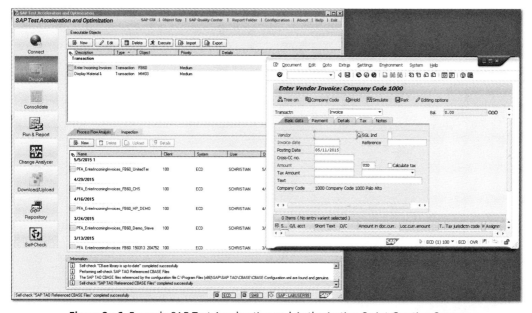

Figure 8.46 Example SAP Test Acceleration and Authorization Script Creation Screen

SAP TAO provides several key capabilities that differentiate it in the marketplace. The first scenario includes the ability to execute automated test scripts based on the results from the BPCA (discussed in Section 8.1). Additionally, it provides the capability to update automated test scripts based on the contents of a transport.

This is especially useful because you no longer need to rerecord a test script if a developer adds fields to a screen or creates a user exit within the transaction. SAP TAO enables the update of the specific component updated by the transport. Lastly, SAP TAO enables the update and/or creation of the dynamic TBOM during script execution.

So why would you want to own these tools? It's an opportunity to reduce the risk of resource turnover, remove tribal knowledge testing from your organization, and execute test scripts more frequently. Manual testing is expensive and laborious. No organization should expect to have 70%, 80%, or 90% test automation (although that would be amazing) because it would be costly to maintain. In our experience, starting out with a goal of 20% automation and 80% manual test scripts—all stored in a central repository—is a fantastic solution to common problems with testing SAP solutions. People will know what to test and how to test, and ideally they will spend less time testing because complex or long-running test scenarios will be automated.

8.3.4 Test Option 3: IBM Rational

IBM Rational comprises several tools meant to support requirements collection, testing, documentation, and management. The purpose of this section isn't to explain the IBM Rational products available in the marketplace, but to explain where integration exists between SAP Solution Manager 7.1 and IBM Rational software components. Unlike the SAP Adapter for HP QC, the software required to integrate IBM Rational can be retrieved from IBM directly.

Note	[«]
See SAP Note 1559619 – Installing IBM Rational SAP Connector for the latest information on the installation, configuration, and maintenance of the adapter for IBM Rational.	

After the software from IBM has been installed, you'll need to activate the enhancement within the Switch Framework in SAP Solution Manager (shown in Figure 8.47).

Caution	[!]
After this enhancement has been enabled, it *can't* be disabled.	

415

We aren't aware of any limitations with the activation of this enhancement when the SAP Adapter for HP QC is actively used. Be sure to test this solution in a non-productive instance of SAP Solution Manager before activating in production.

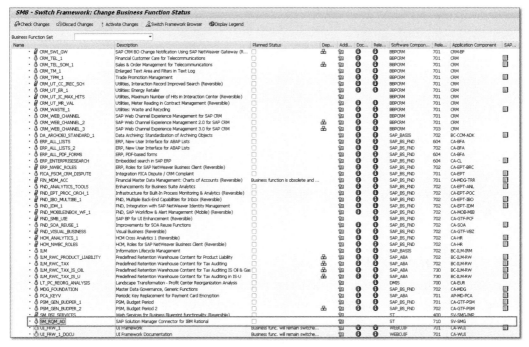

Figure 8.47 Transaction SFW5 Switch Framework Activation

The adapter for IBM Rational includes four main functionalities. The first includes the ability to import business processes from SAP Solution Manager into IBM Rational Quality Manager and IBM Rational RequisitePro. This is a critical component to test planning because SAP Solution Manager can define the test scope and contains information on the transactions and business processes in use in your SAP ERP system to be migrated to SAP HANA.

The second piece of functionality includes the ability to drive testing requirements in IBM Rational using SAP Solution Manager BPCA. You can measure the impact of the enhancement package included in your SAP Business Suite on SAP HANA migration, and then send the results to IBM Rational.

The last two functionalities mimic what is available in the SAP Adapter for HP QC. You can send test plan results to SAP Solution Manager and include defect information within SAP Solution Manager ITSM. The adapter for IBM Rational provides an end-to-end process interface from requirements documentation, testing, defect resolution, and test plan reporting.

In Section 8.4, we'll cover change management tools in SAP Solution Manager that integrate with the testing tools available. All three test options provide integration points with change management.

> **Note** [«]
>
> For the latest information on the SAP Solution Manager Test Options 1, 2, or 3, see the SAP Solution Manager wiki on SDN by navigating to *http://wiki.scn.sap.com/wiki/display/SM/SAP+Solution+Manager+WIKI+-+Test+Management*.

8.4 Change Management with SAP Solution Manager

Change management can mean many things to many different readers. This section focuses on change management as a process for controlling changes within your SAP ERP landscape during the migration to SAP HANA. We know organizational change management tasks will be part of your project, which we'll discuss in Chapter 10. Change management is covered under the ITIL (formerly known as the Information Technology Infrastructure Library), which is a set of practices for ITSM that focuses on aligning IT services with the needs of business. SAP Solution Manager is certified for 15 different ITIL processes as of August 2015. More information is available here: *http://www.pinkelephant.com/PinkVERIFY/PinkVERIFY_2011_Toolsets.htm*. One of those process certifications includes change management.

Change management as a process in SAP Solution Manager is primarily supported by three distinct tools that can be integrated or operated independently. Change Request Management (ChaRM) is the most commonly known tool and supports end-to-end change management, documentation, execution, and reporting. ChaRM is a robust tool for managing both SAP change and non-SAP change. Quality Gate Management (QGM) is a lesser-known tool but very capable at managing the execution of change management. QGM won't associate documentation or change management process approvals to a transportable change, but it will manage the movement of transports from one system to another in a controlled environment. Retrofit, which must be leveraged from within ChaRM or QGM, is the function that enables the movement of transportable changes from one landscape to another across SAP ERP versions. You can imagine how useful this is when you need to move production support changes from an SAP ERP 6 EHP 4 landscape to SAP ERP 6 EHP 7 on SAP HANA. SAP doesn't officially support cross SAP ERP version imports but does support the Retrofit of changes from one landscape to another on different versions. Let's explore these tools over the next several sections so you can understand how they might support your organization's SAP Business Suite on SAP HANA migration project.

[»] | **Note**

For detailed information on the configuration of ChaRM and QGM, see the SAP Solution Manager wiki on SCN or reference IT Service Management in SAP Solution Manager (SAP PRESS, 2013) by Nathan Williams.

8.4.1 Change Request Management

Whether managing change during an eight-week migration or a six-month SAP Business Suite on SAP HANA migration, you'll need to support normal business activity in your SAP landscapes while also maintaining an SAP Business Suite on SAP HANA project landscape. In Chapter 2, we discussed the different approaches to a system and client strategy, so we won't cover those scenarios again. We'll highlight that ChaRM can support any landscape strategy that follows a common software development lifecycle. ChaRM as a component of SAP Solution Manager has been included since SAP Solution Manager 3.x. It has only been Pink Elephant ITIL Certified since SAP Solution Manager 7.1 and remains part of an SAP Standard and SAP Enterprise Support Agreements for customers. The tool can be configured and used in all SAP landscapes.

ChaRM provides the ability to manage both the request for change and the change document (execution of the change event). The change event can be transportable, a set of manual tasks, or a process change that doesn't impact configuration within SAP systems. A change document is referred to as a normal change, urgent change, general change, administrative change, or defect correction. Normal changes and urgent changes are transportable changes, whereas the others aren't. Change documents can be logically organized into projects. A project can represent an actual project such as your SAP Business Suite on SAP HANA migration project, or it can represent a repeated weekly release into a production environment. There is no limit on the configuration of projects in ChaRM; however, ideally you've defined some standards for governance. Let's start by exploring the change document types included with ChaRM:

▸ **Request for change**
Documentation supporting the reason for a change. Includes the ability to manage request for change approvals with custom approval schemes.

▸ **Normal change**
A transportable change within an ABAP or Java system. A normal change includes the ability to leverage transport of copies to reduce the number of transports imported into a production environment.

▸ **Urgent change**
A transportable change with a streamlined process flow when compared to a normal change. It doesn't leverage transport of copies and assumes the quickest path to production.

▸ **General change**
A nontransportable change that can cover manual tasks in SAP but more commonly is used to manage non-SAP changes. Examples of general changes include firmware changes at the hardware level or OS patching.

▸ **Administrative change**
A nontransportable change specific to a manual SAP task. Examples include editing a number range or completing client-specific configuration while a client is open for configuration.

▸ **Defect correction**
A change document that can only be created when in the test phase of a project in ChaRM. This is meant to track the defect correction transport related to a request for change or normal change.

ChaRM is accessed via the SAP CRM UI within a web browser (Figure 8.48). This web-based client can be accessed via Internet Explorer or Chrome, the only options supported by SAP. The content and actions available within the UI are controlled via ABAP security roles. Although the UI is accessed using a web browser, it doesn't run on the SAP Solution Manager Java stack. It's configured, managed, and patched from the SAP Solution Manager ABAP stack.

Tip	[+]
If you need example SAP security roles to access ChaRM within SAP Solution Manager, see the SAP Solution Manager security guide at *http://help.sap.com/solutionmanager71/*. Once there, click on SECURITY INFORMATION • SECURITY GUIDE.	

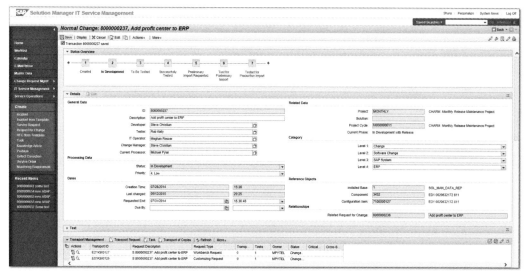

Figure 8.48 Example Change Request Management User Interface

ChaRM centralizes the management and tracking of change by associating the people, documentation, and technical objects related to a specific change. Within ChaRM, you can configure a project to manage the changes related to production support and another project for the transportable objects created as part of the SAP Business Suite on SAP HANA project.

In Figure 8.49, you have two ChaRM projects configured. Any maintenance activity you complete in the support project would need to be manually applied to development SAP Business Suite on SAP HANA and associated to the SAP HANA migration project within ChaRM. (We'll talk later about the Retrofit tool, which can simplify this process.) As you advance the SAP HANA migration project in ChaRM from development to QA, the collection of transports from the project and production support are moved together. When the SAP HANA migration project advances to production, it includes the production support transports as well. This package of changes has been regression tested in QA SAP Business Suite on SAP HANA and validated as a functional code base.

How does ChaRM control transports to ensure consistency in the landscape? Within SAP Solution Manager, each ChaRM project represents a Change and Transport System (CTS) project in the Transport Management System (TMS), as shown in Figure 8.50. Within each system managed by ChaRM, SAP Solution Manager can set flags that enable or disable transport creation, transport release, or transport import.

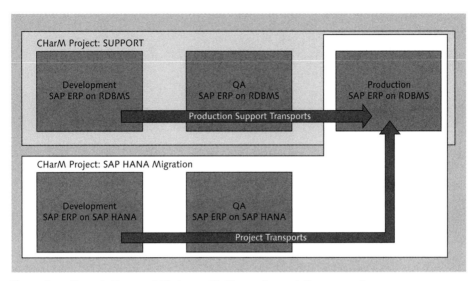

Figure 8.49 Example Transport Strategy with Change Request Management

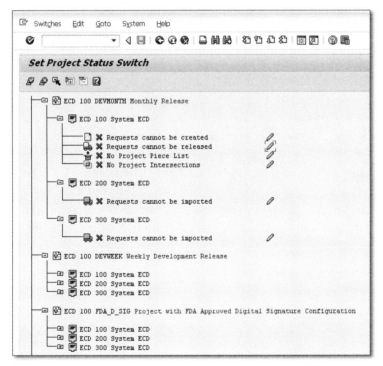

Figure 8.50 Example Change and Transport System Status Switch Set in Transaction SPRO_ADMIN

421

On a properly configured system under the control of ChaRM, no single individual (even someone with SAP_ALL) can manually create, release, or import a transport. All transports fall under the control of ChaRM. This supports the philosophy that no person should be allowed to create a transport without an approved change request. Again, ChaRM within SAP Solution Manager is an ITIL-certified change management tool.

8.4.2 Quality Gate Management

QGM is a relatively underused tool that gives you the transport control of ChaRM without the end-user UI. If you remember, ChaRM provides a central tool for tracking all documentation, approvals, and transports related to a change or group of changes. QGM primarily provides the transport control you want during a project, but QGM doesn't provide the document and approval tracking you get with ChaRM. Using QGM assumes that you're tracking approvals and change documentation in another ITSM tool. QGM is accessed from within SAP Solution Manager via the CHANGE MANAGEMENT work center.

In Figure 8.51, a QGM project has been configured with several quality gates. Think of these quality gates as the mechanisms that enable transports to move between environments based on a project schedule. Based on the project schedule for your SAP Business Suite on SAP HANA migration, a project manager can enable or disable the movement of transports between systems. When leveraging QGM, you still get the control of not allowing transports to be created without approval to start work. This will be essential during your project because you need to ensure consistency between systems. Another benefit of QGM is that it provides transparency to the transport landscape. A project manager isn't dependent on someone else to run a report or export a list of transports by system. When using QGM correctly, there is little risk that someone will accidentally move a transport without being permitted—change control is the name of the game.

Typically, the project team members don't use QGM. Project team members send a request to a change manager or a small group of team leads who then are authorized to create transports using QGM for the project. This might be a potential bottleneck, so it's good practice to define processes or put contingencies in place to prevent slowdowns. You want team member to be able to work on objects related to your upgrade, but you also want everyone to work in a controlled fashion. See the example in Figure 8.52 of creating a transport in QGM. The transport could be linked to a change that might describe the contents or the purpose for that transports.

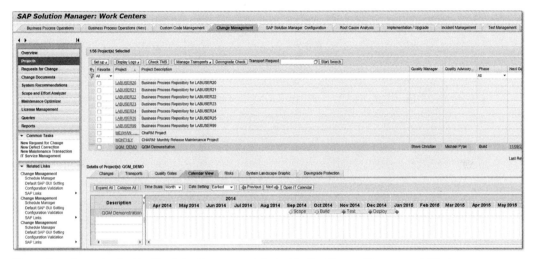

Figure 8.51 Example of a Quality Gate Management Project in the Change Management Work Center

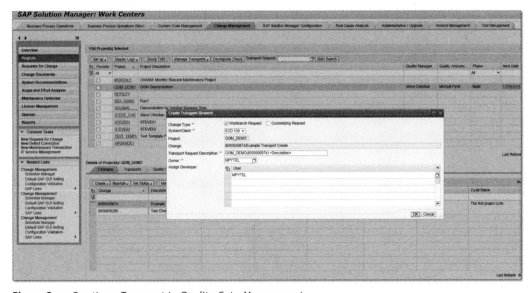

Figure 8.52 Creating a Transport in Quality Gate Management

8.4.3   Retrofit

SAP doesn't officially support cross-version imports, which is why most customers with a project and production support landscape enter a period of dual maintenance during a project. In your SAP Business Suite on SAP HANA migration project, you might choose the scenario where the production support landscape remains on its traditional Relational Database Management System (RDBMS), while the project landscape is on SAP Business Suite on SAP HANA. How do you prevent manual dual maintenance and ensure consistent tracking of objects between landscapes? Retrofit in SAP Solution Manager 7.0 is the sole tool from SAP for managing change across landscapes with different versions of software components.

Retrofit is an additional component that can be configured with ChaRM or QGM. You must be using one of these tools to leverage Retrofit. These tools are required because they both provide the transport tracking necessary to manage objects between the landscapes. The only other dependency Retrofit has within SAP Solution Manager is the use of Cross System Object Locking (CSOL). This is a feature in SAP Solution Manager that locks objects in one landscape while they are being modified in another. Imagine a scenario where a production support request is processed that requires modifications to an ABAP program. The same program is also impacted by your SAP Business Suite on SAP HANA upgrade. How do you ensure the production support change can occur and your object remediation on the project won't accidentally overwrite the production support change later? The first part of the answer comes from CSOL. When the change is started in the development system within the production support landscape, the system creates a lock entry in SAP Solution Manager. This ensures that your project team can't modify the object in the project landscape because it too is configured for CSOL.

Figure 8.53 shows version one of Program A, which exists in both landscapes. The production support developer needs to modify the object. When the developer opens the program in Transaction SE38 or Transaction SE80, the development system uses a trusted RFC to SAP Solution Manager to check the lock table. No lock entry is found, and the developer can continue. In the project landscape, another developer tries to access the same object and gets a message stating that the object is locked and by which person. The locks in CSOL can be overridden by an administrator at any time.

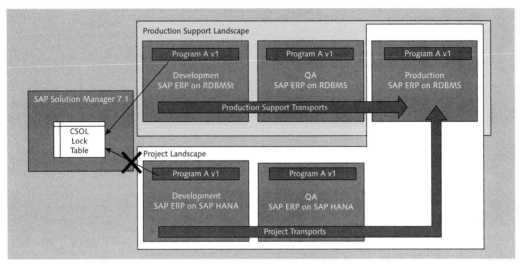

Figure 8.53 Cross System Object Locking – Object in Project Landscape

Figure 8.54 shows the reverse scenario. The project team has locked Program A and created a new version. This locks the object from changes in the production support landscape. In this scenario, the change manager and project manager need to collaborate on a decision. Can the production support change wait until the project is completed? Or does the lock need to be manually overridden and changes retrofitted into the project landscape?

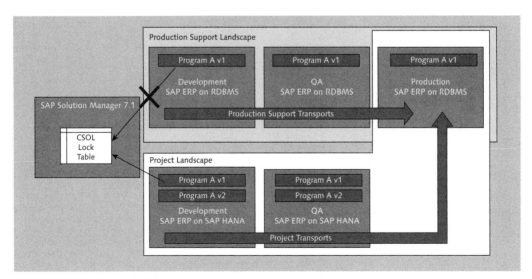

Figure 8.54 Object Lock Maintained by the Project Landscape

Retrofit is a tool provided by SAP and included with your SAP Enterprise Support Agreement. It enables customers to track and manage change through multiple landscapes. This scenario can occur all too often. Manually tracking transports and objects via Excel spreadsheets is insufficient at preventing potential code or configuration overwrites after you move your project into production. CSOL creates awareness of objects in use within the various landscapes. Retrofit then ensures the objects are consistent between systems.

In Figure 8.55, the production support and project landscapes are defined with several transport paths. In the production support landscape, you see the traditional path from development to quality to production. The arrow traversing the production support landscape to the project landscape represents the Retrofit process, which is managed from SAP Solution Manager 7.1. Remember, Retrofit is available when you use ChaRM or QGM. By default, SAP enables the execution of Retrofit after a transport is released from the production support development system. It's also possible to execute Retrofit after the transport has been imported into quality and is ready for production.

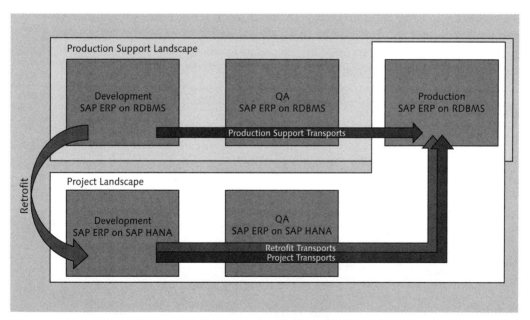

Figure 8.55 Retrofit Process Example

Figure 8.56 shows a collection of transports that have either been processed or are waiting for Retrofit. The tools in SAP Solution Manager are monitoring and tracking transports in the landscape at all times when configured correctly. During your SAP Business Suite on SAP HANA migration project, changes are ideally processed weekly at a minimum—potentially daily if lots of changes are being made to the production support landscape. The person who executes the Retrofit doesn't need to be a developer or a configuration expert—but he does need to be conscious of the objects he is moving and when. Reporting is available to alert project teams when Retrofit objects are being moved into the project landscape.

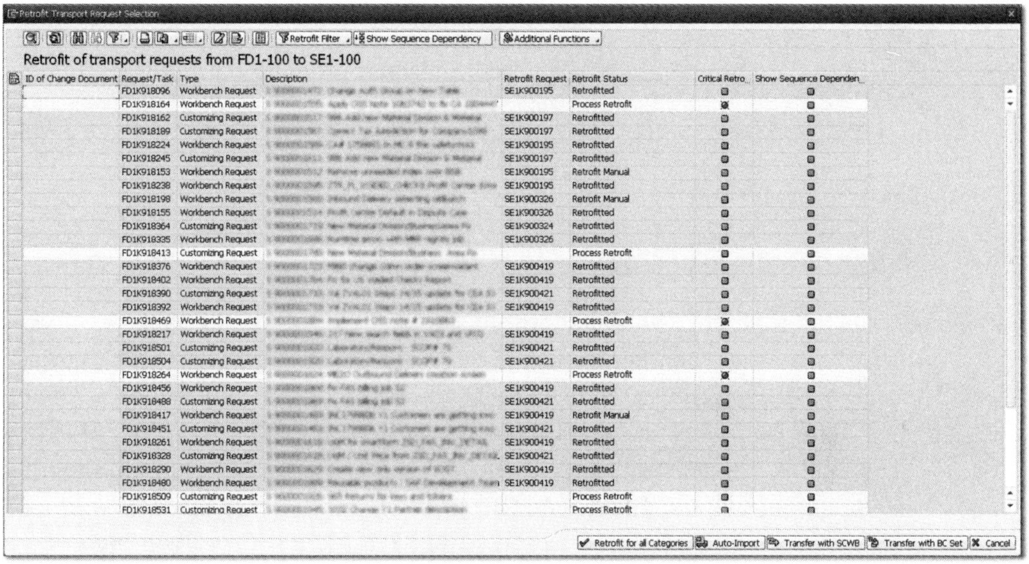

Figure 8.56 Collection of Transports and Their Retrofit Status

In Figure 8.56, the person executing Retrofit highlights the transports and then selects the AUTO-IMPORT button. This button starts functionality that automatically identifies the objects within the production support transport and inserts them into a new transport in the project landscape. During this process, the SAP program inserts the configuration or code changes into the project development system. This Retrofit container transport in the project landscape is then included with the transports, which eventually move to the project landscape QA system and finally the production system. If the AUTO-IMPORT button returns an error, this typically means the SAP utility wasn't able to safely insert the objects. At this point, the person executing Retrofit needs to include development or configuration resources to identify the inconsistencies and manually remediate using the tools in Retrofit. The two other buttons on the screen support this process. The TRANSFER WITH SCWB button is used for workbench objects and provides a side-by-side code editor displaying the object in the production support transport and the object in the project development system. This tool specifically requires development expertise. The button TRANSFER WITH BC SET can be used with Customizing transports; however, we typically see project teams manually completing any configuration that doesn't auto-import and then setting the retrofit item as MANUALLY RETROFITTED.

[»]

Note

To learn more about Retrofit and its configuration, see the SAP Solution Manager wiki on the SCN at *http://wiki.scn.sap.com/wiki/display/SAPITSM/Configuration+and+Administration+of+ITSM.*

8.5 Summary

Throughout this chapter, we discussed the tools and processes available to your project teams as you execute your SAP Business Suite on SAP HANA project. You'll need to be able to manage technical change during your project, and you must have the ability to execute focused testing cycles to achieve the potential value of SAP Business Suite on SAP HANA. After all, what's the point in simplifying your IT landscape if you spend all the savings on testing? During your SAP Business Suite on SAP HANA migration project, the test cycles will involve the greatest number of employees from your organization, so it's imperative that you make the best use of their time. Leveraging test scope identification tools and managing changes to guarantee no repeat test cycles will ensure you run a lean project.

BPCA is an SAP-delivered application that delivers the single greatest value to your SAP Business Suite on SAP HANA migration in terms of narrowing test scope and limiting the amount of time you spend on testing to only those objects that are impacted. There are also third-party tools that compete with SAP Solution Manager BPCA (Panaya and LiveCompare to name two). That said, we've found BPCA to meet or exceed most organizations' impact analysis requirements. And BPCA can integrate directly to third-party testing tools such as HP ALM or IBM Rational. Leverage the tools you already own as part of your SAP

Enterprise Maintenance Agreements because they don't require large amounts of effort to deploy.

Change management during your SAP Business Suite on SAP HANA migration project is key. Whether running the project for eight weeks or eight months, your SAP landscape must remain dynamic to support your organizations. Using SAP Solution Manager ChaRM or QGM will safeguard your SAP landscape from accidental downgrades and overwritten code changes, as well as limit the number of defects related to change control process issues. Coupled with advanced features such as CSOL and Retrofit, you can enable both project and production support teams to work efficiently and with transparency in their activities.

SAP Solution Manager as a software tool has evolved into an important component of SAP software delivery strategy. This is the system from which you can plan, drive, and implement new functionality within your landscape. The success of your SAP Business Suite on SAP HANA migration project can be greatly improved when SAP Solution Manager and its ITIL-certified tools support your project teams' efforts. These tools come with some additional implementation and maintenance effort; however, these upfront costs should pay dividends later during the operation and maintenance of SAP Business Suite on SAP HANA in production.

Manually monitoring systems in the twenty-first century is no longer an acceptable business practice. Tools and software are available as part of your SAP Maintenance Agreements that can monitor systems 24x7 with email, SMS, and IT Service Management integration.

9   Proactive Monitoring

Before going live with SAP Business Suite on SAP HANA, you need to ensure that your teams can monitor both SAP Business Suite and SAP HANA for errors, inconsistencies, or performance issues. As you progress through the lifecycle of your project, you'll want to ensure that the setup and configuration of proactive monitoring keeps pace with the project. You don't want to be in a situation where your production business processes are being executed on a system you can't monitor proactively. You want to avoid responding to issues as a result of a notification from an end user. Ideally, you should get ahead of potential issues by proactively monitoring key areas within SAP Business Suite and SAP HANA to prevent downtime or end-user disruption. Thankfully, you should already own a variety of tools to help monitor your systems.

In this chapter, we'll focus on monitoring your newly migrated SAP Business Suite on SAP HANA system by exploring the various tools available to you. We'll start with the tools delivered in SAP HANA. SAP HANA Studio, SAP HANA Cockpit, and the SAP Database Control Center (DBCC or DCC; we're using DCC in this book) are all SAP HANA-specific components. These tools provide in-depth monitoring for the operation of SAP HANA as a database and application server. We'll cover the different use cases for each tool and who in your organization might have access to each tool. The tools specific to SAP HANA won't provide deep application-level monitoring in SAP ERP, but they will provide you information to diagnose or monitor the system. They bring together operating system (OS) performance information with the database to give you a view of the system as a whole. These tools include SAP HANA-specific capability monitoring for services, high availability (HA) information, backup status, active jobs, memory utilization, and more. Some of these tools can even be accessed by mobile devices.

The Technical Operations process in SAP Solution Manager will enable you to bring together application server, database operations, and SAP ERP application performance information into a single view. Often, monitoring the OS and database isn't enough. For example, we've seen issues where the hardware and database are only 40% utilized, but end-user transactions are still performing poorly. Using SAP Solution Manager, you can monitor end-user dialog performance and correlate that with the system performance. In this example, the issue wasn't the server sizing, but configuration settings that enabled the application to use more resources on the servers. Technical Operations has been available since SAP HANA was initially released and remains the easiest path to email and Short Message Service (SMS) alert notifications for issues (you can configure some email alerts in SAP HANA directly.) SAP Solution Manager is also the mechanism for delivering SAP EarlyWatch Reports for the SAP HANA database as well as SAP ERP. Activating SAP EarlyWatch Reporting is key to maximizing the value of your SAP Enterprise or SAP Standard Support Agreements because SAP services depend on the configuration and data collected by the reporting.

We'll also cover the Database Administration Cockpit (DBA Cockpit) and its potential use cases. You can access the DBA Cockpit from the SAP ERP system or SAP Solution Manager. We'll walk through the setup of the tool, its use case, and who you might grant access to when deployed. The DBA Cockpit can act as a central planning calendar for database-related maintenance activities. When connected to SAP Solution Manager, it gives administrators a single point of entry to manage any database within the SAP landscape regardless of database type or version. The DBA Cockpit has been available for 15+ years, so it's a familiar interface, even though the platform it's managing is new.

Proactive monitoring will position your team and your organization for a successful deployment of SAP Business Suite on SAP HANA. After all, you want to keep the system up, available, and running at high performance levels to further cement SAP Business Suite on SAP HANA as the platform for innovation within your organization.

9.1   SAP HANA Studio

SAP HANA Studio will be your initial go-to application for SAP HANA monitoring and maintenance. It's important that your SAP HANA Studio client is always maintained to the same release level or higher than your SAP HANA database version. By default, when you open SAP HANA Studio, you have two monitoring overviews available. The first is called System Monitor, which provides an overview of the systems you've connected to from SAP HANA Studio. You can immediately see the instance operational state, alerts, and general performance metrics for disk, CPU, and memory. Double-clicking a line item opens the second overview, Administration, which provides you with eight more tabs to drill down into more information. On the OVERVIEW tab, you immediately see information related to services status, the system start time, release levels, alert overviews, and performance statistics. Clicking MORE INFORMATION under any area will link you to the LANDSCAPE tab for more information about services and their hardware consumption.

Let's navigate the monitoring options within SAP HANA Studio:

1. Open SAP HANA Studio from your computer. If you don't have it installed, connect to *http://support.sap.com/swdc*, and then select SUPPORT PACKAGES & PATCHES • A-Z • H • SAP HANA PLATFORM EDITION • SAP HANA PLATFORM EDIT. 1.0 • ENTRY BY COMPONENT • HANA STUDIO • SAP HANA STUDIO 2.

2. If you haven't connected to a SAP HANA system before, you'll need to select FILE • NEW • FOLDER. Give the folder a name, highlight that folder, right-click, and select ADD SYSTEM.

3. If prompted, log on as the SYSTEM user or any administrative user with the role `sap.hana.admin.roles::Monitoring` assigned.

4. Click the SYSTEM MONITOR button, which is the second icon from the left next to ADD A SYSTEM.

5. The right pane will open the SYSTEM MONITOR overview, as shown in Figure 9.1.

Figure 9.1 Example System Monitor Screen

6. You can double-click on the data within a specific column to get additional details. For example, if you double-click the DATABASE RESIDENT MEMORY column, you're immediately brought to the SERVICES tab within the LANDSCAPE ADMINISTRATION view.

Two tabs are displayed on the top row. One tab displays SYSTEM MONITOR, and the other tab displays the SAP HANA instance ID, as shown in Figure 9.2.

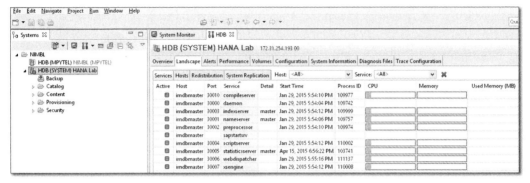

Figure 9.2 The Landscape Tab Displayed in SAP HANA Studio

7. Navigate to the OVERVIEW tab where you'll see the following components (Figure 9.3):

 ▶ GENERAL INFORMATION: This gives you some general information about the instance, the number of hosts, and the database version.

 ▶ CURRENT ALERTS AND MESSAGES: Here you can see some high-level alert information. Clicking here will take you to the detailed ALERTS tab.

 ▶ SAP HANA USED MEMORY: Here you have three memory-related fields:

  – USED MEMORY indicates the total amount of memory used by SAP HANA.

  – PEAK USED MEMORY records the highest used memory value.

  – ALLOCATION LIMIT defines the limit of memory before SAP HANA runs out of memory.

 ▶ RESIDENT MEMORY: The amount of memory the OS sees as in use.

 ▶ CPU USAGE: This measurement compares the percentage of CPU used by SAP HANA to that used by the entire OS.

 ▶ DISK SPACE: This provides detailed information about the disk space used by SAP HANA for the data files, log files, and trace files.

8. Navigate to the LANDSCAPE tab, and then click the SERVICES subtab. Here you can see the status of services that are installed and start when the system is started. You can also see individual service memory consumption in the event you need to troubleshoot system performance (Figure 9.4). For example, the indexserver is consuming 168GB of memory.

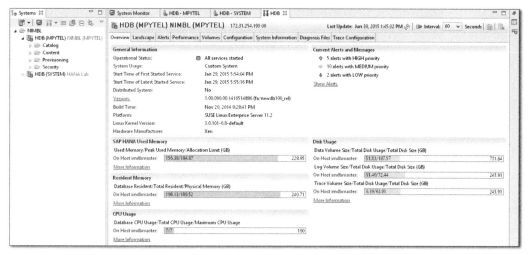

Figure 9.3 Overview Tab within System Administration

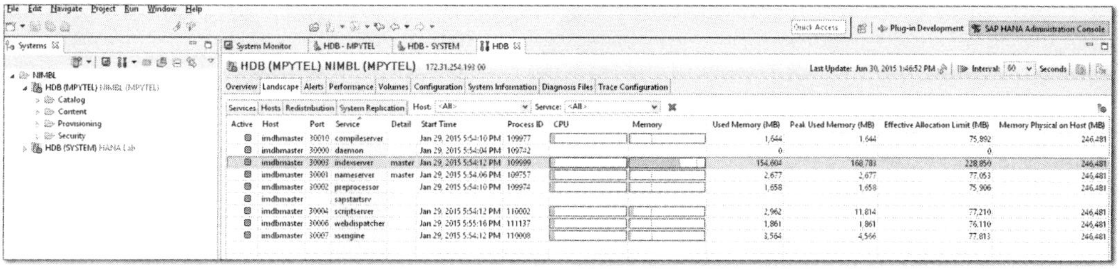

Figure 9.4 Viewing the Status of Services in the Landscape Tab

9. Click on the HOSTS tab to see information about the hosts supporting the SAP HANA system you've connected to (Figure 9.5). In the scale-up scenario supported with SAP Business Suite on SAP HANA, you'll only see one host potentially in your nonproduction systems. In a production scenario, you'll see your active host supporting the SAP Business Suite on SAP HANA database and another host with its auto-failover status displayed.

Figure 9.5 Example Showing One Host Supporting the Nonproduction SAP Business Suite on SAP HANA Instance

10. Navigate to the ALERTS tab to find system level alerts, as shown in Figure 9.6. These alerts are typically resolved by the Basis or SAP HANA administrator.

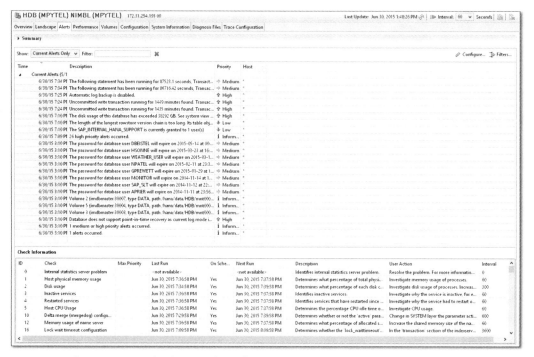

Figure 9.6 Example Alerts Displayed from System Administration in SAP HANA Studio

11. If you want to change the threshold for specific alerts, select the CONFIGURE CHECK SETTINGS button.

12. To enable email alerts directly from SAP HANA, enter the email address of alert recipients, and enter an SMTP server and port, as shown in Figure 9.7.

13. Click the CONFIGURE CHECK THRESHOLDS tab to adjust thresholds for specific alerts (Figure 9.8).

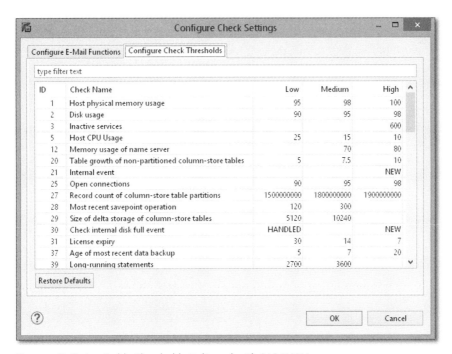

Figure 9.7 Configuration for Email Alerts from SAP HANA

ID	Check Name	Low	Medium	High
1	Host physical memory usage	95	98	100
2	Disk usage	90	95	98
3	Inactive services			600
5	Host CPU Usage	25	15	10
12	Memory usage of name server		70	80
20	Table growth of non-partitioned column-store tables	5	7.5	10
21	Internal event			NEW
25	Open connections	90	95	98
27	Record count of column-store table partitions	1500000000	1800000000	1900000000
28	Most recent savepoint operation	120	300	
29	Size of delta storage of column-store tables	5120	10240	
30	Check internal disk full event	HANDLED		NEW
31	License expiry	30	14	7
37	Age of most recent data backup	5	7	20
39	Long-running statements	2700	3600	

Figure 9.8 Customizable Thresholds Delivered with SAP HANA

14. After you've accepted or changed the check thresholds, click OK to return the ALERTS tab.

15. Click on the PERFORMANCE tab to get access to seven additional subtabs providing detailed information for the following areas:

    ▶ THREADS: This tab provides detailed information about the different operational threads within SAP HANA. For example, if a program or job continues to run, you might need to check for blocked threads. A warning icon is displayed when any thread has an error or lock condition.

    ▶ SESSIONS: This tab shows active and inactive sessions with the ability to filter by the application type using the APPLICATION column. You can display blocked sessions and diagnose problems.

    ▶ BLOCKED TRANSACTIONS: This tab provides another representation of the THREADS tab specific to those threads that are blocked.

    ▶ SQL PLAN CACHE: This tab displays statistical information about the compiled SQL statements and their usage.

    ▶ EXPENSIVE STATEMENTS TRACE: This tab displays active trace information. By clicking the CONFIGURE button, you can also set up a trace by table or application.

    ▶ JOB PROGRESS: This tab displays information about long-running processes. These could be database-level jobs such as delta merges or data compression jobs. Jobs displayed here aren't jobs within SAP ERP.

    ▶ LOAD: This tab enables you to select a host and several key performance indicators (KPIs). You can then view the performance of those KPIs over a period of time. It's an opportunity to perform some event correlation. Figure 9.9 graphs CPU, TOTAL RESIDENT MEMORY, and ACTIVE THREADS.

16. Now that you've explored all the tabs under PERFORMANCE, move to the VOLUMES tab. This tab enables your team to monitor disk usage supporting the different SAP HANA services.

17. Select STORAGE in the SHOW dropdown to get a breakdown of the data and log files by service (Figure 9.10). You can also easily see the available storage.

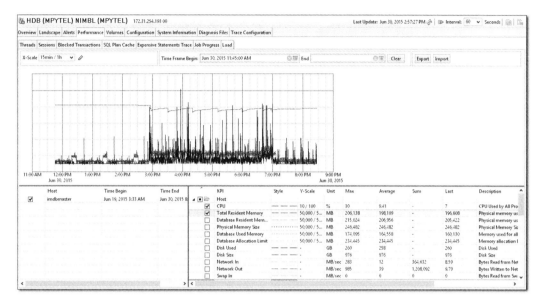

Figure 9.9 Deep Performance Analysis by Time Period in the Load Tab

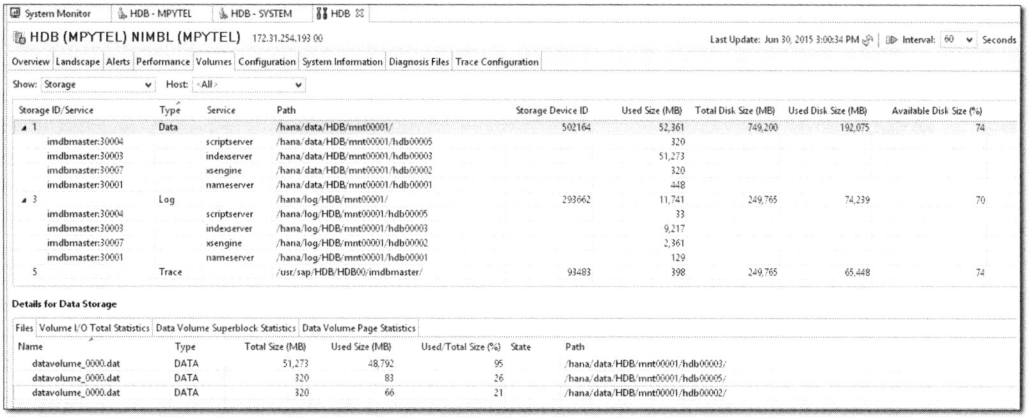

Figure 9.10 Example Storage Information for Single Host SAP HANA Instance

The remaining tabs within ADMINISTRATION are for configuration of the SAP HANA instance, as well as direct links to diagnostics and trace files. Those specific tabs support system administration and not proactive monitoring. SAP HANA Studio is a good application for both monitoring the system as-is and historically. In terms of proactive monitoring, you can enable email alerts. SAP HANA Studio is primarily a tool to be used by the resolvers after they are alerted to a potential issue by SAP Solution Manager. You can assign resources to use SAP HANA Studio in a system operator type mode; however, you'll find the tools we cover later in this chapter to be more suited for operations.

9.2   SAP HANA Cockpit

The SAP HANA Cockpit is a SAP Fiori launchpad delivered with SAP HANA SP 09 and above. It's a web application accessible from any HTML5-enabled browser, including mobile browsers for on-the-go information about system performance, alerts, errors, bottlenecks, and general SAP HANA performance information. Mobile access doesn't work for all applications, but access on a tablet is a little more reasonable. The SAP HANA Cockpit is more suitable for operational type resources who are responsible for monitoring the general health of the SAP HANA systems supporting SAP ERP. From the SAP HANA Cockpit, you can instantly see the status of services and the latest alerts. This is the best barometer of system performance, and it's all accessible in a browser with no client installation to deploy.

Let's navigate some of the features within the SAP HANA Cockpit to help your team monitoring SAP Business Suite on SAP HANA proactively:

1. Log on to the SAP HANA Cockpit (*http://<host_FQDN>:<port>/sap/hana/admin/cockpit*) using a valid user ID and password. You'll need either the `sap.hana.admin.roles::Monitoring` role or the `sap.hana.admin.roles::Administrator` role.

2. After logging in, you'll be presented with a SAP Fiori launchpad containing several tiles that link to additional SAP Fiori applications presenting similar information displayed in SAP HANA Studio, as shown in Figure 9.11.

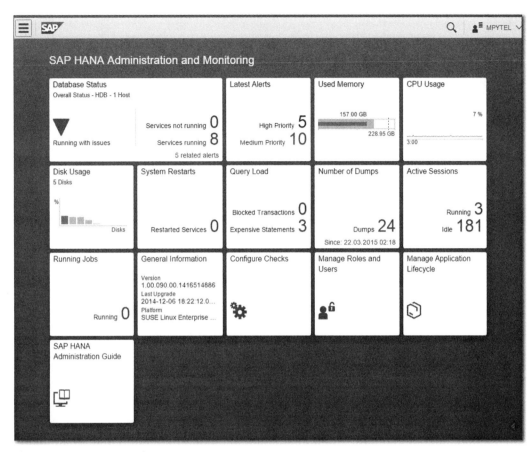

Figure 9.11 SAP HANA Cockpit

3. Let's explore some of the applications. Click on the DATABASE STATUS tile. This displays the service status on the specific host and its memory consumption. Clicking the SETTINGS icon in lower right allows you to add or remove columns.

4. You can see in Figure 9.12 that the system has five alerts. Click GO TO LATEST ALERTS in the lower right to go directly to the alert application.

5. From here, get additional details on the alerts, their frequency, and proposed solutions. In Figure 9.13, we're directed to table that will help solve the specific problem.

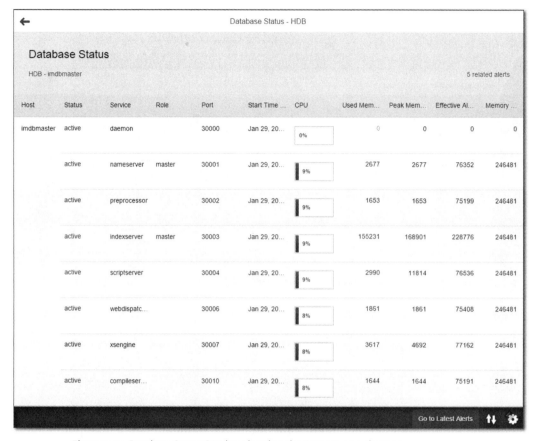

Figure 9.12 Database Status Displayed within the SAP Fiori Application

6. Click the Settings icon in the lower left to enable/disable specific checks performed and their thresholds, and maintain email recipients.

7. Click the Home button in the upper left to go back to the SAP Fiori launchpad. Click the tile Latest Alerts to go to the alert display you viewed in Figure 9.14.

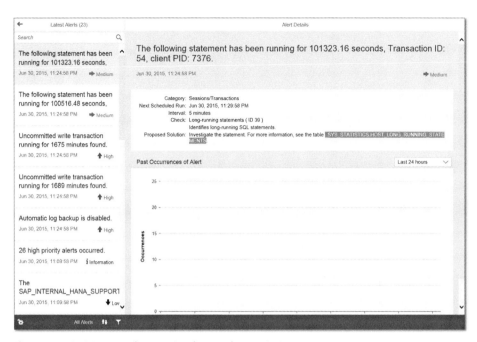

Figure 9.13 SAP Fiori Application Displaying Alerts in SAP HANA

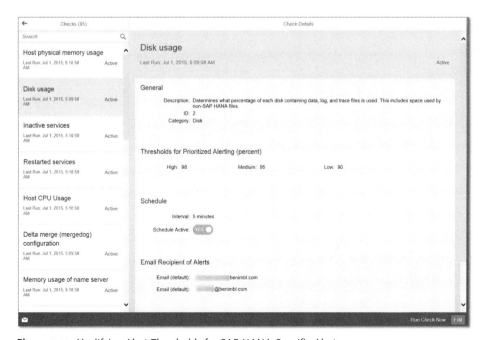

Figure 9.14 Modifying Alert Thresholds for SAP HANA-Specific Alerts

8. Next, click the USED MEMORY tile to open a new application that graphically displays the usage of PHYSICAL MEMORY, SAP HANA USED MEMORY, MEMORY USAGE OF TABLES, AND MEMORY USAGE OF DATABASE MANAGEMENT (Figure 9.15).

9. Select the HOST or UNIT dropdown to change the displayed values.

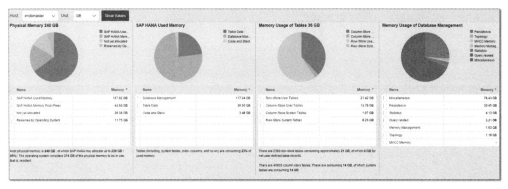

Figure 9.15 Memory Usage Graphically Displayed in Your Web Browser

10. Click the CPU USAGE tile or DISK USAGE tile to essentially go to the same application where you can select different measurements and see them graphically displayed. Figure 9.16 shows the GLOBAL MEMORY ALLOCATION LIMIT, PHYSICAL MEMORY AVAILABLE, and PHYSICAL MEMORY USED measures.

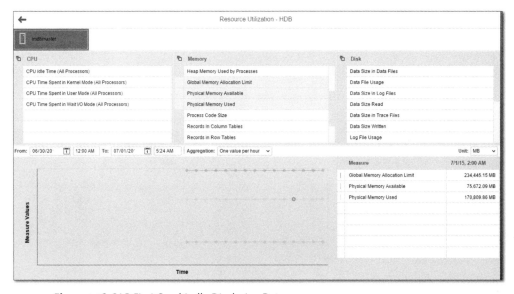

Figure 9.16 SAP Fiori Graphically Displaying Data

11. Click the back arrow in the upper left to return to the launchpad.

12. Click on the NUMBER OF DUMPS to open the trace and log viewer application in a new browser window.

13. View technical details within the SAP HANA application server logs by selecting the log file on the left (Figure 9.17). Errors and Warnings are color-coded within the log file display on the left.

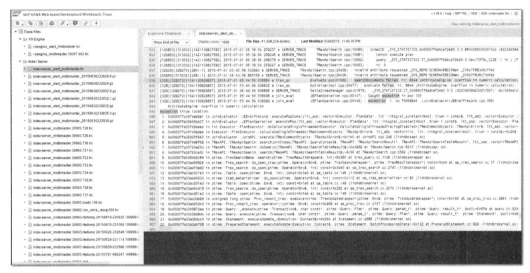

Figure 9.17 Log File Viewer Accessed from the SAP HANA Cockpit

14. The remaining tiles are focused on the administrative aspects of SAP HANA:

   ▶ MANAGE ROLES AND USERS: Opens an application where you can create or update users within SAP HANA.

   ▶ MANAGE APPLICATION LIFECYCLE: Opens the Lifecycle Management applications. This is where you can perform SAP HANA-specific transports and install delivery units from SAP among other administrative tasks.

The SAP HANA Cockpit is accessed via a web browser and provides quick access to important monitoring information. It does provide some proactive monitoring when using the GUI and some email notifications (using the same infrastructure you configured in SAP HANA Studio). Although not all applications will display correctly on a mobile device, the high-level performance data can be displayed. We typically see the SAP HANA Cockpit deployed to those users who require frequent access to performance information and basic troubleshooting information (viewing logs only). The SAP HANA Cockpit can even be accessed by mobile browser (see Figure 9.18). A majority of the configuration and issue-resolution activities your team performs will still be done in SAP HANA Studio. The features and screenshots provided in this section were delivered with SAP HANA 1.0 SP 09. In light of the SAP HANA SP 10 release, you can assume that SAP will deliver additional applications. We know from demonstrations that you'll have additional applications for backup execution and backup history analysis, in addition to new applications for the security team and managing certificates. With the release of SAP HANA SP 10, SAP continues to enhance the SAP HANA Cockpit.

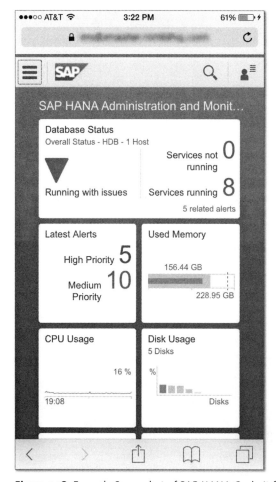

Figure 9.18 Example Screenshot of SAP HANA Cockpit from a Mobile Browser

9.3   SAP Database Control Center

SAP Database Control Center (DCC) is an optional component you can install within your landscape to aggregate information from multiple SAP HANA instances. The SAP HANA Cockpit can be accessed and used for a single system database. If you're using the multitenant database scenario, the SAP HANA Cockpit will work for either the system or the tenant database. DCC is another tool SAP has delivered to customers to ensure visibility and transparency in the SAP HANA landscape, and it will bring all data together for each system or tenant into a single dashboard. In this section, we focus on using SAP HANA Studio and the SAP HANA Cockpit to monitor the database supporting for your SAP Business Suite on SAP HANA migration. Later, Section 9.4 will focus on end-to-end monitoring of SAP ERP and SAP HANA.

Four high-level content areas are delivered with DCC as of August 2015. DCC can provide data center details on availability, performance, capacity, and alerts. Are you meeting Service Level Agreements (SLAs) to your customers? Are there any high-priority alerts open? Is the system response time acceptable? These are all questions you can answer using DCC. DCC can be installed on any SAP HANA database running SP 09 and newer. Remember, one DCC can monitor multiple tenant and system databases. The installation is performed using the lifecycle manager accessed from the SAP HANA Cockpit or using SAP HANA Studio. The installation file is downloaded from the SAP Support Portal and then imported into the SAP HANA system. The process can be completed in under an hour. You'll need the security team's support as multiple accounts will need to be created on all systems to be monitored.

> **Note**   [«]
>
> Detailed information on the DCC installation can be found at *http://help.sap.com/hana.* Once there, select SAP HANA PLATFORM (CORE) • SYSTEM ADMINISTRATION • SAP DB CONTROL CENTER. The installation requires some administrative knowledge of SAP HANA.

1. After the DCC is installed, access the launchpad using either the SAP HANA Cockpit or a direct URL.

    To access the DCC directly, log on to the following URL with a valid user ID and password: *http://<HANA_FQDN>:<port>/sap/hana/dbcc.* You'll need a user ID with one of two roles assigned:

> ▸ Administrative access: `sap.hana.dbcc.roles::DBCCAdmin`

> ▸ User access: `sap.hana.dbcc.roles::DBCCUser`

To access the DCC from the SAP HANA Cockpit, log on to the SAP HANA Cockpit with the following URL: *http://<host_FQDN>:<port>/sap/hana/admin/ cockpit.*

2. Click the HOME button in the upper left to add a new group to the SAP HANA Cockpit launchpad.

3. Click the NEW GROUP button, and name it "DCC".

4. After you've entered a name for the group, click the plus sign on the transparent tile to the right to open the tile catalog.

5. If you've installed the DCC correctly and assigned the role correctly, you'll see five available tiles specific to the DCC.

6. Click the plus sign under each tile, and add the tile to the DCC group you created, as shown in Figure 9.19.

Figure 9.19 Adding Tiles to the SAP HANA Cockpit Launchpad

7. Click the BACK button within the SAP Fiori launchpad. You'll now see your SAP HANA Cockpit applications and the DCC applications (Figure 9.20).

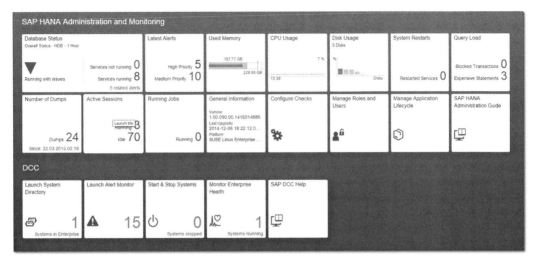

Figure 9.20 Example Launchpad with Multiple Applications Displayed

The first application is the LAUNCH SYSTEM DIRECTORY. From this application, you can connect the DCC to other SAP HANA instances to manage alerts and view performance-related information.

8. Click the ADD SYSTEM button on the lower right of the screen shown in Figure 9.21 to add new systems. You'll be prompted for hostname, port, and a user ID/password to be used, using the same account covered in the DCC guide we mentioned previously.

Figure 9.21 Example System Directory Screen in the Database Control Center

9. In the screen shown in Figure 9.21, you can create logical groupings of systems that will be displayed on other applications. For example, you could create one group for nonproduction systems and another for production systems. This is only a logical grouping and does not affect how DCC collects data.

10. Click the Back arrow in the upper left to return to the launchpad.

11. Click the LAUNCH ALERT MONITOR tile to centrally view alerts for multiple SAP HANA systems.

12. Click on an alert to open another browser window with that SAP HANA system's specific SAP HANA Cockpit and detailed alert display (shown in Figure 9.22).

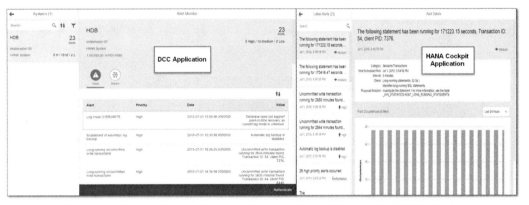

Figure 9.22 Example Screen Flow from Database Control Center to SAP HANA Cockpit Application

13. Close the SAP HANA Cockpit log view, and return to the DCC ALERT MONITOR application.

14. Click the BACK arrow in the upper left to return to the launchpad.

15. Click the START & STOP SYSTEMS tile to open a simple SAP Fiori application to display the systems that are running or are stopped. From this application, you can stop and start SAP HANA systems.

16. To do so, select the AUTHENTICATE button on the lower right of the screen to enter the OS user required to stop and start systems. This prevents SAP HANA users with access to the application from being able to start and stop SAP HANA systems.

17. Click the BACK arrow, and select the ENTERPRISE HEALTH MONITOR tile. Here again you get a simple display of the SAP HANA systems connected to the DCC

and their general status. The circles in Figure 9.23 represent potential errors or issues on the select SAP HANA system.

18. The ALERTS column displays the count of high priority (HP) and medium priority (MP) alerts for that specific system.

19. Clicking the link under the ALERTS column redirects you to the Alert Monitor application described previously.

20. Clicking on one of the error or warning icons in the grid row connects you to that system's SAP HANA Cockpit.

Figure 9.23 Enterprise Health Monitor Showing High Priority Alerts for All Three Categories

21. Click the BACK arrow to return to the launchpad.

22. Click the SAP DCC HELP tile. This is a quick link to the guide for the SAP DCC on *http://help.sap.com*.

DCC centralizes the display of high-level performance and alert information for multiple SAP HANA systems. As you continue your deployment of SAP HANA within your landscape beyond SAP Business Suite on SAP HANA, these tools may become more useful as your landscape becomes more complex. DCC is also useful for the operational team members who are responsible for monitoring, but not necessarily resolving, issues. With SAP HANA Studio, you have a client to deploy and maintain, and the software installation consumes resources on the client machines. DCC can be displayed in any HTML5-compliant browser.

9.4   SAP Solution Manager Technical Operations

You've learned a lot about SAP Solution Manager in this book. It's a critical component supporting the implementation and operation of your SAP landscape. SAP Solution Manager is particularly important during and after the SAP Business Suite on SAP HANA migration. Ideally, you'll include the setup and configuration of SAP Solution Manager for SAP Business Suite on SAP HANA during your project, and not after, as that will allow your team to be prepared at go-live with ready-to-use, out-of-the-box alerts that can help predict an outage before it occurs. These could be hardware- or software-related errors, and no other monitoring solution goes as deep into the application as SAP Solution Manager. Technical Operations within SAP Solution Manager is an advanced monitoring application that supports different time zones, work hours/shifts, notification types, and integration with multiple IT Service Management (ITSM) solutions.

SAP has made documentation and services available to customers to help them implement SAP Solution Manager correctly. For example, SAP customers with Enterprise Support are entitled to multiple Expert Guided Implementations (EGIs), which are remotely delivered educational sessions between a SAP Solution Manager expert and the customer SAP Solution Manager resource configuring the customer's SAP Solution Manager within its data center. There is a substantial amount of training material provided as part of the SAP Solution Manager Ramp-up Knowledge Transfer (RKTs) site within the SAP Support Portal. See the note on how to access the services and content mentioned here.

[»]
> **Note**
>
> SAP EGIs for SAP Solution Manager are prescheduled throughout the year. To find out more, navigate to *http://support.sap.com/solutionmanager*, and select TRAINING AND SERVICES • LEARNING FROM EXPERTS TO EXPERTS • EGI PORTFOLIO. To access the SAP Solution Manager RKTs, head to *http://service.sap.com/rkt-solman*, and select SAP SOLUTION MANAGER 7.1 (INCL. SP 10) or SAP SOLUTION MANAGER 7.1 SP 12.

SAP Solution Manager 7.1 SP 13 was made available in Q2 2015, and with each Support Package Stack (SP Stack), SAP has been enhancing the monitoring and integration capabilities between SAP Solution Manager and SAP HANA. This is part of SAP's Central Operations Concept. SAP Solution Manager is required to efficiently support your SAP ERP and SAP HANA landscape. One SAP Solution Manager can monitor dozens of SAP systems, databases, and even non-SAP systems. It should act as the central repository for both technical and functional documentation related to the business processes within your organization support by and outside of SAP. SAP Solution Manager has the ability to monitor from the hardware to the individual user transaction at the application layer. You can define SLAs by transactions response, background job runtime, or a multitude of metrics collected by SAP Solution Manager when connected to various SAP components.

To download the SAP ERP and SAP HANA support packages during your project, your system has to be managed by SAP Solution Manager. One of the prerequisites to deploying Technical Operations is that the target SAP ERP and SAP HANA systems successfully be configured during managed system configuration as part of Transaction SOLMAN_SETUP.

Note **[«]**

If you want to learn more about managed system configuration, see the wiki on SDN at *http://wiki.scn.sap.com/wiki/display/SMSETUP/Home*.

The next step in setting up monitoring requires you to define what metrics to collect from SAP ERP or SAP HANA. Lastly, when you use an alert based on a threshold, where does it go and what type of alert is sent? There is a wizard for this configuration in Transaction SOLMAN_SETUP, which is executed in SAP Solution Manager. It walks your technical team members through the process and guides them on what to select. The EGIs and RKTs also include content specific regarding the setup of Technical Monitoring. At a high level, here are the steps required to configure Technical Monitoring and to gain access to the screens we highlight in this chapter:

▸ Diagnostic agents are deployed to both SAP ERP and SAP HANA hosts (typically installed with SAP ERP and SAP HANA out of the box).

▸ SAP ERP and SAP HANA are registered to SAP Solution Manager's System Landscape Directory (SLD).

▸ Managed system configuration is executed for SAP ERP and SAP HANA.

▸ The Technical Operations configuration wizard is completed.

▸ Metric and alert templates are defined and assigned to SAP ERP and SAP HANA.

▸ SAP EarlyWatch Reporting is activated for both SAP ERP and SAP HANA.

9.4.1 Accessing Technical Monitoring

As we mentioned, each support package SAP releases for SAP Solution Manager and SAP HANA includes new capabilities and integration scenarios. Specific to SAP Business Suite on SAP HANA, you want to be running SAP Solution Manager 7.1 SP 12+ and SAP HANA SP 09, which provides advanced Root Cause Analysis capabilities. This has the capability to trace a user activity across multiple systems to find a slowdown or error in the process. For example, if a user logs on to the SAP Enterprise Portal to enter a timesheet, that data is passed to SAP ERP and then stored in the SAP HANA database. In the traditional monitoring and analysis scenario, you would have to log on to each system to perform a trace and manually consolidate. Using the Root Cause Analysis tools provided by SAP Solution Manager, you'll centralize all logs and break down performance bottlenecks. Was the timesheet entry slow at the SAP Enterprise Portal, SAP ERP, or the database? With Root Cause Analysis, you can find the answer. Table 9.1 describes the version dependencies between SAP Solution Manager and SAP HANA.

Monitoring Capability by Release		
▶ Availability monitoring and host usage ▶ DBA Cockpit alerts	▶ Availability monitoring and host usage ▶ DBA Cockpit alerts ▶ Real-Time replication monitoring	▶ Complete end-to-end monitoring ▶ DBA Cockpit alerts ▶ Real-Time replication monitoring ▶ Complete Root Cause Analysis
▶ SAP Solution Manager 7.1 SP 4 ▶ SAP HANA 1.0 SP 4	▶ SAP Solution Manager 7.1 SP 8 ▶ SAP HANA 1.0 SP 6	▶ SAP Solution Manager 7.1 SP 12+ ▶ SAP HANA 1.0 SP 9

Table 9.1 Version Dependencies between SAP Solution Manager and SAP HANA

In the following steps, we'll show you how to access monitoring information for SAP Business Suite on SAP HANA from SAP Solution Manager. Every alert shown can be displayed in real time via a web browser or mobile device, can be accessed via historical reporting in SAP Solution Manager, and can trigger an action such as an email, text message, or incident within the ITSM solution. The solution is based on a predefined set of metrics and alerts delivered by SAP (and updated regularly), which is applied to a specific system or systems. Alerts can be modified based on the priority of the system and can be completely customized. All screenshots in this section are based on systems running SAP Solution Manager 7.1 SP 13 and SAP HANA SP 09.

1. Log on to SAP Solution Manager using the SAP GUI, and run Transaction SM_WORKCENTER. Or, for direct access in a browser, go to *http://<solman FQDN>:<port>/sap/bc/webdynpro/sap/ags_workcenter*.

2. A browser opens with your assigned SAP Solution Manager work centers displayed. Navigate to the Technical Monitoring work center, as shown in Figure 9.24.

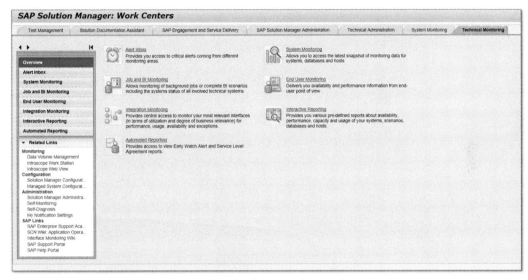

Figure 9.24 Initial Technical Monitoring Screen within SAP Solution Manager

3. Multiple types of monitoring are available with SAP Solution Manager:

   ▷ ALERT INBOX: This is a central repository for all alerts created/collected by SAP Solution Manager. This enables administrators and operators to view alerts, confirm them, or investigate further.

   ▷ SYSTEM MONITORING: This is the real-time application, database, OS, and hardware monitoring that you'll explore.

   ▷ JOB AND BI MONITORING: Here you can monitor the start, stop, duration, and status of background jobs and process chains. Certain background jobs might have critical timing, which requires them to start or stop at a specific time. SAP Solution Manager can monitor and respond to these conditions.

   ▷ END USER MONITORING: Typically, monitoring is done from the data center out to the end user. SAP Solution Manager can work with remote agents to monitor the performance of a system from the perspective of the remote location.

   ▷ INTEGRATION MONITORING: SAP has developed advanced interface monitoring, which can be paired with SAP Process Integration (PI)/SAP Process

Orchestration (PO). This enables you to perform detailed interface monitoring for runtime, errors, and performance bottlenecks.

► INTERACTIVE REPORTING: Here you can explore specific metrics about the system and generate historical reports. For example, you could create an ad hoc report on the disk, CPU, and memory usage of SAP ERP and then correlate that to the number of users on the system.

► AUTOMATED REPORTING: SAP has long provided SAP EarlyWatch Reports as a tool for customers to measure the performance of their systems against SAP-defined KPIs. You can also create custom service level reports for any metric collected by SAP Solution Manager.

4. Start by selecting SYSTEM MONITORING from the left side navigation.

5. Select multiple rows by clicking one row and holding the ⎡Ctrl⎦ key. In Figure 9.25, an SAP ERP and SAP HANA system have been selected.

6. After you've selected the rows for the systems to monitor, click the SYSTEM MONITORING dropdown, and select START NEW WINDOW.

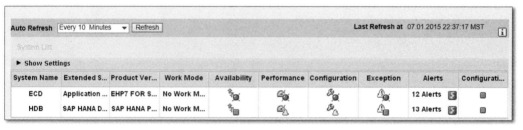

Figure 9.25 General System Status Displayed with a Dashboard

7. Double-click on a specific row to open the monitoring details for that system. Click within the ALERTS column to open the ALERT SUMMARY for that specific system.

8. In Figure 9.26, you can see the single SAP ERP instance broken down into four components:

► The product system sits at the top level. At this level, system-wide information appears related to performance, exceptions, availability, and configuration.

► The technical system and the database sit on the second level. The Technical System represents a specific application instance on a host. There can be multiple hosts supporting application servers for the product system.

▸ The database system is below the technical system. It represents the database supporting the SAP ERP instance, which could be on one or many hosts.

▸ The physical or virtual host supporting the technical instance or database as part of the product system sits on the lowest level.

Figure 9.26 Real-Time Detailed Monitoring for SAP ERP in SAP Solution Manager

9. In our example scenario, a single system is acting as the SAP central instance, dialog server, and database server.

10. On the right side of Figure 9.26, you can see multiple metrics displayed with a corresponding color representing their status:

▸ Green ❶: The metric is operating below the given threshold or normally.

▸ Yellow (does not appear in graphic): The metric is reporting data above Green but below Red. This is a warning.

▸ Red ❷: The metric is reporting above the specified threshold or an error.

▸ Gray ❸: No data has been collected or reported.

11. Hover over an alert on the right to see more information, as shown in Figure 9.27. As you can see for this example scenario, the threshold for long-running dialog processes is set to 1.

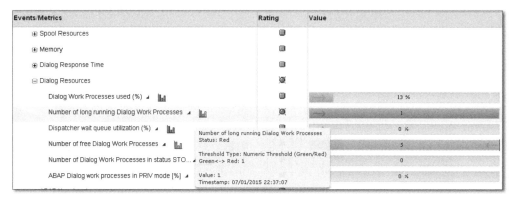

Figure 9.27 Hovering over an Alert for More Information

12. Click SYSTEM LIST in the upper right to return to the dashboard listing of systems. Double-click the SAP HANA database.

13. Display the metrics by category: SYSTEM AVAILABILITY, SYSTEM PERFORMANCE, SYSTEM CONFIGURATION, and SYSTEM EXCEPTIONS. Much like the SAP HANA Cockpit and DCC, you can see general SAP HANA performance information (shown in Figure 9.28). The difference here is that you can also access SAP ERP performance information.

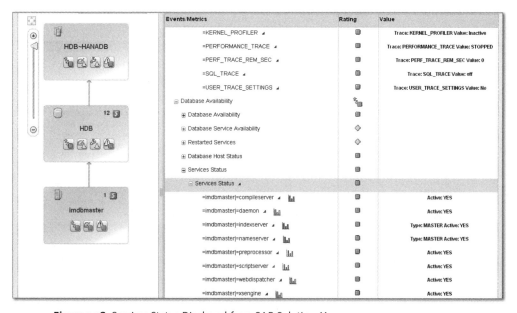

Figure 9.28 Services Status Displayed from SAP Solution Manager

14. As part of SAP Enterprise Support, SAP has delivered both iOS and Android applications that connect directly to SAP Solution Manager without the need for SAP Mobile Platform or SAP Mobile Secure.

These mobile applications are free to download from their respective online stores (Apple Store or Google Play) and can be configured quickly. The same real-time monitoring information displayed in Figure 9.29 can be quickly accessed using the mobile app. This includes integration with the alerts summary.

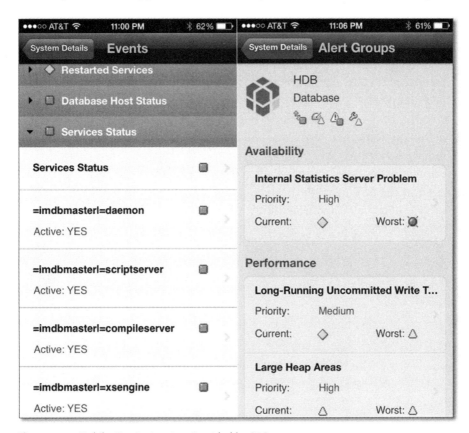

Figure 9.29 Mobile Monitoring App Provided by SAP

<table>
<tr><td>**Note**</td><td>**[«]**</td></tr>
</table>

To find out more about the SAP Solution Manager mobile apps, head over to *http://help.sap.com/sm-mobileapps/*. Common deployment scenarios and the application details are discussed there.

9.4.2 Accessing SAP EarlyWatch Reports

We've shown you how to access the real-time monitoring in SAP Solution Manager for both SAP ERP and SAP HANA. This access can be given to administrators and operators, allowing them to view information anytime. SAP EarlyWatch Reports also provide your organization's support team with a barometer to measure the health of your SAP ERP and SAP HANA systems. These reports are automatically scheduled in SAP Solution Manager after your SAP Solution Manger administrator completes the managed system configuration for the SAP ERP and SAP HANA systems as described. SAP EarlyWatch Reports in SAP Solution Manager not only provide information about the health of your environment, they are also the key to specific service delivery from SAP as part of SAP Enterprise and SAP Standard Support. As part of your SAP Enterprise Support, you can order a remotely delivered service called the SAP EarlyWatch Check. For example, perhaps you receive the SAP EarlyWatch Report with a red rating for system performance. In addition to your own internal resources, you can engage SAP Support to remotely perform an SAP EarlyWatch Check. The output of this check is a list of recommendations or suggestions on how to resolve the performance problems identified in the SAP EarlyWatch Report. SAP EarlyWatch Reports are essential for both the data they provide and the maximization of your support dollars.

To access SAP EarlyWatch Reports, follow these steps:

1. Open the TECHNICAL MONITORING work center as you did earlier in Section 9.4.1. Log on to SAP GUI with a valid user ID, and run Transaction SM_WORK-CENTER.

2. When the browser opens, navigate to the TECHNICAL MONITORING work center, and then select AUTOMATED REPORTING from the left-side navigation.

3. Remove any entries in the SOLUTION or SOLUTION ID fields. Enter a date range for the SAP EarlyWatch Report you want to view. They are typically run every seven days.

4. Click SEARCH, and select the row for the SAP ERP or SAP HANA system you want to view. Click DISPLAY HTML REPORT.

5. SAP EarlyWatch Reports can also be generated in Microsoft Word format by clicking the GENERATE WORD REPORT button.

6. After clicking DISPLAY HTML REPORT, another browser window opens showing the SAP EarlyWatch Report content (Figure 9.30).

Figure 9.30 SAP EarlyWatch Report of the SAP HANA Database

7. The SAP EarlyWatch Report is organized into multiple sections:

▷ Service Summary: Displays red, yellow, or green alerts on an executive dashboard. (It's very rare to have a consistent green light because releases happen so quickly you get a yellow light when your patch level falls behind current.)

▷ Landscape: Provides details information about the hosts and their respective hardware.

▷ Service Preparation: Displays whether the data required for the report generation was collected correctly.

▷ Software Configuration: Displays the primary installed SAP application and the current patch level.

▶ HARDWARE CAPACITY: Provides a general average of the system performance over the time period.

▶ BUSINESS KEY FIGURES: Displays information related to Business Process Monitoring (BPMon) in SAP Solution Manager. Remains empty until you configure BPMon and isn't required for SAP EarlyWatch Check service delivery.

▶ SAP HANA: Provides SAP HANA-specific content related to alerts, configuration, performance, workload, size, growth, and administration. This section provides the most value specific to the SAP HANA database.

9.5 SAP Database Administration Cockpit

The DBA Cockpit is an SAP-specific function delivered within the ABAP stack to monitor and administer databases supporting SAP systems. Its platform-independent monitoring means you can monitor any SAP-supported database from this central console. From the DBA Cockpit, you can perform administrative tasks, run backups, analyze performance problems, and display the status of specific components in the database. As you migrate to SAP Business Suite on SAP HANA, this is another tool accessible by the team. After your team has added your SAP Business Suite on SAP HANA system to SAP Solution Manager as part of the managed system configuration process, you can immediately begin using the DBA Cockpit from SAP Solution Manager. You can also open it locally on the SAP ERP system running on SAP HANA. There are two views provided by SAP when using the DBA Cockpit. One is browser based, and the other is an ABAP transaction. The screenshots in this section are taken from the ABAP transaction, which seems to perform better. The same navigating paths described here work within the web-based view as well.

1. Log on to your SAP Solution Manager or SAP Business Suite on SAP HANA system with a valid user ID and password. You'll need administrative access or one of the following roles assigned:

   ▶ SAP_BC_S_DBCON_ADMIN

   ▶ SAP_BC_S_DBCON_USER

2. Run Transaction DBACOCKPIT.

3. Initially, you'll see the web-based view for the DBA Cockpit. Click the SWITCH TO SAPGUI button.

4. The overview screen shows the current status of the SAP HANA database. From here, you can see memory and CPU utilization, disk usage, current alerts, and the services status for SAP HANA (Figure 9.31).

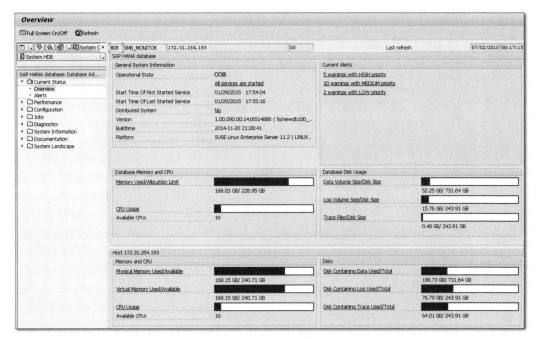

Figure 9.31 SAP HANA Database Current Status Displayed in the DBA Cockpit

You'll notice the information displayed here is organized somewhat like SAP HANA Studio.

5. Click on ALERTS from the upper left to see the alert information in an easy-to-read grid row (Figure 9.32). The checks being performed are shown at the bottom of the screen.

6. Moving to the PERFORMANCE node, you can see multiple areas that give you additional details on the performance of your database.

7. Click STATISTICS SERVER under PERFORMANCE to select from a series of predefined views/tables that collect and store performance information (Figure 9.33). For example, you might want view HOST_LONG_RUNNING_STATISTICS to view statements executed within a time period that took the longest time.

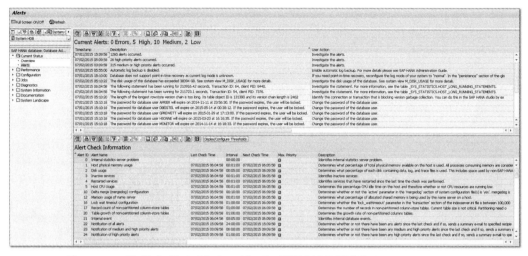

Figure 9.32 Multiple Alerts Displayed for the HDB SAP HANA System

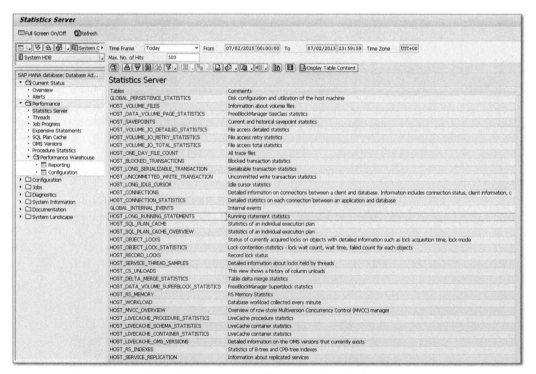

Figure 9.33 Predefined Tables Storing Performance-Related Information

8. Select CONFIGURATION • TRACE CONFIGURATION to define traces and set them to active or inactive (Figure 9.34). In a troubleshooting scenario, you might activate the EXPENSIVE STATEMENTS trace to find troublesome processes.

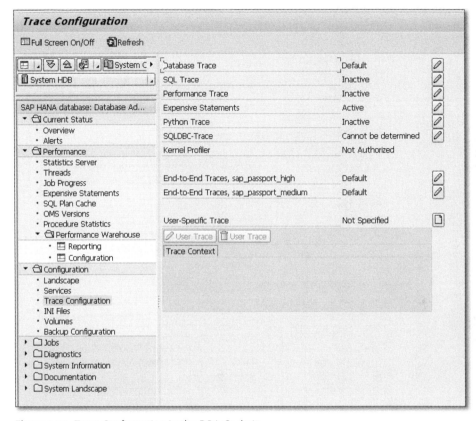

Figure 9.34 Trace Configuration in the DBA Cockpit

9. Click on CONFIGURATION • INI FILES to get a similar view of the configuration files for SAP HANA that you would see in SAP HANA Studio.

10. Click on CONFIGURATION • SERVICES to get another view of the services running and their respective performance metrics.

11. Navigate TO DIAGNOSTICS • LOCKS • BLOCKED TRANSACTIONS or TABLE LOCKS to access additional information about potential bottlenecks in the system.

Some other useful views are available under SYSTEM INFORMATION • OTHERS. For example, the COLUMN TABLES MEMORY USAGE shown in Figure 9.35 displays the tables with the highest memory usage in megabytes.

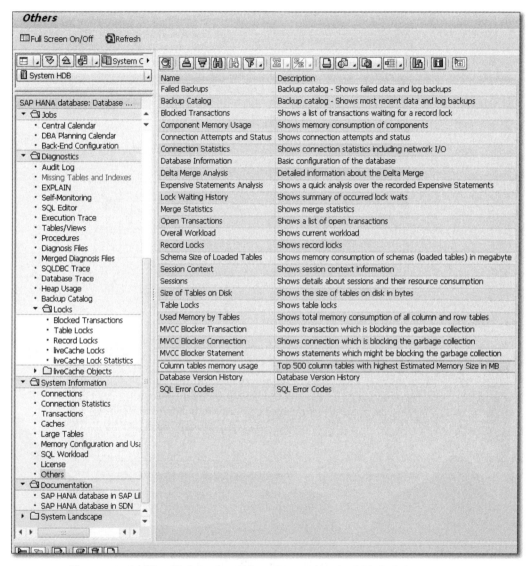

Figure 9.35 Additional Informational Views Accessed by the DBA Cockpit

9.6   Summary

Throughout this chapter, we've described a multitude of tools your team will have access to during your SAP Business Suite on SAP HANA migration project. Each monitoring tool has a specific use case and will become part of your proactive monitoring strategy. Establishing the usage of these tools during your project will ensure that your team members have access to the required information to solve problems. You'll obviously do everything you can to follow SAP recommendations, but you'll encounter various errors during your project and operating SAP Business Suite on SAP HANA. The ability to quickly identify the root cause of issues will give your team a significant advantage on meeting or exceeding your business users' expectations.

SAP HANA Studio remains the go-to utility for configuration, administration, and real-time application monitoring in SAP HANA. It lacks specific capabilities around alert management and holistic system performance monitoring that are delivered with SAP Solution Manager. Neither SAP Solution Manager nor SAP HANA Studio can replace each other. Both will be part of your landscape monitoring and issue-resolution strategy. The SAP HANA Cockpit should prove valuable for support team members who need quick access to high-level information. It loads faster than SAP HANA Studio and can be accessed from any HTML5-compliant browser. Some mobile capability exists, however, the SAP HANA Cockpit applications weren't written specifically for mobile browsers. Access to the SAP HANA Cockpit via the desktop is solid and quick. System operators and operational staff should be able to adapt and quickly glean information from the SAP Fiori applications with little training. Think of the DCC as an extension of the SAP HANA Cockpit. Both can be accessed via the SAP Fiori launchpad. This streamlines the access of the tools and further reduces complexity.

SAP Solution Manager will exist in your landscape for the foreseeable future and is required for the maintenance and operation of SAP Business Suite on SAP HANA. SAP has delivered multiple monitoring templates, hundreds of metrics specific to SAP HANA, and dozens of out-of-the-box alerts that can be directed to email and SMS, or can be integrated into an ITSM solution. SAP Solution Manager is the go-to platform for deep application and database monitoring. You have the ability to customize thresholds and selectively activate alerts based on your requirements. The ability to customize new metrics specific to those scenarios that only exist in your landscape is invaluable. Every metric that is collected by

SAP Solution Manager is stored in a data warehouse that is aggregated and maintained over time, enabling your teams to analyze the performance and growth of your systems over longer time periods. Configuring SAP Solution Manager before, during, and after your go-live will enable your team to measure the existing SAP ERP system performance, which can then be compared to the performance once you've migrated to SAP Business Suite on SAP HANA.

SAP EarlyWatch Reports should be configured for any SAP system in your landscape. These reports not only provide high-level performance, growth, and alert information, but they are also a requirement for specific service delivery from SAP as part of your SAP Enterprise Support Agreement. You can maximize the value of your support agreements with SAP by including these services in your project and then setting up regular intervals throughout the year to use SAP Support for additional performance evaluations. Some of the data reported by SAP EarlyWatch Reports is collected using the DBA Cockpit. This familiar interface, which has been available for multiple releases of SAP ERP, has been extended to SAP HANA. From this ABAP-based application, you can perform most of the functions you perform within the administrative features of SAP HANA Studio. Checking locks, monitoring backups, measuring system performance, and troubleshooting issues can all be done centrally from SAP Solution Manager or locally on the SAP ERP system. For those support team members that have used the DBA Cockpit before, it will aid in the transition to SAP HANA administration. Each of the tools described in this chapter will play some part in your project and the longer support of the SAP Business Suite on SAP HANA landscape.

When running a cutover from one database to another, nothing should be left to chance. Cutover planning starts with the first sandbox migration.

10 Cutover Planning

By now, your team has completed multiple SAP Business Suite on SAP HANA migrations, and you must begin planning for the migration of production SAP ERP. Throughout the project, your team members completed the technical activities recommended by SAP and have no doubt identified the activities specific to your organization. In this chapter, we'll describe how you can capture those tasks to ensure that they are replayed when you perform the migration of production SAP ERP to SAP HANA. As you approach the production go-live, you need to include all systems in your landscape in your planning. We'll not only talk about the technical tasks your team members will complete but also provide some questions you can ask your team to ensure you've considered all of the interfacing systems.

Every step in the process should have an owner, a validation task, and a decision matrix to determine the execution of a rollback procedure if something fails. When you review your landscape, you'll have performed the migration to SAP Business Suite on SAP HANA at least two, if not more, times before the actual production run. What is the right balance of practice migrations and cutover dry runs? It's a risk-based decision based on the output and success of the prior migrations. You want your resources to be confident in the process and know the tasks to be completed. However, you don't want to over-practice the migration to the point where people are overconfident, and little tasks are missed. During the very first migration to SAP HANA, you probably just want to see if it will work, but you should have documented each subsequent migration to ensure that you follow the same steps in the correct order for each migration you complete. This type of documentation should be stored in a shared location such as SAP Solution Manager, SharePoint, SAP StreamWork, or a file share. You can use time stamps from the logs created by the Software Update Manager (SUM) or the Software

Provisioning Manager (SWPM) process outlined in earlier chapters to develop the time line.

Planning for the cutover to SAP Business Suite on SAP HANA not only includes technical planning but also planning for business downtime. Your technical downtime can be measured easily using the tools provided by SAP, but planning for your business downtime can be more complex. Businesses use a variety of functions both within and outside of SAP, and simply because SAP ERP is started, doesn't mean the business is operational. You need to take into account the postupgrade processing tasks your teams will complete, including those tasks which might be executed in SAP Process Integration (PI), SAP Business Warehouse (SAP BW), Master Data Management (MDM), Master Data Governance (MDG), SAP Global Trade Services (GTS), or any other SAP ERP interfacing SAP system. When reviewing your technical downtime, you need to ensure plans include incoming and outgoing interfaces, analytical processes (data loads), background job processing, and planned manual tasks that might exist somewhere in your organization.

Planning for support resources is key to your cutover plan. Keep in mind that SAP Enterprise and Standard Support services should be part of your support model. We know your technical and functional team members will be part of the support plan for cutover and beyond. As an insurance policy, you might engage third-party support as well. Did you know SAP provides services as part of your Maintenance Agreement? You have your SAP GoingLive Support in addition to the SAP OS/DB Migration Check. Both services are broken down into two phases: analysis and verification. The analysis services will be executed well before your cutover and planned go-live. The verification services occur about a month after go-live and will include recommendations on improvements. Using these services is one component of maximizing the value of your SAP Support Agreements. When planning for support of the project, and specifically go-live, you need to ensure your plan includes all resources available to your organization.

10.1 Building Cutover Plans

Your cutover plan is the single playbook from which your teams will operate on the go-live weekend for SAP Business Suite on SAP HANA. The playbook should consist of at least three basic components. The first is the migration task list, which is a comprehensive list of tasks to be completed as part of the preparation, execution, and postprocessing for the SAP Business Suite on SAP HANA migration. Tasks can be automated, manual, or verbal. The second component of your playbook is your rollback plan, which is a list of the tasks you need to perform to restore the production environment to its predowntime status. The third and final component of your playbook is the communication plan, which defines the communication types throughout the cutover weekend, including the recipients, contact information, and the frequency of updates. If a team member needs to know where to log a defect or who to call when his task is done, the communication plan should provide the answers. The communication plan will maintain all details to ensure clear communication between the team members involved. Let's break down each component of your playbook.

10.1.1 Migration Tasks

Ideally, you aren't reading this section just before cutover when you need to decide what to do. Cutover planning starts after the first migration completes. After you complete that first migration from source database to SAP HANA, your team has a framework for the technical activities to be completed. They understand the tasks they executed to prepare the system for migration. They've lived through each phase of the migration and will have completed some initial postprocessing tasks before handover to the functional and technical teams for validation. It's at this point where you define a document, template, or SharePoint site to begin capturing the tasks completed by your teams. Initially, this document or site will be a dumping ground of information. People will have held or released background jobs, interfaces, extracts, exports, and imports. The first task really is to just capture all of the initial data; you'll sort through the content later to get it organized. It's much easier to remove content later than try to remember everything you did after the fact.

How detailed does your plan need to be? If one activity depends on another activity, then you should document it. If a group of activities is going to be completed by one person, you might have one task on the cutover plan with a link to a document that defines in detail the activities to be completed. The documentation detail level doesn't need to be such that someone with no SAP experience can perform it. Ideally, the process is documented at a level where another resource with a similar skillset or skill level can perform the tasks. In a real-world scenario where an organization has specific gaps in support or where only one individual can support a task, then this should be documented as a risk item. Not all organizations can sustain two individuals for each skillset that SAP support requires, so you document this risk and adjust your plan if that risk becomes a reality.

All migration tasks need to be completed for you to return the production system to normal operations. Should you have a validation step for each task in the plan? This is a risk tolerance-based decision specific to your organization. If sequential tasks have a dependency, meaning one task can't complete without the prior task being complete, then you can assume the dependent task is the validation step. When tasks and dependent tasks span hours or days, you need to add a manual verification step. For example, if one task requires you to open a client to perform manual configuration, and the next task is to perform the configuration, you'll know very quickly if one step wasn't completed. If, on the other hand, you have a task to disable a communication channel in PI or an interface will fail and that first task doesn't happen, you might not know of a failure until later that day or beyond. In this scenario, you might ask for a screenshot as validation or a secondary resource to validate the task completion. When building your task list, challenge your team members to really think about the details and consequences if something doesn't occur or doesn't end on time. Some example interview questions include the following:

▸ What was required after the upgrade completed to allow users to log in?

▸ How did we ensure missing background jobs were rescheduled?

▸ Did the SAP BW team run their processes before the upgrade?

▸ During functional regression testing, what defects required a background job or manual task to be executed to resolve?

▸ Was there a change to any logon information for SAP GUI?

▸ Do interfaces use the same hostname and post to connect?

▸ What did we do to check table consistency after the upgrade?

In Figure 10.1, we chose not to show a list of technical tasks. Instead, we wanted to reinforce the business communication tasks that should be part of your SAP Business Suite on SAP HANA cutover plan. You need to not only tell the business users that specific systems are unavailable but also identify the business processes that won't be available. Some examples of the type of business communications that need to be part of your cutover plan include warnings that materials requirements planning (MRP) jobs will be held, the interfaces to SalesForce.com will be unavailable, and transactions within the SAP Enterprise Portal won't function at all.

ID	Status	Title	System	Start Date	End Date	Est. Hours:Mins	Owner	Notes
B		*MileStone 2 : Pre-Phase IT Communication Tasks*						*Additional Notes*
B1		Internal IT						
B2	Pending	Communication to Business that Scheduled jobs in ECP will not run. Weekend jobs will be rescheduled to run late Monday or early Tuesday.	None	5/19/2015	5/19/2015	0:30:00	Shannon/Dave	
B3	Pass	To get/Prepare the list of Important Batch job which needs to be Pre-Processed	None	5/19/2015	5/19/2015	0:30:00	Henry	
B4	Pending	Communication to Business Regarding System Validation after EHP6 Upgrade	None	5/19/2015	5/19/2015	0:30:00	Shannon/Dave	
B5	Pending	Discuss with Business for any data availability requirements during downtime.	None	5/19/2015	5/19/2015	0:30:00	Shannon/Dave	
B6	Pending	Ask THQ for their Monday business on Sunday : target that for 8pm Sunday. Plan to coordinate with Rinako, hiroko. Ask Andy to organize.	None	5/19/2015	5/19/2015	0:30:00	Shannon/Andy	
B7	Pending	Create Master Ticket to Monitor the Progress of EHP6 Upgrade	None	5/19/2015	5/19/2015	0:30:00	Henry	
		To Sales Team						
B8	Pending	Communication to Business regarding Esource, other interfaces, EDI, BW queues downtime. Orders will not be created and Customers will see Pop Message regarding downtime.	None	5/19/2015	5/19/2015	0:30:00	Shannon/Dave	
B9	Pending	To communicate that Normal Sales/Returns Transactions will not be queued up	None	5/19/2015	5/19/2015		Shannon/Dave/Henry	
B10	Pending	Work with josephine's team, sort out how to get 'live' orders in after system is up	None	5/19/2015	5/19/2015	0:30:00	Shannon/Dave/Henry	
		To Service					IT Team	
B11	Pending	Communication to Business regarding SFDC downtime. Orders will not be created. Returns Transactions will not be queued up	None	5/19/2015	5/19/2015	0:30:00	Shannon/Dave/Henry	
		Operation					IT Team	
B13	Pending	Communication to business to reschedule replenishment in order to bring inventory to stock ahead of time.	None	5/19/2015	5/19/2015	0:30:00	Shannon/Dave	
B14	Pending	All Business functionalities like Reporting, Goods movement etc will not be available during downtime window	None	5/19/2015	5/19/2015	0:30:00	Shannon/Dave	
		Warehouse/Shipping					Shannon/Dave	
B15	Pending	All Business functionalities like Reporting, Goods movement, Cycle Count etc will not be available during downtime window	None	5/19/2015	5/19/2015	0:30:00	Shannon/Dave	
B16	Pending	Goods Issue & Goods Returns will not be available. Delay in Inbound/Outbound Shipments	None	5/19/2015	5/19/2015	0:30:00	Shannon/Dave	
		Finance					Shannon/Dave	

Figure 10.1 Example Cutover Plan Built in Microsoft Excel

10.1.2 Rollback Plan

Your organization's rollback plan should be defined in the same document as the migration plan to ensure a single point of access for both sets of tasks. The decision to execute a rollback plan could happen at any point in the cutover process. In fact, you should identify decision points in your cutover plan where you have check steps for a rollback decision. A rollback refers to returning the system to its operational state before the downtime. This doesn't mean a rollback to the point in time where the SUM or SWPM processes were started. The upgrade tools will start processes while your system is up and available. You only restore up to the point where the downtime phase started. After you restore the system to this downtime step, you then begin playing through some of the tasks in your migration plan to start services.

The decision criteria to roll back will differ by organization, The two most common reasons include longer than expected processing times and table inconsistency. When your migration runs longer than expected, the determination to roll back will be based on the time required to roll back. For example, if you planned to turn the migrated system over to the business users for validation at 7AM on Saturday, but the migration is still running Saturday night, you potentially won't have time for validation and a rollback if necessary. You should document or estimate the runtime for the rollback tasks to develop that point in time where you must decide to continue forward or roll back. Choosing to roll back due to data consistency isn't as common as it used to be primarily because SAP has improved the migration tools so much. The preprocessing phase within the SUM Database Migration Option (DMO) will validate which tables can be migrated well before the actual migration. The preceding advice is true in this scenario. Define the time required to roll back and ensure your validation procedures can finish prior to the point of no return.

If you think about the activity executed in a rollback plan, you begin to realize it's very similar to the cutover tasks postmigration. You need to restart services, start interfaces, restart background jobs, and so on, that is, all of the same tasks you would have completed had the migration to SAP Business Suite on SAP HANA completed. The only main difference in the rollback plan when compared to the migration plan is the technical tasks. In the rollback scenario, you're restoring SAP from backup devices (ideally, disk-based backups for speed). This potentially includes the file system and database. In the scenario where you used the SWPM to heterogeneous system copy SAP ERP, you essentially start SAP as-is using normal processes without the need to restore the database. If you opted for the scenario using SUM, you need to restore the database to the point in time before the downtime activity started. You also restore the SUM working directory to restart the migration activities at a future date. A decision to roll back isn't permanent. In an ideal situation, you identify the error, notify SAP Support, and resolve the issue prior to executing another cutover attempt.

10.1.3 Communication Plan

The communication plan consists of a contact list, communication methods, and a schedule of communications to be sent and by whom. During a deeply technical activity such as the migration to SAP Business Suite on SAP HANA, you want your technical resources to be focused on their tasks. You prefer communications come from those who have the time and patience to validate information being shared with the business. In terms of communication media, typically email, SMS, and telephone are identified as the primary methods. It's possible that you'll start seeing more instant messaging (IM) added to the plan as corporate IM takes a foothold.

Another common approach is to include a schedule within the communication plan that defines the scheduled opening and closing of a conference bridge during the cutover activities. Conference bridges are useful when you want to include multiple geographically dispersed resources on technical discussions, although they tend to get overwhelming when you have more than one conversation occurring at the same time. As you build out your communication plan, begin to think about the media your team will use.

When running the SAP Business Suite on SAP HANA migration, you'll have stakeholders at all levels of the organization. Implementing SAP HANA is a major milestone for any organization because it's viewed as (and rightly so) the platform for innovation. Your SAP ERP system is traditionally the backbone of your business processes within a business unit or the company globally. When thinking about the communication types, you need to take into account the types of resources that will consume the information you send. That's not to say that you should limit technical details because people won't understand them, but it's a good practice to limit information to those services and functions that are unavailable and include a time for the anticipated restoration of those services. Instead of sending status communications titled "SAP Business Suite on SAP HANA Migration Status," you might simply reference an upgrade to SAP ERP, which will enable future enhancements and a platform for growth. Technical teams will want the detailed status, which could be posted internally or distributed via email. In terms of communication to the business users, think simple.

Let's walk through some common communication points during your cutover:

1. **Migration planning**
   In the weeks or months coming up to the migration weekend, you've informed the business of the production system downtime. This enables the business to schedule resources, change production plan, or make the required decision to support the system downtime.

2. **Migration preparation**
   This phase might start days or hours before the downtime. You'll want to notify the business when interfaces, background jobs, or specific business processes will be disabled or delayed.

3. **Migration downtime**
   At this point, you need to tell all parts of the organization that the SAP ERP system is unavailable. IT will need to know when to stop interfacing systems. The business will need to know when to stop work and log off the system.

4. **Migration completion**
   The technical migration activities are complete, and the postmigration tasks need to start. This includes rescheduling missing background jobs, restarting interfaces, and starting data validation. The length of this phase might overlap

with the next phase. You might continue startup tasks even when the system has been released to the business users.

5. **Migration finalization**

At this point, you've completed validation and have initiated all startup tasks. The system has been migrated to SAP Business Suite on SAP HANA. Final communications about system and process availability are sent.

10.1.4 Planning for Business Downtime

After your technical team completes two or three migrations to SAP Business Suite on SAP HANA, they will have a good idea on the downtime required for the migration. In terms of reducing the downtime, we covered the options to use multiple processing servers with both the SUM DMO and SWPM. If using multiple processing servers still doesn't reduce the downtime to an acceptable window, then you do have the option of leveraging even more hardware and software by using the Near Zero Downtime (nZDM) functionality within the SUM DMO (see Chapter 5). How do you know how much downtime the business can sustain?

Ideally, as you begin planning the SAP Business Suite on SAP HANA migration, you'll include a survey to your key business stakeholders about upcoming business activities to determine the best weekend for maintenance. If you're able to use the 12-week strategy defined in Chapter 2, then this means you should be able to give the business a 2–3 day advance notice on required downtime. You know your business better than anyone, but here are some questions to ask just in case you need some support:

▶ Where is our corporate financial calendar stored? And what weeks are planned for month-end, quarter-end, or year-end close?

▶ Do we have any special accounting periods that will be closed in the next three months?

▶ Does manufacturing have any weekend inventory activities planned?

▶ If our business is seasonal, what months are the considered peak times?

▶ Does marketing or sales have any special promotions or rebates that will drive an increase in sales orders over the next few months?

▶ Will we be acquiring any new businesses or divesting a business unit in the next three months?

While some of the questions above may seem silly, not applicable, or will never get answered, take the opportunity not only to survey the business users about possible downtime for the migration but also to start a discussion with the business users on potential benefits and enhancements with this new SAP Business Suite on SAP HANA system.

10.2   Cutover Support Resources

When you begin to visualize the cutover weekend, its flow, and the people involved, you realize there will be lots of involvement from various team members. During the project, infrastructure, SAP NetWeaver (Basis) administrators, security, development, business analysts, and even business users will be involved. If you're not including enhancements or modifications to user transactions as part of the upgrade, then the support teams during the cutover weekend will likely be mostly technical. For those customers that are upgrading and migrating to SAP HANA from older releases by SAP ECC 5.0 or SAP R/3, then you're not only introducing a new database platform but new transactions and a new user interface (UI). The support resources involved will differ.

For those customers on a relatively recent enhancement package version, you'll likely not have new transactions or a new UI. Your users will continue to use the system as-is because you didn't activate enhancements during your migration project. When you do introduce new transactions or enhancements, then you'll need to add functional power user type support to your cutover plan to support those initial users logging in to the system. As you know, a power user is someone in the business that is an expert at a business process and how to use SAP to accomplish a job function. A power user won't know (typically) the technical details behind the system or a transaction, and the power user isn't required to support system dumps. But a power user will be useful for answering the "how to" type questions you typically get when enhancing SAP.

As for technical resources, you'll need SAP NetWeaver administrators, developers, security administrators, and technical SAP business analysts supporting you over the weekend cutover. In terms of the support by the SAP NetWeaver administrators, you need to avoid having a single resource work the entire weekend or work for abnormally long periods of time. When resources get tired, they make mistakes. We've seen multiple instances where an organization with a single

Basis resource required that individual to work the entire evening or weekend during a cutover. We've also seen where individual resources volunteer to work the long hours, and they commit to getting the work done. In the scenario, where you're converting your production SAP ERP system to a new database, it's worth the investment (even as an insurance policy only) to secure resources to support the primary SAP NetWeaver administrator. Additional resources can be used to verify and validate the SUM/SWPM processing without the need for that person to execute tasks. The migration using either tool is the culmination of testing and pre-configuration. The actual migration is more of an execution with verification steps and procedures. A technical resource can be trained to monitor the logs and processing information and alert the primary resource in the event some task fails or doesn't process in the correct time frame. While specific customer environments will be different, the upgrade and migration tools remain standard across all SAP customers. Securing external resources with experience using SUM or SWPM won't be an impossible task.

10.2.1 SAP Enterprise Support Services

Your cutover planning (begins after the first test migration) should include scheduling SAP Enterprise Support Services, which are delivered as part of an SAP customer's Enterprise Support Agreement. Your SAP Enterprise Support Agreement entitles you to multiple services each year that cover a broad spectrum of support. If you're an SAP customer with a Standard Support Agreement, the following sections highlight which service offering you'll be entitled to execute. It's important as SAP customers to consider including SAP Support as part of your cutover planning to maximize the value of your support contract and to ensure that SAP is aware of the migration you're executing. Your SAP account executive (who sold you the SAP Business Suite on SAP HANA runtime licenses) will no doubt provide support and be a link to SAP as well. Scheduling the support services for GoingLive Support and SAP OS/DB Migration Check will formalize the communication to SAP that you're migrating to SAP Business Suite on SAP HANA and potentially including an upgrade in the process.

Continuous Quality Check: GoingLive Support

This service is often referred to as a GoingLive Check. This is a remotely delivered service that uses SAP Solution Manager. You schedule the service using the incident process on *http://support.sap.com*, ideally 45–90 days before your production migration. This enable SAP Support to schedule the required resources and for your team to ensure the configuration and connectivity exists between SAP Solution Manager and SAP Support. The service is commonly broken down into two phases: preparation and remote monitoring.

During the preparation phase, you'll complete a survey that provides details on the systems in scope, scheduled data and time for the migration, contacts, and software versions. The SAP Support person responsible for the service will then validate connectivity and information within the SAP Support Portal. During the service delivery, the service includes monitoring for the following areas. If SAP recognizes an issue with a specific component or process, you'll be notified, and a solution will be provided.

- ▸ Hardware utilization
- ▸ System stability
- ▸ System performance
- ▸ Interface activity
- ▸ Performance of business-critical process (you define these)

> **Note** [«]
>
> Want to know more? Head over to the SAP Support Portal at *http://support.sap.com/enterprisesupport* to view an example report and a summary of the prerequisites. Choose AVAILABLE SERVICES • CONTINUOUS QUALITY CHECKS • GOINGLIVE SUPPORT. Both Enterprise Support and Standard Support customers are entitled to one GoingLive Support service per calendar year per SAP landscape.

Continuous Quality Check: SAP OS/DB Migration Check

This service can be executed when an SAP customer changes the underlying OS or database from any release to any release. The SAP Business Suite on SAP HANA migration qualifies for this service, which provides another set of eyes on the tools, processes, performance, and execution of the migration. Unfortunately, the service is only included with an Enterprise Support Agreement. The service is a check on the system(s) to be migrated and validation of the procedures your team plans to follow. The service is delivered remotely and consists of two primary phases: analysis and verification. The analysis session will be delivered four to six weeks before your production migration. This part of the assessment will analyze the system to be migrated, the planned hardware to be used, and the parameters within the system to ensure that any risks are avoided. The verification session is executed six weeks after the production migration to validate that the configuration is in place and to make recommendations on performance improvements. Here's a quick summary of the service scope and details:

- **Analysis Session**
  - Migration project-related issues:
    - Technical data of the source system environment
    - Technical data of the target system environment
    - Migration project schedule
  - Hardware sizing feasibility
  - Load distribution (if necessary, optimization recommendations are given)
  - Configuration of the new system:
    - SAP system parameters
    - Database parameters
    - User/load distribution
  - Performance before migration
  - Transaction profiles
  - Number and distribution of users

- **Verification Session**
  - Comparison of response time before and after migration
  - Performance analysis on the new OS/DB combination
  - Verification of whether all the required SAP recommendations were implemented:
    - SAP system parameters
    - Database parameters
  - User/load distribution
  - Optimization of load distribution and identification of potential bottlenecks

This service and the GoingLive Support service are meant to add value to your team's support during the migration. The prerequisites require an SAP Early-Watch Report to be available for any system to be analyzed and that basic SAP Solution Manager functionality be deployed (see SAP Note 1172939 – Technical Prerequisites for Service Delivery in SAP Solution Manager 7.1). These prerequisites don't require an extraordinary amount of effort, and the reports provided by SAP will either inform your support team of parameters they should use or validate the activities already performed by your team.

> **Note** [«]
>
> For more information about the OS/DB Migration Check from SAP, navigate to *http://support.sap.com/enterprisesupport*, and choose Available Services • Continuous Quality Checks • OS/DB Migration Check.

10.3 Summary

Cutover planning is typically the responsibility of the overall SAP Business Suite on SAP HANA project manager in small- to medium-sized environments. For large environments, we often see a dedicated cutover manager whose sole focus is to catalog, document, execute, and manage the entire cutover process. Dedicating a resource to this activity has proven on countless project to be a worthwhile investment. Importantly, it doesn't need to be a technical resource who performs this role. Ideally, it's someone who can document details and excel at cross-team communication. Your team will have executed multiple successful SAP Business Suite on SAP HANA migrations before the actual production cutover. Defining the person responsible and the centralized location for documentation is a critical first step.

The other key component of successful cutover planning is the maximization of resources available to your organization. This includes the human capital required to both execute and validate a successful migration. SAP Support Services should be part of your planning and execution of the project. Services provided by SAP specific to OS/DB migrations are based on the numerous migrations previously executed by other SAP customers. By leveraging SAP Support Services, you access the knowledgebase of countless projects, conversions, and successes from other technical resources around the world.

Starting cutover planning early in your project is the primary message of this chapter. You have a variety of tools to use, services from SAP, and opinions on how to execute a successful cutover. The foundation for any successful SAP Business Suite on SAP HANA migration is the inclusion of cutover definition as part of every migration you complete in the nonproduction environment. We can't stress enough the importance of cataloging, organizing, and documenting each task your team will perform before, during, and after the migration. We even suggest implementing SAP security around transports within the newly migrated system so that changes are properly captured in project-created transports rather than allowing transports to be freely created.

The second most important message in this chapter is defining a communication plan. A successful migration will include a communication plan that defines the communication types and occurrences, as well as the escalation procedures to follow when a process or task fails. The communication plan will include both IT and business stakeholders. It should identify regular update intervals with clear and consistent messaging, and provide clear direction to any member of the team working during the cutover on when and to whom to communicate a specific task's status. With the information provided in this chapter, you have what you need to build a successful, comprehensive, cutover plan that defines the task sequence, dependencies, rollback requirements, and communication required as the various phases and tasks complete.

PART IV
Optimizations

Optimizing your ABAP code will drive real value after the migration to SAP HANA. Changing the way people work—moving tasks from batch to interactive—will provide tangible value.

11 ABAP Optimizations

Developing secure, well-performing code is a complex task. This chapter won't be a reference guide for ABAP syntax and how to build well-performing code, but it will help you find custom application code that might cause disruptions in service to your business users as a result of the migration. We'll also provide you with some guidance on finding ABAP code to be optimized after the migration to SAP Business Suite on SAP HANA.

You know from previous chapters that the conversion to SAP Business Suite on SAP HANA will transform cluster and pool tables to transparent tables. This conversion can affect the operation of custom ABAP application code, so we'll provide step-by step-guidance on finding affected programs. ABAP applications that use Native SQL as opposed to the SAP-recommended Open SQL is the other potential impact to your custom code postmigration. The concept behind Open SQL is that it abstracts the database-specific SQL statements from the developer. A developer can use Open SQL statements without fear that his code won't run on specific databases. When you move to SAP HANA, you need to find the application code that uses Native SQL commands. Native SQL use cases include the execution of a stored procedure within MS SQL, Sybase, DBA, or Oracle for a specific task or function and the execution of database-specific operations, which provided some performance benefit over Open SQL. Native SQL should be the exception and not the rule.

> **Note**　　　　　　　　　　　　　　　　　　　　　　　　　　　　　　　　 **[«]**
>
> After the migration to SAP Business Suite on SAP HANA, you want ABAP developers to use SAP HANA-specific capabilities for better performing applications with increased capabilities. *ABAP Development for SAP HANA* (SAP PRESS, 2014) goes into great detail on the new paradigms with ABAP on SAP HANA. Be sure to grab a copy for your favorite developer.

To wrap up this chapter, we'll talk about the tools you can use to find ABAP application code to optimize postmigration to SAP Business Suite on SAP HANA. Your users will see some benefits postmigration with the inclusion of SAP HANA optimized transactions by SAP: their background jobs will run faster, and they might see improvement in dialog transactions where large datasets are analyzed and displayed in an ABAP List Viewer (ALV) grid. This is awesome, but what if you want to do more? What if you want to really make an impact? You can do this by changing the way people work, by optimizing background jobs so they can be run interactively, and by changing ABAP reports so they can be run more open-ended and require fewer selection criteria. When you can remove the fear of long runtimes from your end users and enable then to access more data more quickly, then you'll have made an impact. Optimizing your application code will drive more value from the SAP Business Suite on SAP HANA migration, and it provides the opportunity for people to change how they work.

11.1   Noncompliant Code

As previously stated, the migration to SAP HANA will convert cluster and pool tables to transparent tables. You don't need to adjust applications for the migration; everything will convert as-is. However, the runtime behavior of the application might change. The default sort defined at the database level for cluster and pool tables is ORDER BY PRIMARY KEY. The developer could have relied on this behavior in his code, which will require the addition of the ORDER BY statement postmigration. When the table is converted to a transparent table, the data within the table will have no defined sort order. SAP recommends finding and resolving these statements because they are programming errors. These cleanup activities can occur months prior to the migration or immediately after the migration. It's your decision on when to perform them. The tool we'll use to find these objects is called the SAP Code Inspector. Let's walk through an example.

11.1.1   Finding SELECT without ORDER BY

1. Log on to your development SAP ERP system with a valid user ID and password.

2. Run Transaction SCI. When you enter the screen, all fields will be blank (see Figure 11.1).

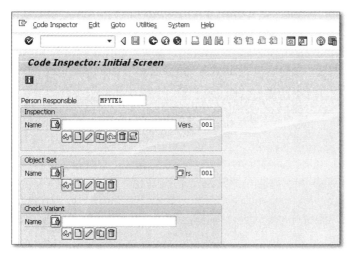

Figure 11.1 Initial Screen for the Code Inspector

Before you can analyze code for the specific statement, you need to define the set of application code to be analyzed.

3. In the OBJECT SET area, enter a name. In our example scenario, we'll analyze all custom code, so we entered the name "All Customer Objects" (see Figure 11.2). You can analyze code by name, package, type, and so on. If you feel searching all custom code is too broad, then provide a name that ties to your search type.

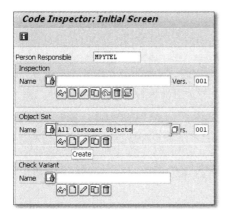

Figure 11.2 Creating a New Object Set in SAP Code Inspector

4. After entering the NAME, click the CREATE button.

5. Here you're defining the selection criteria for the custom objects to be analyzed. You can analyze by individual object, but your goal here is to select a group of objects to be analyzed in bulk.

6. For our example scenario, we've selected all classes, interfaces, function groups, and programs beginning with "Z" as shown in Figure 11.3. If you're not sure that all objects begin with a Z, then you can input package names.

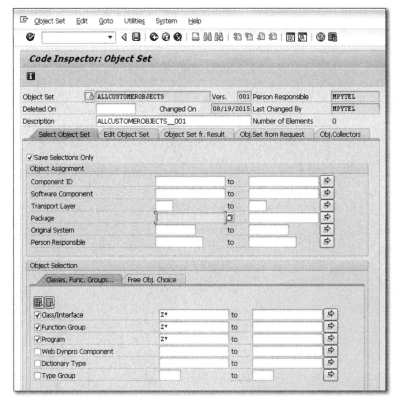

Figure 11.3 Selection Criteria for the Objects to Be Analyzed

7. Determine the best scenario for your environment based on your development standards.

8. When you're finished, click the SAVE button.

9. Click the BACK button.

10. Within the INSPECTION section, click the CHANGE button (see Figure 11.4).

11. Select the OBJECT SET radio button, and input the OBJECT SET NAME you created.

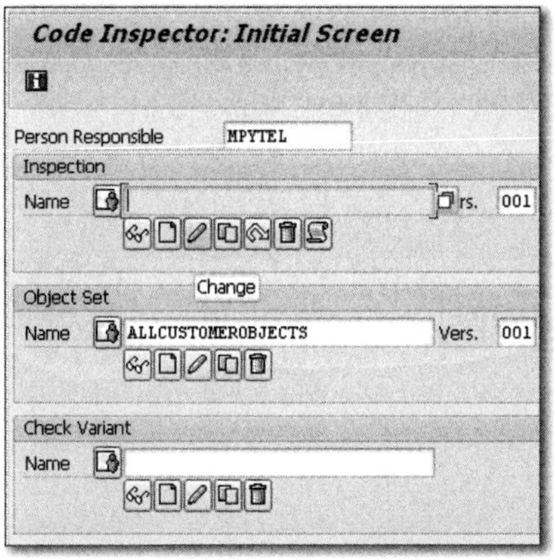

Figure 11.4 Executing an Inspection

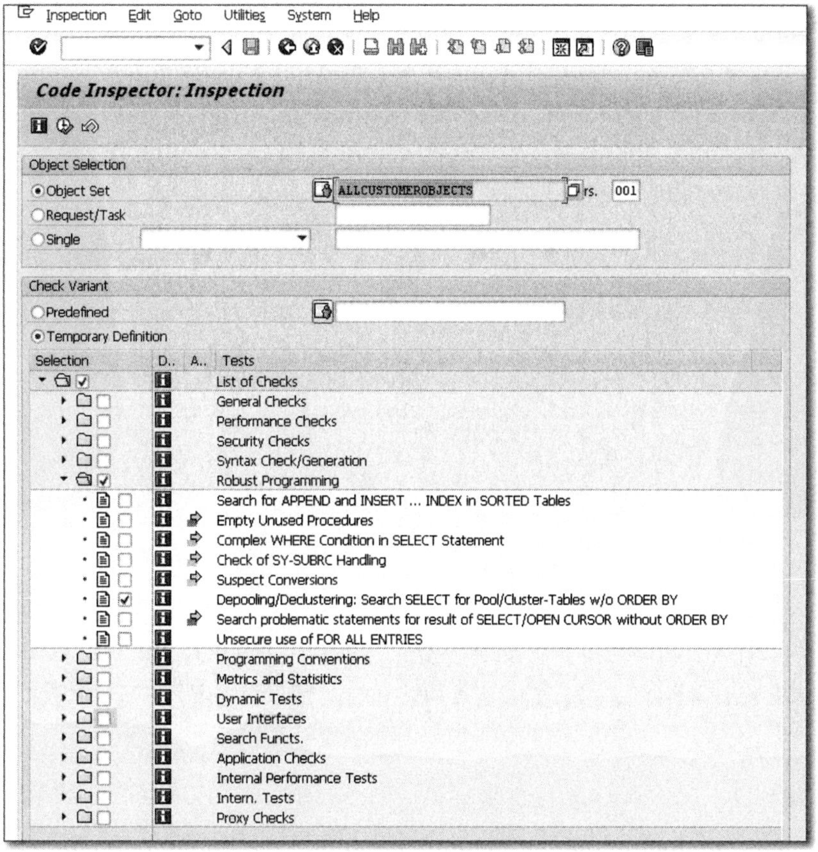

Figure 11.5 Executing an SAP Code Inspector Inspection

12. Under CHECK VARIANT, deselect all options, and then navigate to ROBUST PROGRAMMING • DEPOOLING/DECLUSTERING: SEARCH SELECT FOR POOL/CLUSTER-TABLES W/O ORDER BY (see Figure 11.5).

13. Check the box, and click EXECUTE.

14. Depending on the number of objects selected, this process can take some time. If the process reaches the timeout parameter, then try changing the object set to look at objects by development package.

15. When the results are displayed, you can open the tree display (see Figure 11.6).

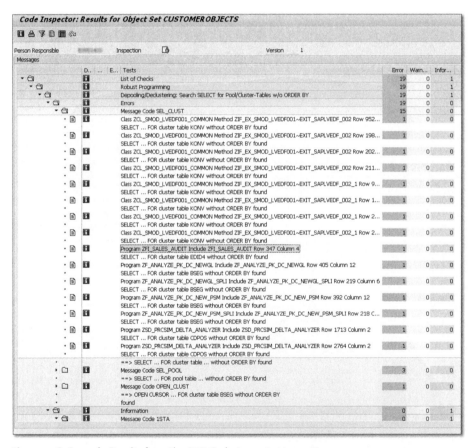

Figure 11.6 Example Results from the SAP Code Inspector Inspection

16. In Figure 11.6, you see a program called ZFI_SALES_AUDIT, which reads the cluster table EDID4 without an ORDER BY function. Although we don't know in

detail how the program works or if it will break the program postmigration, we do know that SAP recommends you remediate by adding the ORDER BY.

> **Note**   [«]
>
> Learn more about the effect of ORDER BY for transparent tables in SAP Note 1788664 – SELECT for Transparent EDID4, CDPOS, PCDPOS without Sorting.

17. Double-click the program to highlight where in the application code the SELECT statement exists (see Figure 11.7). Providing access to this transaction enables your developers to quickly resolve any issues before or after migration.

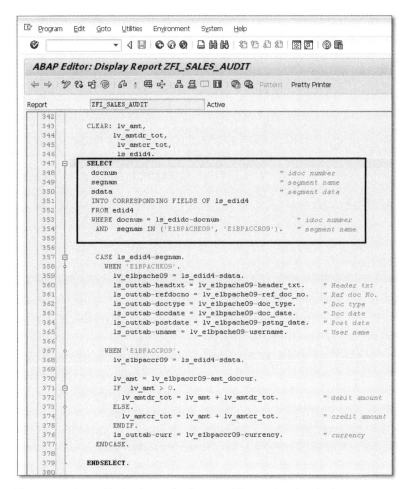

Figure 11.7 Direct Navigation to the Program Editor to Resolve the Issue

11.1.2 Finding Native SQL Statements

Next, you need to find programs that use Native SQL, which could potentially cause issues with a migration to SAP HANA.

1. Log on to your SAP ERP development system with a valid user ID and password.

2. Run Transaction SCI.

3. Click the CHANGE button under the INSPECTION section (see Figure 11.8). You don't need to enter a name.

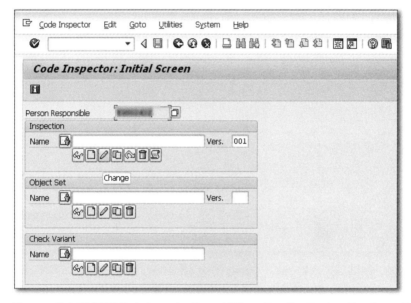

Figure 11.8 Initial SAP Code Inspector Prompt Where You Can Create a New Inspection

4. Select the OBJECT SET radio button, and input the OBJECT SET NAME you created earlier.

5. Navigate to CHECK VARIANT • LIST OF CHECKS • SEARCH FUNCTS. • SEARCH ABAP STATEMENT PATTERNS, as shown in Figure 11.9.

6. Click the SELECTION button next to the INFORMATION button.

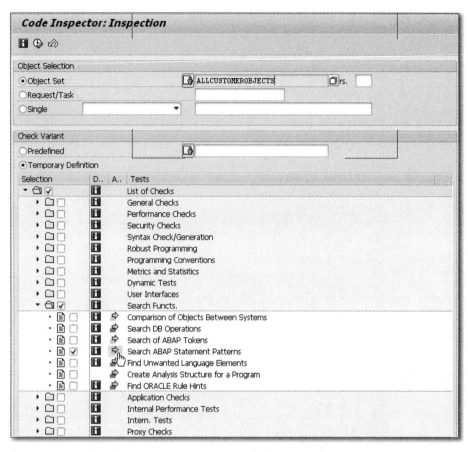

Figure 11.9 Searching for Native SQL Statements with the SAP Code Inspector

7. When prompted for the STATEMENT PATTERN, enter "EXEC SQL" (see Figure 11.10).

   ▶ EXEC SQL is one identifier for Native SQL execution.

   ▶ You can also search for EXECUTE PROCEDURE.

8. Click the CONTINUE button, and then execute the inspection.

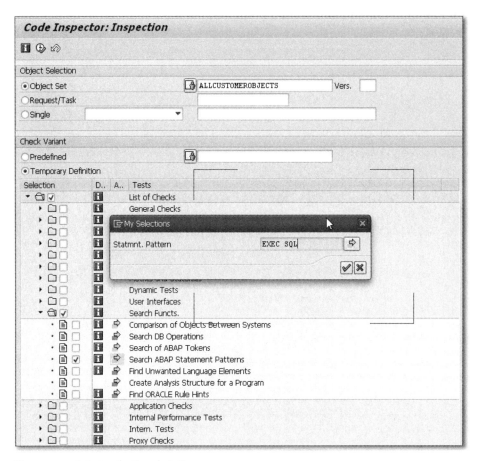

Figure 11.10 Entering the Search Pattern

9. When the results screen is displayed, open the tree navigation to see the objects impacted (see Figure 11.11).

10. From here, you can export the list, which will provide work instructions for the development team on objects to remediate.

11. You have two options when reviewing these objects:

   ▶ Convert to Open SQL

   ▶ Adapt to SAP HANA using Native SQL

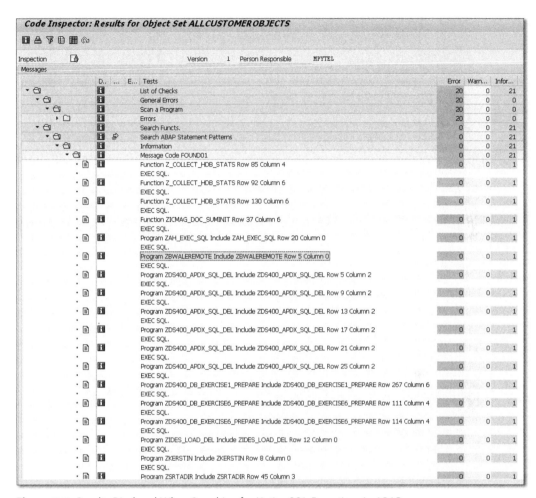

Figure 11.11 Results Displayed When Searching for Native SQL Executions in ABAP

In addition to the manual search instructions provided in this section, SAP has included some search variants you can use. These search variants would be put into the initial SAP Code Inspector screen after you've defined the OBJECT SET. These SAP-provided variants include the following:

▶ FUNCTIONAL_DB
Searches Native SQL, DB Hints, ABAP Database Connectivity (ADBC) connections, cluster/pool tables without Order BY, and so on.

495

► FUNCTIONAL_DB_ADDITION
Not related to SAP HANA but this executes searches related to programs using SELECT without a WHERE clause.

► PERFORMANCE_DB
Performance-related SQL checks from the static code analysis perspective.

[»]

Note

Need to know more? Check out *http://help.sap.com/nw74*, and choose Development Information • Developer's Guides • Custom Application Development (ABAP) • More information: Application Development on AS ABAP • ABAP Test and Analysis Tools • SQL Performance Monitoring • ABAP Test Cockpit and Code Inspector in Context of HANA Migration.

11.2 Optimization Opportunities

ABAP application code optimization won't be a simple task. Improving the database performance won't be the silver bullet, but it does offer a large opportunity for improvement, which is why we typically focus on the database response time back to the application. In this section, we'll highlight some tools your team can use to find those ABAP programs that need to be optimized. We won't focus on SAP-delivered applications, which are typically handled by SAP Support. Your goal is to find those customer-created objects that might provide an opportunity for improvement. We won't be covering how to modify the individual programs or when to use specific SAP classes. The goal of this section is to get thinking about performance and how to find objects to be reviewed.

11.2.1 Workload Monitor

The workload monitor provides the best option to review system performance with the broadest criteria. It enables you to look at a specific day in recent history or view aggregated data over the week or month. Within this transaction, you can also break down the analysis by task type. Was the object run in dialog mode, as a background job, or accessed via remote function call (RFC)? You can also break down the response time distribution. What is mostly CPU time, database time, or client time (network)? Let's explore this transaction.

1. Log on to SAP ERP with a valid user ID and password.

2. Execute Transaction ST03N.

3. Navigate the WORKLOAD section by double-clicking your selected time period.

4. You'll notice the statistics are organized by server. Select a specific application server, or choose all of them.

5. In Figure 11.12, we've chosen the last full month as the time period.

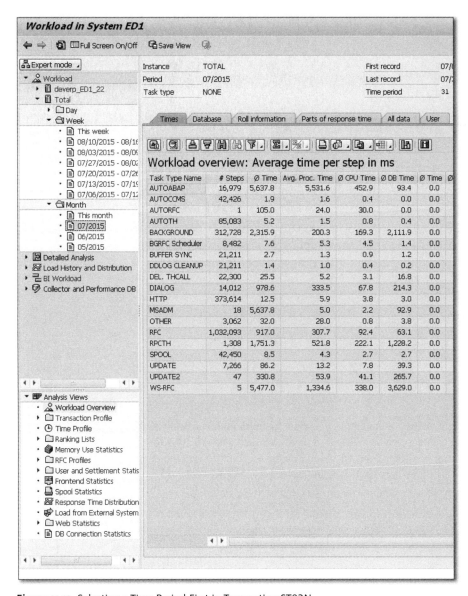

Figure 11.12 Selecting a Time Period First in Transaction ST03N

6. Next you need to navigate to Analysis Views • Transaction Profile • Standard. Double click Standard (see Figure 11.13).

Figure 11.13 Select the Standard transaction profile in ST03N

7. Select the Task Type button. You can chose to narrowly define the task type you want to analyze. For example, if you want to improve end-user transaction performance, you would select Dialog (see Figure 11.14).

Instance	TOTAL		First record	07/01/2015	00:00:00
Period	07/2015		Last record	07/31/2015	23:59:59
Task type	NONE		Time period	31 Day(s)	00:00:00

Times | Database | Parts of response time | GUI times | All data

	Name of Background Job	# Steps	T Response Time	Ø Time	Process.	Avg. Proc. Time	T CPU~	Ø CPU~	T DB Time	Ø DB Time	T Time	Ø Tim
AUTOABAP			: Times: T Total time (s), Ø Time/step (ms)									
AUTOCOMS												
AUTORFC	NNECT	28	630,110	22,503,927.2	19,942	712,217.3	26,904	960,848.2	610,157	21,791,306.6	0.0	0.C
AUTOTH	RT=====CP	EFWK ANALYSIS JOB FOR SIMILARITY	8,482	509,493	60,067.6	407	48.0	66	7.8	28	3.3	0.0	0.C
BACKGROUND		155,692	122,548	787.1	102,517	658.5	38,001	244.1	19,618	126.0	0.0	0.C
BGRFC Scheduler		16,979	95,724	5,637.8	93,921	5,531.6	7,699	452.9	1,586	93.4	0.0	0.C
BUFFER SYNC	=======CP	15,319	80,563	5,259.1	80,560	5,258.8	509	35.1	0	0.0	0.0	0.C
DDLOG CLEANUP		132,256	44,334	335.2	26,167	197.9	32,005	242.0	17,766	134.3	0.0	0.C
DEL. THCALL		71,888	39,801	553.6	38,879	540.8	1,136	15.8	776	10.8	0.0	0.C
DIALOG	=======CP	11,396	39,328	3,451.0	6,624	581.3	364	32.0	11	0.9	0.0	0.C
HTTP		605	35,766	59,150.6	4,783	7,906.2	7,696	12,720.5	16,304	26,949.1	0.0	0.C
MSADM	CHING	SAP_CCMS_MONI_BATCH_DP	711	28,082	39,497.0	3,778	5,314.0	5,673	7,979.0	24,283	34,152.6	0.0	0.C
OTHER		31,938	16,301	510.4	16,011	501.3	28	0.9	5	0.2	0.0	0.C
RFC		11,926	13,133	1,101.2	10,430	874.6	4,010	336.2	2,633	220.8	0.0	0.C
BPCTH		EU_REORG	30	10,072	335,727.2	3,485	116,151.0	4,510	150,324.0	6,587	219,557.7	0.0	0.C
SPOOL	=======CP	SAP_COLLECTOR_PERFMON_RSDB_TDB	60	8,163	136,053.6	1,008	16,806.7	1,933	32,221.8	7,155	119,241.8	0.0	0.C
UPDATE		1,675	6,687	3,992.3	4,525	2,701.6	4,123	2,461.3	2,159	1,289.1	0.0	0.C
UPDATE2		41,914	5,936	141.6	5,914	138.7	180	4.3	111	2.6	0.0	0.C
WS-RFC		OCS_QUEUE_IMPORT	7	5,825	832,299.6	5,472	781,742.6	258	36,888.6	352	50,347.4	0.0	0.C
All		RSPARAGENERBM	1	5,284	5,283,851.0	5,251	5,251,077.0	2	2,460.0	33	32,772.0	0.0	0.C
		134,999	4,629	34.3	3,235	24.0	1,406	10.4	1,054	7.8	0.0	0.C
	=======CP	372,938	4,436	11.9	2,089	5.6	1,345	3.6	986	2.6	0.0	0.C
		8,461	4,022	474.3	4,010	472.8	13	1.6	0	0.0	0.0	0.C
SAPLQOWK		1,744	3,646	2,090.5	91	52.1	46	26.4	61	35.2	0.0	0.C
RDDEXECL	RDDEXECL	4	3,235	808,818.0	2,518	629,582.0	2,580	645,105.0	692	172,884.8	0.0	0.C
RSBTCRTE		88,911	3,186	35.8	2,168	24.4	1,344	15.1	845	9.5	0.0	0.C
SWNCCOLL		711	3,087	4,341.9	2,670	3,755.4	2,336	3,285.2	413	580.3	0.0	0.C
SWNC_TCOLL_STARTER	SAP_COLLECTOR_PERFMON_RSAMONA0	711	2,715	3,819.2	1,684	2,368.9	1,669	2,346.8	1,728	1,445.6	0.0	0.C
RSTPDAMAIN		169	2,681	15,861.1	13	75.6	3	16.0	5	30.0	0.0	0.C
SAPLBBE_ICDD_EXT		94	2,642	28,109.9	706	7,511.6	877	9,334.8	1,935	20,588.9	0.0	0.C
FCC_STD_BACKGROUND_PROGRAM	FCC_STD_BACKGROUND_JOB/800	3,000	2,056	670.5	730	236.0	1,011	329.9	1,304	425.4	0.0	0.C
SESSION_MANAGER		1,016	2,019	1,987.3	1,585	1,559.6	88	87.0	151	149.6	0.0	0.C
/1CADMC/SAPLDMC100000000000361		124,978	1,881	15.0	1,718	13.7	369	2.9	144	1.2	0.0	0.C
/1CADMC/SAPLDMC100000000000363		122,739	1,859	15.1	1,700	13.8	361	2.9	141	1.1	0.0	0.C

Figure 11.14 Selecting Dialog to See Interactive Transactions

8. A standard ALV grid display is provided for you to sort and filter. In Figure 11.15, we've filtered for any object that begins with "Z" and sorted descending on the AVERAGE DATABASE TIME PER DIALOG STEP column.

Report or Transaction name	# Steps	T Response Time	Ø Time	Process.	Avg. Proc. Time	T CPU~	Ø CPU~	T DB Time	Ø DB Ti	T Time	Ø Time	T Roll Wait Ti	Ø Roll Wait Ti	Ø WaitTime	# Trips	Ø Time Ø
ZDN_WRONG_CP_VER_NEW	122	3.222	26.411,5	16	127,2	4	30,9	3.170	25.981,5	0,0	0,0	36	294,1	1,3	146	126,6
ZAB_SCM_DEL_PREQS	714	9.675	13.551,0	3.007	4.211,0	792	1.108,	6.034	8.451,5	0,0	0,0	85	119,1	745,1	1.222	114,2
ZSD_CUST_SPEC_PRICE_E	1	3	2.653,0	0	298,0	0	150,0	2	2.350,0	0,0	0,0	0	0,0	0,0	1	421,0
ZSD_MOB_INV_LOG_BATC	1	2	1.848,0	0	361,0	0	100,0	1	1.482,0	0,0	0,0	0	0,0	0,0	1	423,0
ZSD_UPDT_PARTNERS	1	1	871,0	0	165,0	0	20,0	1	700,0	0,0	0,0	0	1,0	1,0	1	423,0
Z_DEFIBTECH	1	1	534,0	0	46,0	0	20,0	0	481,0	0,0	0,0	0	1,0	1,0	1	286,0
ZPMPAY_OAR	25	23	923,9	5	210,3	1	56,4	11	449,0	0,0	0,0	5	194,3	0,4	68	111,9
ZMB25	41	16	394,0	5	113,5	1	27,1	7	175,8	0,0	0,0	3	62,1	0,8	94	83,2
ZAB_CONSOLIDATE_PURC	30	7	239,2	1	38,3	0	9,3	5	154,2	0,0	0,0	1	41,5	2,0	38	162,3

Figure 11.15 Transactions That Are Candidates for Optimization

9. You can also double-click each transaction or program to identify the users who accessed the transaction.

11.2.2 SAP Workload Analysis

Using analysis from the previous section, we've now identified a program or transaction that requires some deeper analysis. The next tool you can use is Transaction STAD. Within this transaction, you can select a time period from history to analyze the runtime further by following these steps:

1. Log on to your SAP system with a valid user ID and password.

2. Run Transaction STAD.

3. Enter a time period to analyze.

4. In Figure 11.16, we've chosen to display any program beginning with "Z" for our example scenario.

5. Check both boxes under TOOLS, and click OK.

6. The data requested is displayed on screen. Focus your attention on the DATABASE REQUEST TIME column. Figure 11.17 shows a program that is a serious offender.

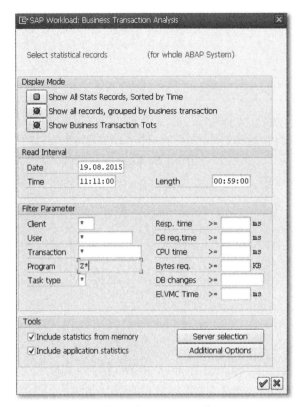

Figure 11.16 Example Analysis Criteria Selection Screen in Transaction STAD

Started	Server	Transaction	Program Function	T	Scr.	Wp	User	Response time (ms)	Time in WPs (ms)	Wait time (ms)	CPU time (ms)	DB req. time (ms)	VMC elapsed time (ms)	Memory used (kB)	Transferred kBytes
		*	Z*	*		*	*	0			0	0	0		0
11:12:25			ZBC_CHECK_FOR_ACTIVE_JOB	B		44	BATCHUSER	55	55	0	10	12	0	4.255	5,4
11:12:38			ZAB_PP_PROXY_NON_CHICAGO	B		44	BATCHUSER	1.028.929	1.028.929	0	2.070	1.024.696	0	4.255	4.379,4
11:12:50			Z_MATERIAL_SEQ_POSTING	B		48	BATCHUSER	1.639	1.639	0	330	1.321	0	4.255	28.367,1
11:14:50			Z_MATERIAL_SEQ_POSTING	B		48	BATCHUSER	1.923	1.923	0	340	1.550	0	4.255	28.369,4
11:16:53			Z_MATERIAL_SEQ_POSTING	B		50	BATCHUSER	1.704	1.704	0	340	1.374	0	4.255	28.371,6
11:18:51			Z_MATERIAL_SEQ_POSTING	B		50	BATCHUSER	1.712	1.712	0	320	1.392	0	4.255	28.373,9
11:20:53			Z_MATERIAL_SEQ_POSTING	B		48	BATCHUSER	1.725	1.725	0	340	1.370	0	4.255	28.376,2
11:22:50			Z_MATERIAL_SEQ_POSTING	B		48	BATCHUSER	1.481	1.481	0	310	1.188	0	4.255	28.378,5
11:24:50			Z_MATERIAL_SEQ_POSTING	B		52	BATCHUSER	2.149	2.149	0	390	1.797	0	4.255	28.380,8
11:26:51			Z_MATERIAL_SEQ_POSTING	B		50	BATCHUSER	1.857	1.857	0	340	1.519	0	4.255	28.383,1
11:28:51			Z_MATERIAL_SEQ_POSTING	B		50	BATCHUSER	1.539	1.539	0	320	1.239	0	4.255	28.385,3
11:30:14			ZAB_ARIBA_DIR_CHECK	B		44		1.645	1.645	0	140	95	0	4.092	20,8
11:30:14			ZAB_ARIBA_DIR_CHECK	B		49		1.816	1.816	0	160	84	0	4.092	20,8
11:30:25			ZBC_CHECK_FOR_ACTIVE_JOB	B		50	BATCHUSER	42	42	0	0	13	0	4.255	5,4
11:30:52			Z_MATERIAL_SEQ_POSTING	B		50	BATCHUSER	1.528	1.528	0	310	1.230	0	4.255	28.387,6
11:32:25			ZBC_CHECK_FOR_ACTIVE_JOB	B		50	BATCHUSER	33	33	0	0	9	0	4.255	5,4
11:32:30			ZAB_PP_PROXY_NON_CHICAGO	B		50	BATCHUSER	1.007.475	1.007.475	0	1.660	1.004.745	0	4.255	4.379,4
11:32:52			Z_MATERIAL_SEQ_POSTING	B		48	BATCHUSER	1.798	1.798	0	340	1.470	0	4.255	28.389,9
11:34:50			Z_MATERIAL_SEQ_POSTING	B		52	BATCHUSER	1.741	1.741	0	330	1.428	0	4.255	28.392,2
11:36:50			Z_MATERIAL_SEQ_POSTING	B		44	BATCHUSER	1.757	1.757	0	340	1.417	0	4.255	28.394,5

System:
Analysed time: 19.08.2015 / 11:11:00 - 19.08.2015 / 12:10:00
Display mode: All statistic records, sorted by time
Number of RFCs which responded (without errors): 1 (1)
Application statistic is included

Figure 11.17 Example Output from Transaction STAD Analysis

7. Double-click on the object to drill down for more information (see Figure 11.18).

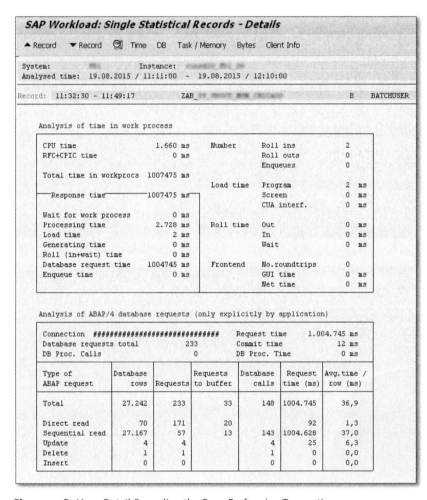

Figure 11.18 More Detail Regarding the Poor-Performing Transaction

8. In Figure 11.18, several points are evident:

▸ The database request time is the longest part of the transaction.

▸ The transaction is spending most of its time on sequential reads.

▸ The transaction has made 57 specific requests to the database, which returned 27,000+ records.

Now that you know this program is an opportunity for enhancement, a developer or system administrator might schedule time with the user to set up a trace of the activity to capture detailed performance information. The most common trace tools you'll use are Transaction SAT, Transaction ST05, and Transaction ST12.

[»] **Note**

For an exceptionally well-written book detailing each of these tools and their usage, see *SAP Performance Optimization Guide* (SAP PRESS, 2013).

11.2.3 Database Administration Cockpit

Next, we want to explore another option to find long-running or expensive SQL statements. Transaction DBACOCKPIT might be known as a Basis transaction, but it offers some excellent diagnostic and troubleshooting utilities. Within Transaction DBACOCKPIT, you have a subtree with multiple performance-related utilities. Let's drill into one tool that might help you find application code to optimize by following these steps:

1. Log on to SAP ERP with a valid user ID and password.

2. Execute Transaction DBACOCKPIT.

3. Navigate to PERFORMANCE • SQL STATEMENT ANALYSIS • TABLE ACCESS (see Figure 11.19).

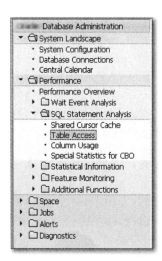

Figure 11.19 Accessing SQL Statement Information in the DBA Cockpit

4. Double-click Table Access.

5. You're presented with a grid displaying some performance data related to SQL statements executed within your system. Navigate to the SQL Module column, and choose the Filter button. Filter on objects that start with "Z*".

   Now you have a display of SQL statements specifically issued by your custom code (see Figure 11.20).

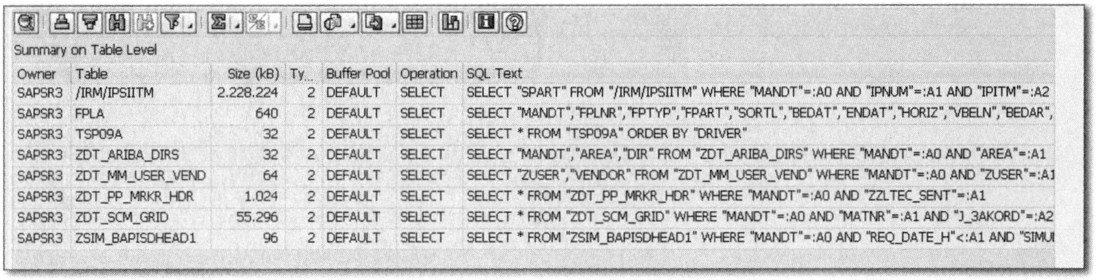

Owner	Table	Size (kB)	Ty...	Buffer Pool	Operation	SQL Text
SAPSR3	/IRM/IPSIITM	2.228.224	2	DEFAULT	SELECT	SELECT "SPART" FROM "/IRM/IPSIITM" WHERE "MANDT"=:A0 AND "IPNUM"=:A1 AND "IPITM"=:A2
SAPSR3	FPLA	640	2	DEFAULT	SELECT	SELECT "MANDT","FPLNR","FPTYP","FPART","SORTL","BEDAT","ENDAT","HORIZ","VBELN","BEDAR",
SAPSR3	TSP09A	32	2	DEFAULT	SELECT	SELECT * FROM "TSP09A" ORDER BY "DRIVER"
SAPSR3	ZDT_ARIBA_DIRS	32	2	DEFAULT	SELECT	SELECT "MANDT","AREA","DIR" FROM "ZDT_ARIBA_DIRS" WHERE "MANDT"=:A0 AND "AREA"=:A1
SAPSR3	ZDT_MM_USER_VEND	64	2	DEFAULT	SELECT	SELECT "ZUSER","VENDOR" FROM "ZDT_MM_USER_VEND" WHERE "MANDT"=:A0 AND "ZUSER"=:A1
SAPSR3	ZDT_PP_MRKR_HDR	1.024	2	DEFAULT	SELECT	SELECT * FROM "ZDT_PP_MRKR_HDR" WHERE "MANDT"=:A0 AND "ZZLTEC_SENT"=:A1
SAPSR3	ZDT_SCM_GRID	55.296	2	DEFAULT	SELECT	SELECT * FROM "ZDT_SCM_GRID" WHERE "MANDT"=:A0 AND "MATNR"=:A1 AND "J_3AKORD"=:A2
SAPSR3	ZSIM_BAPISDHEAD1	96	2	DEFAULT	SELECT	SELECT * FROM "ZSIM_BAPISDHEAD1" WHERE "MANDT"=:A0 AND "REQ_DATE_H"<:A1 AND "SIMU

Figure 11.20 Detailed Records Displayed within the DBA Cockpit

6. In Figure 11.20, you can multiple SQL statements where no column was specified in the SELECT statement. This might be acceptable if the table only has 5–10 columns.

7. You can sort based on a variety of fields within this transaction. Use the Select Layout button to modify.

11.3 Summary

In this chapter, we identified how to find ABAP code that might have errors at runtime postmigration using the SAP Code Inspector, and we navigated specific applications within SAP ERP that you can use to find ABAP application code to be optimized. SAP provides a variety of tools that can be used in this process. We demonstrated three high-level tools that can be used by a developer or system administrator. For detailed code remediation and analysis, you'll need a trained ABAP developer. Ideally, that resource is trained in the transactions discussed in this chapter but is also aware of the SQL Monitor (Transaction SQLM) available with recent releases of the ABAP add-on ST-PI and now delivered as part of SAP NetWeaver 7.40. The SQL Monitor application can be enabled selectively on your production system to capture all executed SQL statements, which can then be downloaded and uploaded to a development system for further analysis with Transaction SWLT (SQL Performance Tuning Worklist). This tool identifies the enhancement points made by your organization within standard SAP transactions.

In the examples in this chapter, we looked exclusively at the custom objects directly executed by users or background jobs. What about the custom search help in Transaction VA01? The SQL Monitor will help you identify those opportunities for improvement as you continue to operate and improve your SAP Business Suite on SAP HANA instance.

Not all optimization for SAP Business Suite on SAP HANA requires SAP S/4HANA Finance. With EHP 7, SAP delivered hundreds of enhancements, some of which are SAP HANA-specific. It's important to see how these optimizations can drive more value from the upgrade.

12   SAP Business Suite Optimization

In this chapter, we focus on the functional enhancements that are delivered by SAP with a move to SAP ERP 6 EHP 7 on SAP HANA. At this point, enhancement packages delivered by SAP are installed but not activated. However, there are specific cases where SAP has delivered new transaction codes that you can selectively begin using to improve the user experience when running SAP Business Suite on SAP HANA. In Section 12.2.1, we'll talk about some of these transactions and the tenfold improvement in performance just by using a new version of transactions your users access every day.

SAP changed the way it delivers new functionality with the SAP Business Suite using the enhancement package concept. Each enhancement package contains groups of business functions that lie dormant in your system until you turn them on. Some enhancements activate changes that might increase or reduce the number of steps in a business process; these have higher impact because they require updates to end-user training and documentation. Other enhancements are just that—enhancements using new transactions or reports that exist alongside the transactions your users access every day. Many enhancements can easily be activated without business process change. In this chapter, we'll talk about the Switch Framework and specific enhancements available with the move to SAP HANA that have minimal process impact.

We'll also talk about two new user interface (UI) enhancements available to customers as part of their maintenance when running SAP ERP 6 EHP 7 (on SAP HANA or any database). The first of these, SAP Fiori, is based on SAPUI5 (SAP's version of HTML5). This is truly a new and innovative interface to SAP ERP because it's browser independent and, in some scenarios, is immediately available via mobile web browsers, which is a first for SAP. No middleware required to enable mobile transactions in SAP ERP? Tell me more!

The second UI enhancement available with SAP ERP 6 EHP 7 SAP Screen Personas (or Personas for short). The Personas enhancement is also HTML based but not mobile enabled (as of August 2015). This UI technology has a faster development and deployment time than SAP Fiori, but it's less flexible. You can essentially redraw SAP screens to simplify the user experience. We'll review some common use cases, how to get started developing new screens, and where to find more information.

Our goal in this chapter is to highlight some key enhancements within SAP ERP Financials (FI), Materials Management (MM), and Sales that will be available to your organization after the migration to SAP Business Suite on SAP HANA. These enhancements will enable your users to process more data more quickly and efficiently. The enhancements we highlight won't require large amount of business process change. A new transaction code will require an update to security roles and potentially some end-user training; our goal here is to provide you with some quick wins post-migration to SAP HANA. Lastly, we'll talk about a new application from SAP to help you find even more enhancements specific to your organization, licenses owned, and your new SAP Business Suite on SAP HANA platform.

12.1 Technical Check

The steps in this section are based on real-world experience and aren't part of the system copy procedures. SAP will continually optimize and enhance the operation of SAP Business Suite on SAP HANA. These steps are good to check on each system after a migration to SAP Business Suite on SAP HANA to ensure that the functional enhancements (that we'll talk about next) will function as they should. All of the steps are related. We want to ensure all views that exist in the ABAP Dictionary exist at the database level. Follow these steps to perform three necessary technical checks:

1. Log on to your SAP Business Suite on SAP HANA system with a valid user ID and password.

2. Open Transaction SE16, and input Table Name "SNHI_DUP_PREWORK" (see Figure 12.1).

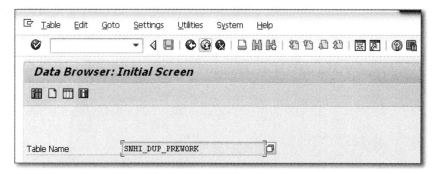

Figure 12.1 Entering the Table Nme in the Data Browser: Initial Screen

3. Click the Table Contents button ▦.

4. Click the Execute button to view all entries (see Figure 12.2).

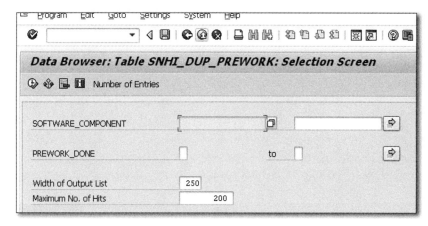

Figure 12.2 Clicking the Execute Button to View All Entries

5. When the list of table entries is displayed, ensure that there is an X in the PRE-WORK_DONE column for all in-use SAP components (SAP_APPL, SAP_BASIS, etc.) as shown in Figure 12.3.

6. If not, see SAP Note 2048896 – Hana Content Activation Check.

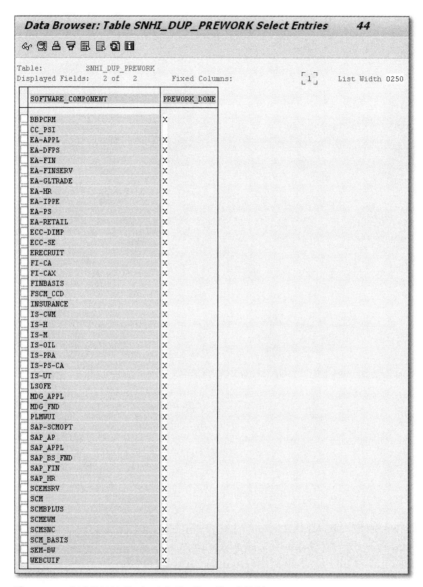

Figure 12.3 SAP HANA Content Activation Check Table

7. Click back to the main menu.

8. Next, enter Transaction HDBVIEWS. In Figure 12.4, you can see multiple views that aren't active or not generated in the database.

Analysis and Repair Tool for Views Generated by HDB
View
Status
Problem description
V_GLPOS_C_CT
V_GLPOS_C_DEB_CT
V_GLPOS_C_VEN_CT
V_GLPOS_C_GL_CT
V_GLPOS_N_CT
V_GLPOS_N_GL_CT
V_GLPCA_CT
Calculation View Not Generated
V_GLPCA_T_CT
Calculation View Not Generated
FIN_GLPOS_C
Calculation View Not Generated
FIN_GLPOS_V
Calculation View Not Generated
/1FIGL/VGLFUNCA
Not Active in DDIC
/1FIGL/VGMAVCA
Not Active in DDIC
/1FIGL/VJVPSC010
Not Active in DDIC
/1FIGL/VTRACTSL0
Not Active in DDIC

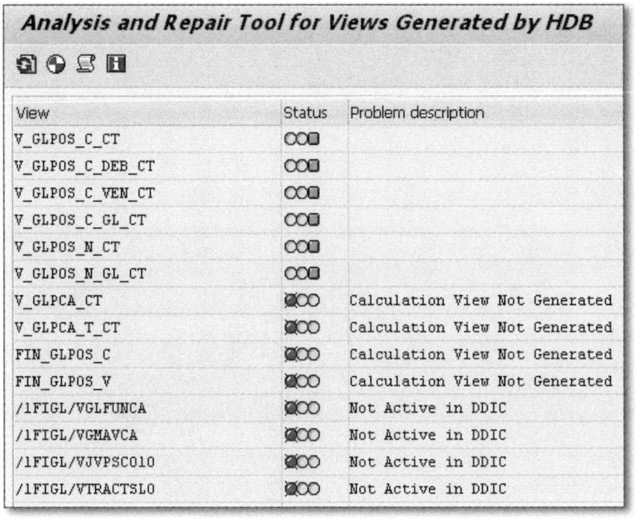

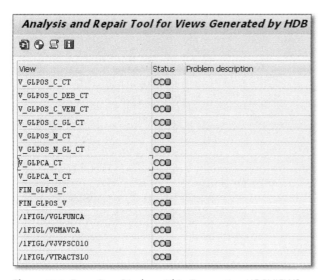

Figure 12.4 Errors Displayed in Transaction HDBVIEWS

9. Click the GENERATE button to resolve the errors. After the process completes, it should look like Figure 12.5.

Analysis and Repair Tool for Views Generated by HDB
View
Status
Problem description
V_GLPOS_C_CT
V_GLPOS_C_DEB_CT
V_GLPOS_C_VEN_CT
V_GLPOS_C_GL_CT
V_GLPOS_N_CT
V_GLPOS_N_GL_CT
V_GLPCA_CT
V_GLPCA_T_CT
FIN_GLPOS_C
FIN_GLPOS_V
/1FIGL/VGLFUNCA
/1FIGL/VGMAVCA
/1FIGL/VJVPSC010
/1FIGL/VTRACTSL0

Figure 12.5 Error-Free Display within Transaction HDBVIEWS

10. Click back to the main menu.

11. Enter Transaction DBACOCKPIT.

12. Navigate to Diagnostics • Missing Tables & Indexes.

13. Click the Refresh button to execute the check.

14. The errors displayed will be specific to your environment (see Figure 12.6). In our scenario, we had to remove some indexes at the database layer.

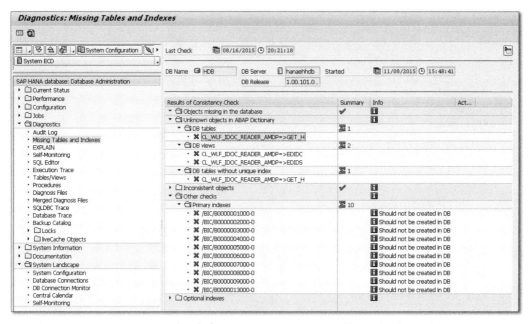

Figure 12.6 Errors Displayed after Executing the Missing Tables and Indexes Check

These checks ensure that the SAP-delivered SAP HANA views are active and functioning correctly. These transactions should be executed whenever you apply Support Package Stacks (SP Stacks), apply enhancement packages, or enable new business functions using the Switch Framework.

12.2 Functional Enhancements

Although we may advertise the SAP Business Suite on SAP HANA migration as a technical project, there can be opportunities to include some enhancements as part of the project. Using the migration methods described in this book will allow the business users to work as they did before (unless this was a major upgrade from SAP R/3 or SAP ECC 5.0), and we don't want to expand the scope so far that the project extends beyond a reasonable time period. However, we do want to offer some benefits to the end users for all their support with testing and business downtime during the migration. Many of the enhancements we talk about in this section don't require a change in their business processes. You can update existing transactions or move to a new transaction code that will function similar to the original transaction but has been enhanced by SAP to use SAP HANA views instead of joining tables at runtime. Let's dive into some enhancements by functional area. If you don't see a specific area listed, we'll also talk about how you can find more information.

12.2.1 Finance

At this point in your migration, your system is either running SAP ERP EHP 6 or SAP ERP EHP 7 on SAP HANA and you don't have SAP S/4HANA Finance activated. However, that doesn't mean you don't get any enhancements. In fact, some fantastic enhancements are available in SAP ERP Financials (FI). For example, in the line item view transactions, we have seen 100x performance improvements. What can you do with all this new speed? Accountants and analysts are so used to restricting search criteria that it can almost be paralyzing to have so much speed! The items listed here are enhanced or created when you migrate to SAP Business Suite on SAP HANA. To leverage these transactions or reports, you don't need to activate any new functionality. The following examples are enhancements to existing transactions and provide the same functionality as before—only faster:

- Transaction FBL1H: Display Vendor Line Items
- Transaction FBL3H: Display GL Account Line Items
- Transaction FBL5H: Display Customer Line Items
- Transaction FAGLL03H: GL Account Line Items (New)
- Transaction F110: Parameters for Automatic Payment
- Report RFCHKN10: Check Register
- Report RFBILA00N: Financial Statement
- Transaction AR01: Asset Balances
- Transaction KEPM: CO-PA Planning

[»] **Note:**

The transactions in this section are just a sample. To view the 100+ enhancements to FI with SAP ERP EHP 7 on SAP HANA, check out SAP Note 1761546 – SAP ERP Powered by SAP HANA: Optimizations. Open the PDF attached to the SAP Note to see all enhancements by functional area. You can cross-reference the PDF content with your own users' transactions in Transaction ST03N to find opportunities to use SAP Business Suite on SAP HANA even more.

12.2.2 Materials Management

The enhancements with MM for SAP ERP EHP 7 on SAP HANA are divided between enhancements you automatically get when migrating and those that require the activation of a business function within the Switch Framework. Let's start out with a quick list of common transactions that have been improved with SAP Business Suite on SAP HANA:

- Transaction MMBE: Stock Overview
- Transaction MB5L: List of Stock Values: Balances
- Transaction MIDO: Physical Inventory Overview
- Transaction MIGO: Goods Movement
- Transaction MB51: Material Document List
- Transaction MB52: Display Warehouse Stocks of Material
- Transaction MIRO: Enter Incoming Invoice

Again, this is only a subsection of the out-of-the-box enhancements when running SAP ERP EHP 7 on SAP HANA. Check the attachment to the SAP Note 1761546 we talked about in the previous section.

Next, let's look at three enhancements delivered with EHP 7 that have considerable impact on performance improvements within MM. These enhancements not only impact traditional MM transactions, but also Procurement and materials requirements planning (MRP). Here are the three business functions we recommend activating because they have minimal business process impact and maximum technical impact to improve performance:

- LOG_MM_OPTIMIZATIONS: Materials Management, UI, and Performance Optimizations
- LOG_PPH_MDPSX_READ: Performance Optimizations for MRP
- LOG_MM_OPT_POH: Optimization for Purchase Order History

SAP has delivered hundreds of enhancements using business functions, so it's difficult to narrow down a list that works for as many readers of this book as possible. We know these offer significant performance improvements, they don't change business processes, and, more importantly, they are reversible so they are lower risk to your landscape. When migrating to SAP Business Suite on SAP HANA, your technical team can activate these functions prior to regression testing and then determine whether they remain on after you regression test your SAP Business Suite on SAP HANA environment.

Let's step through the process of activating these enhancements:

1. Log on to SAP ERP with a valid user ID and password.

2. Run Transaction SFW5. Click CONTINUE TRANSACTION when prompted with a warning.

3. Check the PLANNED STATUS box for the following three enhancements (or any enhancements you choose to enable), as shown in Figure 12.7.

   ▸ LOG_MM_OPTIMIZATIONS

   ▸ LOG_PPH_MDPSX_READ

   ▸ LOG_MM_OPT_POH

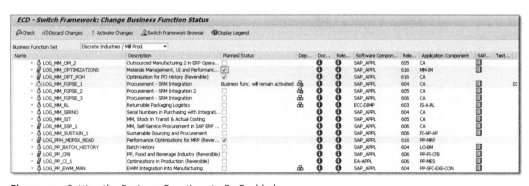

Figure 12.7 Setting the Business Functions to Be Enabled

Tip			**[+]**
Want to know more about these business functions? Click the ❶ button under the DOCUMENTATION column. This will redirect you to the *http://help.sap.com* site to learn more about the specific changes made when activating the object.			

4. Click the ACTIVATE CHANGES button, and then click the button again to begin the process. Confirm the popup box when it appears (see Figure 12.8).

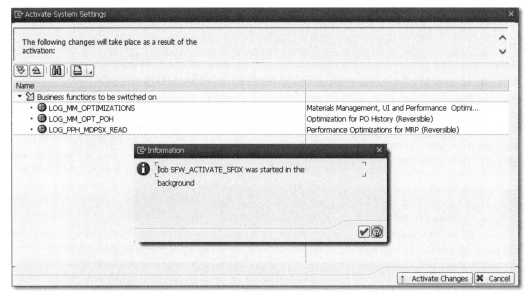

Figure 12.8 Activating Changes

5. Validate that the background job completes without error by using Transaction SM37. An example job log is shown in Figure 12.9.

Job Log Entries for SFW_ACTIVATE_SFOX / 21581600

Job log overview for job: SFW_ACTIVATE_SFOX / 21581600

Date	Time	Message text
08/16/2015	21:58:25	BW processing for Switch : Global time stamp was set to 20,150,817,035,825
08/16/2015	21:58:25	BW processing for Switch : Global time stamp was set to 20,150,817,035,825
08/16/2015	21:58:25	BW processing for Switch MM_SFWS_OPTIMIZATION: Global time stamp was set to 20,150,817,035,825
08/16/2015	21:58:25	BW processing for Switch MM_SFWS_OPT_POH: Global time stamp was set to 20,150,817,035,825
08/16/2015	21:58:25	BW processing for Switch PPH_MDPSX_READ_OPT: Global time stamp was set to 20,150,817,035,825
08/16/2015	21:58:25	Call start of BAdI SFW_SWITCH_CHANGED
08/16/2015	21:58:25	Call end of BAdI SFW_SWITCH_CHANGED (durations: 0 sec.)
08/16/2015	21:58:25	End of Switch Framework Activation (Duration: 9 s).
08/16/2015	21:58:25	Job finished

Figure 12.9 Confirmation That the Activation Job Completed Sucessfully

Some of the most common transactions impacted by enabling the functions listed previously are given in the following list. Accessing the documentation link in Transaction SFW5 for each business function will provide more information.

- LOG_MM_OPTIMIZATIONS
  - Transaction MI20
  - Transaction MI24
  - Transaction MB5B
  - Transaction MB90
- LOG_PPH_MDPSX_READ
  - Transaction MD01N
  - Transaction MD02
  - Transaction MD03
  - Transaction MD04
  - Transaction MD07
  - Transaction MD44, MD47
  - Transaction CO46
  - Transaction MF50
- LOG_MM_OPT_POH
  - Transaction ME2N
  - Transaction ME2L
  - Transaction ME2M
  - Transaction ME2K

> **Note:** [«]
>
> MRP is significantly enhanced with the LOG_PPH_MDPSX_READ business function. When searching SAP Help or the SAP Community Network to find more information, search for MRP Live. Here's a great blog on some of the new MRP functionality and speed improvements:
>
> *http://scn.sap.com/community/erp/manufacturing-pp/blog/2015/03/15/mrp-on-hana-whats-new*

12.2.3 Sales and Distribution

In the area of Sales and Distribution (SD), you have a handful of out-of-the-box, documented improvements. A majority of the enhancements are delivered in one business function that requires activation to be used. Here again, you have a business function that provides more performance improvements than business process changes. We recommend activating it as part of the SAP Business Suite on SAP HANA migration project to implement performance improvements with the database change. Let's review some of the improvements out of the box:

- Transactions V.00, V.02, V.03, V.04, V.05, V.06: Incomplete Sales Docs, Orders, Inquiries, Quotes, Schedule Agreements, and Contracts
- Transaction VA15: List of Inquiries
- Transaction VA25: List of Quotations
- Transaction VA45: List of Contracts
- Transaction VA05 – List of Sales Orders

The single business function we recommend activating is LOG_SD_REPORT_OPT (Sales and Distribution Optimization of Lists). It provides enhancements to the Sales, Credit, and Billing modules within Sales and Distribution (SD). You don't need to be running all three to activate. The process to activate is the same as we defined in Section 12.2.2—using the Switch Framework with Transaction SFW5. Here are some of the transactions that are changed or improved with the business function activation:

- Transaction VKM1 through Transaction VKM5: Blocked SD Documents, Released SD Documents, Sales Documents, SD Documents, and Deliveries
- Transaction VF05: List of Billing Documents
- Transaction V23: SD Documents with Billing Block
- Transaction VA05: List of Sales Documents
- Transaction VF31: Output from Billing Documents

[»]   **Note:**

Keep in mind this is only a subset of improvements with SAP ERP EHP 7 on SAP HANA. See SAP Note 1761546 – SAP ERP Powered by SAP HANA: Optimizations, and open the PDF attached to the SAP Note to see all enhancements by functional area.

12.3   Enhancement Discovery

The enhancement package concept is actually very innovative in how it enables customers to selectively activate enhancements and how they are installed using a similar process to patches to reduce downtime when compared to a major version upgrade. The downside of the enhancement package concept is that you're never forced to use the enhancements; therefore, you never get to see the benefits. We talk to customers all around the world who put little effort in discovering what enhancements are available to their organization. Hopefully, the move to SAP Business Suite on SAP HANA can act as a catalyst for further innovation and adoption of enhancements from SAP. One roadblock to using enhancement packages is knowing what's available to use. With more than 1000+ enhancements, it can be overwhelming. We recommend using SAP's online Innovation Discovery Tool. This browser tool is based on the data your SAP Solution Manager system shares with SAP. It then enables you to explore new capabilities specific to your release and the functionality you've implemented. To use the tool, follow these steps:

1. Open a web browser, and navigate to *https://apps.support.sap.com/innovation-discovery.*

2. Log on with your SAP SUSER and password.

3. Click the SYSTEMS button, and select the system you want to analyze for available enhancements. After you select a system, the application tiles display information about enhancement opportunities as shown in Figure 12.10.

4. The following application tiles provide detailed information:

   ▶ SAP FIORI: Describes the SAP Fiori applications available to your organization based on the system data provided to SAP. This should reflect your newly migrated SAP Business Suite on SAP HANA system.

   ▶ INNOVATIONS: Describes new functionality delivered with the ENHANCEMENT Package installed or new functionality delivered via ABAP add-ons.

   ▶ TECHNOLOGY: Summarizes new technical capabilities delivered with the product version of the system you selected. For example, if you're running the latest version of the SAP Fiori components for SAP Gateway, you'll see the enhancement for offline data processing in SAP Fiori.

   ▶ APPLICATIONS: Highlights software licenses you own and new enhancements to those solutions.

The Innovation Discovery application provided by SAP is meant to highlight the opportunities your organization has available to implement. Within each tile, you can filter by enhancement type and specifically select the NO ADDITIONAL LICENSES filter that enables your team members to quickly find enhancements you already own that are applicable. By providing more information on the innovation provided by SAP, you can create some awareness and potentially drive some requirements to begin using this new functionality.

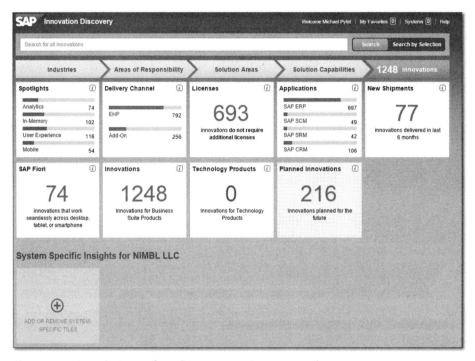

Figure 12.10 Example Output from the Innovation Discovery Application

12.4 Summary

Our goal in this chapter was to highlight some key areas that offer performance optimizations for SAP ERP either out of the box or after activating some simple business functions. There are already numerous enhancements to SAP ERP that you can install as ABAP add-ons. The enhancements we described in this chapter already exist in your system. All you need to do is enable them, and potentially provide end-user access to any new transactions. It's also possible that your organization has customer (Z) versions of the enhanced transactions that might negate your custom version of the transaction. When looking at the enhancements, you also need to keep in mind your system usage. In Chapter 2, you used the Solution Documentation Assistant (SDA) to retrieve a list of transactions used by your users over a time period. That same list could be used as a cross-reference to the transactions covered here to determine if your organization could start using some enhancements today.

All too often, we see environments in which the customer has spent the effort to patch and install enhancement packages but hasn't spent any effort determining which enhancements to activate. This essentially means they're working really hard but never get to enjoy the fruits of their labor. Enhancements are provided as part of a customer's Maintenance Agreements. You drive more value out of your SAP investment by using these enhancements. By using the Business Process Change Analyzer (BPCA) described in Chapter 8, Section 8.2, and the business functions we discussed in this chapter, you can measure the impact of activating these business functions. SAP has helped you remove the risk (fear) of not knowing what will change when activating an enhancement. After all, if you're not using the enhancements delivered within the enhancement packages, you're essentially running the same version of SAP ERP that was available off the shelf eight years ago.

SAP S/4HANA Finance is the next generation SAP Business Suite. It provides a simplification of table structures, a better user experience, and advanced reporting that blends transactional and analytical data. SAP S/4HANA Finance has the ability to change how users work and interact with the SAP Business Suite

13 SAP S/4HANA Finance

For many, the next step after completing the SAP Business Suite on SAP HANA migration is the technical installation of SAP S/4HANA Finance, which essentially brings your environment into the realm of SAP S/4HANA. Without a doubt, SAP S/4HANA Finance is true innovation. In essence, it's the simplification of the tables and functions that support SAP ERP Financials (FI), and it could only happen with an in-memory database such as SAP HANA. Although SAP S/4HANA Finance may initially sound like a single product with one installed component, in this chapter, you'll find out it's much more than that and requires multiple components to be installed. We'll walk through the Maintenance Planner transaction to get SAP S/4HANA Finance installed with the Software Update Manager (SUM) and all of the preparation steps.

SAP S/4HANA Finance not only includes updates to tables in the database but a simplification of the user interface (UI) to common financial transactions. You'll have the opportunity to leverage SAP Smart Business Applications for SAP S/4HANA Finance, which are SAP Fiori applications that blend analytical and transactional data into one UI. This is truly revolutionary because prior to this innovation, a FI super user might have multiple login screens to SAP ERP and then another to SAP Business Explorer (BEx) for analytical reports. SAP S/4HANA Finance pushes this content together using SAP Fiori, so it's accessed via web browser—another great enhancement freeing IT departments from SAP GUI and frontend client maintenance. In this chapter, we'll talk about the architecture behind these new capabilities so you're informed as to what's required.

This chapter isn't intended to be your functional enhancement guide to all things SAP S/4HANA Finance, but we'll cover the details needed so your team can get started with SAP S/4HANA Finance in a sandbox environment.

[»] **Note**

For detailed information on the capabilities and new functionality, check out *SAP Simple Finance: An Introduction* (SAP PRESS, 2015).

In this chapter, you'll discover that SAP S/4HANA Finance has a similar implementation path to that of functions within an enhancement package. It's installed first and then activated with a defined migration path. This migration to full use of SAP S/4HANA Finance might run several weeks because it needs to be coordinated with financial period-end activities. Let's review the architecture and then dive into the technical details of SAP S/4HANA Finance.

13.1 Why SAP S/4HANA Finance?

This question will be answered differently based on who you ask. We see tremendous value in the simplification of tables within SAP S/4HANA Finance, reduction in storage, increased analytical capabilities, and an awesome new HTML5-based UI with SAP Fiori. If you ask a controller about the value of SAP S/4HANA Finance, he might talk about its capability to support real-time profitability analysis; the reduction in errors among the General Ledger (GL), Controlling (CO), and Asset Accounting (AA); and how it provides transparency into business transactions with a simplified UI in SAP Fiori. With SAP S/4HANA Finance, we'll move to the Universal Journal, which is at the core of the enhancements delivered by SAP. An example of this simplification is shown in Figure 13.1.

Why couldn't SAP do this on any database? The Universal Journal (technical name: ACDOCA) has hundreds of fields and, without columnar storage, would be a massive table that any application would have difficulty managing. At present, it only runs with SAP Business Suite on SAP HANA. So what happens to all the tables it replaces? SAP created what are called *compatibility views*, which redirect any request to a specific table to the respective data in the Universal Journal (shown in Figure 13.2). Therefore, your custom applications that make direct calls to table FAGLFLEXA will still work after the migration to SAP S/4HANA Finance. (Table FAGLFLEXA is just one of the many tables that no longer exist when migrating to SAP S/4HANA Finance.)

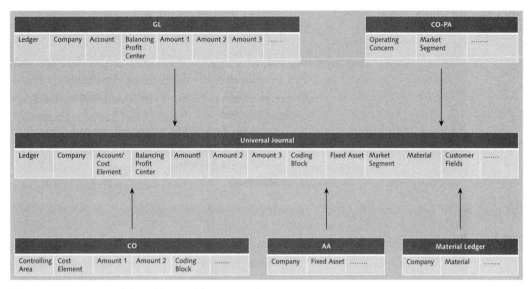

Figure 13.1 Overview of the Table Simplifications with SAP S/4HANA Finance

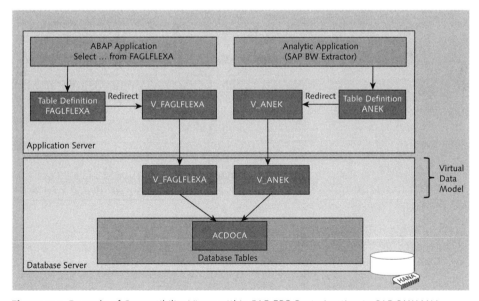

Figure 13.2 Example of Compatibility Views within SAP ERP Postmigration to SAP S/4HANA Finance

13.2 Requirements

In this section, we're going to break down the requirements for SAP S/4HANA Finance into functional and technical requirements. The installation of SAP S/4HANA Finance isn't complex, but it does have a few more moving parts because SAP S/4HANA Finance is comprised of SAP Accounting powered and SAP Cash Management, both powered by SAP HANA. It requires content in ABAP as well as the SAP Gateway and SAP HANA Live (see Chapter 14 for more on SAP HANA Live). Let's make a high-level review of the installation process, which is one component of your roadmap to SAP S/4HANA Finance (shown in Figure 13.3.)

[»] **Note**

Need to know more about the functional enhancements with SAP S/4HANA Finance? Check out the following SAP Notes:

▸ SAP Note 1946054 – SAP Simple Finance, On-Premise Edition: Transaction Codes and Programs – Comparison to EHP 7 for SAP ERP 6.0

▸ SAP Note 2119188 – Release Scope Information: SAP Simple Finance, On-Premise Edition 1503

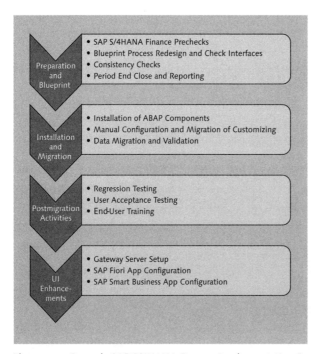

Figure 13.3 Example SAP S/4HANA Finance Implementation Process Overview

Again, this is meant to be a technical installation guide of SAP S/4HANA Finance. The steps here don't outline the transactional and reporting changes made by the move to SAP S/4HANA Finance.

13.2.1 Functional Requirements

In Section 13.2.2, we'll talk about the technical components and versions needed to install SAP S/4HANA Finance. In this section, we want to give an overview of the functional tasks to be completed by the business analysts (or FI configuration resource) prior to the technical team performing any installations. It's important to note that you can migrate to SAP S/4HANA Finance from any version of GL. You can migrate from any combination of classic GL, new GL, old AA, or new AA to SAP S/4HANA Finance in one step using the migration tools provided by SAP, which are accessed via the Implementation Master Guide (IMG) using Transaction SPRO. The following is a list of tasks to be completed by the functional teams before the technical teams can move forward with the technical installation (e.g., within a sandbox):

1. Implement Report RASFIN_MIGR_PRECHECK from SAP Note 1939592, and test whether the necessary prerequisites for new AA have been fulfilled.

2. Check if new asset depreciation is active. If not, then you need to activate.

3. Implement Program ZFINS_MIG_PRECHCK_CUST_SETTNGS from SAP Note 2129306 to check the consistency of settings between GL and CO.

4. Check consistency between documents and reports using Report RFINDEX_NACC.

5. Reconcile AA with GL using Transaction ABST and Transaction ABST2.

6. Reconcile Accounts Payable/Accounts Receivable (AP/AR) subledgers within GL using Report SAPF190 or Report FAGLF03.

7. Reconcile the Materials Ledger (ML) with GL using Report RM07MBST and Report RM07MMFI.

8. Reconcile ledgers within the new GL (Transaction GCAC).

9. Execute Report RAPERB2000 and Report RAPOST2000 to close AA (no asset postings afterwards).

10. Close previous years in AA (only current year open).

11. Process or delete all held documents.

12. Initialize valuation differences from currency valuation (known from the new GL migration).

13. Ensure all balances have carried forward in the GL and subledgers.

After those tasks are complete, your team might want to execute some standard reporting for validation purposes after the migration. Some example reports follow:

▸ Financial statement

▸ Asset history sheet

▸ Customer and vendor sales list and open item lists

▸ Totals for cost centers

Lastly, your team will want to ensure any delta extracts related to FI for the SAP Business Warehouse (SAP BW) system have been processed completely. As part of the technical upgrade and installation activities, the technical team will hold all background jobs and interfaces.

[»]

> **Note**
>
> For the most up-to-date SAP S/4HANA Finance preparation tasks, go to *http://help.sap.com/sfin200* Once there, choose INSTALLATION AND UPGRADE INFORMATION • MIGRATION GUIDE • <LANGUAGE> • PRIOR TO INSTALLING.

13.2.2 Technical Prerequisites

First let's run through some important notes you'll need to read prior to the installation. Ideally, your functional team is completing the preparation tasks while the technical team ensures that you have everything required to perform the installation.

▸ **SAP Note 2103558**
SAP Simple Finance, On-Premise Edition: Compatible Add-Ons

▸ **SAP Note 2117481**
Release Information Note: SAP Simple Finance, On-Premise Edition 1503

> ▹ This note is very important because it lists the prerequisite notes to be installed prior to the technical installation via SUM.

> ▹ It also lists the SAP Notes to be installed prior to the migration to SAP S/4HANA Finance.

▶ **SAP Note 2100133**

SAP Simple Finance On-Premise Edition: Compatible Partner Products

▶ **SAP Note 2035994**

SAP Simple Finance, On-Premise Edition: Installation with Components/Products Not Yet Released for SAP Simple Finance

As a starting release for SAP ERP 6 EHP 7 on SAP HANA, you need the minimum component versions indicated in Table 13.1. Ideally, when you executed the SAP Business Suite on SAP HANA migration using the SUM Database Migration Option (DMO), you upgraded to the component versions indicated in Table 13.1 or greater.

Component	Minimum Source Release	Support Package
SAP_BASIS	740	SAPKB74010
SAP_BW	740	SAPKW74010
SAP_APPL	617	SAPKH61707
EA-APPL	617	SAPK-61707INEAAPPL
EA-FINSERV	617	SAPK-61707INEAFINSRV

Table 13.1 Component Versions Included in SAP ERP 6 EHP 7 Support Package Stack 8+

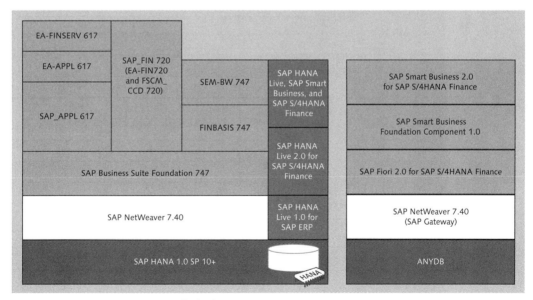

Figure 13.4 Components to Be Installed When Migrating to SAP S/4HANA Finance

In Figure 13.4, you can see the specific component versions that your SAP ERP system will have installed after you complete the SAP S/4HANA Finance installation using the SUM. This is the same installation tool you used to perform the database migration, so the SUM preparation steps defined in Chapter 5 apply here. You need to download the latest version of SUM and the SAP Host Agent to use the Software Logistics Common UI (SL Common UI) for the update to SAP S/4HANA Finance. Let's run through some of tools you'll use during this installation:

▸ **Maintenance Optimizer or Maintenance Planner**
You need to ensure that the system information in the Landscape Management Database (LMDB) is correct and has been synchronized to the SAP Support Portal.

[»] | Note

Maintenance Optimizer was introduced in SAP Solution Manager 7.0, and, as of July 2015, it can be replaced by the Maintenance Planner. Both tools are available for use as of August 2015.

▸ **Software Update Manager**
Maintenance Planner/Optimizer will provide a *stack.xml* file for the installation. SUM will read that file and perform the update/upgrade to the required components.

▸ **SAP HANA client**
You need the SAP HANA Application Lifecycle Management (HALM) application to install the SAP HANA Live content.

[»] | Note

What's in a name? SAP Simple Finance 2.0 was technically named SAP Simple Finance on-premise 1503 as of Q2 2015. You won't find a technical reference to SAP Simple Finance 2.0 when performing the installation. The Support Package Stacks (SP Stacks) are also named unlike other SAP ABAP add-ons. A SAP Simple Finance 1503 support package is comprised of four digits. The version discussed in this book was SAP Simple Finance 1503 Support Package 1508. The technical name for SAP Simple Finance 1503 was SAP SFINANCIALS 1503.

13.3 Installation

By now, you've prepared the system both technically and functionally. We'll start with the Maintenance Planner for this task because it's not as easy as selecting an add-on installation. After you have the *stack.xml* and download basket, you'll start SUM to complete the installation.

13.3.1 Maintenance Planner

In this section we will focus on the execution of the Maintenance Planner to define the target stack and your download basket.

1. Log on to the Maintenance Planner with a valid SUSER and password via *https://apps.support.sap.com/sap/support/mp*.
2. Click the EXPLORE SYSTEMS tile.
3. Select the SYSTEM ID, which is the target for the SAP S/4HANA Finance installation (see Figure 13.5).

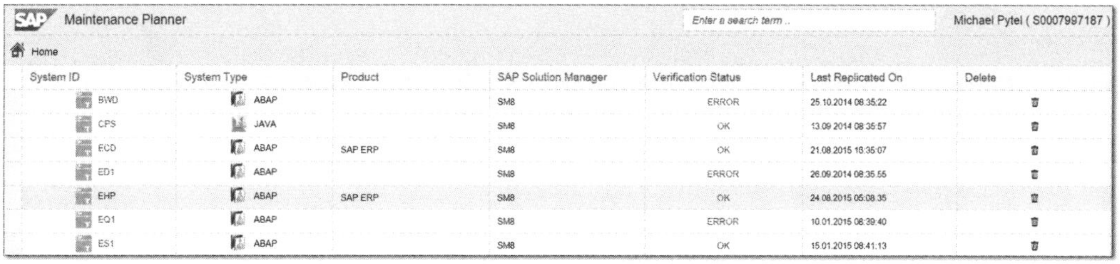

Maintenance Planner
Enter a search term ..
Michael Pytel (S0007997187)
Home
System ID | System Type | Product | SAP Solution Manager | Verification Status | Last Replicated On | Delete
BWD | ABAP | | SM8 | ERROR | 25.10.2014 08:35:22
CPS | JAVA | | SM8 | OK | 13.09.2014 08:35:57
ECD | ABAP | SAP ERP | SM8 | OK | 21.08.2015 16:35:07
ED1 | ABAP | | SM8 | ERROR | 26.09.2014 08:35:55
EHP | ABAP | SAP ERP | SM8 | OK | 24.08.2015 05:08:35
EQ1 | ABAP | | SM8 | ERROR | 10.01.2015 08:39:40
ES1 | ABAP | | SM8 | OK | 15.01.2015 08:41:13

Figure 13.5 Selecting a System in Maintenance Planner

4. Click the PLAN button to begin identifying the target installation (see Figure 13.6).
   - If your VERIFY button is red, you must click it first to verify the installed components.
   - After the verification is complete, you can then click the PLAN button.

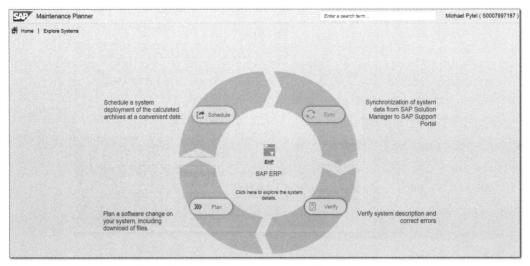

Figure 13.6 Defining the SAP S/4HANA Finance Installation

5. Click the INSTALL OR MAINTAIN AN ADD-ON button (see Figure 13.7).

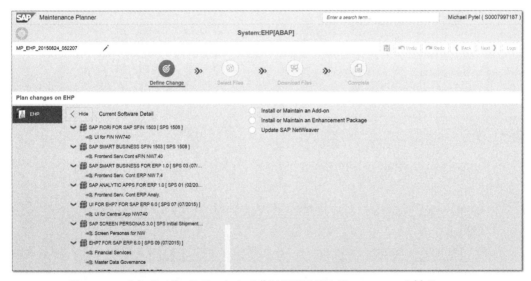

Figure 13.7 Selecting the Option to Install SAP S/4HANA Finance as an Add-On

6. Scroll down in the list of components, select SAP SFINANCIALS 1503, and then the latest target SP Stack (see Figure 13.8).

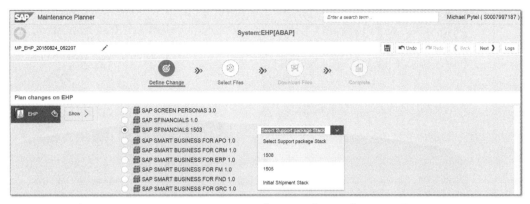

Figure 13.8 Selecting SAP S/4HANA Finance 1503 as the Target for Installation

7. If you don't see SAP SFINANCIALS 1503, follow these steps.

  ▸ Return to the DEFINE CHANGE step, and select INSTALL OR MAINTAIN ENHANCEMENT PACKAGE.

  ▸ Choose your EHP target stack, and check the box for APPLICATIONS FOR FIN 700.

  ▸ Select CONFIRM, and then select INSTALL OR MAINTAIN ADD-ON where you'll select SAP SFINANCIALS 1503.

8. When prompted, select the CENTRAL APPLICATIONS (FIN) checkbox, and click the CONFIRM SELECTION button (see Figure 13.9).

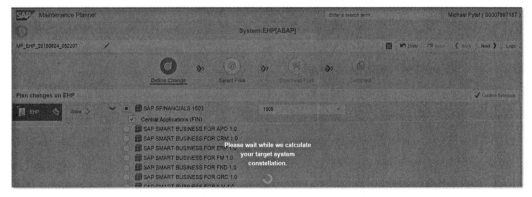

Figure 13.9 Confirming the Selection Defines the Target Stack to Download

9. On the left-hand side of the screen, you should see a green notepad icon with the plus sign. This confirms that SAP Simple Finance 1503 has been identified as the target (see Figure 13.10).

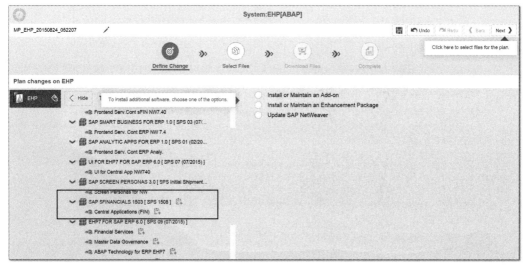

Figure 13.10 Confirmation of the Target Component to Be Installed

10. On the SELECT FILES step, choose your application server operating system (OS) version and kernel patch (see Figure 13.11).

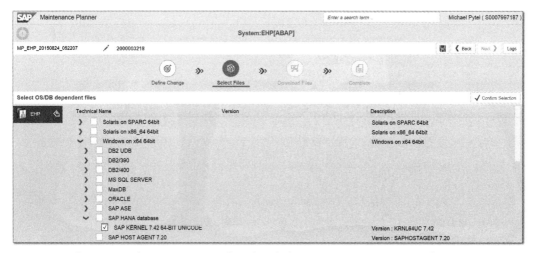

Figure 13.11 Choosing Your Kernel Stack with the SAP S/4HANA Finance Stack

11. On the next screen within the Select Files step, open the Select Stack Independent Files item.

   ▹ If you don't see SAP FINANCIALS 1503 with the ABAP components listed like those in Figure 13.12, you have an error calculating your stack.

   ▹ Return to the Define Change step, and select Install or Maintain Enhancement Package.

   ▹ Choose your EHP target stack, and check the box for Applications for FIN 700.

   ▹ Select Confirm, and then select Install or Maintain Add-on where you'll select SAP SFINANCIALS.

Note [«]

In certain customer environments, we had to select the add-on for SAP SFINANCIALS 1.0 first in addition to SAP SFINANCIALS 1503.

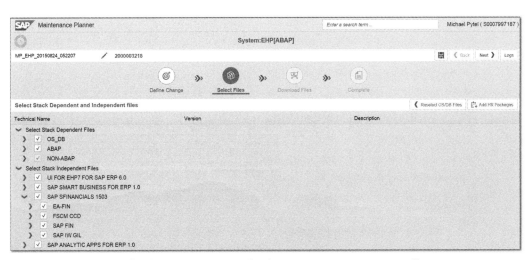

Figure 13.12 Correctly Defined ABAP Components for the SAP S/4HANA Finance Installation

12. Click Next, and then click the Push to Download Basket button (see Figure 13.13).

13. Click the Download Stack XML button, and save to your local machine.

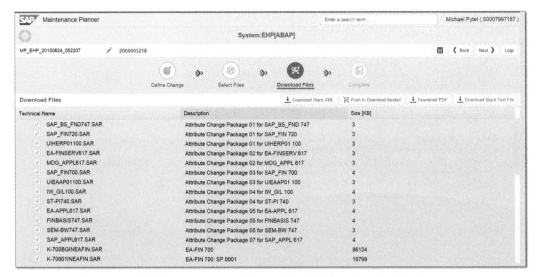

Figure 13.13 SAP S/4HANA Finance Objects Placed in Your Download Basket

14. Download the necessary files to the primary application server (PAS), and save the *stack.xml* to the same folder.

Next, you'll perform the SAP Simple Finance 1503 installation.

13.3.2 Running Software Update Manager

At this point, you'll use the SAP Download Manager to download the necessary files on the PAS. By this time, you've already downloaded, installed, and prepared SUM as described in Chapter 5.

Follow these steps to install SAP S/4HANA Finance:

1. Connect to *http://<hostname>:1128/lmsl/sumabap/<SID>/doc/sluigui/*, and log on as the <SID>ADM account for the PAS.

2. Enter the path to the *stack.xml* file, and click NEXT (see Figure 13.14).

3. When prompted, enter the passwords for the system accounts listed.

4. Next the system checks for the latest SPAM version available. If you already have the latest installed, click SKIP SPAM UPDATE (see Figure 13.15).

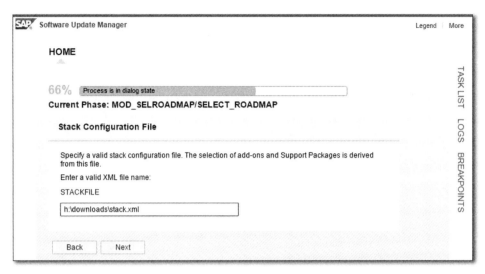

Figure 13.14 Entering the Path to stack.xml for the SAP S/4HANA Finance Installation

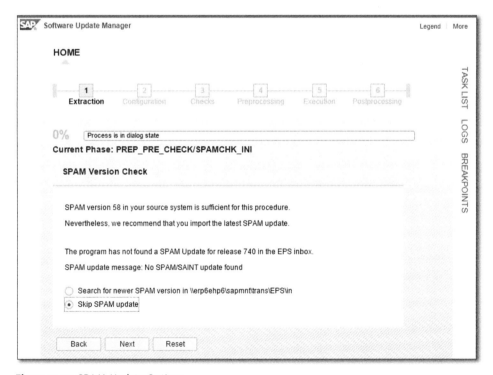

Figure 13.15 SPAM Update Options

5. You might be prompted with the screen shown in Figure 13.16 if additional schemas are found by the installer.

6. In this step, it's checking for Multiple Components One Database (MCOD). The two schemas listed are related to SAP HANA system administrators. Confirm the messages, and click NEXT.

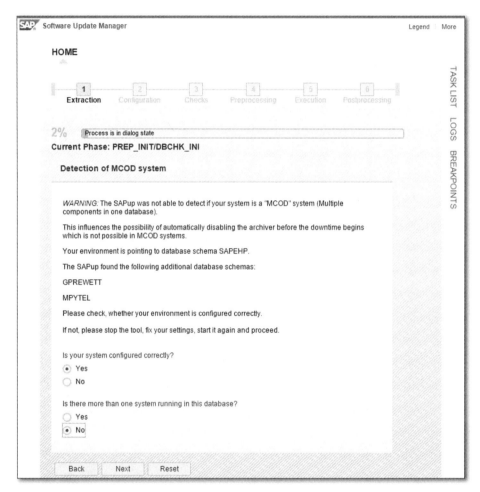

Figure 13.16 Software Update Manager Checking for Multiple Components Installed in the Database

7. This should be the end of the EXTRACTION step. Confirm your *CHECKS.TXT* file by clicking the *LOGS* button.

8. If the check file is free from errors, click NEXT to start the CONFIGURATION step.

9. On the next screen, choose what mode you'll use for the installation. Earlier in the book, we covered Standard and Advanced.

   ▶ In this sandbox example scenario, we'll use SINGLE SYSTEM. It has the shortest duration but the longest downtime.

   ▶ Select STANDARD if want to reduce the system downtime.

10. Click NEXT (see Figure 13.17).

Figure 13.17 Choosing Your Installation Mode

11. In the PROCESS CONFIGURATION step, you input the number of processes to be used during the procedure.

12. Enter the values based on your system, and click NEXT. The values in Figure 13.18 are based on a four-core application server with 32GB memory.

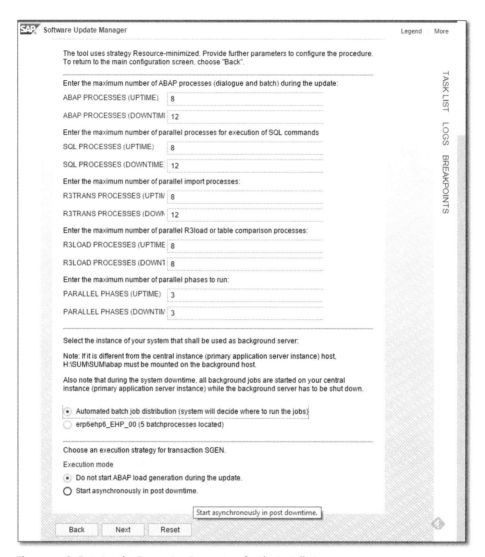

Figure 13.18 Entering the Processing Parameters for the Installation

13. Validate the add-on versions in the next step, and click NEXT (see Figure 13.19).

14. Next you need to validate the target versions for the components being installed (see Figure 13.20). In this example scenario, we validate that SAP_FIN will move to RELEASE 720 for SAP S/4HANA Finance.

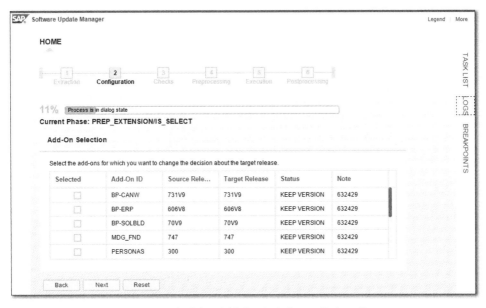

Figure 13.19 Opportunity to Upgrade Other Add-Ons in Software Update Manager

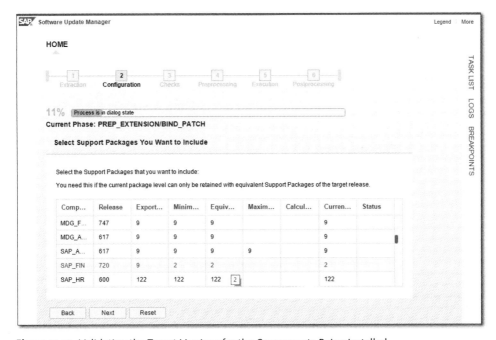

Figure 13.20 Validating the Target Versions for the Components Being Installed

15. Click NEXT here and on the following two screens. When prompted to, include customer transports.

16. At the end of the CONFIGURATION step, validate your *CHECKS.TXT* file to verify that no errors exist, and click NEXT.

17. At the start of the CHECKS step, you're prompted to run the command /n/ASU/ UPGRADE within SAP ERP.

18. Run the transactions, return to the screen shown in Figure 13.21, and click NEXT.

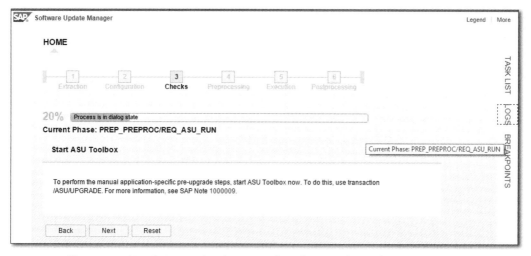

Figure 13.21 List of Notes and Tasks to Complete Shown in the Application-Specific Upgrade Toolbox

19. After executing the ASU Toolbox and clicking NEXT, you'll enter the PREPROCESSING step.

20. On the screen shown in Figure 13.22, click NEXT to lock changes to the repository. No transports can be created after this step.

21. Next you're prompted to have all users log off the system and to hold all background jobs (see Figure 13.23).

   ▸ Remember, you can use ABAP Program BTCTRNS1 to hold all scheduled background jobs.

   ▸ The ABAP Program BTCTRNS2 will release any jobs held by the program.

Figure 13.22 Locking the System So No Changes Can Be Made

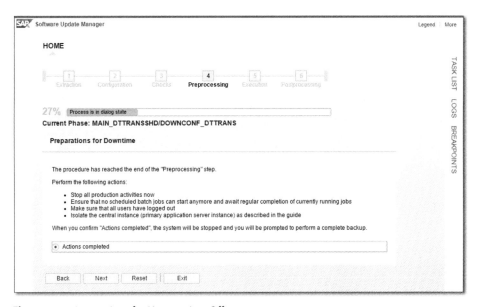

Figure 13.23 Instructions for Users to Log Off

22. After clicking NEXT, you'll get a prompt to enter the EXECUTION step as shown in Figure 13.24. Validate that the *CHECKS.TXT* file doesn't contain errors, and click NEXT.

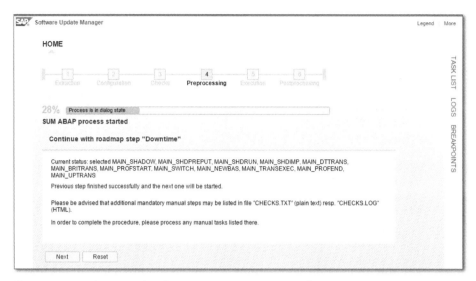

Figure 13.24 Confirmation That the Preprocessing Step Is Complete

23. When prompted, take a backup of your SAP HANA database. Then return to SUM, and click NEXT. This will start the downtime portion of the installation. When processing, you should see a screen like the one shown in Figure 13.25.

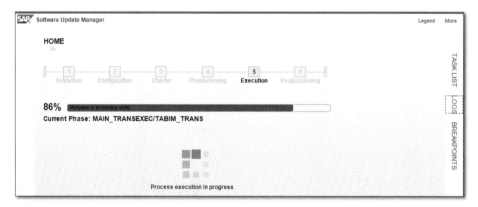

Figure 13.25 Example Screen from the Execution Step for the SAP S/4HANA Finance Installation

24. When the EXECUTION step completes, you'll be prompted to click NEXT (see Figure 13.26).

25. You'll want to take another backup at this point and return the database to NORMAL log mode if you switched to OVERWRITE.

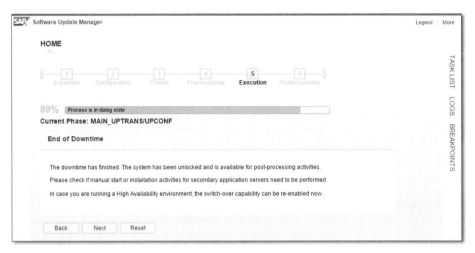

Figure 13.26 Confirmation of the End of System Downtime

26. Review the *CHECKS.TXT* file for errors (see Figure 13.27).

Figure 13.27 Clean CHECKS.TXT File with No Errors or Warnings

27. After the installation is completed within SUM, you enter the CLEANUP step and click NEXT (see Figure 13.28).

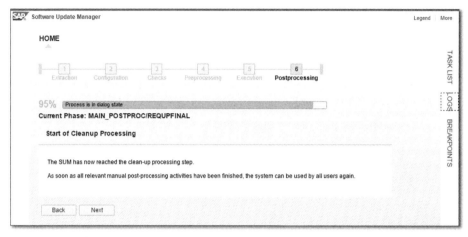

Figure 13.28 Software Update Manager Cleaning Up the File System Used during the Install

28. Lastly, you need to validate that SAP Simple Finance 1503 was actually installed.

29. Log on to the SAP ERP system, and click SYSTEM • STATUS from the toolbar. Then select the COMPONENT UNDER PRODUCT VERSION button.

30. Click the INSTALLED PRODUCT VERSIONS tab to verify that SAP SFINANCIALS 1503 is listed (see Figure 13.29).

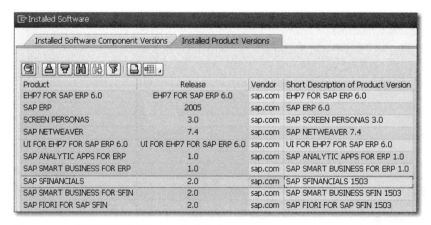

Figure 13.29 SAP S/4HANA Finance Installed

31. You can perform another verification by navigating to the IMG using Transaction /NSPRO.

32. You should immediately see an IMG menu for MIGRATION FROM SAP ERP TO SAP ACCOUNTING POWERED BY SAP HANA (see Figure 13.30).

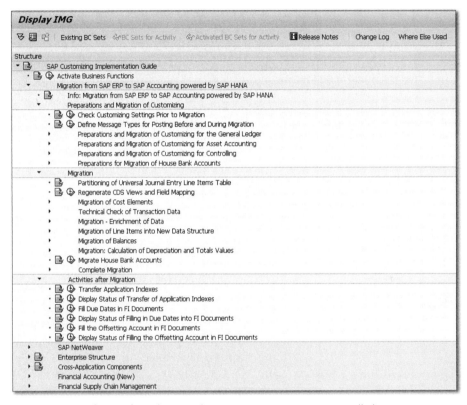

Figure 13.30 Verification from the IMG That SAP S/4HANA Finance Is Installed

13.4 Summary

In this chapter, we took a very tactical approach to the installation of SAP S/4HANA Finance. This is only the first step in the migration to SAP S/4HANA Finance. In the next chapter, we talk about the SAP HANA Live installation. For a full deployment of SAP S/4HANA Finance, you'll need to install the SAP HANA Live components: SAP HANA Live 2.0 for SAP S/4HANA Finance and SAP HANA Live 1.0 for SAP ERP. Lastly, you'll need to deploy the SAP Fiori components: SAP Fiori 2.0 for

SAP S/4HANA Finance and SAP Smart Business 2.0 for SAP S/4HANA Finance. The installation of SAP Fiori application components is well documented and follows a similar process to installing ABAP add-ons for SAP NetWeaver 7.4.

At this point in the book, you've completed multiple migrations to SAP Business Suite on SAP HANA and are well on your way to a go-live. SAP S/4HANA Finance introduces technical changes to your landscape by requiring additional SAP NetWeaver instances to support SAP Gateway and the new SAP Fiori ABAP add-ons. SAP S/4HANA Finance is a new UI for both transactional and analytical FI users. This installation will no doubt be completed in a sandbox environment and unit tested before being applied to development. SAP S/4HANA Finance will change your release level of SAP_FIN prior to the activation of SAP S/4HANA Finance, so you need to be aware of the ABAP versions when installing in a development system that also provides production support. The installation and configuration of SAP S/4HANA Finance will require a project landscape and/or a code freeze to ensure a consistent support and project landscape.

[»] **Note**

For the latest information on the migration to SAP S/4HANA Finance, head over to the SAP Help site, which defines each migration step in detail. The online guide will act as a complement to the IMG activities. Go to *http://help.sap.com/sfin200*, and choose INSTALLATION AND UPGRADE INFORMATION • MIGRATION GUIDE.

SAP HANA Live bridges the gap between transactional and analytical reporting. It enables you to remove the traditional extract-and-store data warehouse strategy. SAP HANA Live is real innovation for SAP Business Suite customers.

14 SAP HANA Live

SAP HANA Live for the SAP Business Suite, specifically SAP ERP, is another licensed product (although it was bundled with SAP Business Suite on SAP HANA licenses in 2014 and 2015) that will likely later become part of your landscape if it wasn't also included in the scope of your migration project. Essentially, SAP HANA Live contains predefined data models for the tables supporting SAP ERP in SAP HANA. What is commonly referred to as SAP HANA Live Content is installed at the database level within SAP HANA and then can be accessed by both ABAP applications and external analytic toolsets. Because your data now resides in memory, you'll start to see a blend of online analytical processing (OLAP) and online transaction processing (OLTP) transactions in a single database. When you hear about real-time access to business data, SAP HANA Live is one tool that supports this goal.

SAP HANA Live provides views at the SAP HANA database layer, which SAP describes as the future of SAP analytic development. There are multiple view types—SAP Query Views, Value Help Views, Reuse Views, and Private Views—and they all can have hierarchal relationship to one another. This isn't a replacement for SAP Business Warehouse (SAP BW), but it's another capability your organization will have access to after you complete your SAP Business Suite on SAP HANA migration.

In this chapter, we'll not only step through the SAP HANA Live installation but also talk about two other tools. SAP HANA Live Explorer will help your business users find views over the data they want to access. And SAP HANA Live Authorization Assistant will help your security team efficiently grant access to SAP HANA

Live views. The SAP HANA Live views are SAP-defined virtual data models that can provide data to a variety of analytical user interfaces (UIs): SAP Business-Objects, SAP Lumira, SAP Fiori, and so on.

SAP HANA Live content is similar to the predefined extractors, cubes, and queries delivered within SAP BW. The content is created by SAP, and it can be installed and selectively activated. With SAP HANA Live, a query view that brings together customer orders, customer returns, and customer payment information into a single SAP HANA view can then be exposed to an analytical application. Using the traditional data warehouse strategy, this could require developing extract programs, storing data in a data warehouse, and then writing reports. With SAP HANA Live, you create a virtual data model for the data you need and then expose it to some UI. You avoid the extract process and duplicate storage of data. Figure 14.1 shows an overview of SAP HANA Live Architecture.

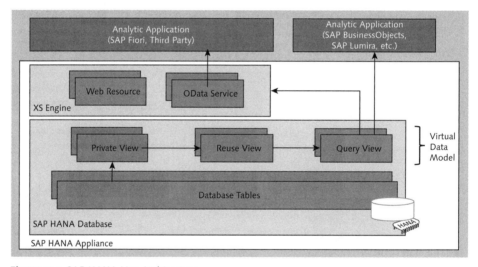

Figure 14.1 SAP HANA Live Architecture

One thing most customers don't realize is that SAP HANA Platform and SAP HANA Live are open. The content with SAP HANA Live is accessible via SQL or multidimensional expressions (MDX). There is no requirement to use a specific application to access the SAP HANA Live content. SAP also enables its customers to model their own SAP HANA Live content. SAP customers can define database views operating directly over the SAP Business Suite on SAP HANA tables, enabling unprecedented access to real-time transactional data. How do you create your own query views or extend the ones provided by SAP? SAP delivers the SAP HANA Live Extension Assistant, which is an Eclipse-based tool. In this chapter, we'll help you get SAP HANA Live installed and show you how to setup the SAP HANA Live Extension Assistant. This step isn't required as part of the SAP Business Suite on SAP HANA migration, but it will help reinforce the value of the migration to SAP Business Suite on SAP HANA.

14.1 Installing SAP HANA Live Content

In this section, we'll walk through installing and activating SAP HANA Live content. When you read the SAP Help HANA Live documentation, you'll find reference to two installation scenarios: integrated and replication. The integrated scenario applies to the use case where the SAP ERP database resides in SAP HANA. The replication scenario applies to those customers who choose to operate SAP HANA as a standalone database and leverage SAP real-time replication to move data between SAP ERP and the SAP HANA Live database. The next obstacle to getting SAP HANA Live installed is deciding what content to install. SAP is continually enhancing SAP HANA Live and creating new content specific to industries, business scenarios, and new products. Following is a sample of the SAP HANA Live content available for SAP ERP as of the first half of 2015:

▸ SAP HANA Live 1.0 for SAP Business Suite foundation component

▸ SAP HANA Live 1.0 for Commodity Management

▸ SAP HANA Live 1.0 for SAP CRM and SAP ERP cross-analytics

▸ SAP HANA Live 1.0 for SAP ERP

▸ SAP HANA Live 1.0 for EHP 4 for SAP ERP

▸ SAP HANA Live 1.0 for EHP 7 for SAP ERP

▸ SAP HANA Live 1.0 for Event Management

▸ SAP HANA Live 1.0 for Event Management and Transportation Management cross-analytics

▸ SAP HANA Live 1.0 for Extended Warehouse Management

▸ SAP HANA Live 1.0 for Financial Close

▸ SAP HANA Live 1.0 for Flexible Real Estate Management

- SAP HANA Live 1.0 for SAP Global Batch Traceability
- SAP HANA Live 1.0 for Insurance
- SAP HANA Live 1.0 for Manufacturing
- SAP HANA Live 1.0 for SAP PLM
- SAP HANA Live 1.0 for Policy Management
- SAP HANA Live 1.0 for Production Revenue Accounting
- SAP HANA Live 1.0 for Reinsurance Management
- SAP HANA Live 1.0 for Retail
- SAP HANA Live 1.0 for Utilities, edition for SAP ERP

[»] | **Note**

Need more information on SAP HANA Live? Check out SAP Note 1778607 – SAP HANA Live for SAP Business Suite. You can also search the Product Availability Matrix (PAM) by visiting *http://support.sap.com/pam* and searching for "SAP HANA Live."

Next, let's install SAP HANA Live 1.0 for SAP ERP.

14.1.1 Prerequisites

Follow these steps to take care of any prerequisites:

1. Check SAP Note 1778607 for the latest release information about SAP HANA Live for the SAP Business Suite. SAP HANA Live content requires EHP 6 or EHP 7 on SAP HANA. In our example scenario, we have EHP 7 installed.

2. Confirm that the following tables are set to column store.

   - DD02L
   - DD02T
   - DD07L
   - DD07T

3. Log on to the development or sandbox SAP ERP on SAP HANA system. Run Transaction SE11, and click Display to validate table DD02L (Figure 14.2).

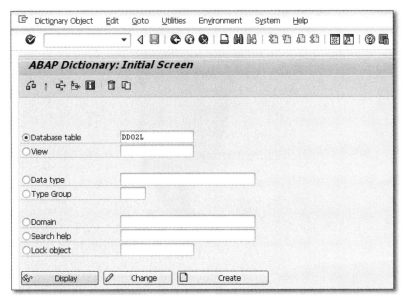

Figure 14.2 Validating the Storage Type

4. Click Goto • Technical Settings (see Figure 14.3).

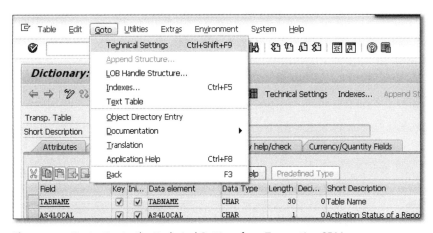

Figure 14.3 Navigating to the Technical Settings from Transaction SE11

5. Click on the DB-Specific Properties tab to validate that the storage type is Column Store (see Figure 14.4).

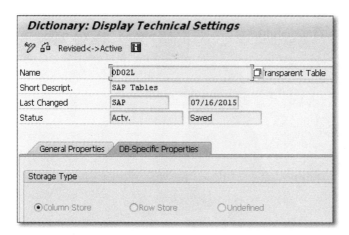

Figure 14.4 Storage Type Correctly Set to Column Store

6. If the table is still set to ROW STORE, you'll need to enter change mode, select the COLUMN STORE button, and then SAVE and ACTIVATE your changes.

7. Repeat the validation steps for the other three tables defined in the previous step.

8. Download the SAP HANA Live for SAP ERP content from the SAP Support Portal. To do so, navigate to *http://support.sap.com/swdc*, and choose INSTALLATIONS AND UPGRADES • BROWSE OUR DOWNLOAD CATALOG • SAP IN-MEMORY (SAP HANA) • SAP HANA ADD-ONS • SAP HANA ANALYTICS FOR ERP • SAP HANA ANALYTICS FOR ERP 1.0 • INSTALLATION (see Figure 14.5).

9. Download the latest file displayed.

10. Download SAP HANA Live Tools 1.0, which provides you with the SAP HANA Live Browser, SAP HANA Live Authorization Assistant, and SAP HANA Live Extensibility Assistant.

11. Navigate to *http://support.sap.com/swdc*, and choose INSTALLATIONS AND UPGRADES • BROWSE OUR DOWNLOAD CATALOG • SAP IN-MEMORY (SAP HANA) • SAP HANA ADD-ONS • SAP HANA CONTENT TOOLS • SAP HANA CONTENT TOOLS 1.0.

12. Download the latest version of the files displayed (see Figure 14.6).

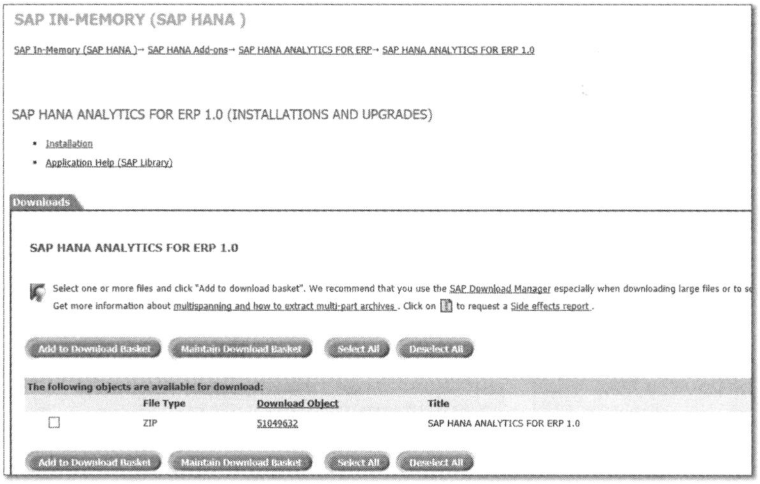

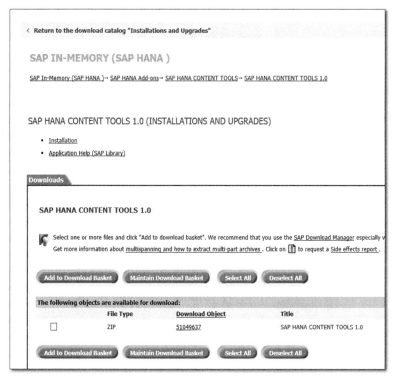

Figure 14.5 Download Path for SAP HANA Live for SAP ERP

Figure 14.6 Downloading the SAP HANA Live Tools for Installation

13. Save the compressed file to your computer, and transfer the file to the SAP HANA database server.

14. Extract the ZIP file on the server to a directory accessible by the <SID>ADM user.

15. Within the extracted directory contents, navigate to the *DATA_UNITS/SAP_ HANA_ANALYTICS_FOR_ERP_1.0* folder, and ensure that you see the *HCOHBAECCXX_0.ZIP* file, as shown in Figure 14.7. (*XX* = current release level.)

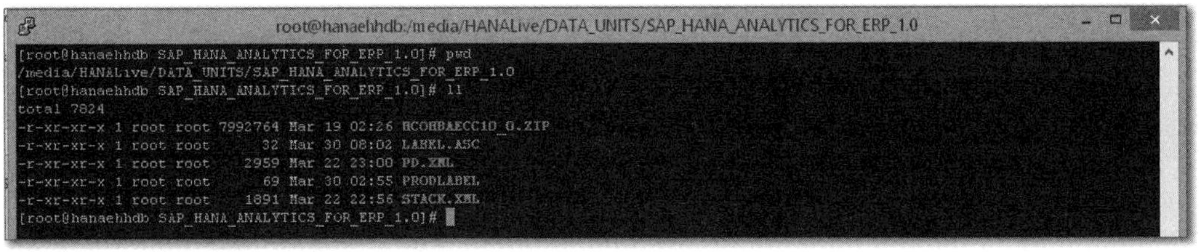

Figure 14.7 Required Files for the SAP HANA Live for SAP ERP Installation

16. Repeat the extraction steps for the SAP HANA Live Tools download.

14.1.2 Installation

Next you'll use the SAP HANA Application Lifecycle Management (HALM) utility to install the SAP HANA Live packages:

1. Validate that your SAP HANA user has the following role assigned to perform the installation:

```
sap.hana.xs.lm.roles::Administrator
```

2. From the SAP HANA server, navigate to the SAP HANA client directory.

   ▸ You can run the installation from any computer with the SAP HANA client installed and the downloaded package.

   ▸ For this example scenario, we chose to install from the SAP HANA server to centralize all content. Either approach is supported.

3. Within the SAP HANA client directory, you'll see an executable named *hdbalm*. You can learn more about the hdbalm utility by running `./hdbalm help` from the command line.

4. Use the following command to perform the package install:

   ▸ `./hdbalm -u <user> -h <host> -p 80XX install <path to media>`, where XX is your SAP HANA instance ID

   ▸ Example: `./hdbalm -u MPYTEL -h hanaehhdb.nimblhq.com -p 8010 install /media/HANALive/DATA_UNITS/SAP_HANA_ANALYTICS_FOR_ERP_1.0/`

5. When prompted to install the package, type "yes", and press ⌷Enter⌷ as shown in Figure 14.8.

Figure 14.8 Installing SAP HANA Live with hdbalm from the Command Line

6. The process will run for a few minutes. Confirm the results, and close the window (see Figure 14.9).

7. Repeat the steps for the SAP HANA Live Tools.

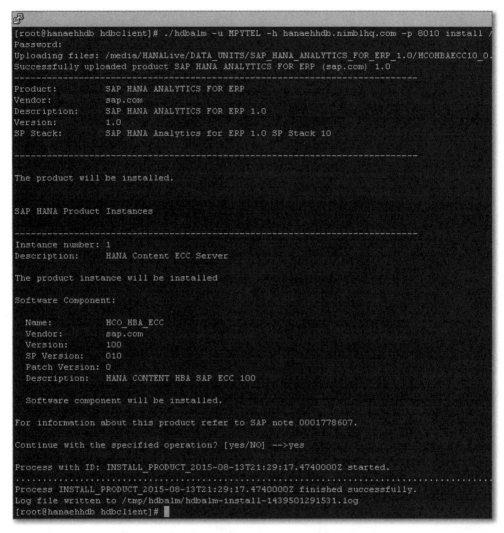

Figure 14.9 Confirmation That the Installation was Successful

8. When completed, you can execute the following command to validate the installation as shown in Figure 14.10:

▶ `./hdbalm -u <user> -h <hostname> -p 80XX get product list`, **where** XX is the SAP HANA instance ID

▶ **Example:** ./hdbalm -u MPYTEL -h hanaehhdb.nimblhq.com -p 8010 get product list

```
[root@hanaehhdb hdbclient]# ./hdbalm -u MPYTEL -h hanaehhdb.nimblhq.com -p 8010 get product list
Password:
SAP HANA ANALYTICS FOR ERP (sap.com) 1.0
SAP HANA CONTENT TOOLS (sap.com) 1.0
[root@hanaehhdb hdbclient]#
```

Figure 14.10 Example Usage of Get Product List from hdbalm

14.1.3 Validating Installation

To validate the installation, follow these steps:

1. Open SAP HANA Studio, and log on to your SAP HANA system.

2. Choose WINDOW • OPEN PERSPECTIVE • SAP HANA MODELER from the toolbar (see Figure 14.11).

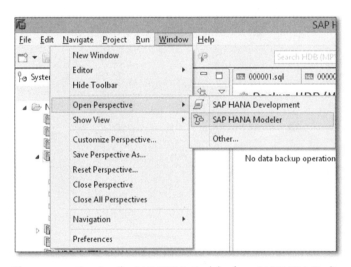

Figure 14.11 Opening the SAP HANA Modeler from SAP HANA Studio

3. Expand your SAP HANA node, and choose CONTENT • SAP • HBA. You should see SAP HANA Live Content displayed under CALCULATION VIEWS.

4. Right-click one of the calculation views, and select DATA PREVIEW (see Figure 14.12).

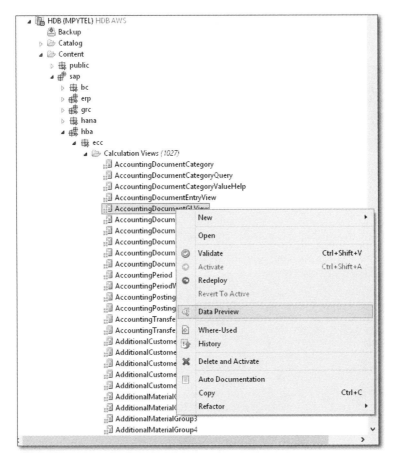

Figure 14.12 Validating the SAP HANA Live installation

5. Click on the RAW DATA tab to view data within the view. If you see your data, then the SAP HANA Live installation was successful. Note: you need to choose a calculated view that relates to data in your system. Figure 14.13 shows CHARTOFACCOUNTS, which displays master data in SAP ERP Financials (FI).

[»] **Note**

Want to know more about installing SAP HANA Live? SAP provides documentation as part of *http://help.sap.com*. SAP has provided even more content as part of its Rapid Deployment Solution (RDS) for SAP HANA Live. The RDS at *http://service.sap.com/rds-shl*includes step-by-step guides and additional content to help make your SAP HANA Live deployment a success.

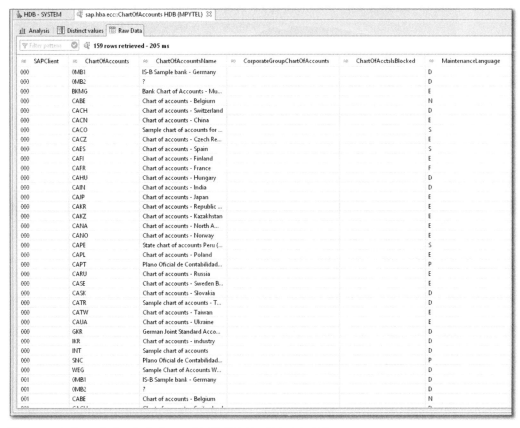

Figure 14.13 Example Raw Data from a SAP HANA Live Calculated View

14.2 SAP HANA Live Explorer

SAP HANA Live Explorer is a useful tool to find content that can be consumed in SAP Lumira, SAP BusinessObjects, or using the Open Data protocol (OData) to SAP Fiori. Access to the application is governed by two main roles delivered when you install the package in SAP HANA. As you explore SAP HANA Live with the Explorer application, you'll get a sense of how organizations can truly start to deliver self-service analytics. In the example in this section, SAP Lumira is installed on the desktop. Follow these steps to find a query and then open it in SAP Lumira:

1. Before logging on to the SAP HANA Live Explorer, make sure you have one of the following roles assigned in SAP HANA.

559

▸ `sap.hba.explorer.roles::Developer`

▸ `sap.hba.explorer.roles::Business`

2. There are also two URLs you can use to access the SAP HANA Live content depending on your intended audience. We'll plan on using the developer view.

   ▸ Developer (Report Developer): *http://<HANA Server Host>:80XX/sap/hba/ explorer*

   ▸ Business User (Power User): *http://<HANA Server Host:80XX/sap/hba/ explorer/buser.html*

   – *XX* is your SAP HANA instance ID.

   – Example: *http://hanaehhdb.nimblhq.com:8010/sap/hba/explorer*

3. When presented with the log on screen, enter your SAP HANA database user ID and password.

4. The next screen is the default screen showing all SAP HANA Live content. Multiple options are available on this screen (see Figure 14.14).

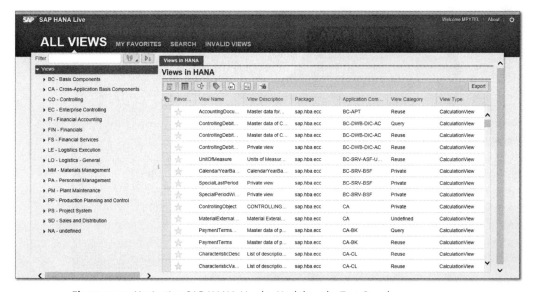

Figure 14.14 Navigating SAP HANA Live by Module or by Text Search

5. After you've selected a view or query, you'll see multiple buttons in the toolbar just above the grid rows:

   ▸ OPEN DEFINITION: Shows you quickly the fields within the query.

   ▸ OPEN CONTENT: Quickly displays the top 1,000 rows of the table.

▶ ⊞ OPEN CROSS REFERENCE: Lets you see in a text view the tables accessed by the query. Click the GRAPH VIEW and EXPAND ALL to see a nice graphical layout of all the table and field relationships.

▶ ◈ ADD TAG: Enables you to add metadata to content displayed.

▶ ⬚ GENERATE SLT FILE: Looks like an export to CSV, but it isn't. It creates a file that you can use as an input for the System Landscape Transformation (SLT).

▶ ⬚ OPEN VIEW IN LUMIRA: Prompts you for a download that will automatically open SAP Lumira on your desktop (if installed).

▶ ⬚ OPEN VIEW IN ANALYSIS OFFICE: Opens SAP BusinessObjects Analysis, Edition for Microsoft Office if installed locally.

6. Click on the OPEN VIEW IN LUMIRA button to get the option to model a report over the query you selected. This feature automatically defines the connection. You provide your SAP HANA user and password in SAP Lumira to begin building analytical reports over live SAP ERP transactional data (see Figure 14.15).

Figure 14.15 Example Report in SAP Lumira Connecting to SAP HANA Live

14.3 SAP HANA Live Authorization Assistant

In the tools package you installed in Section 14.1.2, the package included the SAP HANA Live Authorization Assistant. This utility will help security administrators generate the required SAP HANA database authorizations based on the users defined within the ABAP stack and the required SAP HANA Live content. First, you need to install the plugin within SAP HANA Studio. Then you'll walk through the generation of authorizations for a specific user.

1. Open SAP HANA Studio on your desktop, and log on to the SAP HANA system.

2. Ensure that you have the following role assigned to yourself:

   `sap.hba.tools.auth.roles::AnalyticsAuthorizationAdministrator`

3. Install the plugin to access the SAP HANA Live Authorization Assistant. From SAP HANA Studio, select HELP • INSTALL NEW SOFTWARE.

4. In the WORK WITH field, enter the following URL and press ⏎ Enter:

   ▸ *http://<HANA database server>:80XX/sap/hba/tools/auth*

   ▸ Example: *http://hanaehhdb.nimblhq.com:8010/sap/hba/tools/auth*

5. Select the package for ANALYTICS AUTHORIZATION ASSISTANT, and click NEXT (see Figure 14.16).

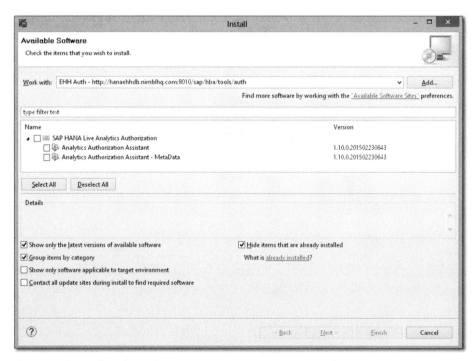

Figure 14.16 Installing the Authorization Assistant in SAP HANA Studio

6. Accept the license agreement, and click FINISH.

7. Restart SAP HANA Studio to see the updated component on the toolbar.

8. From the top of SAP HANA Studio, select ANALYTICS AUTHORIZATION • GENE-RATE ANALYTIC PRIVILEGES.

9. When prompted, select the query views (see Figure 14.17).

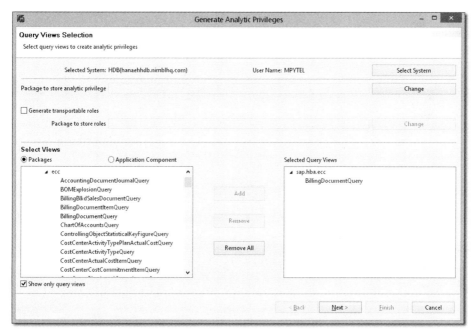

Figure 14.17 Selecting the Query View to Generate Privileges For

10. Select the ABAP System (SAP ERP) schema and the client. A list of ABAP users is displayed. You can also search for a specific user. Then click NEXT (see Figure 14.18).

11. The new role is created with the correct privilege, which you can see in SAP HANA Studio under SYSTEM • SECURITY • ROLES (see Figure 14.19).

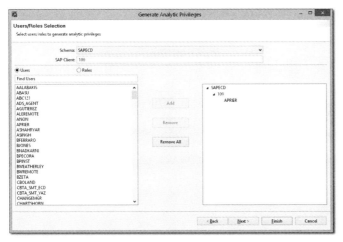

Figure 14.18 Selecting an ABAP User within the Authorization Assistant

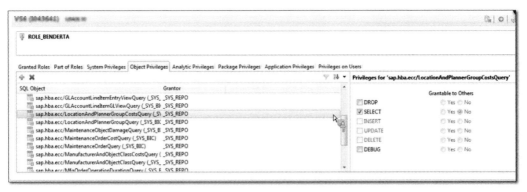

Figure 14.19 The Generated Role

> **[»]** **Note**
>
> Need to know more? Check out SAP Note 1796718 – SAP HANA Live Authorization Assistant. Also see the page *http://help.sap.com/hba*, and choose SAP HANA Live Tools • SAP HANA Live Authorization Assistant.

14.4   SAP HANA Live Extension Assistant

SAP HANA Live Extension Assistant is another utility you can install within SAP HANA Studio to help with the administration of SAP HANA Live. The SAP HANA Live Extension Assistant is a tool meant to simplify the modification of query views in SAP HANA Live. In the scenario where you've found a view but want to add a field from another table (maybe a Z table), then you could use the SAP HANA Live Extension Assistant to modify the SAP-delivered view. Let's quickly cover how you enhance a SAP HANA Live view.

1. Open SAP HANA Studio, and log on to the SAP HANA system. Ensure that you have the following role assigned:

   ```
   sap.hba.tools.extn.roles::ExtensibilityDeveloper
   ```

2. To install the plugin, click HELP • INSTALL SOFTWARE.

3. In the WORK WITH field, enter the following URL:

   ▸ *http://<HANA database server>:80XX/sap/hba/tools/extn*

   ▸ Example: *http://hanaehhdb.nimblhq.com:8010/sap/hba/tools/extn*

4. Select the SAP HANA Live Extensibility Tool, and click NEXT (see Figure 14.20).

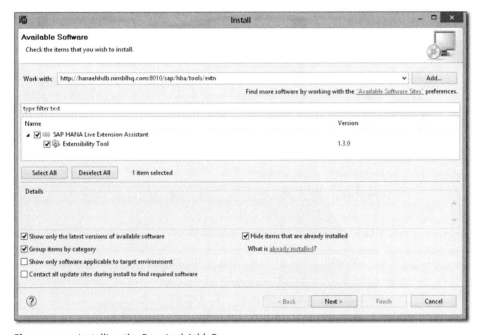

Figure 14.20 Installing the Required Add-On

5. Navigate to SYSTEM • CONTENT • SAP • HBA • ECC • CALCULATION VIEWS, and right-click a view.

6. Select EXTEND VIEW (see Figure 14.21). The add-on installed a new option.

Figure 14.21 Selecting Extended View from the Context Menu

7. On the next screen, you're presented with a list of fields that represent the columns of the view. The utility creates a copy of the original for you to modify. Click NEXT after you've made your selection (see Figure 14.22).

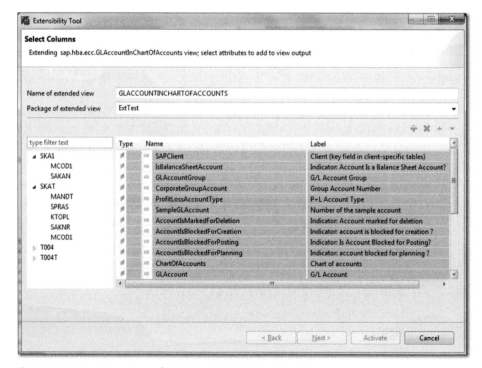

Figure 14.22 Creating a Copy of the View You Want to Extend

8. Clicking NEXT enables you to view tables already defined in the view, or you can add new ones.

9. Figure 14.23 shows a field being added from an existing defined table.

10. After you make your edits, click VALIDATE, and then click ACTIVATE.

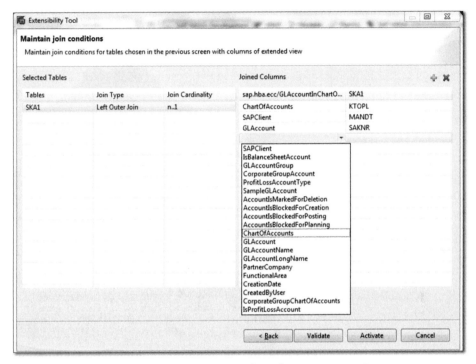

Figure 14.23 Adding an Additional Field to SAP-Delivered SAP HANA Live Content

Now you've extended an SAP-delivered view. The view is available for use within the SAP HANA Live Explorer tool or through an analytical UI such as SAP Lumira.

14.5 Summary

The SAP HANA Live virtual data models provided by SAP can bring real value to your organization's operational and analytical reporting requirements. The installation is straightforward, and the content is continually updated. As of August 2015, SAP has focused on SAP HANA Live content for specific industry solutions. We've also seen multiple new SAP Fiori applications (specifically the SAP Smart

Business Applications) require SAP HANA Live content to be enabled. The same is true for SAP S/4HANA Finance. After you install and activate SAP S/4HANA Finance, you have the SAP HANA Live for SAP S/4HANA Finance package that will be required to fully utilize the new applications delivered by SAP.

SAP HANA Live is true innovation in that it harnesses the power of SAP HANA to provide real-time access to operational data. In the traditional data warehouse environment, when a user wanted access to data for analytics, he had to make a request for IT to create the data model in SAP BW, then design reports, and eventually get access to a copy of the data from a prior time period. With SAP HANA Live, users can browse standard content and immediately access data using off-the-shelf tools, such as SAP Lumira, SAP BusinessObjects, and Microsoft Excel.

In this chapter, we covered the installation of content, which will be a frequent activity as SAP continues to enhance SAP HANA Live. We then showcased how end users can browse content within SAP HANA Live Explorer. After a user knows what data he wants, you need to ensure that he has secure access to only the information specific to his job function. The SAP HANA Live Authorization Assistant will help IT by generating roles based on specific SAP HANA Live views. And lastly, we covered the utility from SAP that simplifies the enhancement of SAP-delivered content.

SAP HANA Live is a new component from SAP with a low risk of negative impact on the migration to SAP Business Suite on SAP HANA and the opportunity to make a big positive impact on the analytic capabilities provided by IT to the business users.

Appendices

A   Project Documents

This appendix includes instructions for creating a Project Charter, along with some sample text, and coverage of your communication plan, your risk plan, and your cutover plan.

A.1   Project Charter

The Project Charter is the high-level statement about the project. In this document, you define the current state, the target environment, and the tangible benefits you expect. In this book, we described the SAP Business Suite on SAP HANA as a technical migration. Your application code and SAP Business Suite can migrate as-is from any database to SAP HANA. However, the Project Charter shouldn't be limited to technical statements about the goals of the project. You can define business goals here as well, such as "Improve MRP runtime and accuracy, which will reduce inventory on hand by 5%." This is a quantifiable goal that can be measured before and after the SAP Business Suite on SAP HANA migration. In the content in this section, we've provided an example Project Charter using a fictional company called Acme Corporation (Acme, for short).

A.1.1   Project Overview

Acme has a requirement to improve its operational and analytical capabilities, which will be driven by process and technology improvements. Acme IT and key business stakeholders believe an upgrade and migration to SAP Business Suite on SAP HANA will provide the software platform to achieve process excellence. The high-level goals include the following:

- Reduce period-end closing time by 50%.
- Reduce inventory on hand by 15%.
- Improve manufacturing capacity by 10%.
- Increase marketing lead product campaigns by 25%.

These goals will be achieved through a process analysis and redesign supported by new technology capabilities that will provide operational staff access to information more quickly with a higher degree of accuracy. If successful, Acme will have shifted resources from tactical execution to more strategic planners, increased IT system automation, and met its goals.

Current Situation

Describe the as-is situation and challenges.

Acme supports 6,000 employees across three continents on a single SAP ERP platform. SAP ERP EHP 4 was originally implemented in 2011 for finance, manufacturing, logistics, and HR. This deployment lasted roughly 10 months and resulted in a system that supported all three business units within a single SAP ERP system. The project centralized accounting and HR functions, which enabled the organization to save considerable operational costs. Acme has continued to operate SAP ERP and maintained a Maintenance Agreement with SAP for its SAP ERP platform. SAP has delivered multiple enhancements to the marketplace, which Acme has been unable to implement even though it's entitled to access. Continuing to forgo these enhancements delivered by SAP has left Acme in a position where its business processes haven't been analyzed or improved in four years.

From an operational standpoint, data volumes have grown considerably in the past four years. With new products being developed, increased sales orders, and a more sophisticated supply chain, end users have been tolerating slower than normal response times due to large data sets. Acme has explored the opportunity to archive data, which will require significant investment from the business in terms of data retention policy creation. Additionally, IT will need to purchase and implement software tools to support the new data-retention policies.

Proposed Resolution

Describe the "to-be" environment consisting of SAP Business Suite on SAP HANA, including what the project will deliver and the resolution to the functional/operating need.

After weighing the potential archival and data-retention capabilities, it's clear that Acme would be better served investing in a new in-memory platform that provides advanced levels of compression. This will enable Acme to continue to retain data online, within one application, available for analysis by end users. The effort and cost saved by not implementing an archive solution will then be applied to business process redesign, new technology implementation, and deployment of new analytical tools that will support quicker and more accurate business planning decisions.

The new environment will consist of SAP ERP EHP 7 on SAP HANA and will include SAP HANA Live and SAP Lumira for advanced self-service analytic capabilities. The initial technology deliverable of the project will be to migrate and upgrade SAP ERP to the latest release running on SAP HANA.

A.1.2 Project Scope

The project scope needs to be defined specific to the technology components being deployed, the affected process areas, and how the enhancements will be rolled out to the end users. Acme wants some enhancements with the SAP Business Suite on SAP HANA project, so by controlling the scope, Acme can specify those items that will be included in the as-is migration.

Solution Description

Describe the proposed solution to the business goals stated earlier.

Acme's upgrade and migration project to SAP Business Suite on SAP HANA will include the installation of EHP 7 with the latest Support Package Stacks (SP Stack). Once installed, the project team will selectively activate business functions included as part of the enhancement package, which will drive process and operational improvement in the following areas:

- ▶ Material Requirements Planning (MRP)
- ▶ Procurement
- ▶ SAP ERP Financials (FI)
- ▶ Production Planning (PP)

In addition to the functionality within SAP Business Suite being activated, Acme will deploy multiple new analytical capabilities in parallel to the SAP Business Suite enhancements. Acme will install SAP HANA Live and SAP Lumira Cloud edition, which will facilitate self-service analytics with cloud-based report and document sharing. This will enable business users to create their own analytical reports and visualizations—with IT on-hand to support when needed.

Project Goal

Describe the overall goal that is to be achieved by the project.

The high-level goals defined in the Project Overview can be quantified using new reporting capabilities defined within the solution scope. The technical details behind each high-level goal include the following:

- Reduce period-end closing time by 50%.
  - Implement SAP Financial Closing Cockpit.
  - Increase financial close task automation.
  - Implement workflow to reduce idle time between tasks.
- Reduce inventory on hand by 15%.
  - Implement MRP Live for SAP Business Suite on SAP HANA.
  - Enable more frequent MRP execution and analysis.
  - Enable planners to make decisions more quickly.
- Improve manufacturing capacity by 10%.
  - Leverage Plant Maintenance (PM) for proactive machine maintenance.
  - Reduce machine downtime by 50%.
  - Implement better consumable planning for shop floor machinery.
- Increase marketing lead product campaigns by 25%.
  - Implement more advanced pricing simulation.
  - Integrate SAP Business Suite availability checks with an ecommerce web site.

Deliverables

Deliverables are produced by the team to ensure success. These are tangible items.

The Acme project team will produce the following major deliverables as part of the project:

- **SAP Business Suite on SAP HANA system**
  Successfully migrated SAP Business Suite on SAP HANA system, including the latest features and functions available. This system must be free from defect conforming to SAP and industry standards.

▶ **Business process documentation and test scripts**
Central repository of business process and test script documentation that provides reusable test scripts for future enhancements. The business process documentation will provide an overall view of decisions made and process design.

▶ **End-user training**
Successfully trained SAP end users are supported by online help and training material.

▶ **Cost savings**
Tangible cost savings are defined in the project goals.

Business Case Summary

Here we want to provide a high-level project budget and expected ROI as percentage.

Table A.1 summarizes the return on investment (ROI) over three years for this project.

Items	Year 1	Year 2	Year 3
Costs			
Hardware	$220,000	$44,000	$44,000
Software	$160,000	$35,200	$35,200
Internal Labor	$144,000		
External Labor	$172,800		
Total Costs	$696,800	$79,200	$79,200
Cumulative Costs		$776,000	$855,200
Value			
Inventory Reduction	$250,000	$100,000	$50,000
Increased Capacity	$100,000	$150,000	$200,000
Increased Sales	$250,000	$350,000	$450,000
Total Value	$600,000	$600,000	$700,000
Cumulative Value		$1,200,000	$1,900,000
Cumulative ROI		55%	122%

Table A.1 ROI Calculation Displaying Cumlative Costs and Value

Out of Scope

Describe what won't be done during this project. As an example, SAP S/4HANA Finance will be excluded from the project scope.

Any technology or software solution that doesn't support the defined goals won't be included in the scope. The project will focus solely on the migration to SAP Business Suite on SAP HANA and those process changes required to meet the defined deliverables. The following components are known to *not* support the defined scope and will be considered out of scope for this project:

▸ Business continuity planning

▸ Employee (SAP end user) hardware upgrades

▸ Local area network/wide area network (LAN/WAN) upgrades

▸ SAP S/4HANA Finance

Implementation Strategy

The implementation approach selected for the project is based on the implementation scope.

The Acme project team will use the SAP ASAP methodology for upgrades combined with SAP's Rapid Deployment Solution (RDS) for the SAP Business Suite on SAP HANA migration. This methodology has been successful at other companies of similar size and complexity. A majority of Acme IT staff are familiar with the methodology and the common deliverables by phase. SAP's ASAP methodology includes the following project phases:

▸ **Project Preparation**
During this phase, the team goes through initial planning and preparation for the SAP project.

▸ **Business Blueprint**
The purpose of this phase is to achieve a common understanding of how Acme intends to run SAP Business Suite on SAP HANA to achieve its project goals.

▸ **Realization**
The purpose of this phase is to implement all the business process requirements based on the business blueprint.

- **Final Preparation**
  During this phase, Acme completes testing, end-user training, system management, and cutover activities to finalize readiness for go-live.

- **Go-Live and Support**
  The purpose of this phase is to move to live production operation with SAP Business Suite on SAP HANA.

- **Operate**
  Sustain and maintain system operation.

Project Planning

The schedule and major milestones of the project make up the project plan.

The project schedule will cover 12 weeks with some procurement tasks completing prior to the official start of the project. A high-level schedule is shown in Figure A.1.

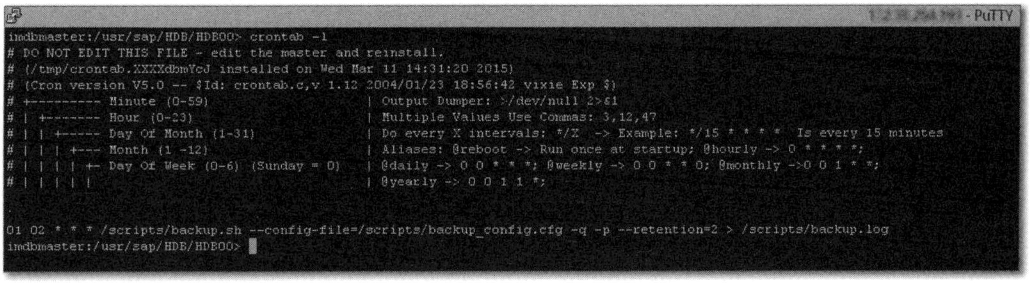

Figure A.1 Project Time line

Project Stakeholders

Individuals and organizations who have an interest in the project are stakeholders.

Project stakeholders include the project sponsors—CIO, VP Manufacturing, COO, VP Finance, VP Sales, and so on.

Project Management – Project Managers name(s)

Constraints

These are items beyond the control of the project team that limit options, such as business activity, acquisitions, year end, and so on.

The project sponsors believe no new business activity will limit the ability for the project team to operate as long as the 12-week time line is kept. This doesn't include a 4-week contingency plan should the initial go-live date not be met. If the time lines aren't met, the project sponsors will meet to determine a course of action. Known business activities include the following:

▶ Annual inventory for all manufacturing sites

▶ New product launch in North America

▶ New rebate plan deployment

▶ Open additional manufacturing plant in Mexico

A.2   Communication Plan

Constant project management is required to keep an SAP Business Suite on SAP HANA project running and focused. The communication plan defines the types of communication, frequency, and the audience. It's important to define a communication plan that includes communication to the business users outside of the project team. Ideally, the external business users should understand the value of the project and why downtime has been requested. Table A.2 provides an example communication plan in matrix form.

Meeting	Frequency	Content of Meeting	Participants
Steering Committee Meeting	Monthly (2h)	▶ Strategic/high-level update ▶ Request for strategic approval	Steering committee members from Acme, including SAP representatives as required and requested
Program and project mgmt. meeting	Weekly (1h)	▶ Update/progress ▶ Verify direction ▶ Project monitoring and progress tracking ▶ Issue resolution ▶ Escalation management	▶ Project managers ▶ Risk management ▶ Quality assurance ▶ Organization Change Management (OCM)

Table A.2 Communication Matrix

Meeting	Frequency	Content of Meeting	Participants
Regular team meeting	Every 2 weeks	▶ Update status/progress of each track ▶ Status, next steps ▶ Critical issues ▶ Latest info ▶ Open issues	▶ Project leads ▶ Project team
Individual meetings for action points responsible	Depending on action point time frame	▶ Detailed status ▶ Next steps ▶ Degree of work break-down structure (WBS) completion ▶ Critical issues ▶ Risks	▶ Project leads ▶ Action point responsible

Table A.2 Communication Matrix (Cont.)

In this matrix, you can add columns to define who is responsible for meeting minutes and who should receive them. The communication plan should also define communication and escalation channels. Figure A.2 shows an example that defines the information and status flow.

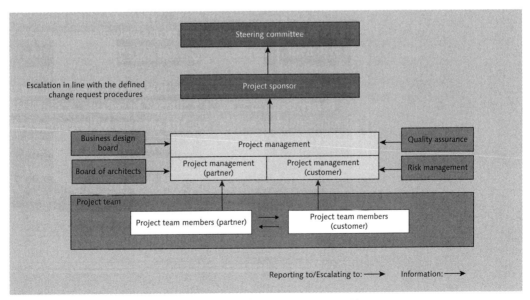

Figure A.2 Example Communication Path as Part of the Communication Plan

A.3 Risk Plan

The risk plan is meant to define those events, tasks, or external activities that might impact the project time line, cost, quality, or scope. In Figure A.3, you can quantify the potential impact. When you combine this information with the likelihood the event will occur, you can develop a risk assessment. After you assess the risk, you can choose what to do about it. Mitigate it, accept it, and watch it are three examples of risk strategy (see Figure A.4).

Project Risk List
Project XYZ
Decision Matrix

For every parameter (time, costs, quality, and functionality/scope) the impact of the risk occuring is valued subjectively on a scale between 1 and 5. The following table has to be used at the assessment to make the classification of the risks per parameter comparable. Definition of Total Impact (resulting from weighting 4 Parameters for Project Success) is project specific.

		Assessments				
		1	2	3	4	5
Parameters for Project Success	Time	Effects on time have to be neglected.	results in a time delay of up to 5% of the total project duration	results in a time delay of up to 15% of the total project duration	results in a time delay of up to 25% of the total project duration	results in a time delay of more than 25% of the total project duration
	Costs	Effects on costs have to be neglected.	results in a cost increase up to 5%	results in a cost increase up to 15%	results in a cost increase up to 25%	results in a cost increase higher than 25%
	Quality	Effects on quality have to be neglected	results in a deterioration of the quality in uncritical areas of the project/product	results in a deterioration of the quality in critical areas of the project/product	results in a considerable deterioration of the quality; the customer must approve this	The product is useless.
	Functionality/ Scope	Effects on function or scope have to be neglected.	results in a deterioration of functionality in uncritical areas of the project/product	results in a deterioration of fuctionality in critical areas of the project/product	results in a considerable deterioration of functionality, the customer must approve this	The product is useless.

Risk List | Risk Matrix | Decision Matrix | Check List | (Formulas)
READY

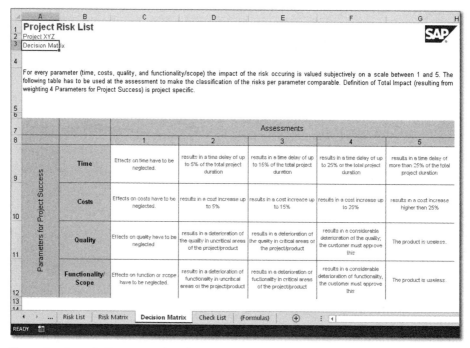

Figure A.3 Example Matrix to Define the Impact of a Risk

Project Risk List
Project XYZ
Risk List

		Identification and Analysis of Risks		Total Impact	Probability of Occurrence	Risk Assessment		Definition of Measures and Monitoring					
No.	Risk Category	Risk Description (IF -> THEN)	Date				Priority (optional)	Risk Strategy	Risk Indicator	Risk Response	Responsible Person	Deadline	Status
1	Infrastructure	Hardware Availability		4	50%	2.0		Mitigate					Open
2	Project Scope	HANA Live Installation		2	30%	0.6		Accept					Open
3	Resources	Business users for testing		4	30%	1.2		Mitigate					Open

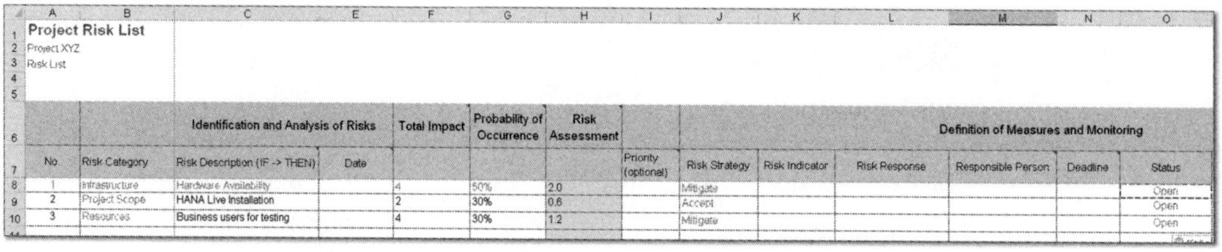

Figure A.4 Example Risk List Which Is Part of the Risk Plan

A.4   Cutover Plan

In Chapter 10, we talked about the cutover plan and the types of activities to document in that plan. Figure A.5 shows an example cutover plan built in Excel. Within this plan, you can clearly see numbered steps, color-coded tasks, start dates, end dates, and planned durations. Any project team member can access this document and immediately identify the remaining tasks to be completed on the project.

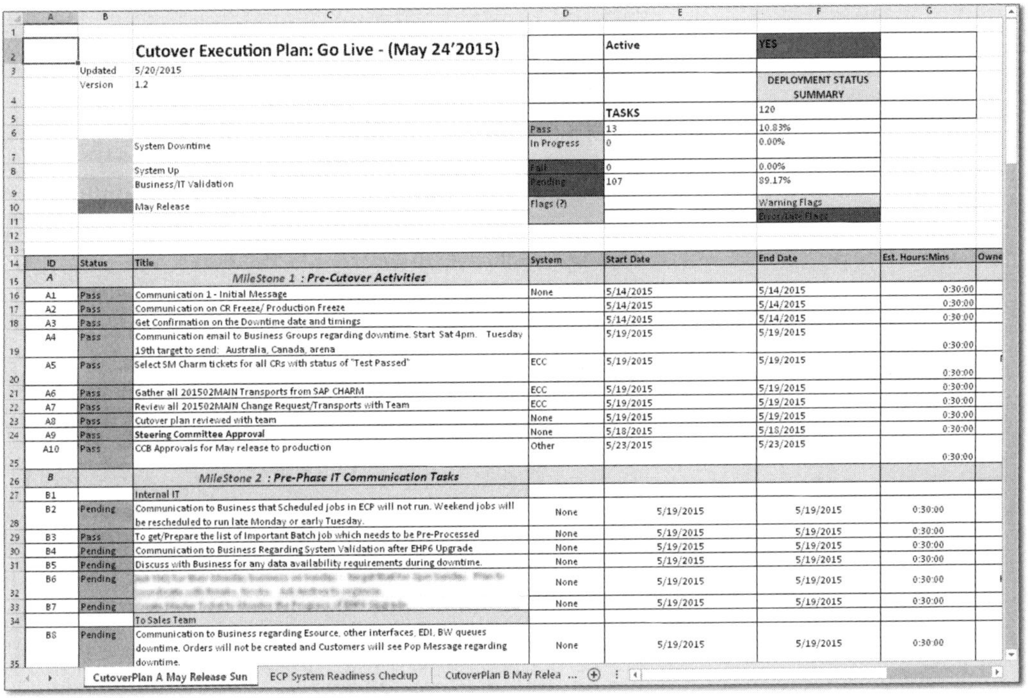

Figure A.5 Example Cutover Plan

> **Note**   [«]
>
> For more example project documents, check out SAP's ASAP roadmaps on the SAP Support Portal by navigating to *https://support.sap.com/support-programs-services/methodologies.html* and choosing IMPLEMENT SAP • ASAP IMPLEMENTATION ROADMAP • HANA ASAP 8 METHODOLOGY.

B   Glossary

ABAP   The high level programming language created by SAP for ERP.

ACID (atomicity, consistency, isolation, and durability)   A concept referring to a database system's four transaction properties to ensure database reliability.

AS ABAP   ABAP Application Server.

BPCA (Business Process Change Analyzer)   A component of SAP Solution Manager that can help identify the impact of a change event at a transaction code and program level.

Business Blueprint   Refers to a phase within the ASAP methodology where you define the business requirements. Can also be used to refer to a comprehensive requirements document.

ChaRM (Change Request Management)   A component of SAP Solution Manager that provides ITIL standards-based change management for SAP and non-SAP components.

DBA Cockpit   Transaction within SAP Solution Manager and SAP BUSINESS SUITE used to view the database status, performance, and health.

Disaster Recovery (DR)   Refers to the procedures and/or components required to restore services or a system in the event of unplanned downtime.

DMO (Database Migration Option)   The capability of SAP Software Update Manager to perform both an update and migration of a system to SAP HANA.

downtime   Refers to the time period where an SAP system is unavailable for use by the business users

dual stack   Refers to the previously supported ability to use an AS ABAP and AS JAVA on one host sharing the same SID. This is no longer recommended by SAP.

EarlyWatch Reporting   A prerequisite for service level reporting and all services delivered by SAP. It provides a set of key performance indicators (KPIs) your system is measured against in terms of maintenance history, performance, growth, and capacity.

enhancement package   Enables customers to electively implement software innovations from SAP and activate the software upon business demand.

enqueue service   Critical component of the SAP system and consists of the enqueue server process and the lock table. It administers locks on objects during SAP transactions.

ERS (Enqueue Replication Server)   Provides the System Replication functionality for the enqueue service to prevent a single point of failure (SPOF).

GUI (Graphical User Interfaces)   Leveraged by end users to facilitate a business process in software.

HA (High Availability)   Refers to a system or component that is continuously operational relative to a 100% operational measurement.

ICF (Internet Communication Framework)
A component of the ASP ABAP that facilitates communication from and to SAP systems.

IMDBMS (In Memory Database Management System) Stores the entire database structure in-memory with all operations (such as select, insert, update) occurring in memory without the need for an I/O instruction to disk.

JSON (JavaScript Object Notation)
A syntax for storing and exchanging data using an XML-like schema.

Maintenance Optimizer A tool within SAP Solution Manager that reads from the Landscape Management Database (LMDB) to plan the target definition for technical components.

Maintenance Planner Online planning tool provided by SAP that supports the definition of a target system at the component level.

MRP (material requirements planning)
The function that includes Production Planning, Scheduling, and Inventory Controlling systems used to manage manufacturing processes.

nZDM (Near Zero Downtime) Refers to the ability to keep downtime to a minimum during a system update using advanced tools from SAP.

OLAP (online analytical processing)
A system that performs multidimensional analysis of business data and provides the capability for complex calculations, trend analysis, and sophisticated data modeling.

OLTP (online transaction processing)
A class of systems that facilitate and manage transaction-oriented applications, typically for data entry and retrieval transaction processing.

OpenSQL Provides a unified syntax and unified semantics for all database systems supported by SAP.

PAS (primary application server) Refers to the SAP component where the SAP Central Services instance resides.

QGM (Quality Gate Management)
A component of SAP Solution Manager that facilitates a controlled method to transport creation and movement throughout the SAP landscape.

Quick Sizer Online application provided by SAP that enables customers to perform a t-shirt based sizing or a throughput-based sizing.

RDBMS (Relational Database Management System) A database management system that is based on the relational model.

RDS (Rapid Deployment Solution) A set of tools, procedures, and processes to implement SAP solutions on a defined time line.

REST (Representational State Transfer)
A current software architecture for building scalable web services.

RPO (recovery point objective) The period of time where a potential for data loss might occur during a disaster recovery.

RTO (recovery time objective) The targeted duration of time that a business process must be restored after a disaster event.

SAP Fiori Application platform provided by SAP that enables device-agnostic software development focused on simple, easy-to-use, user interfaces.

SAP HANA Live SAP-provided virtual data model based on the transactional and master data tables of the SAP Business Suite.

SAP MaxAttention Provides customers with an embedded support team, tailored engineering services, enhanced back-office support, and attention from SAP executives.

SAP Screen Personas Software tool that provides a simple, drag-and-drop approach to modify many common SAP GUI screens to make them more usable as well as more visually appealing.

SAP S/4HANA Finance Next-generation SAP Business Suite component focused on the simplification of tables and user interface specific to SAP ERP Finance (FI).

SAP Solution Manager Software solution provided by SAP as part of a customer's maintenance agreement to support the implementation, upgrade, update, and maintenance of the customer's SAP systems.

savepoint Changed data that is automatically saved from memory to disk at regular intervals in SAP HANA.

SEA (Scope and Effort Analyzer) A component of SAP Solution Manager that helps SAP customers estimate the effort related to development and testing for an SAP upgrade.

SDA (Solution Documentation Assistant) A component of SAP Solution Manager that enables customers to reverse-document and continuously validate their documentation of business processes.

SID (System Identifier) Represents the unique SAP system or instance.

SL Toolset (software logistics toolset) A set of tools provided by SAP that aids the installation, update, and maintenance of SAP components.

SLT (SAP Landscape Transformation) Provides real-time replication from any database to any other database using native database triggers.

SoH (Suite on HANA) Refers to any SAP Business Suite component running on SAP HANA. This includes SAP ERP, SAP CRM, or SAP SCM.

SP Stack (Support Package Stack) Sets of support packages and patches for a product version that must be used in the given combination.

SUM (Software Update Manager) SAP-developed application that supports the upgrade, update, and migration of SAP systems to SAP HANA.

SWPM (Software Provisioning Manager) SAP-developed application that supports the installation of new SAP systems.

System Replication Provides the ability to build a copy of a system either in the same location or remote location for purposes of Disaster Recovery or High Availability.

TDI (Tailored Data Center Integration) Refers to the standards and design principles SAP has made available for those customers who choose not to purchase a certified SAP HANA appliance and instead use existing resources within their own data center.

Transaction SGEN   Transaction within SAP AS ABAP to generate all SAP objects to reduce compiling at runtime for the end users.

UDA (Upgrade Dependency Analyzer) An online application provided by SAP to help customers understand the dependencies between components during an upgrade.

UME (User Management Engine)   The central store for user IDs, their credentials, and the roles or profiles assigned.

Unicode   An international encoding standard for use with different languages in the same database supporting an SAP component.

uptime   The time period during maintenance on an SAP system when the system is available to business users.

Work center   A user interface within SAP Solution Manager that provides a task-based view into a specific component of SAP Solution Manager.

C The Author

Michael Pytel is a speaker, blogger, and SAP-certified consultant focused on education for SAP Business Suite on SAP HANA and SAP Solution Manager. He is passionate about sharing his experiences and the lessons he has learned from numerous technical projects driving value from SAP software. A frequent presenter at ASUG, SAP Insider, and SAP conferences, Michael continues to share the knowledge he has gained implementing SAP Business Suite on SAP HANA across the country.

Index

T

W

X

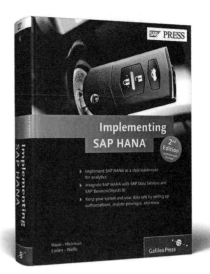

- ▶ Implement SAP HANA as a data warehouse for analytics

- ▶ Integrate SAP HANA with SAP Data Services and SAP BusinessObjects BI

- ▶ Keep your system and your data safe by setting up authorizations, analytic privileges, and more

Jonathan Haun, Chris Hickman, Don Loden, Roy Wells

Implementing SAP HANA

If you're ready to implement SAP HANA as a data warehouse for analytics, you'll want this book along for the ride. Explore the steps in a complete SAP HANA implementation, and then play with downloadable sample data that you can use to test your skills. Become an expert in data provisioning with SAP Data Services, data modeling, and connecting to the BOBJ platform. Take your SAP HANA knowledge to the next level!

860 pages, 2nd edition, pub. 12/2014
E-Book: $69.99 | **Print:** $79.95 | **Bundle:** $89.99

www.sap-press.com/3703

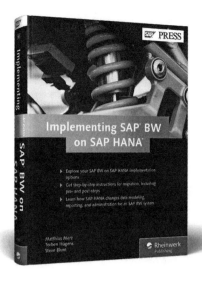

▶ Explore your SAP BW on SAP HANA implementation options

▶ Get step-by-step instructions for migration, including pre- and post-steps

▶ Learn how SAP HANA changes data modeling, reporting, and administration for an SAP BW system

Matthias Merz, Torben Hügens, Steve Blum

Implementing SAP BW on SAP HANA

If you're making the leap from SAP BW to SAP HANA, this book is your indispensable companion. Thanks to detailed pre-migration and post-migration steps, as well as a complete guide to the actual migration process, it's never been easier to HANA-ify your SAP BW system. Once your migration is complete, learn everything you need to know about data modeling, reporting, and administration. Are you ready for the next generation of SAP BW?

467 pages, pub. 04/2015
E-Book: $69.99 | **Print:** $79.95 | **Bundle:** $89.99
www.sap-press.com/3609

www.sap-press.com

Interested in reading more?

Please visit our website for all new
book and e-book releases from SAP PRESS.

www.sap-press.com